Readings in

Severely and Profoundly Handicapped Education

Irving Newman

Assistant Professor and Coordinator of the Mentally Retarded and Severely/Profoundly Handicapped Programs, Southern Connecticut State College, New Haven, Connecticut.

Robert Piazza

Assistant Professor Department of Special Education, Southern Connecticut State College, New Haven, Connecticut.

Special Learning Corporation

42 Boston Post Rd. Guilford, Connecticut 06437

SPECIAL LEARNING CORPORATION

Publisher's Message:

The Special Education Series is the first comprehensive series designed for special education courses of study. It is also the first series to offer such a wide variety of high quality books. In addition, the series will be expanded and up-dated each year. No other publications in the area of special education can equal this. We stress high quality content, a superb advisory and consulting group, and special features that help in understanding the course of study. In addition we believe we must also publish in very small enrollment areas in order to establish the credibility and strength of our series. We realize the enrollments in courses of study such as Autism, Visually Handicapped Education, or Diagnosis and Placement are not large. Nevertheless, we believe there is a need for course books in these areas and books that are kept up-to-date on an annual basis! Special Learning Corporation's goal is to publish the highest quality materials for the college and university courses of study. With your comments and support we will continue to do this.

John P. Quirk

©1978 by Special Learning Corporation, Guilford, Connecticut 06437

All rights reserved. No part of this book may be reproduced, stored, or communicated by any means--without written permission from Special Learning Corporation.

First Edition
1 2 3 4 5

ISBN 0-89568-079-3

Manufactured by the Redson Rice Corporation, Chicago, Illinois

CONTENTS

Therapeutic approaches to problems in feeding children with abnormal muscle tone and poor muscle coordination is outlined, with attention being given to means of assessment, intervention, and treatment.

3. Instruction and Model Programs

4. Teacher Training

FOCUS   154

5. Future Trends

GLOSSARY OF TERMS

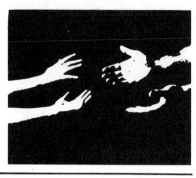

adaptive behavior The effectiveness or degree with which the individual meets the standards of personal independence and social responsibility expected of his age and cultural group. Three aspects of this behavior are: (1) maturation (2) learning; and/or (3) social adjustment. These three aspects of adaptation are of different importance as qualifying conditions of mental retardation for different age groups. There are levels of adaptive behavior defined by the American Association on Mental Deficiency, the Balthazar Scales of Adaptive Behavior, et cetera.

advocacy A program in which agencies or volunteers act on behalf of the interests of other persons who are in some way developmentally disabled. The interests of others may range from the services the individual needs, the exercise of his full human and legal rights, representation in society, to becoming a foster or adoptive parent.

amentia An obsolete term previously used to describe that level of severe mental retardation for individuals obtaining I.Q. scores below 25 or 30.

atrophy A wasting of tissues, organs or the entire body.

babbling Speech sounds which do not convey meaning; as found in vocalization of infants, or in certain severely retarded individuals.

baseline The usual level of functioning proficiency or state of an individual with respect to a particular characteristic. The frequency of occurrence of a behavior before intervention or treatment.

behavior modification Precisely planned, systematic application of methods and experimental findings of behavioral science with intent of altering observable behaviors, including increasing, decreasing, extending, restricting, teaching, maintaining behaviors; some of key concepts are:

OPERANT BEHAVIOR - behavior controlled by its consequences;

RESPONDENT BEHAVIOR - (classical, Pavlovian) reflex behavior, elicited or controlled by its antecedents;

POSITIVE REINFORCER - a stimulus which, when presented as a consequence of a response, increases or maintains the response;

NEGATIVE REINFORCER - an aversive stimulus which, if removed as a consequence of a response, increases or maintains the response;

birth injury A temporary or permanent trauma sustained during the birth process.

custodial care Archaic term used to mean the 24 hour supervision (medical, social, physical, psychological) of a person usually provided by an institution with the purpose of maintaining the person's present condition rather than providing treatment or therapeutic function; generally contrasted to active treatment.

diagnostic services Include, but are not limited to the educational, medical, psychological, and the social aspects of the individual that identify the presence of mental retardation as well as other related conditions. Diagnostic services examine the causes, complications and the consequences of the problem.

institutionalized 1) The end result of a habit of behavior or pattern of organization by a society in which the pattern or behavior become integrated into the expectations of the society; 2) the process or result of an individual's internalizing routine and regulated activities commonly found within a residential facility until he functions as if by rote without making independent choices or decision; 3) the state or condition of having been placed in an institution, and organization of some aspect of collective life controlled by rules, customs, rituals or laws.

residential facility Public or private facilities offering 24 hour service which may include short term, long term, diagnostic, or special programs and may be used in a continuum of community services.

secondary service system An array of service components which apply to certain extraordinary needs of certain primary clients but do so within the context of a target clientele composed of persons most of whom are identified as handicapped or disabled.

stereotyped behaviors Complex, repetitive movements which appear non-functional, especially repetitive hand movements, rocking, object twirling, or head banging; "blindisms". Stereotyped behaviors are not uncommon in more severely retarded individuals, particularly nonverbal ones.

task analyses The ability to describe, isolate, and sequence all the necessary subskills of a major objective.

TOPIC MATRIX

Readings in Severely and Profoundly Handicapped provides professionals in the Special Education field an overview of the nature, needs, assessment and educational techniques in teaching the severely/profoundly handicapped population.

COURSE OUTLINE:

Teaching the Severely/Profoundly Handicapped

I. Definition
II. Legislation and litigation
III. Determining skill levels
IV. Educational materials and strategies
V. Training professionals
VI. Research needs and future considerations

Readings in Severely/Profoundly Handicapped

I. The Right to Educational Services—Insight and Perspective
II. Diagnosis and Assessment
III. Instruction and Model Programs
IV. Teacher Training
V. Future Trends

Related Special Learning Corporation Readers

I. Readings in Special Education
II. Readings in Mental Retardation
III. Readings in Mainstreaming
IV. Readings in Physically Handicapped Education
V. Readings in Psychology of Exceptional Children

PREFACE

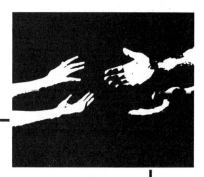

The content of this reader has been compiled and organized to meet the needs of professionals, students and others interested in the challenge of working with the severely and profoundly handicapped.

With the passage of P.L. 94-142, The Education of All Handicapped Children Act, the right of severely and profoundly handicapped individuals to a free appropriate public education to meet their unique needs has been mandated. However, between mandated and delivered services reside many obstacles.

The primary objective of this anthology is to provide the reader with relevant articles that focus on the responsibility of the educational establishment to move toward a more human system of instructional alternatives for the severely and profoundly handicapped. The articles chosen represent current viewpoints and strategies from professionals concerned with the plight of this long neglected population. We felt that there was a need within our field to bring together and more widely disseminate useful literature in this area.

The severely and profoundly handicapped do not learn quickly or easily. To overcome this problem new efforts are needed to develop effective and useful instructional programs and evlauative instruments. Teacher training institutions must also re-examine their priorities. It is hoped that this volume will lend some insight and perspective to the challenge that lies ahead. It has been organized as a textbook or reference for college students at the undergraduate and graduate level. In addition, teachers, administrators, other professionals and nonprofessionals will find it a valuable reference source.

The educational rights of this population have been recognized, but they will not be secured until those professional educators and others charged with this task take the responsibility to enforce them. Legal rights are useless unless they are implemented.

Irving Newman

Robert Piazza

The Right to Educational Services:

Until recently, those classified as severely and profoundly handicapped had a bleak prognosis for a reasonable social adjustment. Usually housed in isolated and dehumanized back wards of institutions, they were left to atrophy in both body and mind. Despite the great social and educational gains made by other handicapped individuals, the severely and profoundly handicapped remained in the middle ages with respect to care and treatment.

In the past several years, however, profound changes have taken place in this area. Spurred by a number of court decisions and the enactment of P.L. 94-142, The Education of All Handicapped Children Act, a rapid movement of the educational community toward a more humane system of instructional alternatives has begun. After years of work by parents, educators and advocates of handicapped individuals public schools are being asked to accommodate severely and profoundly handicapped children who were previously kept at home or received training in private schools and institutions. P.L. 94-142 is designed to:

> ". . .assure that all handicapped children have available to them . . .a free appropriate public education which emphasizes special education and related services designed to meet their unique needs, to assure that the rights of handicapped children and their parents or guardians are protected, to assist States and localities to provide for the education of all handicapped children and to assess and assure the effectiveness of efforts to educate handicapped children."

There is little doubt that the spirit of the times requires that severely and profoundly handicapped students be allowed to grow within the least restrictive developmental environments. There is also little doubt that the creation of less restrictive developmental environments will require changes of a large magnitude in our educational system. Providing appropriate accommodations for the severely and profoundly handicapped is now the charge. Is the professional community ready to meet that challenge? The answer lies in the attitudes and values that we place on human life. We all have a responsibility to work toward this end, but more importantly, success or failure of this challenge rests squarely on our shoulders.

Definitions of severely handicapped: A survey of state departments of education

Joseph E. Justen III
Gregory E. Brown

State departments of education were surveyed to determine the definitions of severely handicapped currently in use and also to determine whether the provision of education services to this population was mandatory or permissive. It was found that while the majority of states required that education services be provided to all children, fewer than half had a definition of the severely handicapped. Of the states surveyed which had definitions, the majority referred to either the mentally retarded or the multiply handicapped.

Because of recent litigation and legislation, more and more states have begun to recognize and provide services for a group of children loosely referred to as the "severely handicapped." However, the exact composition of this group is often difficult to ascertain. In viewing programs across the nation supposedly designed specifically for the "severely handicapped," one can readily conclude that there is little consensus regarding the parameters of this population.

Undoubtedly, various administrative and political constraints contribute to the lack of consistency in the populations served by these programs. For example, the patterns and sources of funding, or the difficulty of serving low incidence populations in a low density population area, may determine what services are provided to whom. However, this lack of consensus about who should be included in the *severely handicapped* population undoubtedly goes beyond mere administrative concerns to reflect some basic philosophical differences.

The lack of consensus reflected in the programs for the severely handicapped across the nation is also reflected in the positions taken by leading professionals in the field. While most of these individuals have not provided operational definitions of the population to which they are referring, it is clear in their writings and presentations that many are using the term *severely handicapped* in quite different contexts (AAESPH, Note 1; NARC, Note 2). While some have used the term in a rather restricted context to refer to individuals with the most profound forms of retardation, others have used it quite loosely to refer to a wide range of debilitating conditions, often including individuals some might contend are more moderately handicapped. At the most general level, the term *severely handicapped* has probably been most used to refer to any and all children excluded from public schools in the past because of a handicapping condition. Thus, in a real sense, for many states and profes-

"Definitions of Severely Handicapped: A Survey of State Departments of Education," Joseph E. Justen III and Gregory E. Brown, *AAESPH Review*, Vol. 2, No. 1, March 1977. 1977 AAESPH Review.

sionals the term *severely handicapped* is synonymous with *unserved handicapped*.

While the designation *unserved* may be useful in identifying a population in need of special services, it probably is not very useful as a construct for service delivery. In addition, as more and more services become available it will probably not continue to serve as a useful diagnostic construct. As states develop and implement service delivery models for individuals previously denied services, it apparently will be necessary to more adequately describe the population for whom these services are intended and, thus, to resolve definitional problems. The purpose of this study was to ascertain the definitions in current use by state departments across the nation, in order to find viable directions for future efforts to define this population.

PROCEDURE

In October, 1975, letters were mailed to the directors of special education in the 50 state departments of education. Information regarding the following questions was requested in these letters.

1) Does your state have legislation pertaining specifically to the education of the severely handicapped? If yes, are services mandatory or permissive?
2) Does your state have a definition(s) of the severely handicapped for educational purposes? (You may have more than one categorical definition.) If you do, what is that definition? Is it statutory or provided through administrative regulations?

It was also requested in these letters that, if a state had neither a definition nor legislation, this fact be indicated since this information was also important.

In January, a second letter requesting the same information was mailed to those who did not respond to the first letter. A total of 45 states (90%) replied.

In analyzing the information received from the states, the authors attempted to answer the following questions:

1) How many of the states have definitions of the severely handicapped?
2) How many of the states have legislation pertaining to services for the severely handicapped?
3) Is there a relationship between a state having a definition and the mandatory provision of services?
4) What elements do the definitions used by the various states have in common? What are the major differences?

RESULTS

Of the 45 states responding to the survey, 29 (64.4%) indicated that the provision of educational services to the severely handicapped is mandatory in their state. On the basis of the information available, an attempt was made to distinguish between mandatory educational services provided by the local school board or comparable agency and those services provided through the traditional state institutions. Only the former were included in the category of mandatory services.

All but one of these 29 states have legislation which mandates the provision of educational services; the exception, Pennsylvania, is required by U.S. District Court order to provide educational services. With few exceptions, the state laws requiring educational services are general in nature and refer to "all children" or "all handicapped children." Only nine of the 29 states mandating services make specific reference to the *severely handicapped*.

Less than one-half of the states responding (22 of 45) have some sort of definition of the severely handicapped. Of these, only three are statutory and 19 are part of administrative rules, regulations, and guidelines. Two states indicated that the definition provided was only proposed and had yet to be formally adopted.

A fourfold point correlation or phi correlation was computed to determine the relationship between a state having mandatory services and a definition. This relationship is represented graphically in Table 1. A weak positive correlation was found ($r = .17$). Thus, states which have mandatory legislation are somewhat more likely to have a definition as well. However, when tested for statistical significance, this correlation was not found to be significant ($t = 1.12$, $p < .05$).

The insignificance of this correlation and the general lack of consensus in the

1. EDUCATIONAL SERVICES

field regarding the definition of the severely handicapped is reflected in the fact that 13 of 45 states (28.9%) report the mandatory provision of services but lack a definition. Another six (13.3%) have a definition but do not report mandatory services.

The types of definitions used by the various states were categorized on the basis of their main features and emphasis. The categories and the number of states using these definitions are reported in Figure 1. Two types of definitions are used most frequently by those 22 states which have definitions. Nine states refer primarily

Table 1 *States with permissive or mandatory services and with or without a definition*

	Permissive services	Mandatory services	Total
Definition	6	16	22
No definition	10	13	23
Total	16	29	45

to the *mentally retarded,* usually to the *severely* and/or *profoundly retarded*; another nine refer to the *multi-* or *multiply handicapped*; three states use both of these definitions. Therefore, while only 22 states indicate that they have definitions, 25 different definitions of the *severely handicapped* are presently in use in those states.

Three states take an open-ended approach and attempt to focus on those children not currently receiving services. Two take a categorical approach, referring to traditional diagnostic labels, e.g., *deaf-blind, autistic.* And another two attempt to define the *severely handicapped* by referring to the intensity of services required, e.g., staffing patterns.

In order to provide the reader with a feel for the type and range of definitions used by states in working with the severely handicapped, an example of each type is provided.

1) Definitions which focus primarily on the *severely* and *profoundly retarded* (nine states):

    Rhode Island (proposed)—"The severe and profound mentally retarded [includes] a child who, at the time of school evaluation, obtains a score on an individually administered test of intelligence 4 or more standard deviations below the mean . . . and who manifests a pervasive severe or profound impairment in adaptive behavior." (Rhode Island State Board of Regents, Note 3). Some states use the AAMD levels of *mild, moderate, severe,* and *profound* retardation while others use the traditional educational categories, *educable, trainable,* and *custodial.* Although some states indicated that some severely handicapped children are being served in existing programs for the trainable retarded, a definition which referred solely to the *TMR* was *not* considered as constituting a definition of the *severely handicapped.*

2) Definitions focusing primarily on the *multi-* or *multiply handicapped* (nine states):

    New York—"Multiply handicapped: a child who, because of the multiplicity of his handicapping conditions, requires intervention by more than one certified specialist in the area of education of the handicapped. For purposes of the section, visually impaired children shall be included, but those children whose second handicap is solely in the area of speech shall not be included" (New York State Education Department, Note 4).

3) Definitions which focus on those who are not currently being served by any existing educational program (three states):

    Missouri—"'Severely handicapped children,' handicapped children under the age of twenty-one years who, because of the extent of the handicapping condition or conditions . . . are unable to benefit from or meaningfully participate in, programs in the public schools of a regular or special nature" (Vernon's Annotated Missouri Statutes, Note 5).

4) Definitions which did not fit one of the preceding categories and which refer

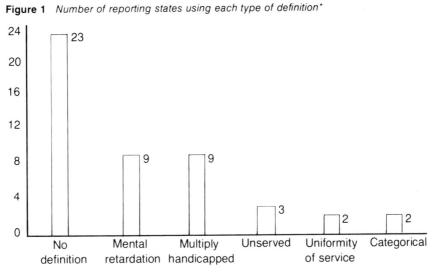

Figure 1 *Number of reporting states using each type of definition**

*Totals to 48 because some states had more than one definition; 45 states reported.

primarily to the intensity and/or extent of service(s) required by the severely handicapped (two states):

Iowa—"The severely handicapped are those pupils also termed 'profoundly handicapped' who have special education needs which require intensive special education programs and services" (Iowa Department of Public Instruction, Note 6).

5) Definitions which define the severely handicapped by enumeration of a number of traditional categories (two states):

Idaho—"The severely handicapped are those children who are profoundly retarded, seriously emotionally disturbed, deaf, blind, and deaf-blind" (Idaho Department of Education, Note 7).

While none of the states surveyed had adopted the BEH definitions of the severely handicapped, programs with federal funding will undoubtedly take this definition into account. It is included as an example in this discussion for two reasons: (1) it cuts across and includes a number of the different types of definitions discussed earlier, and (2) it is likely to have nationwide impact. This definition states:

A severely handicapped child is one who because of the intensity of his physical, mental, or emotional problems, or a combination of such problems, needs educational, social, psychological, and medical services beyond those which have been offered by traditional regular and special education programs, in order to maximize his full potential for useful and meaningful participation in society and for self-fulfillment. Such children include those classified as seriously emotionally disturbed (schizophrenic and autistic), profoundly and severely mentally retarded, and those with two or more serious handicapping conditions such as the mentally retarded-deaf, and the mentally retarded-blind.

Such children may possess severe language and/or perceptual-cognitive deprivations, and evidence a number of abnormal behaviors including: a failure to attend to even the most pronounced social stimuli, self-mutilization, self-stimulation, durable and intense temper tantrums, absence of even the most rudimentary forms of verbal control, and may also have an extremely fragile physiological condition. (United States Office of Education, Bureau for Education of the Handicapped, 1974).

1. EDUCATIONAL SERVICES

DISCUSSION

As evidenced by this survey, relatively few states have attempted to develop a definition(s) of the *severely handicapped* in both functional and operational terms. Even more surprising was the finding that over half of the states surveyed said they had no definition of the *severely handicapped* and yet 56.5% of these same states claimed to have legislation mandating services to all exceptional children. Thus, several states are in the process of serving children they have not even defined.

With the recent passage of PL 94-142, The Education For All Handicapped Children Act (Senate Bill 6), states soon will be required to provide educational services to all children. This national educational mandate will insure that no more children will fall between the cracks of the traditional educational categories and thus be excluded from educational services. This law will not, however, determine what types of educational services are provided to whom.

If appropriate educational programs are to be developed for the severely handicapped, it is necessary to examine systematically what is known about this population. In order to accomplish this, it is important to define clearly the population in question so that all those concerned can communicate with a minimum of confusion and misunderstanding. Thus, as Kolstoe (1972) has noted, at the most elementary level it is important to develop or to accept some definition in order that a common conceptual basis exists for further discussion, research, and program implementation. Without this common frame of reference, it is possible that many professionals within the same state will hold widely divergent views about who should be included in which program.

Undoubtedly, the lack of state definitions observed to date is due to the relative newness of mandatory legislation and the lack of previous programs for the severely handicapped. Hopefully, states will not be complacent in reacting to the new legislative mandates for the severely handicapped but will rather take leadership roles in formulating and implementing effective plans. While they may seem a small issue, initial definitions established by the various state departments may well set the stage for the effectiveness and efficiency of future service delivery models.

REFERENCE NOTES

1. American Association for the Education of the Severely/Profoundly Handicapped. *Second annual conference.* Kansas City, Mo., November 12-14, 1975.
2. National Association of Retarded Citizens. *Proceedings: National training meeting on the education of the severely and profoundly mentally retarded.* New Orleans, La., April 1975.
3. State of Rhode Island, State Board of Regents. *General regulations of the state board of regents governing the special education of handicapped children.* Providence, R.I., 1975.
4. State of New York, State Education Department. *Commissioner's regulations.* Albany, N.Y., 1974.
5. *Vernon's Annotated Missouri Statutes,* 162.670 (Supp. 1975).
6. State of Iowa, Department of Public Instruction. *Rules of special education.* Des Moines, Ia., 1974.
7. State of Idaho, Department of Education. *Administrative rules and regulations: Handbook for special education.* Boise, Idaho, 1975.

REFERENCES

Kolstoe, O. P. *Mental retardation: an educational viewpoint.* New York: Holt, Rinehart and Winston, 1972.

United States Office of Education, Bureau for Education of the Handicapped. *Definition of severely handicapped children.* (45 CFR 121.2), 1974.

On Justice Douglas and Education for the Severely/Profoundly Handicapped

EDWIN W. MARTIN, Ph.D.
*Acting Deputy Commissioner
of Education
Director, Bureau of Education
for the Handicapped*

If I asked you to name the persons responsible for our being here today to discover and determine the educational challenges for severely/profoundly handicapped children, you might very well tell me: Norrie Haring, Lou Brown, the Brickers, Ed Sontag, Paul Thompson, and many others. I'd like to suggest two others: a black man named Brown who lived not far from here—Topeka, Kansas, I believe—who felt his daughter should not have to go to separate and unequal schools; and a man who in 1953 listened to this argument, helped his colleagues decide to end the system of segregated schools in this nation, and so touched off the individual rights movement which led us here today—Justice William Douglas.

My interest is not simply to honor Justice Douglas as he retires, or the courageous Mr. Brown, but to share with you my personal feelings about this meeting of the American Association for the Education of the Severely/Profoundly Handicapped.

JUSTICE DOUGLAS AND INDIVIDUAL RIGHTS

I see this Association—more specifi-

cally, the cause to which it is devoted—as a most significant indicator in the evolution of this nation's character. It is an affirmation of the rights of an individual, however humble, over the forces in the State or Establishment which would deny him an education. This affirmation of individual rights was Justice Douglas's central philosophic tenet, one which involved him in controversy during his more than 36 years on the Supreme Court. He fought complacency; he extended the legal rights of the poor, the criminal, the racially oppressed. As the *Washington Post* said this morning, "Any case attracted his interest if it contained what he saw to be a social or political injustice."

He grew up in Yakima, Washington, in a poor family. He began mountain climbing to regain strength after he contracted polio—another tie to our situation. He worked in the wheat fields, and from this background he became a champion of the individual and of his rights in our society, particularly the right to free speech, even if others considered that speech radical or the community called it "dirty" literature.

PROTECTING THE FEW FROM THE MANY

There are many reasons for not educating the severely and profoundly handicapped. Educating these children is often enormously costly. The class sizes have to be small. In traditional education terms, the gains may be small as well. I have heard the argument that such programs are not fair to the majority. They

rob resources: many more "normal" or even mildly handicapped children could be educated with the same dollars. The only protection a severely handicapped child has against such thinking is a government of laws which is fiercely devoted to the intrinsic right of a given individual. Providing equal opportunity for education to a deaf–blind child does not mean providing only equal dollars. The fundamental issue is the same as it is in the case of providing a tax-paid attorney for an impoverished migrant worker.

I heard the late Justice Black once speak on the Bill of Rights and on its strict construction as he saw it. He talked of its role in trying to keep an individual from going to jail—the protection against self-incrimination and the protection against unreasonable search and seizure. Such protections are not always admired today as we face the threat of growing crime, but the framers of our Constitution knew too well of governments that jailed persons all too easily or that violated the rights of the individual in the name of the State.

The real horror of Watergate and of the current CIA and FBI investigations is how little concern was aroused, and how long it took for people to become concerned. The concepts seem so abstract: a little invasion of privacy in the name of national security; "Well, it's pragmatic, it's necessary."

To my mind, what has made this country great, and what holds our promise for the future, is the preservation of our commitment to the individual

"On Justice Douglas and Education for the Severely/Profoundly Handicapped," Edwin W. Martin, *Journal of Special Education*, Vol. 10, No. 2, 1976. 1976 Journal of Special Education.

9

1. EDUCATIONAL SERVICES

even if, as with our commitment to the profoundly handicapped, it is expensive or unpopular.

OUR RESPONSIBILITIES TO THE HANDICAPPED MINORITY

Within our constitutional framework there are many responsibilities as well as rights. Today, we are promising to fulfill the right of the handicapped individual to an education. As educators or related specialists *we* have responsibilities as well. I would like to mention several of these as I see them.

Need for professional expertise: Knowledge

First, we have the responsibility to know more about how to teach these youngsters and how they learn. The turnout for this meeting is heartening and impressive, because we all know that our universities are not crowded with experts in this area. We are already offering course work in the area, but sometimes without real expertise behind those offerings. As professionals, we must pay the price, even if it is somewhat embarrassing, of learning new skills and attitudes before we teach others. We must not succumb to passing along "book learning" only—an all-too-frequent failure of education.

Need for affective-domain expertise: In emotions, attitudes

Second, we must examine more carefully and systematically the emotional base of our work. We have focused too long on cognitive knowledge alone. What feelings and emotions do teachers of the severely handicapped have? Will they need support systems to cope with their feelings as they work with children who respond somewhat differently than do less severely handicapped children? In my experience, teaching can be a lonely business—one where you must face your failures as well as your successes. Frequently, we have failed to provide the help that teachers need to face these feelings, to share their struggles and problems, to admit to the human frailties we all have. In our quest for rationality we have denied emotion. Surely this work with profoundly handicapped persons will not allow us to continue that pattern.

Need for better evaluation and accountability

Third, I think we must pay greater attention to the effectiveness of our work. This is perhaps the most painful challenge of all. It is so hard to evaluate ourselves. Our fears are great, as are our technical limitations. Yet if we are to mature as a profession we must begin to look at our results in quantitative and qualitative terms. The temptations to ignore this will be great. It's hard, it's costly, it's scary. Further, society will not press us too hard. The charitable orientation toward the handicapped and the history of custodial care suggest to me that society will not look a gift horse in the mouth and challenge those willing to take on this task. The question will really become one of our own self-esteem, of our commitment to know.

Need for interdisciplinary work

More than many areas of human service delivery, education of the profoundly and severely handicapped calls for interdisciplinary efforts. I believe that while examples of successful efforts do exist, in general we are still caught up in parochialism. Each discipline values itself more highly than it honors others. Each knows a little bit more about the real truths.

I don't believe these patterns will be broken down by administrative arrangements, through super agencies or the like. I think we will have to build a new professional literature and new education programs—programs which stress collaborative experiences, not just words about the values of interdisciplinary efforts. What we know as professionals is more than just information and skills. We have a system of values, a system of constructs which guides the way we think, the way we perceive. Unless we can share with other professions some common constructs, some common values, unless we can view human behavior and arrive at some common meanings about that behavior, I doubt that interdisciplinary efforts will work. Essentially, we face a problem concerning the way knowledge is organized by discipline. Our actions are determined by the meanings we give to events. If an educator sees only a need to read, a psychologist sees only a need to be ac-

cepted, a physician sees only a need to be healed, and they cannot see the common core of these processes and ways to achieve all of them simultaneously, then working in the same center or for the same employer will not help.

JUSTICE DOUGLAS'S RIGHTEOUS INDIGNATION—OUR MODEL

Finally, I want to return to Justice Douglas. As the *Post* reports, Justice Black once said of him that his first cry as an infant must have been one of outrage at some injustice. That is a model for each of us. The group of children you strive to serve have had their rights violated. They have been excluded. They have been segregated. They have been placed in dehumanizing situations. They are only beginning to be admitted to the human race as beings with rights.

The road will not be smooth. There will continue to be violations and abuses, conscious and unconscious. Discrimination against the handicapped is generally unconscious in our society. While we have had people who would speak out against blacks or religious groups, no one speaks out against the handicapped. Yet discrimination exists, and it is not entirely a societal accident.

As professionals and as citizens, you must help protect the rights of these citizens. You must use your courage to speak out in public and in your professional groups against such outrages. Many will not understand. They will see only a profoundly damaged organism—"a near vegetable," they might say. They will speak of higher priorities.

What you know, however, is that equity for these citizens is essential to our national security. It is essential for our fidelity to our Bill of Rights. If we violate these persons, we violate our commitment to the principle which protects us all. In this year of our Bicentennial as a nation, your work affirms not only the rights of the severely and profoundly handicapped, but strengthens the rights and protections of every citizen. That principle is what Justice Douglas understood and protected so well.

The Severely Handicapped: A New Horizon

R. PAUL THOMPSON

R. PAUL THOMPSON *is Chief, Special Services Branch, Division of Assistance to States, Bureau of Education for the Handicapped, US Office of Education, Department of Health, Education, and Welfare, Washington, D.C.*

Few parents would be ready to accept Karen as their child. A beautiful, 2 year old with tresses of blond hair, but a twisted body, mere bony stubs for legs, and arms hanging motionless to the side. All this and no response to sound. There might be similar difficulty with loving 15 year old Kevin, who seems to be only a hulk, his brain cells too badly damaged to provide guidance. There is no speech and no control of bodily function; grimaces arising from periodic seizures and pain are the only emotions evoked.

What can the thousands of Karens and Kevins in our society expect out of life? More than most people might have expected, thanks in large part to a developing awareness of human potential. Encouragement of that awareness, particularly as it relates to the needs and possibilities of the many severely handicapped persons in the nation, has been a basic mission of the Bureau of Education for the Handicapped (BEH). Its goal is to help the most severely handicapped children and youth become as independent as possible, thereby reducing their requirements for institutional care and providing opportunity for self development.

A Working Definition

One of the early efforts of a task force created to develop strategies for achieving this objective was to formulate a working definition for the specific population involved. Ultimately, the members of the group agreed upon the following:

> Those children who because of the intensity of their physical, mental, or emotional problems, or a combination of such problems, need educational, social, psychological, and medical services which will make it possible for them to maximize their full potential for meaningful participation in society and for self-fulfillment.

That would include such children as those with severe language deficits, those whose responses to sight, sound, and touch are minimal, and those who abuse their bodies.

A National Campaign

BEH estimates made shortly after the appointment of the task force placed the number of such severely handicapped children and youth at almost 1.5 million, including over 460,000 severely to profoundly retarded, 41,000 severely multihandicapped, and approximately 900,000 seriously emotionally disturbed (autistic or schizophrenic). In short, the number of severely handicapped young needing specialized services was staggering, requiring not only BEH leadership in launching a national campaign, but the vigorous participation of local, state, and private agencies as well. In an effort to strengthen the role of these agencies, BEH requested proposals from creative educators for model demonstrations of efficient, cost effective procedures.

Initial Programs

The result of these requests was the launching in July 1974 of 15 exemplary projects covering such matters as child assessment, training, and education; teacher inservice training; parent counseling and assistance; and community involvement. Through the programs funded, carefully designed services were provided to more than a thousand severely handicapped children and youth. Most of them experienced their constitutional right to an education for the first time. They benefited from new ways developed to determine sensory losses, and new ways of teaching those who had been thought to be unteachable.

Included in the new programs were 5 ingenious ideas for education through the use of electronic aids. Among the innovations coming out of these projects were video taped presentations for assisting parents of severely handicapped infants and small children; counseling and instructional packets for parents living in rural areas, with telephone service available from the home to the master

"The Severely Handicapped: A New Horizon," R. Paul Thompson, *Exceptional Children*, Vol. 43, No. 3, November 1976.
1976 Exceptional Children.

11

1. EDUCATIONAL SERVICES

teacher at no expense to parents; closed circuit television shows for slightly higher functioning children; stimulation programs for severely handicapped children and infants in Appalachia; and closed circuit, computerized home instruction for severely emotionally disturbed children.

Additional Projects

In January 1975, when BEH invited proposals for additional projects, 69 were formally submitted and 7 were funded. Their collective contributions have included models of community coordination, community placement of the severely handicapped, curriculum enrichment, prevocational training, infant stimulation, and use of volunteers.

Encouraged by the national response to the initial 2 years of programs for the severely handicapped, BEH issued 6 requests for new proposals in January 1976, from which over 140 responses were received. Educational specialists who reviewed the proposals were deeply impressed by the high quality that now seems to characterize projected programs in this field.

Added Dimensions

It is becoming increasingly evident that something can be done for the severely handicapped and, more importantly, that they can do something for themselves if they are provided appropriate educational services. Estimates are that by 1980 over 40,000 severely handicapped children and youth will be receiving those services through federally sponsored programs; but, with 1.4 million youth involved, there will have to be even greater activity on the part of state and local agencies. That added dimension is both the challenge and the promise of Public Law 94-142. To meet this challenge, BEH will continue to fund exemplary projects for the severely handicapped, provide technical assistance for programs under way, and facilitate greater accomplishments among the increasing number of agencies that are playing a role.

In this expanding effort, costs represent a major source of concern. However, the issue is not simply one of money. We are learning that the severely handicapped are human beings who were once rejected as ineducable and who are demonstrating today that with the proper kind of training, they can lead satisfying, dignified lives.

Educational Services for the Severely and Profoundly Handicapped

NORRIS G. HARING, Ed.D.
University of Washington

THE PROBLEM

Christmas in Purgatory by Burton Blatt (1966) and *Willowbrook* by Geraldo Rivera (1972) brought the secret, locked, back wards of state institutions for the severely handicapped out into the open—into newspaper headlines, in fact. Burton Blatt denounced institutional care in his pictorial essay which showed the forgotten children, young adults, and others living in deplorable conditions in state institutions. The public was outraged. Blatt gave reasons for these conditions (e.g., understaffed, over-populated institutions) and announced commitments to provide more acceptable standards. His view seemed to be that in the middle of the 20th century, with space exploration in full swing, it was patently absurd to fail to solve some of these relatively simple problems.

But then Geraldo Rivera investigated the state institutions of New York, where at first glance conditions *seemed* to be better. The children were clean, and the rooms were clean. Yet unmistakable gloom hovered over these institutions too. Further investigation uncovered the reality: back wards, locked doors, forgotten people. The scene was reminiscent of the early 1900s or even the early 1800s.

"Why should this be?" was the question asked by many people. "What other choice is there?" was one reply. Were there no alternatives to hospitalization or institutionalization for such citizens as these?

Rivera's 1972 exposure of deplorable conditions was adamant proof that widespread commitment to the educational and social development of the severely handicapped had not been made. Available information that would have offered alternatives—especially the information derived from behavioral technology—had not been applied in teaching even such basic skills as toileting or self-feeding. The children and young adults were left alone. Consequently, they began to exhibit "institutional" behaviors, thereby rendering transition into society an even more dubious, if not impossible, objective to establish for them.

In one sense, speaking about "transition into society" is always problematical. One can examine present society and understand to some extent what skills a handicapped person will need as bare minimum "entrance requirements." But the task of anticipating by 20 years the structure of a society now moving so swiftly that it generates in its citizens a nostalgia for music, events, and customs only 2 years old is better left to astrologers or soothsayers or economists (all of whom seem to operate with about the same rate of success). To further anticipate what specific skills a severely handicapped individual will need 20 years hence to produce a given product in that society—indeed, to anticipate what that product might be—is better left to providence.

Yet in attempting to talk about future improvements in the education and quality of life for the severely and profoundly handicapped, we must confront two variables—both of which are unpredictable and yet so interrelated that change in one is inextricably bound to change in the other. That is, before we can develop an educational system to offer increased academic, vocational, and technical skills that will enable a severely handicapped person to live independently or semi-independently in the community, we must know what that community will require of that individual. We must also know what that individual is capable of, what amount of stress he can sustain, what skills he can acquire, what responsibilities he can handle. At present the potential of this society and its severely handicapped citizens is an open-ended question. Hopefully, as some of the severely handicapped infants now in early intervention programs progress to young adulthood, through programs tailored to their individual needs, we can speak with more confidence about what such

"Educational Services for the Severely and Profoundly Handicapped," Norris G. Haring, *Journal of Special Education,* Vol. 9, No. 4, 1975. 1975 Journal of Special Education.

13

1. EDUCATIONAL SERVICES

citizens can do.

Of course, there are no graduates yet from any of the current individualized programs and there may not be for nearly 20 years; by then the skills necessary to cross a street may have changed. Nevertheless, to repeat the Chinese proverb that John F. Kennedy was so fond of quoting: A journey of a thousand miles begins with a single step. And it is a fact that we have the technology now to begin concerted efforts towards educating severely/profoundly handicapped children.

The behavioral technology developed during the last 25 years should enable these children to develop, maintain, and strengthen new behaviors, and to modify or eliminate inappropriate behaviors (Krumboltz & Krumboltz, 1972). This technology is now being used with severely handicapped children in federally funded demonstration centers. But the challenge we face is to implement available technology in developing even wider-ranging quality programs for all severely handicapped children.

THE CHALLENGE

This challenge was articulated in the Pennsylvania courts during the 1971 suit brought by the Pennsylvania Association of Retarded Citizens. The outcome clearly indicated that free public school education should be provided for mentally retarded persons. Then, in Mills vs. Board of Education of the District of Columbia in 1972, "the ... decision expanded the implications of the Pennsylvania right to an education situation in that *all* handicapped children, not just those labeled as mentally retarded, have a right to a public education. In addition, the Mills case is considered 'a final and irrevocable determination of plaintiffs' constitutional rights' [Friedman, 1972] ..." (Sontag, Burke, & York, 1973).

These federal court mandates prompted the United States Office of Education to establish priority objectives to insure equal educational opportunities for all handicapped children and youth. Efforts in this regard are being coordinated by the Bureau of Education for the Handicapped (BEH) through the design and implementation of six objectives:

1. To assure that every handicapped child is receiving an appropriately designed education;

2. To assist the states in providing appropriate educational services to the handicapped;

3. To assure that every handicapped child who leaves school has had educational career training that is relevant to the job market, meaningful to his career aspirations, and realistic to his fullest potential;

4. To assure that all handicapped children served in the schools have a trained teacher or other resource person competent in the skills required to aid the child in reaching his full potential;

5. To secure the enrollment of preschool-aged handicapped children in federal, state, and local educational and Day Care programs; and

6. To encourage additional educational programming for severely handicapped children, so they may become as independent as possible, by providing opportunities for self-development and thereby reducing their requirements for institutional care.

To meet these objectives, federally funded research, demonstration, and personnel preparation programs have been established across the nation. With advances in technology, and with demonstration centers providing educational services to the severely handicapped, school districts now have both the responsibility and the opportunity to provide reasonable educational services within public school systems.

In short, we have changed our attitudes about our responsibility to provide educational services to all children, regardless of handicap. Programs are being implemented on behalf of children for whom institutionalization was formerly the only available placement. This change in attitude and orientation is owing to the cooperation of parents, professionals, and paraprofessionals in many disciplines working to make the education of severely handicapped children open-ended and free from presuppositions that these children are limited in their behavioral patterns and potentialities.

Still, a critical need exists to change any conceptual limitations placed on future growth of the severely/profoundly handicapped: Their potential is practically unknown because effective intervention programs have not existed until recently. Thus, all statements related to "innate potentialities" should be held in abeyance.

Certainly one of the first steps we must take in finding out more about the potential of severely handicapped persons is to sharpen our diagnostic and assessment skills *so that we can identify as early as possible those children who are in fact at risk.* By identifying these children at birth or early in infancy, we can intervene immediately with systematic educational procedures to help these children develop to their fullest potential, whatever that potential may be. It is critical to intervene early enough, both to counteract the effects of the child's handicap and to prevent development of secondary or associated handicaps that can result from neglect of the primary one. Our diagnostic skills could be sharpened by something as simple as a checklist, based on normal infant development, of responses (or lack of responses) that can alert us to those deviations from normal that signal potential impairment. The checklist should emcompass findings from work with nonhandicapped children, establishing developmental norms from the moment of birth. Fetal development is usually monitored by obstetricians; this is especially critical if there is reason to think a woman might bear a handicapped child.

The Expanding Population

Personnel in special education must not only incorporate the developments of a rapidly changing environment and technology, but must also deal with a rapid expansion of the number, type, and age-range of the handicapped population to be served. An increasing number of states (e.g., Wisconsin, Pennsylvania, Missouri, and Washington) have legislated mandatory preschool education for the severely handicapped. With more and more states likely to follow suit, special education teachers are increasingly finding themselves in roles other than traditional ones: Rather than remedial reading, they are teaching such things as self-feeding, toileting, dressing, and even walking. And though we have the behavioral technology to effect significant behavior change, there have been few standardized curricula developed to teach these fundamental life skills to the severely handicapped.

In addition to preschool education now provided for the severely handicapped, research in early identification and intervention techniques with "high risk" infants is also being undertaken in 34 federally-funded, university-affiliated hospitals and clinics. These programs are designed to intervene as early as possible with the infant in order to remediate the handicapping condition or to prevent further handicaps. With ever-improving screening and diagnostic techniques, most severely handicapping conditions should be diagnosable within 2 to 3 months of birth, with the exception of those virally-caused diseases (e.g., multiple sclerosis) that have long latency periods.

Meeting The Challenge

In order to meet the challenge of providing high quality programs for educating the severely handicapped, our first priority is to develop teacher competencies. We must implement precise instructional procedures: comprehensive curricula, systematic application of behavioral technology, and systematic programming. Traditional methods which may be successful in a classroom for normal children are not sufficient for the special classroom. How are these competencies to be realized? What kinds of skills will be required for teaching the severely handicapped? In responding to these questions, we must establish some guidelines.

Teachers must have *at least* the following basic skills and competencies if they are to achieve success with the severely handicapped. They must be able to:

1. Sequence instructional curricula and perform analyses of tasks related to curricular objectives. The teaching sequence should include a precisely defined set of prerequisite behaviors; a statement of terminal behaviors, with examples of correct performance; and a list of intermediate behaviors, from beginning to end, that are required to meet the final behavioral objectives.

2. Evaluate changes that occur in the child's performance each day. This requires direct and continuous measurement that yields a day-by-day comparison of performance in order to show the child's progress. As the child acquires responses, the learning tasks, as specified, may be recorded as "go" or "no go." The frequency of responses—for example, any that occur at a rate of 1 or more times per minute—should be recorded.

3. Select, purchase, construct, or have constructed adequate instructional materials for teaching tasks, skills, and facts that are needed by these children. In many cases teachers may be able to design and build specially tailored prosthetic devices to assist children in tasks which are difficult or impossible to perform without these aids.

4. Involve parents in the teaching process. This relationship can prove to be most effective if parents are given instruction and demonstrations that enable them to work productively with their children. Teachers should work with parents in establishing the teaching objectives and the procedures to be used, and should instruct them in the skillful application of behavioral principles. Parents will learn to improve their teaching skills as they observe the teacher modeling the teaching task. Following that, parents should be given an opportunity to teach while the teacher observes and provides suggestions. Parents usually become very good teachers and, as they do, they are able to exert significant positive influence on the management of their own children.

5. Arrange and manage reinforcing contingencies which are often required to persuade the child to attend to tasks in individual and group instruction. Having children attend and respond productively in groups of six to eight requires an ingenious arrangement of teaching and reinforcing events.

6. Engage in teamwork. Any comprehensive instructional program for severely handicapped children requires teamwork. The other members of the team—for instance, the communication disorders specialist, the occupational therapist, the physical therapist—should apply their intervention skills together in the same setting. The opportunity for each to see other colleagues apply their own skills and competencies increases the effectiveness of the overall management strategy because each professional person learns from the other. This builds respect and cooperation (Haring, 1975).

Personnel Preparation Programs

The establishment of programs to prepare personnel for educating the severely/profoundly handicapped will be a decisive factor in implementing the above considerations within the public school environment. Federal BEH guidelines recommend four basic components of personnel preparation programs: (a) research design, (b) high quality service and demonstration, (c) professional and paraprofessional training, and (d) dissemination of effective procedures and materials.

With the support of the BEH, federal funding has been used to establish these personnel preparation programs nationwide. Urgent priority has been given to those trainees who are preparing to educate the severely/profoundly handicapped. Demonstration centers have programs based on behavioral technology, including: infant learning programs, parent training programs, pre-academic and academic programs, applied academic programs, prevocational and vocational training, community placement for young adults, and programs for developing leisure time and recreational activity skills.

It is encouraging to be able to list some schools and agencies which are already providing teaching models: University of Kansas; University of Kentucky; Maryland State Department of Special Education; University of Miami, Florida; University of New Mexico; Oregon State System of Higher Education; University of Oregon; Pennsylvania State Department of Special Education; University of Vermont; and the University of Wisconsin at Madison. All are concerned specifically with identification, and with diagnostic/pre-

1. EDUCATIONAL SERVICES

scriptive and follow-up services, the object of which is to involve as many segments of the community as possible in integrating the handicapped child to his society. Within a controlled setting, procedures are tested and evaluated, specific skills are taught, and packets of materials are prepared for use in the community. Therapeutic, recreational, educational, and social needs are all met within the demonstration center. It must be stressed that these are not merely self-contained worlds where the severely handicapped may take refuge. Rather, they are centers whose primary concern is the re-entry of the handicapped child into the world. Therefore, these centers place high priority on providing him with skills necessary for that re-entry and on providing the public with the means to facilitate his integration.

Parent Involvement and Training

It must be emphasized that personnel preparation includes preparing and training parents. We have discussed how parents should be included as much as possible in instructional activities, as they are in demonstration centers. Parent training programs must continue to investigate critical variables in home and community management of severely/profoundly handicapped children in order to develop complete and relevant parent instruction. Like paraprofessional training, parent training should be established in all communities through special courses.

Parent training programs must not only provide training in caring for the severely/profoundly handicapped child; they must also be able to deal with primary difficulties that inhibit the parents' ability to meet their child's needs. Consider the plight of a family with several children when the parents are unemployed and when one child is severely handicapped and needs intervention. Without a financial base, the family could be literally starving. Therefore, the first priority is to help the family obtain food stamps, health care, and other support, in order to meet their most basic needs. Only after these primary needs are met can the parent training program profitably begin individualized instruction for the parents

with their child.

Considerations for parent training programs will have to expand to include such variations from the traditional "nuclear family" in our society as the communal home, e.g., a foster parent program or a group home, with several parental figures and several children. Evaluation and possible revision of adoption procedures for severely/profoundly handicapped children and youth should also be considered. Additionally, parental training may be directed by the courts as a means of rehabilitating parents involved in child abuse cases. Two common child abuse situations that call for involving professionals serving the handicapped are: abuse of a severely/profoundly handicapped child, or (more commonly) the extreme abuse of a child that results in his becoming severely/profoundly handicapped. Finally, the administrator implementing parent training programs obviously must consider the appropriate facilities available for dealing with handicapped parents. For example, communicating with the deaf parents of a deaf/severely retarded child cannot be expediently facilitated by telephone. Alternative methods for efficient, quick communication have to be established.

The Need for Essential Community Support

Even if we perfect an educational system which can optimize a severely handicapped person's functioning in this society, that person still could not function even semi-independently if certain external support services were not available to him. What, for instance, happens to a severely handicapped person who lives at home when his parents die? Is that individual forced to be institutionalized (even though he is able to hold a job) simply because he can't "afford the rent"? What respite care services are now available to parents of severely handicapped children? What are the difficulties in obtaining life insurance, dental care, and medical care for a severely handicapped person? These are questions which must be addressed.

Clearly, what is required is an assignment of priorities, a kind of global "task analysis" applied to society's significant

responses toward such a support system. Dr. Marc Gold (1974) of the University of Illinois at Urbana-Champaign has discussed the concept of "power," which means whatever it takes to perform a given task: in this case, however much energy, creativity, money, time, hard thinking, and work society will have to expend to insure an effective system for delivering comprehensive services to the severely handicapped. We need especially to assess how much and what kind of "power" is required if effective and realistic legislation for the severely handicapped is to be passed through local, state, and federal legislatures.

Given our unstable economy, dwindling food supplies, rising unemployment, the impact of environmental pollutants—given so very little that can be held constant, the task of analyzing the individual skills and societal support systems to improve the quality of life for the severely handicapped may seem insurmountable. In chess circles, however, there is a rule of thumb generally adhered to by players when the game becomes too complex, or when there are too many variables to take into consideration: Essentially the strategy is to "reduce and simplify." That is, when the play gets too complex, it is wise to begin trading pieces until the board has been reduced to a point where moves are more easily anticipated. Similarly, we can begin our task of determining what to teach by delineating only those skills which must be taught, which are transportable across a variety of situations, and which are *absolutely essential* to marginal functioning in society on an independent or semi-independent basis. The same is true of the support we can fairly expect or ask of the community and the society at large to provide for the severely handicapped individual who progresses through individualized programs of instruction from early infancy to childhood to adolescence and who wishes to take his rightful place in society. In other words, we are talking not only about individual skills but also about community support services which, if not provided, will result in the institutionalization of those severely handicapped individuals who cannot function without them.

National Dissemination of Information

In order to support activities that will meet the challenge of supplying comprehensive services for the severely handicapped, there must be a national effort to disseminate current technology expediently to those who are directly and daily involved with this population. It is common knowledge that publishing materials is a slow process—usually there is an 18 month delay. As we consider the mandates for immediate service, the problem is even more evident. Information is needed now, personnel preparation is needed now, and we dare not waste time reinventing the wheel. One answer to this problem is to share information, especially on a multi-disciplinary basis. This sharing can help us to expand our technology.

There has not until recently been a formal organization advocating quality services for all severely/profoundly handicapped people, supported by all of the people who may be involved with this population (educators, parents, allied health personnel, and those providing community-based services).

One group involved in preparing personnel to educate the severely/profoundly handicapped attended an informal information exchange in November, 1974. As the 2-day seminar continued, others became involved: representatives of BEH, university-based educators, pediatricians, businessmen, parents, psychologists, public school teachers and administrators, state directors of special education, and graduate students. This remarkably diverse group recognized a common interest and voted to form the American Association for the Education of the Severely/Profoundly Handicapped.

Since that first meeting, the Association has become a legally incorporated non-profit organization. A monthly newsletter is published to provide information on the very latest research, technology, programs, and resources concerning the severely/profoundly handicapped. The Association also disseminates materials to members five times a year—the latest information about programs being used, resources available, and annotated bibliographies of other published materials.

We hope that this Association will augment all that has been organized previously in behalf of the severely/profoundly handicapped and contribute significantly to future activities, including developing a national network for communication and dissemination. This article, the first in a continuing series, is one effort in support of a national network for disseminating information. The series will review the work of the Association and other agencies and individuals pioneering in services to the severely/profoundly handicapped.

Summary

Special educators have been challenged to provide services for the severely/profoundly handicapped; and to be responsible we must continue programs at each developmental stage of the person's life. In addition to infant learning programs, we need vigorous programs for teaching self-help skills, as well as prevocational and vocational training for older severely handicapped children and young adults. The individual cannot be abandoned at age 21. All interdisciplinary services must be coordinated and continued as we deal with the realities of today's world. The implications of these realities demand that we develop a process for systematic follow-up so that no severely/profoundly handicapped individual gets "lost" to service at any point during his lifetime. This challenge cannot be met without national dissemination of materials so that quality services can be available in any part of the United States.

This is the direction we must take. The foundations have been established: We know what should be accomplished with regard to early identification, early intervention, preschool and school-age programs, vocational training, personnel preparation, parental and interdisciplinary involvement, and national dissemination. What we don't know are the future implications of such programs as they relate to the changing direction of society. It is difficult to predict the skills which will be needed 20 years from now. But this is why it is so important to remain flexible in our approach and sensitive to the changing relationship of the handicappped individual to his society.

References

Blatt, B. *Christmas in purgatory: A photographic essay on mental retardation.* Boston, Mass.: Allyn & Bacon, 1966.

Gold, M. Inservice training for Experimental Education Unit staff, University of Washington, Seattle: November 1974.

Haring, N. G., & Brown, L. (Eds.). *Teaching the severely handicapped—A yearly publication* (Vol. 1). New York: Grune & Stratton, 1976, in press.

Krumboltz, J. D., & Krumboltz, H. B. *Changing children's behavior.* Englewood Cliffs, N.J.: Prentice-Hall, 1972.

Rivera, G. *Willowbrook.* New York: Vantage Books, 1972.

Sontag, E., Burke, P., & York, R. Considerations for serving the severely handicapped in the public schools. *Education and Training of the Mentally Retarded,* 1973, 2(8), 20–26.

A Bill of Rights for the Handicapped

Public Law 94-142 will bring schools closer
to the principles of democracy on which
the Nation was founded by opening classrooms to a
new student clientele

By any standards, Public Law 94-142—enacted last November as the Education for All Handicapped Children Act and scheduled for full implementation in Fiscal Year 1978—is blockbuster legislation. Schools in every part of the Nation are destined to feel its impact, and to be sturdier and more broadly "American" as a consequence.

The most recent in a series of refinements of the Education of the Handicapped Act, P.L. 94-142 has been hailed as a "Bill of Rights for the Handicapped," promising an end to the inglorious custom of treating persons with disabilities as second-class citizens.

It gives national imprimatur to the proposition that the claim of a handicapped individual to first-rate schooling (and by extension to all other privileges offered by our society) is no less compelling than that of any other American.

It opens the way for the Nation's schools to broaden their horizons, no longer focusing their operations solely on "regular" students but giving equal consideration to those with handicaps—including placing such youngsters in regular classrooms to the fullest extent that doing so would be in their best interests.

P.L. 94-142 is remarkable among Federal education laws for being permanent, voted by margins of 404 to 7 in the House and 87 to 7 in the Senate to serve the Nation's schools in perpetuity.

Moreover, many of the advances it calls for have specific implications for the education of nonhandicapped youngsters as well. Two are especially noteworthy. The first, adopting a practice that enlightened educators have been advocating for many years, requires that children served by the Act be educated in accordance with individual plans tailored to their particular needs and capacities. The second calls for making what is now termed "preschool" education a standard part of the elementary-level operation, providing free public education to all handicapped children starting at age three. Over the next few years these important innovations can be expected to receive careful study not just by the special education community but by educators in general, and doubtless by parents as well.

Mr. Goodman is Executive Secretary for the National Advisory Committee on the Handicapped.

LEROY V. GOODMAN

P.L. 94-142 is in any case a big, ambitious law—representing in the view of one of its distinguished sponsors, Sen. Harrison Williams (D.-N.J.), "the most significant development" in Federal school legislation since the enactment of Title I of the Elementary and Secondary Education Act of 1965. Its magnitude is suggested by the scope of some of the challenges it sets out to deal with, as cataloged in its opening passages:

"There are more than eight million handicapped children in the United States today," and those children have special educational needs that are not being fully met.

"More than half" of them "do not receive appropriate educational services."

"One million" are in fact "excluded entirely from the public school system."

Many other handicapped children are not "having a successful educational experience because their handicaps are undetected."

The State and local agencies have the responsibility for solving such problems as these, the law declares, and advances in the training of teachers and in developing improved diagnostic and instructional procedures and methods assure that the States and localities could do the job. The hitch, P.L. 94-142 says, is that they can't tackle it properly because they do not have the resources.

Against that background—and picking up on guarantees introduced in P.L. 93-380 enacted two years ago—P.L. 94-142 sets out to make certain that without exception, eve-

ry one of the Nation's handicapped children (defined as "mentally retarded, hard of hearing, deaf, speech impaired, visually handicapped, seriously emotionally disturbed, orthopedically impaired, or other health impaired children, or children with specific learning disabilities") receives "special education and related services."

The scope of assistance inherent in this goal might seem to suggest that the most noteworthy aspect of the bill is the size of the outlays it implies, and in fact the numbers do get big. What most observers see as being of greater significance, however, is the fact that the policies expressed in the law are binding irrespective of what happens as regards the size of appropriations. Those policies clearly are worth noting, and they include the following:

□ A free public education will be made available to all handicapped children between the ages of 3 and 18 by no later than September of 1978 and all those between 3 and 21 by September of 1980. Coverage of children in the 3-to-5 and 18-to-21 ranges will not be required in States whose school attendance laws do not include those age brackets. Nevertheless, it is now national policy to begin the education of handicapped children by at least age three, and to encourage this practice P.L. 94-142 authorizes incentive grants of $300 over the regular allocation for each handicapped child between the ages of three and five who is afforded special education and related services.

□ For each handicapped child there will be an "individualized educational program"—a written statement jointly developed by a qualified school official, by the child's teacher and parents or guardian, and if possible by the child himself. This written statement will include an analysis of the child's present achievement level, a listing of both short-range and annual goals, an identification of specific services that will be provided toward meeting those goals and an indication of the extent to which the child will be able to participate in regular school programs, a notation of when these services will be provided and how long they will last, and a schedule for checking on the progress being achieved under the plan and for making any revisions in it that may seem called for.

□ Handicapped and nonhandicapped chil-

Reprinted from *American Education*, November 1976. U.S. Department of Health, Education, and Welfare, Office of Education.

dren will be educated together to the maximum extent appropriate, and the former will be placed in special classes or separate schools "only when the nature or severity of the handicap is such that education in regular classes," even if they are provided supplementary aids and services, "cannot be achieved satisfactorily."

Tests and other evaluation material used in placing handicapped children will be prepared and administered in such a way as not to be racially or culturally discriminatory, and they will be presented in the child's native tongue.

There will be an intensive and continuing effort to locate and identify youngsters who have handicaps, to evaluate their educational needs, and to determine whether those needs are being met.

In the overall effort to make sure education is available to all handicapped children, priority will be given first to those who are not receiving an education at all and second to the most severely handicapped within each disability who are receiving an inadequate education.

In school placement procedures and in fact in any decisions concerning a handicapped child's schooling, there will be prior consultation with the child's parents or guardian, and in general, no policies, programs, or procedures affecting the education of handicapped children covered by the law will be adopted without a public notice.

The rights and guarantees called for in the law will apply to handicapped children in private as well as public schools, and youngsters in private schools will be provided special education at no cost to their parents if the children were placed in these schools or referred to them by State or local education agency officials.

The States and localities will undertake comprehensive personnel development programs, including inservice training for regular as well as special education teachers and support personnel, and procedures will be launched for acquiring and disseminating information about promising educational practices and materials coming out of research and development efforts.

In implementing the law, special effort will be made to employ qualified handicapped persons.

The principles set forth a few years ago in Federal legislation aimed at the elimination of architectural barriers to the physically handicapped will be applied to school construction and modification, with the Commissioner authorized to make grants for these purposes.

The State education agency will have jurisdiction over all education programs for handicapped children offered within a given State, including those administered by a noneducation agency (a State hospital, for example, or the welfare department).

An advisory panel will be appointed by each governor to advise the State's education agency of unmet needs, comment publicly on such matters as proposed rules and regulations, and help the State develop and report relevant data. Membership on these panels will include handicapped individuals and parents and guardians of handicapped children.

Many of these policies have at one time or another been advocated by individual educators or by professional associations. Several have in fact been established within particular States, either by legislative action or as a consequence of court suits brought on behalf of handicapped children. And for more than five years, OE's Bureau of Education for the Handicapped (and particularly its Deputy Commissioner, Edwin W. Martin) have been urging a national goal of providing education for all handicapped children and of doing so by 1980—a principle and a target date now spelled out in the law. In short, the concepts involved are not new. The difference is that through P.L. 94-142 they have become requirements, and accommodation to them is a condition of being eligible to receive support under the Act's funding provisions.

Like so many other aspects of the Act, those provisions are both lofty and innovative, entailing some noteworthy changes in the ways by which Federal education dollars have traditionally been distributed. Allocation of the current $100 million annual appropriation for the State grant program, for example, is based on a funding formula by which the number of children in

---

P.L.94-142 has been voted to serve the Nation's schools in perpetuity

---

a State between the ages of 3 and 21 is multiplied by $8.75. Starting with FY 1978, however, State allocations are to be determined by a radically different formula which at the same time rewards extra effort to educate handicapped children and calls upon the Federal Government to take on an increasing share of the cost.

The first element of the new formula's equation again involves the 3-to-21 age range but includes only those youngsters in that range who are handicapped and who are receiving special education. Thus the

more handicapped children the State sets out to educate, the more money it will be entitled to. The second element is a specified percentage of the national average public school expenditure per child. For FY 1978 the proportion of the overall allocation for which a given State will be eligible is to be determined by multiplying the number of handicapped children being served by five percent of the national average expenditure. At the current expenditure rate that would translate into an estimated overall authorization of $378 million.

For FY 1979 the multiplication factor doubles, with the number of children being served multiplied by *ten* percent of the national per pupil expenditure. Thereafter it continues to rise by an additional ten percent annually for another three years, to a permanent level of 40 percent—that is, the number of handicapped children being served in the State times 40 percent of the National average per pupil expenditure.

Based on the current per pupil expenditure, that could mean a FY 1981 authorization of more than $3.16 billion, and even that figure might be low, depending on whatever changes inflation or other factors might work on national average expenditures during the next four years. It is important to note, however, that the actual amounts of money to become available will depend in large measure on the President's budget and the subsequent actions of the Congressional Appropriations committees. Authorization amounts frequently far exceed actual appropriations.

Accompanying the new formula is a new system by which funds are to be distributed. As has been the arrangement since the launching of the State grant program, all grants made this year and next are to be directly controlled by the States. Under the new formula, however, the States are to pass along 50 percent of the FY 1978 funds they receive to their local education agencies, and in FY 1979 and thereafter the States are to retain only 25 percent of their total, with the local districts receiving 75 percent.

State and local education agencies alike must take into account certain limitations in how the new formula may be applied in determining allotments. As regards the first part of the equation—the number of handicapped children receiving special education—Congress sought to deflect any temptation to stack the deck by limiting the total to no more than 12 percent of the State's overall 5-to-17 population (a provision also aimed at discouraging questionable identification of youngsters as being handicapped). Similarly, not more than one sixth of the 12 percent may include children identified as having "specific learning disabilities" (a term the law incidentally instructs the Commissioner of Education to more clearly define).

1. EDUCATIONAL SERVICES

Such limitations aside, P.L. 94-142 portends a major expansion of the Nation's commitment to handicapped children. To participate in that expansion the States must have taken two steps. First, they must have adopted a "full service" policy of assuring all handicapped children the right to a free appropriate public education. And second, they must have prepared for submission to the Commissioner of Education a plan for implementing that policy. In essence the State plan—it must be revised annually—is a document reporting on the current situation in the States as regards education of the handicapped and spelling out the methods, procedures, and resources it pledges to employ toward putting into practice the various policies set forth in the law—serving all handicapped children, opening up regular classrooms to such children, the September 1978 and September 1980 benchmarks, priorities for unserved and severely handicapped children, and the like.

For its part the local education agency (LEA) must submit a formal application to the State education agency (SEA) similarly endorsing these policies and giving assurance that it will carry them out. This application must then be supplemented by regular reports to the SEA. If along the way the State finds evidence that an LEA is failing to comply with all the provisions of the law, it may, after having given proper notice, hold up further payments to the district until the problem is corrected, meanwhile using these funds to make other arrangements for serving the affected children.

The Office of Education is similarly made responsible for riding herd on the States through mechanisms which begin with notifying a noncomplying State of OE's intention to take action. This could go as far as the Federal circuit court in the instance of a State that appealed an adverse OE ruling.

If the Commissioner finds there to be a "substantial" failure to meet the various provisions of P.L. 94-142—either by a State or by an intermediate or local agency within the State—the law says he "shall" withhold further payments under the Act and that he "may" withhold funds earmarked for education of the handicapped under the Elementary-Secondary and Vocational Education Acts.

Action also might be taken by the parents of individual children, for the Congress went to considerable pains to spell out various procedural safeguards. It is now required, for example, that parents or guardians have an opportunity to examine all relevant records bearing on the identification of children as being handicapped, on evaluating the nature and severity of their disability, and on the kind of educational setting in which they are placed. The latter issue is expected to be of particular concern

to parents who feel their handicapped children have unfairly been denied access to regular classes. Schools are called upon to give written notice prior to changing a child's placement (and a written explanation if it refuses a parent's request for such a change), and statements of this kind are to be in the parents' native tongue.

In the event of objections to a school's decision, there must be a process by which parents can register their complaints. That process must also include an opportunity for an impartial hearing which offers parents rights similar to those involved in a court case—the right to be advised by counsel (and by special education experts if they wish), to present evidence, to cross-examine witnesses, to compel the presence of any witnesses who do not appear voluntarily, to be provided a verbatim report of the proceedings, and to receive the decision and findings in written form.

As a result of the Act, Congress expects substantial, sustained progress

---

The advances called for in P.L. 94-142 entail such a break from the traditional suppression of the handicapped that some people in education might imagine that the Act's language represents only the ideal. Not so. Congress plainly expects specific, substantial, sustained progress, and it calls upon the Commissioner to report at least annually and in detail as to precisely what gains are being made.

For each State and within each disability, for example, there are to be data for the overall number of handicapped children "who require special education and related services;" the number receiving a "free appropriate public education" contrasted with the number who should be but aren't; and the number participating in regular classrooms together with the number who have been placed in separate classrooms or "otherwise removed from the regular education environment." And there must be figures for the number of handicapped children enrolled in public and private institutions, with a breakdown in each for those receiving an appropriate education and those receiving something less than that.

In addition to providing this statistical information, OE is called upon to evaluate the Act's overall annual performance.

Among other things that evaluation must include an assessment of the effectiveness of procedures established by the States and education agencies within the States to assure that handicapped children are placed in the least restrictive environment commensurate with their needs; and a report on arrangements made to prevent erroneous classification of children as eligible to be counted (and thus funded) under the Act.

In short, Congress is four-square for accountability, and it has instructed OE to keep score on how the States and local education agencies are doing. That's quite an assignment, given the fact that there are more than 16,000 school districts in the United States, and the Bureau of Education for the Handicapped is busy now trying to gear up for carrying it out.

Members of the BEH staff also are busy preparing the various regulations required by Congress as a preliminary step to the law's full implementation. In all, these regulations will address a dozen or so different topics, some minor and some of general impact. The drafting process involves numerous steps, including a series of ten "input" conferences held last March and April to get comments and suggestions from State and local education officials, teachers, handicapped individuals, parents of handicapped children, advocacy groups, State legislators, and others with a direct stake in the law.

These and other suggestions received by BEH were then used as the basis for deliberations by an "input" team of some 100 persons from around the Nation chosen to represent the broadest range of "consumers" and "users" of P.L. 94-142. The documents they produced are now being reviewed and where necessary refined by officials of BEH and the HEW Office of General Counsel, and final versions will be published in the *Federal Register* by no later than December of this year.

Meanwhile in State departments of education and local school districts across the country, planning is similarly under way toward preparing for the day on which all of the P.L. 94-142 revisions of the Education of the Handicapped Act will be in effect. That would be October 1, 1977—the start of the 1978 Fiscal Year and the date on which American education will enter a new era.

P.L. 94-142 will most obviously affect the 10 to 12 percent of the school population who are handicapped. But its benefits will be felt by all other students as well, and by all teachers and administrators. The fundamental promise of P.L. 94-142 is that it will strengthen public education in general by strengthening what has been one of its weakest links. And in opening classroom doors to a new student clientele, it will bring the Nation's schools far closer to the principles of democracy and justice on which the Nation was founded.

Education:
An Inalienable Right

THOMAS K. GILHOOL

☐ Litigation is busting out all over. In increasing numbers handicapped citizens—citizens who are different and citizens who are thought to be different—are turning to the courts to secure their rights, to secure to themselves that which is due them.

GROWING LITIGATION

In San Francisco an 18 year old high school graduate who is dyslexic and who after graduation is only able to read at the fifth grade level has gone to court for damages against the school system for failure to teach. In San Francisco, a number of citizens, some of them handicapped and some of them family, friends, and associates of the handicapped, have gone to court to strike down a zoning ordinance which would exclude from certain neighborhoods small group residences for handicapped citizens. In Washington, D.C., handicapped citizens have gone to court to insure that the subway system that is being built there will accommodate physically handicapped citizens.

Right to Treatment

Among the cases now in litigation and in significant number decided, three lines may be discussed. The first line of cases has come to be called the right to treatment cases. These cases, in contemporary terms, began in Alabama when Judge Johnson of the northern district of Alabama in the case of *Wyatt v. Stickney* was called upon to look at certain state institutions for the mentally ill and for the mentally retarded.

Judge Johnson in that case ruled that citizens residing at state schools and hospitals indeed have certain rights. They have the right to a humane physical and psychological environment. They have the right to treatment or, if you will, habilitation, or, if you will, program. They have the right to an individual program fitted to their capabilities, a program which is designed individually and reviewed often and a program which, of course, includes education. They have a panoply of other rights such as the right to privacy, the right to use the telephone and to

receive and send letters, and finally the right to receive their programs in the least restrictive setting, that is, in the community or perhaps in the public school rather than in a remote and isolated institution. Right to treatment cases similar to this Alabama case are pending now in Massachusetts, New York, Nebraska, Minnesota, and Wisconsin.

Question of Standards

The second line of cases began in California against the backdrop of the following facts: While 9% of the school population in California is Black, 27% of the children enrolled in educable retarded classes are Black; while 13% of the school population in California is Chicano, 26% of the educable class population is Chicano; and while in New Mexico, for example, 7,000 of the school population enrolled in special education are girls, 11,000 (4,000 more) are boys. Those figures, of course, do not merely characterize California or New Mexico. That discrimination, that overbalance, can be found in each one of our states. In a line of cases that began with the case of *Diana v. State Board of Education* (1970) and was followed by the case of *Larry P. v. Riles*, 343 F. Supp. (1972) and recently by the case of *Ruiz v. State Board of Education* (1971), the courts have addressed the question of the standards applied to assign children to special education. Those cases have resulted in such things as an injunction against group testing, the requirement that tests be standardized— indeed be developed and standardized for cultural and language subgroups in our society— and the requirement that no one be assigned to a special program without the consent of the parent.

Right to Education

This second line of cases bears directly upon the third, to which I especially want to attend. They are the cases that have come to be called the right to education cases, and they are concerned with the access to free public education for all exceptional children. They seek and have secured zero reject education. This third line of

1. EDUCATIONAL SERVICES

cases is concerned as well with the role of parents and children themselves in the design of their education. They are concerned with, as we have come to call it, securing the right to a due process hearing.

The third line of cases began in Pennsylvania with the case of the *Pennsylvania Association for Retarded Children v. the Commonwealth of Pennsylvania*. It was a historical accident, of course, that in the beginning the class of children suing was the retarded. In subsequent cases, of which there are now a great number, the class of children suing to secure their rights include all exceptional children. The Pennsylvania case and the decision therein was followed shortly by a decision in the District of Columbia. That was followed by litigation against the New Orleans Parish School District and the State of Louisiana. In turn, that case has been followed by four or five cases in the state of North Carolina and by cases in Maryland, Kentucky, Rhode Island, Maine, Delaware, New York, Massachusetts, North Dakota, Colorado, Nevada, and Wisconsin. Within the next several weeks the states of Hawaii, Arizona, New Mexico, and California will be in court on the right to education.

TURNING TO THE COURTS

In a sense, resort to the courts by those in the movement of which we are members is new, but it should not be strange. There are, I suspect, too many who think that the resort to litigation is an act of hostility, just short of a declaration of war. That, of course, is not the case. The use of the courts to secure one's rights is not really different from the things we have been doing for many decades. It is not different from resorting to the legislature by lobbying or from resorting to the executive by way of negotiations with statewide or local school officials. To be sure, the language may be a bit different and that is what lawyers are for—to translate the claims of children, parents, and others into language that the courts can address. But then, the language with which one speaks to the legislature is slightly different from the language with which one speaks to administrators. It is essentially the same, however; we are after our rights.

The courts also have slightly different powers than do the legislature and the executive. For example, it is the art of accommodation that characterizes decisions in the legislature and in the executive. In the courts it is not a question of accommodation; it is the art of the necessary. If the Constitution requires it, if the statutes require it, it shall be done; there is no question of accommodating. Perhaps most significantly, it is important to understand what has now been made most clear by the United States Supreme Court, which in the case of *Shapiro v. Thompson* held unconstitutional the one year resi-

dence requirement for public assistance. The point is that the absence of money is no defense for the failure to deliver rights as required by the Constitution and by the laws. The state cannot grant services to some and withhold them from others merely because it would cost more to give services to all. So, there are some special advantages in turning to the courts.

Many persons concerned about the hostility of which I spoke have eschewed the courts for a good period of time. They have been concerned in the school context, for example, with the difficulties presented by suing those administrators and teachers upon whom they depend for services, a fear appropriate to the situation. The experience in the Pennsylvania case and other cases indicates that that fear too is misplaced. I need not remind you of what The Council for Exceptional Children proclaimed in a draft policy statement on the organization and administration of special education (CEC Policies Commission, 1971). CEC—you—said that there is no dividing line which excludes some children and includes others in educational programs. Mentally retarded children of yesteryear who were excluded because they were "unteachable" are now recognized to be teachable. The point is that lawyers and parents turning to the courts are doing nothing special or unusual. Essentially, what they have done is to adopt the agenda long since set by the best of the professionals and shared by the parents' movement, and they have taken that agenda to court. And so, the experience in the litigation has been that those named as defendants, if they are good professionals, welcome litigation as an opportunity to advance the agenda which they share.

AN OLD TRADITION

In going to the courts, exceptional citizens have joined an old tradition in the United States. That tradition, the use of the courts to achieve social change, to achieve justice, dates back at least to 1905 when W. E. B. Dubois and his associates founded the National Association for the Advancement of Colored People (NAACP). From the very beginning they articulated among their strategies the use of the courts to achieve the rights that they were claiming. In pursuit of that strategy, for over 50 long years the NAACP turned again and again to the courts. That effort culminated in the decision of the US Supreme Court in 1954 in *Brown v. Board of Education* which held unconstitutional segregated schooling.

You are familiar, of course, with the use of the courts in the late 1950's and in the early 1960's by the civil rights movement. In the early 1960's, as lawyers became available in some significant number to low income citizens, the poor, welfare recipients, public housing tenants, and low income consumers resorted to the courts. As the 1960's wore on, the courts were used by the women's movement, a use not unlike that by the labor movement some 30 years before. More recently, the elderly have turned to the courts to assert their rights.

That is the tradition into which 13 retarded children in January of 1971 stepped and placed all of us. It is a tradition that is bound not merely by historical accident but rather by a certain common experience shared by each of the groups. It is the experience of being on the wrong end of the judgment made so widely in our society that *we* are superior and *they*—the poor, the women, the aged, the handicapped—are inferior.

That judgment has had, of course, enormous consequences. It means that they are not persons. It means that they need not be heard. It means that they need not be listened to. It means that we need not act on what they say to us (which has, of course, characterized official behavior toward each of those groups for a considerable period of time). It means that attached to them is a certain stigma, and following on the stigma is prejudice, discrimination, finally the tendency to separate them out—to institutionalize them.

There are other consequences as well. When that judgment is being fed back to those of us who are on the wrong end of it, again and again and again by people and by institutions, we come to believe it; we come to believe, as the retarded and their families have come to believe, that indeed we are inferior. We tend then to feel ashamed, to feel guilty, and to be most timid in the face of authority, to be timid too often in asserting our rights.

This tradition, which in some sense has characterized the experience of each of those groups in contemporary society, is a tradition which has a jurisprudence, a set of facts of which the courts have taken account. For example, in perhaps the clearest and most famous statement of the duty of the court to such citizens, Chief Justice Stone, in the famous footnote 4 of the US Supreme Court's decision in *United States v. Carolene Products*, 304 U.S. 144, 152 (1938), set out the jurisprudence to which we are now addressing ourselves. Chief Justice Stone said that "prejudice against discrete and insular minorities may be a special condition which tends seriously to curtail the political processes ordinarily to be relied upon and which therefore may call for a correspondingly more searching judicial inquiry."

USES OF LITIGATION

Against that background, I want to ask you to walk with me through the Pennsylvania experience, although we could, of course, be looking with equal care at any one of the cases which I have mentioned. As we look at the Pennsylvania

experience, let me ask you to bear in mind at least four uses to which litigation may be put. First, citizens may use litigation in order to secure certain substantive rights, in this case, zero reject education, access to free public education by all. Second, litigation may be used to create a new place, a new forum, where citizens may turn to enforce their rights and perhaps create new rights. In any case, they can make real in their particular experience the rights that have been declared otherwise. Third, the courts may be used to bring to the attention of the public—the public-at-large, legislators, decision makers, the ordinary citizen—certain facts that have not had great visibility before. In the right to education cases, for example, the essential fact that all children are capable of benefiting from an education would be brought out. Fourth, the courts may be used by a citizen, as indeed may any other means of petitioning the government for redress of grievances, to express himself, to act out, to tell others who and what he is, or, in another sense, to redefine, change, or alter his notion of himself.

SECURING ACCESS TO EDUCATION

In the Pennsylvania case, those four uses of litigation can be seen in the course of that litigation. First, those 13 children, on January 7, 1971, went to Federal district court with the Pennsylvania Association for Retarded Children, and they went on behalf of every excluded child in the Commonwealth of Pennsylvania. They took with them to court the Commonwealth of Pennsylvania, the Secretary of Education, the Secretary of Public Welfare, 13 individual school districts, and all of the school districts of the Commonwealth of Pennsylvania. They went, in the first instance, to secure access to free public schooling. Why did they go? Well, despite the declaration in Pennsylvania law that Pennsylvania shall provide a proper education for all of its exceptional children and despite the considerable efforts of those who manned that system (people like Bill Ohrtman and Joe Lantzer, who for many years labored with others to make that declaration real), what the law gave on the one hand, it took away on the other. And what it did not take away in the words of the law, practice managed to take away. While Pennsylvania statutes said the Commonwealth shall provide a proper education for all of its exceptional children, a few paragraphs later the law said that children who are uneducable and untrainable may be excluded from the public schools and that children who have not yet attained a mental age of 5 years may be postponed in admission to the public schools. Consider that a mental age of 5 can mean an IQ of 35. For a child with an IQ of 35 or below, admission to public schools can be postponed. Postponed until when? A person with an IQ of 35 or below may never achieve a mental age of 5. Forever, therefore, can that

...that the Pennsylvania law and the law of each state, yours included, requires that the schools maintain a census of children in school and children out of school. But that law has not been respected. As it turned out, and as Mr. Lantzer can report to you, there were at least 14,267 retarded children who had been denied

That was the circumstance those 13 children faced when they turned to the courts to claim, first of all, access to education. What arguments did they make? Their claim rested on two rather straightforward arguments, the first legal and the second factual. First, the legal basis of their claim was the decision of the Supreme Court in *Brown v. Board of Education* in which the Court wrote unanimously as follows:

> Education is required in the performance of our most basic public responsibilities. It is the very foundation of good citizenship. It is a principal instrument for awakening the child to cultural values, in preparing him for later training.

Note these words some years before Gunnar Nirje and others formulated the normalization theory:

> If education is a principal instrument in helping the child to adjust normally to his environment, it is doubtful that any child may reasonably be expected to succeed in life if he is denied the opportunity of an education. The opportunity of an education, where the state has undertaken to provide it to any, is a right which must be made available to all on equal terms.

If it is doubtful that any child may reasonably be expected to succeed in life when denied the opportunity of an education, is it now even more clear that an exceptional child without an education may not be expected to succeed? For the ordinary child may learn willy nilly, wandering in the street, watching television, riding the school bus, but the exceptional child, by definition, if he or she is to learn, requires a formal, structured program of education.

The exceptional child without an education is not merely in jeopardy "of success," as the Supreme Court put it, but of liberty and life itself. You know very well that the rate of institutionalization among those children who have

been deprived of public education is considerably higher. And you know as well that the death rate at those institutions is higher among children who have not had the opportunity of an education which would produce for them those self help skills that enable them, for example, to avoid scalding hot water.

Benefiting Each Child

The factual argument for right to education was equally straightforward. It rested on the now clear proposition that without exception, every child, every exceptional child, every retarded child, is capable of benefiting from an education. There is no such thing as an uneducable and untrainable child. To put it another way, for example, for every 30 retarded children with a proper program of education and training, 29 of them are capable of achieving self sufficiency, 25 of them in the ordinary way in the marketplace and 4 of them in a sheltered environment. The remaining 1 of every 30 retarded children is capable, with a proper program of education and training, of achieving a significant degree of self care.

This fact was presented to the Court in many and diverse ways—in the testimony of Ignacy Goldberg, Columbia Teachers College; James Gallagher, recent Director of the Bureau of Education for the Handicapped; Donald Stedman of the University of North Carolina; and Burton Blatt of Syracuse University. The moment before Jean Hebeler was to take the stand the Attorney General, in the face of that factual evidence, said, "We surrender." The Court in its final opinion on May 5, 1972, noted that the Commonwealth of Pennsylvania had indeed yielded to overwhelming evidence against their position, and the Court complimented the Commonwealth on its wisdom.

I might note for you in particular how some of that came to be. On August 10, some 10 days before the trial, we served on the Attorney General, as is the custom in Federal litigation, the list of witnesses we intended to call. The Attorney General called together Mr. Ohrtman, Director of the Bureau of Special Education, and his deputy at that time, Mr. Lantzer, and their counterparts in the Department of Public Welfare and said to them, "Who are these people?" The answer was that they were the very best in the profession. The Attorney General asked, "What are they going to say?" Mr. Ohrtman and Mr. Lantzer and the others replied, "They are going to say that all children are capable of benefiting from an education." The Attorney General said, "What do we say?" Our friends said, "We say they are right."

The result of the arguments, both legal and factual, was a series of Court orders and injunctions requiring that as soon as possible and in any event no later than September of 1972, all retarded children should be granted access to a program of free public education and training appropriate to the capacities of each of them. The Court further ordered that access to schooling was to be accorded to all of those children within the context of a presumption that placement in a regular class is preferable to placement in a special class, and placement in a special class is preferable to placement in any other program, whether homebound, itinerant, or institutional.

Finally, the Court said that the right of access to education was to be accorded to all retarded children between the ages of 4 and 21—the age of 4 because in Pennsylvania kindergarten was available to many ordinary children at that age and 21 because free public schooling in Pennsylvania as in most states was available if the parent and the child so chose until that age. Consider, those of you whose concern is vocational education, what that must mean for the schooling of children, particularly for the schooling of those between the ages of 16 and 21 who with appropriate vocational address can realize their capacity to be numbered among those 29 of the 30 who may be self sufficient in the ordinary marketplace and at the very least self sufficient in the sheltered workshop.

CREATING A NEW FORUM: THE RIGHT TO BE HEARD

Let me turn now to the second objective, the creation of a new place, a forum where citizens (parents, in particular, and children) may be heard about the nature and quality of that education. The fact of the matter is that if an exceptional child is assigned to a program not appropriate for him, he might as well be excluded from schooling. An example of this situation can be found in an article by Mortimer Garrison and Donald Hammill (1971), both of the Temple University in Philadelphia. They reported that in five county metropolitan Philadelphia at least 25% and as many as 68% of the children assigned to educable classes were misassigned; they had been misclassified. At least 25% and as many as 68% of those children belonged not in the educable class but in regular classes. That study is not unique. It reported facts that other studies across the country have confirmed, for instance Jane Mercer's study in Riverside County in California.

For a long time it has been clear that when the government extends to a citizen a particular benefit, the government may not take that benefit away from the citizen until and unless that citizen is first given notice and the opportunity to be heard about the deprivation. That is clear from a long line of cases dealing with government employment, dealing with determination and reduction of public assistance benefits, and dealing with eviction from public housing. So, the claim was put to the Court that

before you can deprive any exceptional child of the benefits of education either by initially assigning him to a particular program or by maintaining him in a program which no longer fits, you must give to the parents and the child a notice—a statement of reasons for the assignment or for the continuing placement—and the opportunity to be heard.

The second legal argument presented to the court to secure the right of parents and children to be heard about the appropriateness of their educational assignments was an argument that proceeds from the consideration of stigma. In the winter of 1971, the US Supreme Court decided an interesting case called *Wisconsin v. Constantino*, 400 U.S. 433 (1971). Wisconsin had a law which authorized the sheriffs and other local officials in towns across Wisconsin to note whenever they found a citizen to be drunk publicly too often and to post that person's name in the town square and outside each of the taverns in the town. Mrs. Constantino found her name posted. She did not like it and turned to the courts saying, "They can't do that, at least unless first they give me notice and an opportunity to be heard." The three judge court in Wisconsin and the Supreme Court agreed, and in its opinion the Supreme Court said some things that are germane to us and were germane to the claim of those 13 children and their parents. The Court said:

> The only issue present here is whether the label or characterization given a person by 'posting,' though a mark of illness to some is to others such a stigma or badge of disgrace that procedural due process requires notice and the opportunity to be heard. We agree with the Court below that the private interest is such that those requirements must be met. Only when the whole proceedings leading to the pinning of an unsavory label on a person are aired can oppressive results be prevented.

The result of this argument in the Pennsylvania case was an order of the Court requiring that parents be given notice and the opportunity to be heard before their child's educational assignment can be changed, whether from regular class to special class or among special classes or from special education to homebound instruction or back across that ladder. Before any child's educational assignment can be changed and periodically after assignment, every 2 years automatically and every year if the parents so request, the child and the parent are entitled to notice and the opportunity to be heard. The notice is to set out in detail the reasons for the assignment or the reasons for continuing an assignment. The notice informs the parents of their right to be heard, informs them of the availability of the closest county chapter of the Pennsylvania Association for Retarded Children to assist them in the hearing, informs them of the availability of the mental retardation diagnostic facilities of other departments of the gov-

1. EDUCATIONAL SERVICES

ernment to assist the parent in the hearing and in independent prescription, and informs the parents of how to secure that hearing.

The hearing is to be held in front of the Secretary of Education of the Commonwealth or his designee. The parent is entitled to access to all of the child's school records prior to that hearing and is entitled to an individual independent evaluation. The parent is entitled to be represented at that hearing by any person of his or her choosing, the chairman of the education committee of the local CEC chapter or the local ARC chapter or a neighbor or a minister or a professor or an attorney. At that hearing, the parent is entitled to present whatever evidence the parent or the child may wish to present with respect to the appropriateness of the educational assignment. The parent is entitled to examine, to question, and to cross examine any officials of the school district who may have information with respect to the assignment. The hearing examiner, the Secretary of Education, or his designee is directed to enter a decision, the sole criteria for which shall be: Is this the appropriate program of education and training for this child, and if it is not, what is?

Consider for a moment the implications of the due process hearing. It is clear that the hearing may be used by the children and by the children's parents to secure their rights and to review the quality of the program presented to the child. But consider also the use that the hearing forum may be to the teacher, the school psychologist, and the administrator. Before that forum was invented, the teacher and school psychologist had little recourse. For example, a school psychologist examines a child and designs an educational program for that child. He sends the program to the superintendent of schools and the superintendent of schools calls back and says, "That's a fine program. Beautifully done. I wish we could make that program available to the child, but we're not able to now, maybe in a couple of years." The only course of action available to that teacher or that psychologist is to return to his or her desk and in frustration and anger slam shut the drawer of the desk. Now, of course, there are other options. The professional in the discharge of his professional duties to that child may turn himself to the hearing and encourage that the question of delivery of the proper program to that child be raised at the highest levels of the educational system, that the question be addressed and be resolved.

Your lot of course is not always a happy one. As I suggested, we have with some ease adopted the agenda that you, the professionals, have set and we have taken it to court. I realize that that in no sense begins to cure the sorts of difficulties under which you labor. I suggest, however, that the creation of the due process hearing offers you another forum in addition to the lobbying and negotiating that you do to reach your professional objectives.

I might just parenthetically mention that there is a growing body of law that would begin to protect the professional space, space for professionals to discharge and to act upon their obligations to their clients. I think of Bennie Parish, a public assistance case worker in Oakland, California, who some years ago was ordered to join the department at 4:00 on a Sunday morning in a house to house search of the homes of public assistance recipients to discover, as you can imagine, if there was someone under the bed or whatever. Bennie Parish said to the Oakland department, "No, I won't go; my clients have the right of privacy and I won't invade that privacy." The department said to him, "You're fired," and the Civil Service Commission in California said, "That's right, you're fired." But then the California Supreme Court unanimously said, "No, you're not fired, nor can you be fired because you have the right in the discharge of your professional obligations to assert the rights of your clients."

Okania Chalk, a public assistance case worker in York, Pennsylvania, went after work to a meeting of public assistance recipients and told them that there were things going on at the office that did not accord with the regulations or with the recipients' rights. Therefore, Okania Chalk suggested that they organize and organize some more. Then York said to Okania, "You're fired," and the Civil Service Commission said, "Right, you're fired," but the Pennsylvania Supreme Court unanimously said, "No, you're not fired because you have the right in the discharge of your professional duties to respect, to protect, and to act on behalf of the rights of those who are your clients." These examples demonstrate that the due process hearing, among other things, is a forum where you may act professionally.

BRINGING UP NEW OR LITTLE KNOWN FACTS

The third use of litigation to which I alluded was the use of litigation to get up front new facts or old facts that too many have not perceived. I need not belabor that use of litigation. As you can imagine, when citizens go to court on cases concerned with the public interest, the media goes too. When Ignacy Goldberg and Jean Hebeler come to Philadelphia the media comes with them. And on the steps of the courthouse while they are waiting to testify, they talk into the microphone and the camera, and on the tube that night people who have never heard it before hear, "All children are capable of benefiting from an education." They hear, "There is no such thing as an uneducable or untrainable child," and that new fact begins to work its way into the decisions of the citizens, the legislature, and others.

EXPRESSING ONESELF

Let me turn then finally to the fourth use of

litigation, the use of litigation to express oneself and perhaps to change one's notion of oneself. Two stories may illustrate this use of litigation. On October 7, 1971, the Court ordered that each of the 13 plaintiffs in the Pennsylvania case should be placed within one week in a program of education and training appropriate to them. One of the plaintiffs, a child and her parents, were visited by a school official of one of the defendants and the school official said, "We have the order. Tell you what, we're going to do you a favor, we're going to give Kate another chance." The parents said, and you'll excuse me for translating it, "No, you're not. You're not going to do us a favor; you're not going to give Kate another chance. You're going to give Kate that to which she is entitled."

In the second case, again after that order to place the 13 children in the proper program within one week, another school official defendant came to the house of another plaintiff and said, "We have the order. We will obey it, of course, if you want us to. We have a class for Felix. It is the same class that we had 2 years ago, and we will put him in it if you want us to. You remember, however, what happened a few years ago. Felix went into the class, but the class really wasn't the class for him. In 2 weeks he began to act up. We had to call you and tell you to come and take Felix home. Well, if you want us to, we will obey the order and put him in that class, but we expect that in another 2 weeks we will have to call you again and say, 'Felix is act-ing up; come and get him and take him home.' Of course, we will tell you about your rights to a hearing and all the rest. We will do it if you want us to, but what good parent would put his child through all of that?" The parents said many things to that school official, none of which I will repeat, at least not in exact terms. But essentially what they said was, "Sir, you're talking the wrong language. It is no longer the case that the child must fit the class. It is now the case that the class must fit the child."

And so it is. It is a new language that suggests a new conception of the handicapped citizen, a new conception of that citizen's place in our society, a new conception of those obligations owed to him by those who act in place of the society, a conception that suggests that handicapped citizens no longer have what they may have by the grace or by the good will of any other person but that they have what they must have by right. It is now a question of justice.

REFERENCES

CEC Policies Commission. Organization and administration of special education. *Exceptional Children*, 1971, *37*, 428–433.

Garrison, M., Jr., & Hammill, D. D. Who are the retarded? *Exceptional Children*, 1971, *38*, 13–20.

THE SEVERELY/PROFOUNDLY HANDICAPPED: WHO ARE THEY? WHERE ARE WE?

Ed Sontag, Ed.D.
Bureau of Education for the Handicapped

Judy Smith, M.S.Ed.
University of New Mexico

Wayne Sailor, Ph.D.
San Francisco State University

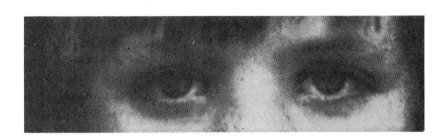

The misunderstanding and misuse of the label "severely/profoundly handicapped" may appear to call for the possible creation of yet another special education category. To create a new category would be a serious error, since it would tend to remove these children from the educational and social mainstream; it also would obscure the fact that the severely/profoundly handicapped exist across all of special education. This article examines various approaches to the problems of definition and categorization of the severely/profoundly handicapped, proposing a service–need definition, with emphasis on teacher competencies. Finally, the authors review what must be done within the profession to make it possible to achieve such a classification system.

THE CHILDREN BEHIND THE LABEL

Children with severe or profound handicaps are children who are divergent in degree, not in kind. The very label "severely/profoundly handicapped" may, however, contribute to the notion that such children are somehow different in kind, since it refers to a very low level of intellectual functioning and therefore suggests that those children so labeled have a homogeneous pattern of neurological impairment. On the contrary, they form an extremely heterogeneous group, comprising not only the organically impaired but also those whose serious emotional disturbance, deafness, blindness, or severe orthopedic impairment renders them *functionally* retarded. These seriously disabling conditions occur with a low incidence in the general population. Thus, when we speak of the severely/profoundly handicapped, we are referring not simply to the severely mentally retarded but to a population of multiply handicapped persons, including the severely emotionally disturbed, the severely health-impaired, and so on.

Inasmuch as a severe or profound handicap is a matter of degree of disability, it follows that children with such impairments may start out both in life and in education at relatively the same point, but their individual potentials will vary spectacularly. An excellent example of a child with a profound functional handicap is the young Helen Keller who, without proper education and training, manifested extreme intellectual impairment but, with enlightened help, became quite another person. Although it now appears that few of the severely/profoundly handicapped (or, for that matter, the gifted) will duplicate the achievements of Helen Keller, these students can make very significant educational gains, and the demonstration of this by special educators has provided the impetus for their intensified public education.

The fact remains, however, that the misunderstanding and misuse of the label severely/profoundly handicapped may appear to call for the possible creation of yet another special education category. To create a new category would

The Severely/Profoundly Handicapped: Who Are They? Where Are They?, Ed Sontag, Ed.D., Judy Smith, M.S.Ed., Wayne Sailor, Ph.D., *The Journal of Special Education*, Vol.11 No. 1, 1977. ©1977 Journal of Special Education, Philadelphia, Pa.

be a serious error for two reasons. First, it would promote the placement of these children in settings away from the educational and social mainstream. In some states, trainable mentally retarded students are finally being included in the regular schools, while severely/profoundly handicapped children are being excluded. By creating another category of students outside the educational mainstream, we may find ourselves in the near future fighting to place them in regular schools, much as we have sought and are still seeking regular school placement for trainables. In the past, placement of the trainable mentally retarded in special schools was partially a result of low expectations concerning their abilities to develop traditional academic skills. However, such current work as that of the University of Washington's Experimental Education Unit has dramatically shown that the trainable mentally retarded, as well as children with far more severe impairments, can indeed acquire primary level reading skills.

Second, use of the label severely/profoundly handicapped has already prompted universities and state departments to create new divisions of special education for a category that we believe cannot and should not be given categorical status. The most crucial step that professionals can take at this juncture is to focus on a group of children who do not fit existing educational labels and who must not be trapped in still another educational classification. The severely/profoundly handicapped exist across all of special education. To view them otherwise is to deny their individuality, their special needs and, most unfortunate of all, their educational potential.

IDENTIFYING A NONCATEGORY

Perhaps, then, we need to take a totally new stance toward the entire issue of defining the population of severely/profoundly handicapped children. To do so, we shall first critically examine three current propositions which reflect various approaches to the problems of definition and categorization. We shall briefly pose arguments for rejection of each of these propositions and conclude with a fourth proposition which represents our position on the issue of determining who are the severely/profoundly handicapped.

Proposition 1. *There is a new disability category entitled "severely and profoundly handicapped" (SPH), or variants thereof.*

According to the proposition, this disability category has specifiable parameters, and through diagnostic assessment procedures, children who are appropriate to a disability class of this type can be identified. This concept reflects the position taken by the Bureau of Education for the Handicapped and by university special education departments in 1974 when services for the severely handicapped began their rapid expansion. Parameters were spelled out: e.g., disabilities so severe or complex that they restrict ambulation or locomotion by means of typical transportation modes; behavior characteristics that are injurious to self or others; hyperactivity, impulsivity; frequently uncontrolled bowel or bladder functions; epilepsy, grossly inadequate communication skills; mixed or multiple sensori-motor disabilities.

When parameters to define a population are necessarily subjective and when no adequate standardized instruments exist, then parameters must include such qualifiers as *"must* be characterized by" or *"may* be characterized by." The first qualifier necessarily creates the possibility of a false negative: A child who is severely handicapped will be rejected for services because of failure to display one or more of the descriptors. The second qualifier can easily produce a false positive: A child who is not severely handicapped is mistakenly identified because he displays one or more of the parametric descriptors. Thus, Proposition 1, in our opinion, should be rejected as a basis for defining the severely handicapped in the absence of a reliable diagnostic classification system based upon standardized observation and assessment. Moreover, there are already too many rigidly defined disability categories. The addition of still another category compounds an already difficult problem in educational service delivery.

Proposition 2. *The severely handicapped do not represent a new disability category. They represent the lower limits of functioning in the continuum which exists in each established disability area.*

This solution to the definition problem represents a current effort by several state education agencies to handle the problem of certification. It represents, in part, a reaction to the pressure to create a new disability category.

Proposition 2 must be rejected on the basis of the inadequacies that exist in the established system of disability categorization. A child who is *very* orthopedically disabled (who represents the lowest extreme of the continuum of crippled and other health-impaired children) would be considered severely handicapped by this definition and placed with children from the lowest strata of the mentally retarded population, even in the absence of any indication that he was academically retarded. The same would hold true for the emotionally disturbed, the deaf, the blind, and others. The potential for misplacement of children in service settings is probably greatest when this solution to the definition problem is adopted.

Proposition 3. *The severely handicapped belong in one of three global instructional areas, under a reorganization plan which would include early childhood education, general special education, and severely handicapped education. Assignment of children to the new areas would consist of reassignment of the existing disability categories.*

This proposition represents a current thrust in solving the definition problem by many state education agencies. Through this solution, the existing disability categories would be collapsed into a dichotomy of general special education and severely handicapped education, with early childhood education, determined primarily by age, representing a broad new component of special education under Public Law 94-142.

The problem with Proposition 3, and the reason that it too should be rejected, rests again with the inadequacies of the existing disability category system. General special education would encompass, for example, the learning disabled, educable mentally retarded, orthopedically disabled, emotionally disturbed, deaf, speech-impaired, and so on. Severely handicapped education would include the trainable mentally retarded, seriously disturbed, deaf–blind, and others. The potential for misplacement of children in terms of homogeneity of services is great. Trainable mentally retarded children typically do not belong in an educational program designed to benefit the profoundly retarded nonambulatory child; their curriculum requirements are substantially different. Nor does the profoundly retarded deaf child belong in a program designed for disturbed children who can deal with an academic curriculum. New subgroupings within each of the areas would no doubt become necessary at the local education agency level, and these subgroupings might well provide less functional service than the existing system of disability categorization provides.

Proposition 4. *Severely handicapped education represents one of three global instructional areas under a reorganization plan which would include early childhood education and general special education as the other two areas. Assignment of children to the new areas would be according to the nature of the children's service requirements and, indirectly, on the basis of the competencies of teaching personnel.*

This proposition resembles Proposition 3, except that reclassification into either the general special education or severely handicapped education categories (with assignment to early childhood education based on age) would be determined by the type of service required. It assumes a clean slate from the outset, as far as disability categories are concerned. Regardless of his handicapping condition, if a child or young (school-aged) adult requires instruction in basic skills, this proposition specifies that the individual belongs in a program for the severely handicapped. If a child, regardless of handicap, primarily requires academic instruction, then he belongs in a program of general special education. Children in need of both types of service would divide their time between programs. Indeed, a prime goal would be to move students gradually from severely handicapped education to general special education programs and, further, into the mainstream of regular education to the maximum extent. Exceptional children below school age would enter early childhood education programs in which the emphasis would also be divided between services for the severely handicapped (basic skill development) and general special education (preacademic instruction).

In addition, teachers whose training has produced competencies in basic self-help, motor, perceptual, social, cognitive, and communication skill development areas would teach classes for the severely handicapped. Teachers whose competencies lie in preacademic and academic instruction would teach general special education.

With this service-need definition we may cut across disability areas and create a truly programmatic and need-centered model of service delivery. Equally important, this manner of identification, placement, and programming should facilitate a progressive inclusion of the low-incidence population into the mainstream of school and community.

HANDICAPS WITHIN THE PROFESSION

Various teacher training and public education programs focusing on low-incidence children are in operation across the United States, in different stages of development. These programs differ in their degree of emphasis on this population's longitudinal needs and problems and on the competencies needed by teachers to deal with these problems: e.g., training to compensate for severe sensori-motor deficits; beginning verbal and nonverbal communication; home management and living skills; parent involvement; use of prosthetic, orthotic, and adaptive equipment to enhance general development; basic social skill mastery; basic self-help and maintenance (including feeding and toileting); behavior management; community mobility skills.

Although these models are in the process of evolving, there continue to be problems that hamper our professional efforts. We need programs that focus not just on one or two longitudinal areas but on all educational requirements of the severely/profoundly handicapped population. We need the kind of information exchange that would enhance work in all aspects of educational programming. And we need coordination and quality control on a national scale.

High on the list of priorities for dissemination is the creation of a matrix of teacher competencies and a means for measuring the attainment of those competencies. Continued research, as well as the full sharing of information among programs, is a requirement in developing competency-based training programs. Moreover, until a full spectrum of those proficiencies can be developed, we must have a system for refining and updating what is currently known. In the meantime, an exchange program for doctoral students, mutual doctoral training programs, and a national exchange of professionals at all levels may encourage programs to impact on one another.

Evident needs exist for coordination: to create skill sequences; to match existing curricula to assessed skill deficiencies; to evaluate existing curricula through systematic measurement for effectiveness; to create curricula where none exist through task analysis; and to evaluate and control the quality of these curricula. The pressing need for national curriculum and assessment programs can be met if we make a concerted effort in identification, evaluation, development, and dissemination.

From a base of such activities, it may well become possible to develop quality control for our training programs. In view of the requirements of Public Law 94-142, standards of quality and continuity become more than ever a pressing issue. We need continuous evaluation and decision making regarding relevant course content and performance skills, as well as the cost-effectiveness of our personnel preparation programs. Many existing evaluation systems simply do not cover both the courses and the experiences designed to provide competencies. We need to generate statements of standards for preservice training in terms of practicum sites, staff qualifications, student–staff ratios, competency statements, evaluation procedures, and professional standards that are exclusionary in the sense of admitting only the most highly qualified people to the task of educating the low-incidence population. A permanent data-monitoring system must also be established as an aid to planning for the rapidly accelerating demand for service delivery. Such a system should generate up-to-date printouts of all enrollment information from state departments, thereby supplying the nation with standardized needs-assessment figures on a current basis.

As we move toward an objective content evaluation system to measure acquisition and toward a series of skill-assessment systems to be administered by independent evaluation teams, we must ensure that the evaluation system reflects child-change data, as well as teacher acquisition. In directly measuring performance change, the trained teacher must be able to assess his own effectiveness in terms of reliable and demonstrable progress on the part of his class.

Related to the evaluation of our training programs, our graduates, and the educational progress of the children they serve is the matter of certification. Several years are required for teacher trainees to complete the typical university training sequence. Yet there is currently a considerable nation-wide demand for people who can work with the severely/profoundly handicapped in public school settings. To fulfill this demand we cannot continue to provisionally certify surplus teachers from other areas of education. While provisional certification may help alleviate the teacher shortage, we cannot expect that it will promote high-caliber educational programming for children. An additional danger is the certification of too many teachers who have an inappropriate range of competencies to serve severely/profoundly handicapped children, thus glutting the market with a surplus of inadequately trained teachers.

To provide a broader certification program for trainees in preservice programs, consistent with Proposition 4, we might consider the merits of a state plan that calls for two types of special educators: those with competencies for high-incidence populations of exceptional children, and those with competencies for low-incidence populations. With the addition of training for preschool programs, certification would follow the attainment of specifiable competencies in one of three areas: general special education, severely/profoundly handicapped education, and early childhood education.

In order to meet the immediate need for staffing, however, we should consider controlled inservice training, in which universities with preparation programs for teachers of low-incidence populations develop a close link with state departments in a coordinated training effort. Two critical factors are the selection of highly qualified professionals to provide such inservice training and the assurance that programs for severely/profoundly handicapped children and their prospective teachers take place within the mainstream of education.

An additional way to meet the demand for personnel is to elevate the paraprofessional within the educational strata. Educational systems have traditionally resisted financing personnel beyond the teaching staff on a local level, and the paraprofessional has been viewed as an assistant, rather than as a therapist or educator in his own right. However, programming for the severely/profoundly handicapped population engenders a teaching situation in which the ratio of professionals to children is optimally around one to three. To help meet this requirement and fulfill a greatly expanded role, paraprofessionals must be trained or retrained, must have professional status as teaching associates, and must be paid in accordance with their contributions, which are often considerable. We must continue, in addition, to make fuller use of occupational, physical, and speech therapists (as well as professionals trained in deafness, blindness, and other specialty areas) as resource persons, teacher consultants, and trainers of children.

For all of these personnel, there must be an effective licensing mechanism, such as peer review or certification by state education agencies, with cooperation from universities. Specialized support personnel (e.g., consultants to programs for the blind) and allied health professionals (e.g., occupational therapists) should be given a coordinated opportunity to enter the competency-based training model. Consortia of training colleges and medical schools, for example, could provide an integrated training program across all the multidisciplinary training components of quality education for the severely/profoundly handicapped. State licensing agencies for specialty educators and support therapists should be encouraged to consider specialized licensing requirements. These would reflect the highly differentiated competencies and expertise acquired by those therapists who complete relevant components of university education preparing them to become effective members of the educational team.

Finally, through the competent people we now have, we must provide technical assistance to localities whose leaders have shown the potential for integrating low-incidence children into the community and into the public schools. That leadership must be reinforced by solid professional support and by the extensive sharing of expertise. Indeed, mutual support and sharing of information are the best and perhaps the only means we have to meet the needs of all professionals who are working to raise the potential of the severely/profoundly handicapped child. Then, perhaps, we will make sure that no Helen Keller goes unrecognized.

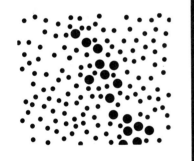

Diagnosis
and
Assessment

The question of accurate diagnosis and assessment of severely and profoundly handicapped children has presented a dilemma to the special education field for some time. In the past this problem has been either ignored or performed in a rather haphazard manner. Often, the final result was the placement of the child in an institution where little educational intervention was arranged.

Now that litigation and legislation has given the right to an appropriate education to all handicapped children, proper evaluative services must be provided. More is needed than a useless label. Teachers must be provided educational descriptors of what skills the child already has, and which skills need to be taught. Diagnostic and assessment services should provide instructional goals that are functional and attainable by the child. Severely and profoundly handicapped individuals who are to receive educational services are not easy to diagnose and assess. Sensory, communication, motor, emotional and other problems may hamper accurate determination. For most children, the identification of problems is based on a comparison between the child's current status or level of performance and some "standard" which describes the level of performance which we would like the child to achieve. Most traditional standards for comparison are based on the performances demonstrated by a child's "normal" chronological peers. The extent and nature of a "problem" is precisely defined as the difference between performances currently demonstrated by the child and the standards which we have established for "acceptable" or "desirable" performances. However, formal instruments which are used widely with other handicapped children often have little utility with the population at hand. Alternate procedures for determining skill levels have to be developed. These new instruments should probably be left unstandardized, since comparison of one severely handicapped individual with another would be inappropriate.

Research has shown that early assessment and intervention with handicapped children is crucial. This fact is magnified when we are speaking of youngsters with very severe disabilities. Diagnostic and assessment tools must have the capability to determine skills at a very low level and get optimum results.

The follwing articles look at various diagnostic and assessment techniques for the severely and profoundly handicapped. Many of the following suggestions can be used by teachers and other specialists directly in the classroom. Task analytic procedures have been found particularly functional and useful.

Task Analytic Assessment of Severe Learning Problems

DENNIS R. KNAPCZYK

DENNIS R. KNAPCZYK *is Coordinator of Research and Evaluation, Indiana University Developmental Training Center [U.A.F.] and Assistant Professor of Education, Indiana University, Bloomington.*

Abstract: Task analytic assessment provides a method which classroom teachers and other community service agents can utilize to assess the level of functioning of severely retarded individuals. Devices can be developed on an individualized basis by those working directly with the severely retarded; these then can be employed to suggest program goals and objectives, and to evidence the attainment of those objectives.

Formal assessment procedures have been developed and utilized to measure a wide variety of pupil oriented tasks, skills, and learning processes. Standardization of these instruments has made it possible to compare a single child's performance with that of a large sample of children of the same age group. Discrepancies observed between one child's responses and those of the comparison group suggest learning strengths or deficiencies. The results of formal diagnostic instruments can be utilized to plan learning activities to maximize learning potential (Bibb, 1972; Buckland & Balow, 1973; Halliwell & Solan, 1972; Waugh, 1973).

However, formal devices have a number of limitations which restrict their applicability to severely retarded populations. Because of standardization requirements, administration must be formalized. Sensory and communication deficits, which many severely retarded children exhibit, require modification of administration procedures (Guthrie, Butler, Gorlow, & White, 1964). Comparison of the results with a target population is therefore often inappropriate (Benton, 1970; Bialer, 1970; Bibb, 1972).

The large number of deficits areas which the severely retarded exhibit requires utilization of comprehensive devices (Gardner 1971). However, time restrictions generally imposed by formal instruments necessitate that only a small sample of behavior characteristic of a particular deficiency area can be included (Gardner, 1967, Sarason & Gladwin, 1958). At best, formal assessment procedures yield only vague indications concerning specific learning problems of the severely retarded (Sarason & Doris, 1969).

Finally, few formal diagnostic instruments can be administered by special class teachers because of the intense training implied by the standardized methods of administration. Thus, the utility of formal instruments is dependent upon a clear channel of communication between the classroom teacher and the diagnostician, usually a school psychometrist or psychologist. Translation of test results into instructional strategies or learning packages requires extensive knowledge of diverse instructional materials and procedures. Often those who administer formal instruments have little formal teaching experience, and generally none with the severely retarded (Gardner, 1971, Stone & DeNevi, 1971).

Task Analytic Procedures

An alternate procedure for assessing performance of the severely retarded involves utilization of task analytic assessment procedures

"Task Analytic Assessment of Severe Learning Problems," Dennis R. Knapezyk, *Education and Training of the Mentally Retarded*, Vol. 10, No. 2, April 1975. © 1975 The Council for Exceptional Children, Division of Mental Retardation.

(Vallet, 1972). Task analysis has been cited as an effective instructional method for teaching skills to handicapped individuals (Minge & Ball, 1967). It involves the selection of a target task (e.g., face washing) and subsequent analysis into its component behaviors (e.g., picking up soap, rubbing soap on hands, rubbing hands on face, etc.). Each component behavior is learned sequentially and separately and is chained to those behaviors previously learned until the complete task can be performed without assistance. Individualized instruction can occur by altering task components and sequence to effectively utilize each child's entry skills (Lent, 1968; Lent, 1970; Toombs, 1971).

Task analytic procedures can also be applied to the assessment of learning performance and evaluation of teaching methodology. The same process of specifying the component behaviors of tasks is employed. However, prior to training each component behavior, the child is requested to perform the task (Tilton, Liska, & Bourland, 1972). Assistance is provided by the administrant when required to insure that the child is given the opportunity to attempt each behavior. Thus, assistance is provided only when the child has made no attempt to perform the required behavior within a specified time interval (e.g. ten seconds). The degree and type of assistance can be coded and entries made for each task component. This process yields a clear profile of a child's strengths and weakness with respect to the specific skills assessed.

Table 1 illustrates a task analysis of the behaviors involved in putting on and buttoning or zipping a coat. Spaces are provided for entering the observed performance of the child along with the duration of task completion. Duration is included as a measure in assessment since some individuals are observed to be able to perform a task, but consume an excessive amount of time. A teacher observing this would focus upon amount of time to complete task as a training objective and not upon the specific behaviors involved. The analysis illustrated in Table 1 could be expanded to include a more discrete listing of behaviors, or be contracted depending upon the individual or group involved. Maintaining the same basic sequence and component behaviors would provide for comparison across children and groups for evaluation purposes.

Use of Profiles

A variety of codes can be utilized to designate the degree of assistance required to perform each component behavior. This coding can also be structured to reflect a sequential progression from complete independence in performance to no attempt at performance. Similarly, this format can be utilized to yield a profile which delineates the type of training appropriate for the individual (e.g., the fading of gestural and verbal cues and prompts). Coding of the degree of performance can be expanded or contracted to achieve the type of information for facilitating instructional programming.

The resulting profile of an individual's performance, as illustrated in Table 3, suggests the amount and type of training which the individual requires. In the sample assessment of a child's dressing skills, it was observed that this individual could pick up his coat and put an arm through a sleeve. However, he required verbal prompts to put the other arm in the coat and gestural prompts to draw it around the shoulders. It was necessary for the teacher to cooperate with the individual in drawing the coat over his chest. For purpose of training, the teacher utilized a fading procedure to substi-

TABLE 1

Task analysis of the behaviors involved
in putting on and buttoning or zipping a coat.

Instructions: "Put your coat on."

Evaluation:

Duration: start _____ stop _____

Behaviors: putting on coat
- _____ picks up coat
- _____ puts one arm in sleeve
- _____ puts one arm through sleeve
- _____ puts both arms in sleeves
- _____ puts both arms through sleeves
- _____ draws coat around shoulders
- _____ draws fronts of coat around chest

Behaviors: buttoning coat
- _____ matches buttons to holes
- _____ puts hole to button
- _____ puts button partially through hole
- _____ puts button completely through hole
- _____ completes buttoning of coat
- _____ number of buttons buttoned
- _____ number of buttons possible to button

Behaviors: zipping coat
- _____ puts ends of zipper together
- _____ inserts ends of zipper
- _____ pulls upward on zipper tab
- _____ holds bottom of coat and pulls tab upward
- _____ zips coat partially
- _____ zips coat completely

TABLE 2

Sample code used for assessing the degree of
assistance required in performing
each task component.

W: child completes behavior without assistance
V: verbal cues are used to assist or prompt child
G: gestural cues are used to assist or prompt child
X: child and administrant cooperate in performing behavior
A: child makes no attempt to perform behavior

2. DIAGNOSIS AND ASSESSMENT

TABLE 3

Task analytic assessment of the behaviors
required to put on and button
or zipper a coat.

Instructions: "Put your coat on."

Evaluation:

Duration:	start	1 min. 30 secs.
	stop	6 mins. 34 secs.

Behaviors: putting on coat

W	picks up coat
W	puts one arm in sleeve
W	puts one carm through sleeve
V	puts both arms in sleeves
V	puts both arms through sleeves
G	draws coat around shoulders
X	draws fronts of coat around chest

Behaviors: buttoning coat

A	matches buttons to holes
A	puts hole to button
A	puts button partially through hole
A	puts button completely through hole
A	completes buttoning of coat
O	number of buttons buttoned
6	number of buttons possible to button

Behaviors: zipping coat

X	puts ends of zipper together
X	inserts ends of zipper
W	pulls upward on zipper tab
A	holds bottom of coat and pulls tab upward
W	zips coat partially
G	zips coat completely

tute verbal and gestural cues for direct assistance, and instructions and chaining of the behaviors for directive verbal and gestural prompts.

The child was unable to perform any of the behaviors involved in buttoning and it was necessary to train each behavior independently and chain the skills to those previously mastered. With zipping it was observed that the child cooperated in the initial fastening of the zipper, not responding to either verbal or gestural prompts. The child could independently pull up the zipper. In structuring a training program for this child, it was unnecessary to include zipping as a component.

Summary

Task analysis can be utilized for assessing a variety of objective skills pertinent to teaching the severely retarded. Some of these include social skills, pre-vocational training, self-help skills, communication, coordination, and others (Lent, 1970; Tilton, Liska, & Bourland, 1972). Likewise, each skill can be sequenced to parallel the progression of child development (Farnham-Diggory, 1972; Mills, 1972; Tilton, Liska, & Bourland, 1972). This would increase the utility of the assessment device in comparison to other groups with different levels of functioning.

In addition to utilizing task analysis for assessment, the same process can be employed for evaluation of programs. Pre-evaluation provides the basis for specifying the areas in which training is required. This assessment facilitates the development of instructional objectives. Re-administration of the assessment device subsequent to training would yield evidence for determining whether an objective has been attained (Knapczyk & Leimohn, 1973; Livingston & Knapczyk, 1973).

Preparation of this paper was partially funded through SRS Project Grant No. 59-P-25293/5-02 awarded to Indiana University Developmental Training Center.

References

Benton, A. L. Interactive determinants of mental deficiency. In H. Haywood (Ed.) *Social - cultural aspects of mental retardation.* New York: Appleton-Century-Crofts, 1970.

Bialer, I. Relationship of mental retardation to emotional disturbance and physical disability. In H. Haywood (Ed.) *Social-cultural aspects of mental retardation.* New York: Appleton-Century-Crofts, 1970.

Bibb, J. J. Measurement and evaluation of the migrant child. In A. B. Cheyney (Ed.) *The ripe harvest: Educating migrant children.* Coral Gables: University of Miami, 1972.

Buckland, P. & Balow, B. Effect of visual perceptual training on reading achievement. *Exceptional Children.* 1973, **39**, 299-304.

Franham-Diggory, S. *Cognitive processes in education.* New York: Harper and Row, 1972.

Gardner, W. I. Use of the California Test of Personality with the mentally retarded. *Mental Retardation*, 1967, **5**, 12-16.

Gardner, W. I. *Behavior modification in mental retardation.* Chicago: Aldine, 1971.

Guthrie, G., Butler, A., Gorlow, L., & White, G. M. Nonverbal expression of self-attitudes of retardates. *American Journal of Mental Deficiency*, 1964, **69**, 42-29

Halliwell, J. W. & Solan, H. A. The effects of a supplemental perceptual training program on reading achievement. *Exceptional Children*, 1972, **38**, 613-621.

Knapczyk, D. R. & Liemohn, W. Theme instruction: an interdisciplinary model for service and training in special education. Working paper. Indiana University Developmental Training Center, Bloomington, 1973.

Lent, J. R. Mimosa Cottage: Experiment in hope. *Psychology Today*, 1968, **2**, 51-58.

Tilton, J. R., Liska, D. C., & Bourland, J. D. (Eds.). *Guide to early developmental training.* Lafayette: Wabash Center for the Mentally Retarded, 1972.

Toombs, L. *Title I project evaluation report.* Parsons, Kansas: Parsons State Hospital and Training Center, 1971.

OCCUPATIONAL EDUCATION FOR SEVERELY HANDICAPPED STUDENTS: ASSESSMENT AND IMPLEMENTATION

Tim Crowner

Recent thinking regarding occupational programming for severely handicapped persons appears to follow two lines of thought. First, if occupational education-special education programs are to be successful they must become more community based. A second line of thought involves the use of applied behavioral analysis to the occupational needs of severely handicapped persons. Unfortunately, community programming advocates and advocates of applied behavioral analysis have not collaborated as well as they might have. The Individual Educational Plan (IEP) may furnish the ground upon which this communication will begin to occur. A systematic application of the available technical concepts underlying both lines of thought may be reflected in IEP's for the severely handicapped. Such plans would include descriptions of the various contexts in which work might be performed in a given community. A delineation of specific skills required to operate within various contexts would follow. Finally, task analysis would be applied to components of these contexts and instructional sequences, leading to the student's acquisition of specific relevant skills.

A useful organization of information on occupational evaluation and instruction will be set forth in this chapter. Discussion will be based upon an operating program in Madison, Wisconsin. It is felt that the Madison program exemplifies the kind of marriage between the two schools of thought about occupational education for the severely handicapped. Emphasis will be placed on three key themes: (a) precision, (b) completeness, and (c) cooperation. Precision refers to how well an IEP details strategies for goal attainment, measurement, evaluation, and delineation of roles and responsibilities for parent, staff, and related agencies. Completeness refers to how thoroughly the IEP deals with those contingencies affecting the environmental context in which the vocational goals must be performed. Cooperation refers to evidence that the plan has been well coordinated across all individuals and relevant agencies.

The phrase "severely and profoundly handicapped" is meant as a functional term to encompass a population of students who require extraordinary medical, therapeutic, and educational prescription in order to compensate for, or habilitate presenting handicaps. It would be unrealistic to assume that one day, all severely and profoundly handicapped persons will be competitively employed. It is therefore necessary to operationally define what is meant by occupational goals for this population. Writers of IEP's must be able to discriminate the aspects of occupational training which are important across all children of any age or degree of handicap.

Occupational education is being used in this paper to convey a broad view of prevocational and vocational education ranging across age and ability. An occupational goal continuum must be established as a conceptual guide in planning for severely and profoundly handicapped persons. This continuum is based on the concept of community effort required to sustain the handicapped individual. It is assumed that, for some handicapped individuals, self-maintenance is a reasonable occupational goal. The economic contributions to society gained by a handicapped person's maintenance are only different in degree from those gained through competitive employment. Certainly, the human dignity a profoundly handicapped individual achieves through self-maintenance is as significant as economic self-support achieved by a mildly handicapped person.

There are obviously many degrees of economic self-support, and self-maintenance. Figure 1 represents a continuum leading from complete reliance on others to complete economic self-support.

Figure 1
Occupational Continuum
Complete Reliance on Others
Self Maintenance
Sheltered Work
Complete Economic Self Support

There is no dichotomy in this continuum. Individual educational plans for occupational goals should identify jobs for severely and profoundly handicapped persons regardless of placement on the occupational continuum. For example, a job may be serving food to oneself. Many

"Occupational Education for Severely Handicapped Students – Assessment and Implementation," Tim Crowner, *Developing Effective Individual Educational Programs for Severely Handicapped Children and Youth*, Topical Working Conference Sponsored by BEH, Washington, D.C., August 1977.

2. DIAGNOSIS AND ASSESSMENT

skills needed and developed for competitive employment by the handicapped are the same as those necessary for self-maintenance. Following directions, being socially appropriate, and self-discipline are examples of such common skills. In particular, rate, endurance, and quality of performance are essential to holding down a competitive job. Enhancing these skills even in a preschooler has direct connection to occupational success in later life. Each of these skills will be discussed in more detail later. They are brought up at this point to imply that IEP's should address occupational goals even for the most profoundly handicapped.

Writers of IEP's should also bear in mind that existing occupational programs often fail. The U.S. Department of Health, Education, and Welfare commissioned a study of occupational preparation programs for the handicapped in 1972. The report of this study, *Improving Occupational Programs for the Handicapped*, cites three basic ways in which existing programs fail:

> They fail to prepare the environment for the student as well as they prepare the student for the work environment. Secondly, they fail to take advantage of or solicit assistance from services or groups outside of the immediate administration of the program. Thirdly, they do not assure the relevance of program content to the job market and environment in which the students will live when they graduate. (HEW, 1972, p.6)

In addition to the above observations, occupational education is too often treated as an isolated goal. It is seen as task oriented. A narrow view of sheltered workshop tasks prevails for the severely handicapped. However, well designed IEP's may help the student avoid many of the deficiencies which have been identified in the past with vocational preparation of the handicapped. Especially as IEP writers recognize the advantages of combining applied behavioral analysis to community based occupational preparation. IEP's can force focus upon long and short range goals for each child and provide parents and advocates with a blueprint from which to check progress. Well written IEP's will, with precision, completeness and coordination, set forth goals to which professionals will be held accountable.

In summary, the literature reviewed indicates that severely handicapped persons can learn complex and sophisticated behaviors. However, service delivery models that assure generalization of learned behaviors are underdeveloped. Diagnostic services have been characterized as overdeveloped and irrelevant. The solution proposed to alleviate service deficiencies involves more active involvement with the community on the part of service purveyors.

Literature addressing the occupational needs of the profoundly retarded is nonexistant. This is maybe due to a narrow definition of what constitutes occupational preparation. Yet, many of the efforts designed to lead a severely handicapped person to gainful employment are applicable to the needs of the profoundly handicapped person.

Before discussing the specific aspects of assessment, prescription, and implementation, an overview of an operating program may prove useful. In an article tracing the evolution of a community-based vocational preparation program, Certo, Brown, Belmore, and Crowner (1977) review the facts that led the Madison Metropolitan School District (MMSD) away from the school house and into the community. Essentially, MMSD found that:

1. A model which prescribed a single teacher and single class (the traditional elementary school model) had administrative convenience as its greatest advantage. That is, the number of variables needing attention by the service purveyors was smallest in this model. Small groups attached to a single teacher were easy to monitor. However, the structures evolved in such environments tended to be static. Thus, students tended to become stimulus-bound to a given teacher and classroom.
2. A departmentalized model – the traditional secondary school model where teachers specialize in a specific subject and students rotate from teacher to teacher – tended to provide for better student generalization. It also allowed for the rapid development of a specialized curriculum because the teacher could attempt to teach the same concepts to a variety of students. This model, however, led to a disjointed program where various skills become isolated.
2. MMSD finally moved to a model which combined the self-contained class with community-based experiences. A brief description of this model will assist the reader in understanding the context from which positions taken in this paper arise. In the community-based training model students spend about a fifth of their instructional time out of the classroom. Certain teachers operate as community-based instructors, and they have flexible schedules which allow them to operate during the evening hours with days free when appropriate. Community-based instructors have six functions: (1) to identify community environments in which students will ultimately function; (2) to analyze the elements of a given environment to determine criteria for survival in that environment; (3) to work with classroom teachers to evolve instructional strategies leading to survival skills; (4) to aggressively prepare the environment for the eventual presence of the severely and profoundly handicapped individual; (5) to implement an instructional program directly within that environment with targeted students; (6) to follow-up into post secondary placement – transition to the Division of Vocational Rehabilitation (DVR).

Community-based instructors, support staff, and classroom teachers work with parents and outside agencies to identify skills which are immediately meaningful to a given student. Activities are then designed for skill development and are executed in the classroom, home and community. Skills immediately meaningful to the student are related to skills ultimately needed. In the classroom, for example, the teacher may work with students on simple meal preparation as a desired skill

while stressing work-site preparation and clean-up duties. At home, the parents are instructed to work with their child in table setting and cleaning skills. In the community the trainer stresses proper arrangement of tools before work is begun.

Cognitive, affective, sensory, motor and language goals are identified for each student, as are ways in which these goals may be achieved through functional activities. For example, language may involve indicating a student's need to use a public bathroom. Cognition for the student may involve learning that soap works better if water is applied to the hands first. Affective learning may involve learning to act unobtrusively, and sensory goals may relate to desired water temperature while washing, while motor goals may relate to the zipping and buttoning of clothing.

One can see the importance of using the precise, complete, and coordinated IEP as a document to guide parents and professionals through the complexity of such interrelated and comprehensive programming. MMSD has observed two great advantages in this community based approach. There has been rapid skill acquisition and retention by students, and the community is becoming increasingly sensitized to the presence and needs of severely and profoundly handicapped persons. However, a main disadvantage to the community based model is that it is administratively inconvenient. Scheduling becomes a horrendous problem; monitoring staff time is very difficult, and liability related to safety factors increases. Of course, our moral obligation does not involve the development of administratively convenient models. Yet, any model should produce individual programs which can be clearly understood and held to account. Thus the significance of IEP's as blueprints or even contracts becomes clear.

Initial Assessment

Initial assessment for occupational skills should occur across the occupational continuum described earlier. Thus, all students should be assessed for functional occupational level. Focus for occupational assessment of a given student will be drawn from information regarding the student's age, ability and need. Age will dictate the amount of time left in school. The shorter the time in school available, the greater the focus on specific occupational goals will be. Ability will dictate the kinds of environments in which occupational information will be collected. That is, will information on student performance occur in a community-based work site, or would a room in a small group treatment facility be a more appropriate site to observe the student's performance? It may be appropriate, for some students, to observe dressing or feeding in the student's home. Need may dictate both emphasis and choice of work site. For example, a seriously behavior disordered student may be 20 years old but have such bizarre behavior that self discipline as a self care objective may dominate his needs. A multihandicapped/hearing impaired student may need a work site where very little verbal direction occurs.

Recent Research

Perhaps the most striking aspect of the literature concerning vocational preparation of severely handicapped persons is that it illustrates the range of complex skills which such persons can acquire. Crosson (1969),

Schoreder and Yarbrough (1972), Bellamy, Peterson, and Close (1975), Gold (1976), among others, have demonstrated that the severely handicapped can learn complex assembly skills through the use of task analysis strategies and chained instructional sequences. Furthermore, Huddle (1967), Brown and Pearce (1970), and Schroeder and Yarbrough (1972), have demonstrated that arrangement of environmental contingencies can enhance the productivity of severely handicapped persons.

Researchers have been successful in proving that severely handicapped individuals can learn rather sophisticated behaviors. However, a number of unresolved issues remain which concern the ability of handicapped individuals to generalize these learned skills. Williams (1975), contends that trainers must determine whether or not these skills can be performed across persons, places, instructional materials, and language cues. In short, are many of the behaviors performed by severely handicapped persons stimulus Bound? If learned behaviors are in fact bound to a specific set of circumstances then there is a danger that skills being taught later in time will be more difficult to teach because of earlier learning. This phenomenon, proactive inhibition, is discussed by Underwood (1964). Underwood has found that habits learned earlier in time will tend to interfere with newly acquired skills, increasing the probability that these new skills will be forgotten.

Furthermore, retention of a given skill may be affected by the importance of that skill to the student. For years, general educators have been calling for "relevant curriculum" in public schools. Ferrara (1975) observes that behaviors learned earlier in time were not retained by a group of severely and profoundly handicapped students. However, when skills were taught which had immediate application to a student's needs, these skills tended to be retained. For example, if a severely handicapped person is taught to go to a refrigerator, and to pour a glass of milk, this behavior has great utility to that individual. Ferrara notes that such behaviors are more readily generalized by severely handicapped students from the classroom to the home setting. Examining educational structures may help explain this phenomena.

Crowner (1977) suggests that there is a relationship between restriction and structures developed to instruct students. A structure is defined as an element constructed in the learner's environment which is designed to direct, guide, or inhibit the learner's behavior. Structures may be physical or behavioral in nature. Physical structures include room arrangements, degree of isolation from normalized environment, or some prosthetic device such as a jig used in an assembly task. Behavioral structures encompass all personal interactions such as social reinforcement, language cues, and home-school relationships. The degree to which such structures are available or natural in many different settings is directly related to how easily a behavior being taught in one environment will be generalized and retained across settings. Thus, structures must be constructed that are available in naturalized environments if the trainer wishes the learner to generalize behaviors.

In an extensive review of the literature on sheltered workshops, Pomerantz and Markolin (1977) state:

2. DIAGNOSIS AND ASSESSMENT

> In general, sheltered workshops are not now using available instructional technology in ways that lead to job placement of severely handicapped clients. Workshop programs rely on production and adjustment training within the workshop, in the hope that a general upgrading of client skills may lead to future placement. (p. 131)

These authors call for more aggressive job placement activities. They suggest a more active involvement with the community. The HEW study of occupational programs for the handicapped (cited earlier) draws this same conclusion.

Wolfensberger (1975) voices disatisfaction with another aspect of services provided to handicapped individuals — diagnosis. He cites a number of "embarrassments in the diagnostic process" (p. 181-185). His observations that are particularly relevant to this discussion are:

1. Diagnosis for the family is quite often a dead end, frequently resulting in a frustrating series of cross referrals instead of leading to a meaningful service assignment.
2. Many diagnostic centers do not provide adequate feedback counseling and consider their duty done when the diagnostic process is satisfactorily completed.
3. Diagnostic services are often overdeveloped in comparison to other available resources.

Occupational assessment should be an integrated part of a general assessment strategy. This is particularly important because much guiding information on ability arises from a general assessment process. Assessment for severely and profoundly handicapped persons is a very complex process because of the multiple needs of the child. Occupational assessment is then a component of a transdisciplinary based evaluation. To clarify, Crowner (1977) makes the following distinction regarding a transdisciplinary model:

> There are three across-discipline service delivery models. Multidisciplinary models join a number of separate disciplines so they are available for evaluation and prescription. Interdisciplinary models enforce interrelationships among each of the disciplines so that there is coordination of effort. Transdisciplinary models not only enforce interdisciplinary cooperation but encourage interchangeability across disciplines. This process can be referred to as a "skills swap", where each discipline must inservice all other disciplines so that all disciplines acquire many "traded" skills. (p.6)

Often a primary professional is designated to carry out the recommendations made by other members of the transdisciplinary team.

Depending on specific circumstances, the community based trainer may be the most logical choice as primary professional. As a specialist, the community based trainer often is involved in making program recommendations to the primary professional (generally a classroom teacher). The IEP can act as a transdisciplinary guide for the primary professional and, if well written, can hold supportive disciplines accountable for their specific responsibilities.

General Assessment Strategies

Severely and profoundly handicapped individuals are usually assessed by the classroom teacher, physical therapist, occupational therapist, speech and language therapist, and the psychologist. If the initial assessment calls for observation in the community environment, the community-based trainer becomes involved. This always occurs with students over 14 years of age. A good assessment is the primary basis for a good IEP. Clear, complete and well coordinated assessment strategies are essential in individual program development. Four assessment strategies are followed within the context of a transdisciplinary model using applied behavioral analysis designs:

1. When assessing a severely and profoundly handicapped student, it is advised that specific activities for the student be created to provide a standard of observation for each discipline.
2. It should also be made clear, initially, who will collect what information so that duplication of duties does not occur. Each discipline should focus upon specific areas for assessment purposes.
3. It is important to determine how information will be collected. For example, it might be decided that the classroom teacher will engage the student in certain activities while the other professionals observe unobtrusively. Or perhaps the occupational therapist will visit the home during mealtime. Some standardized measures associated with psychology or therapy may be deemed appropriate.
4. There must be interdisciplinary agreement. That is, a behavior, or lack of a behavior, must be considered absent or present by two or more disciplines. Often, the parent fills the role of a reliability checker. This strategy is continued throughout the student's schooling.

Use of these strategies will produce guiding information which may be used in developing the initial IEP. Information should be generated regarding cognitive, effective, motor, language, medical, and physical stamina. This information should be based on functional examples such as rate, endurance, and quality of performance in a given environment and across different environments.

Occupational Assessment Strategies

Once again depending on age and ability and need of a given student occupational assessment may be the focus for the general assessment of a student. That is, if age, ability, and need imply it then the transdisciplinary team may decide to make their assessment in a community based site. This would be in accordance with the first assessment strategy discussed earlier. For purposes of this discussion it will be assumed that occupational assessment was chosen as a primary focus.

Applied behavioral analysis comes into play very heavily once the decision on assessment focus has been made. Staff must bring to bear task analysis and observational technique. Measurement will focus on rate, endurance, and quality. Observations must be made under strict baseline conditions. Baseline conditions means that precise objectivity is used in assessments. Information gathered at this point must be standardized in a way which will allow it to be compared with information gathered later in time. Precision then is a key because precision implies detail. Detail which can communicate clear and concise information about the student. Information which can be validated by more than one person. Information which not only verifies the presence of a behavior but also specifies rate and endurance and quality of behavior.

Task analysis is essential. It forms the cornerstone of assessment for severely and profoundly handicapped persons. Task analysis provides information on a task that can be matched against pupil skills. Thus, a pupil's location on a given task at a given level of the occupational continuum can be pinpointed.

Applied behavioral analysis may be overly task oriented but it provides the tightest information on students one can achieve. Its importance to precise IEP's and ultimately to accountability is obvious. Within the context in which it is being applied here, there is far less need for concern over becoming task orientated. Because of the community based and transdisciplinary nature of the program it is important that precision be maintained. Skill transfer, generalization, and reliability of information are enhanced by the community based transdisciplinary approach.

For example, understanding student motivation is of major concern to the trainer. The trainer is interested in why a student performs well in a given work environment. What is reinforcing the student's behavior, and are the reinforcers natural to a given work environment? For example, some severely handicapped students perform only to please a trainer, or because the task is novel and seems fun. These reinforcers are not likely to sustain the learner once the trainer withdraws from the work site. After determining what the natural work site reinforcers are, existing student reinforcers may be paired with natural reinforcers in the environment using basic operant strategies. The probability of a student's sustained performance will then be enhanced. The trainer's understanding of student motivation is essential to other members of the transdisciplinary team. Basically this information is used to form many of the programs for a child. In the example just used, a natural reinforcer would likely be money. Thus, the classroom teacher, acting on this information, will initiate educational programs related to money and its usage.

Assessment Tools

A primary tool for occupational assessment is the check list. Check lists are used extensively in assessing the severely handicapped. Unfortunately, few efforts to publish generalizable check lists have been made to date. Often check lists are location specific and would have little meaning across different communities. This is why understanding how to conduct a task analysis is an important competency for professionals working with severely and profoundly handicapped persons. Not only is it necessary for professionals to develop their own complete check lists through task analysis, but often, existing check lists must be broken down considerably in order to be applied to the severely handicapped. Some task analysis are generalizable across settings.

Understanding the student's potential within a given work site is founded upon a thorough understanding of that work site. In addition, information about community based sites influence curriculum at all levels. Belmore and Brown (1976) describe an analysis format for work sites. An outline of that format appears on the next page. This detailed analysis provides information on related work skills, transportation, legal considerations as well as simple job site descriptions. It is an excellent format with which to collect precise information for IEP's. Also it helps delineate where coordination among disciplines and agencies should logically occur. Teachers of even very young or profoundly handicapped persons may use the information gathered by this tool in developing occupational orientated sections of IEP's for their students. Schwartz (1976) has developed a complete job site and skill analysis for a dishwashing work site. Schwartz's study is an excellent example of the use of the job skills inventory developed by Belmore and Brown.

An Outline of the Madison Job Skill Inventory

A. General Information
    1. Reasons why severely handicapped students are considered for this job.
    2. A general description of the job.
    3. A general description of the work setting.
    4. A general description of the social environment:
        a) Information related to fellow workers.
        b) Information related to supervision.
        c) Information related to special contingencies.
B. Specific Skill Requirements of the Job Under Analysis
    1. A List of the basic physical-sensory motor skills required.
    2. A list of the basic interpersonal skills required.
    3. A list of the basic language skills (verbal and nonverbal) required.
    4. A list of the basic functional academic skills required
    5. A list of the basic machine and tool skills.
    6. A list of the basic hygienic skills required.
C. Supportive Skills and Other Information Required
    1. Transportation skills required.

2. Skills related to work preparation.
3. Basic money management skills required.
4. Time-telling and time-judgment skills required.
5. Health code requirements.
6. Informed consent and legal requirements.

Rating scales are another method for gaining information on occupational needs of the severely handicapped. Ferrara (1977) has designed a rating scale for community survival screening. This scale rates performance across transportation, general behavior, clothing, direction following, staying in a group, frustration level, toilet needs, waiting, walking, locating destinations, and amount of supervisors needed.

Individual Educational Plans

Goals and Objectives

Once occupational information is gathered it must be integrated with general information in order to form a complete and coordinated IEP. Long and short range goals must be stated in the IEP. Because of the functional nature of occupation, many of the goals relating to it are very pragmatic. To begin, a general goal relating to work site should be established. Goals may be evolved by asking key questions. For this first general goal one might answer the following two questions.

1) Was performance in the work site used for initial assessment such that the student is ready for placement in that particular environment? If question one is answered no, then the primary goals may involve reaching criteria for entrance into some particular environment. If question one is answered yes, then goals should be developed which are based on criterion for complete success in the chosen site. Criterion will be set for rate, endurance, and quality of performance as well as affective behavior.

2) How much time does the student have left in school? The answers to this question will relate to emphasis on occupational goals and will dictate the long or short range nature of occupational goals. For instance, should emphasis be on specific job training or on surveys across many work sites, and how much instructional time should be spent in occupational preparation as compared to other activities.

In some regards setting occupational goals is a process of moving from the general (guiding information) to the specific. Once goals related to criterion for rate, endurance, quality and affective behaviors have been determined then relationships between occupational activities and other goals need to be examined. Specifically, what are the general goals in language, cognition, motor, medical, and affective areas and what specific subgoals in each of these areas can be set for occupational preparation? For example, what is the language goal in the work environment?

Writing the IEP

This paper has taken the position that individual educational plans for severely handicapped students should include occupational goals as part of precise, complete, and coordinated statements about pupil needs and programming. Rate, endurance, quality, and affective behavior are seen as relevant occupational goals which may be connected to general educational goals for children. Because of the number and complexity of goals for this population, the IEP becomes an essential blueprint for parents and professionals. The IEP can marry applied behavioral analysis to realistic community based occupational training. It can provide a format for transdisciplinary and interagency planning and cooperation. Individual Educational Plans appear as formal written documents. The IEP document should be a record of past events, and of events which should occur in the future of a student's life. Specifically, the information that must by law, appear in the student's current level of functioning, expectations (goals) for immediate and long range future functioning, and "precisely" how and when the student's goals will be achieved. Writing an IEP provides an opportunity for interested parties to organize and verify information about a student.

Information about a student's occupational functioning both presently and in the future, should be an integrated part of an IEP. A separate IEP dealing with occupational information would encourage discontinuity in a student's program. If there are separate IEP's for general and occupational information, it might be reasoned that the programming implied will occur as distinct and separate. In fact, certain information regarding occupational expectations should be stated in all IEP's. The student's age and time left in school should influence the focus of information, and specifically of information relating to occupational programming. If, for example, a student is graduating at the end of the school year, then general educational and therapeutic activities would all be designated to support occupational goals. This fact would reflect itself in the IEP.

Complete IEP's will contain answers to many occupational related issues which are arrived at through the strategies outlined in this paper. Specifically the complete IEP will address at least these questions:
1. How much time is available before graduation?
2. Where is this student in terms of the occupational continuum?
3. What things may the student be able to do with prosthetic support?
4. What is currently reinforcing this student?
5. Of those behaviors a student has, what are his

rates, levels of endurance, and quality of performance? The well coordinated IEP will spell out how persons will work together to achieve the occupational goals which have been set. For example, with proper coordination desirable recreation could become contingent upon work performance. However, if agencies responsible for recreation have not been involved, it is not likely that such a plan could be worked out. In short, the educational services being provided should be supported and reinforced by as many persons and agencies as possible.

The precise IEP will spell out specifically who will do what by when. It will be based on sound behavioral orientated objective data. It will specify how available instructional sequences will be used to achieve goals. It will delineate measurement strategies, objective criteria, a schedule for examining progress, and dates by which goal achievement might realistically be expected.

Evaluating the IEP

It should be obvious by this point that IEP's should be evaluated on the basis of precision, completeness, and coordination. However, there is a final consideration which is crucial to the evaluation of an IEP. That is, does the IEP reflect a realistic plan for the student? What information will help answer this question? First of all, judgments about precision, completeness, and coordination will help the consumer in assessing the relevancy of a plan. The consumer/evaluator of IEP's must look at the structures that are implied by instructional strategies. Are the structures natural or contrived? Have the educators provided for continued progress to a higher level on the occupational continuum once the most immediate next level is reached (good long range goals)? Does the plan reflect the skills needed for survival in the local community?

Application of Piagetian Sensorimotor Concepts to Assessment and Curriculum for Severely Handicapped Children

Cordelia C. Robinson
University of Nebraska Medical Center

Abstract. People who work with very young handicapped children encounter problems in infant cognitive functioning. Standardized intelligence tests are inadequate tools for the assessment of these children's developmental capacities and the design of appropriate intervention strategies. This paper describes the adaptation of Piagetian sensorimotor concepts to the assessment of severely handicapped infants and toddlers. The objective of this procedure is to develop and validate a curriculum that will aid these children in the acquisition of sensorimotor skills.

The problem of cognitive development in children who are atypical in developmental patterns or developmental level is all too familiar to individuals working with young children with severe handicaps. The early intervention literature is replete with descriptions of the unsatisfactory nature of standardized norm-referenced intelligence tests when one's purpose is the design of intervention strategies to ameliorate developmental problems or enhance developmental functioning with moderately to severely handicapped children. This problem of assessment is difficult with children under two years and particularly difficult with the infant or toddler with a motor or sensory handicap.

Many have discussed the dependence of current means of assessment of infant cognitive functioning upon the child's motor skills (Bruner, 1973; Kopp, 1974; Kopp & Shaperman, 1973). A look at the Bayley Scales of Infant Development or the Cattell Infant Scales reveals the weighting of skills that may be classified as adaptive eye-hand functions. While these skills persist as aspects in the measurement of intelligence throughout life, they comprise a disproportionate amount of the assessment during the first three years of life. The relationship between motor and cognitive skills and their influence upon each other are of interest to developmental psychology and are currently being analyzed from differing perspectives. In Bruner's work we see a very careful analysis of a child's actions as they function to shape instrumental intelligence. A good deal of emphasis is placed upon the correlation of motor and cognitive functioning. Others, most notably Kagan (1970), argue that too great an emphasis has been placed upon maturity of motor abilities as indicators of cognitive structures. His data (citing the consistency in infant autonomic responses to events which violate principles such as object constancy) are certainly suggestive of early discrimination and memory capacities in young infants. His results also suggest the utility of analyzing tasks in an effort to differentiate components as motor skills that are necessary (as opposed to those which are

coincidental) to the problem we present to the child to solve. The techniques developed by Hauesserman (1958) for assessing developmental potential in preschool children are an example of such a strategy. Her use of systematic variation of materials to permit identification of the basis of a child's response has been extremely valuable as a basis for developing teaching strategies appropriate to a child's developmental level. Her techniques emphasize adaptation of the testing materials and mode of presentation to the child's current response repertoire. If the child cannot speak but can point, the test is adapted and questions accommodated to that mode of response.

In this paper I would like to describe our beginning efforts to develop systematic adaptations of Piagetian sensorimotor tasks to the current response repertoires of the severely handicapped infant and toddler-aged children with whom we are working. The objective of such adaptations in assessment is the development and validation of a curriculum designed to facilitate acquisition of sensorimotor schemes in handicapped children.

Among individuals identified as severely handicapped we see a good number who are multihandicapped. While assessment and development of a prescriptive program is difficult with any individual who is severely handicapped, the task becomes still more complex when we are faced with an individual with moderate to severe neuromotor impairment or cerebral palsy. The majority of severely retarded individuals will be functioning as developmentally young individuals with cognitive development in the range of tasks typically achieved in the first three years of life. As was earlier noted the majority of the tasks used to assess a person's cognitive development during those years are heavily weighted with motor accomplishments as well. They are typically tasks requiring gross motor development such as posture control and rotation through different positions, fine motor components such as coordinated reach and grasp, or complex motor schemes such as combining objects at midline, sliding, tearing, crumpling, and examining through physical manipulation.

The very nature of the behaviors which we have used to index the early cognitive development of children makes it impossible to get a reasonable assessment of the extent to which a severely physically handicapped child has developed an understanding of some of the rules of our physical environment.

The development of the concept of object permanence provides an illustration of the manner in which the physically handicapped child is penalized. The typical means of assessing object permanence, or the recognition that an object still exists when we have lost sensory contact with it, is to hide an object with the child observing the hiding and then permit the child to search

"Application of Piagetian Sensorimotor Concepts to Assessment and Curriculum for Severely Handicapped Children,"
Cordelia Robinson, *AAESPH Review*, Vol. 1, No. 8, November 1976. © 1976 AAESPH Review.

for the object. For most young children of 10-12 months of age or more this task presents no difficulty. However, what we frequently do not appreciate is the motor complexity of the task. The child has to visually observe the hiding of the object and then combine visually directed reach and grasp to uncover the object and then reach and grasp to pick up the object. But is that complex motor response necessary for us to infer object permanence or is it just our peculiar means of assessing the concept? If we could not move our limbs, we could still express our knowledge of the concept by telling someone where to look for a missing object. If we could not talk, we might try to convey the same message through directed gaze. It might take awhile for the person with whom we are trying to communicate to learn the meaning of our directed looking, but through trial and error we would eventually establish a means of communication.

Among the severely handicapped individuals we are working with, few have speech. Consequently, development of alternative response strategies, such as directed gaze or pointing, for the individual with slightly better physical control becomes necessary if we are to assess development with respect to the cognitive accomplishments of the first several years.

In our project for handicapped infants from birth to three years of age we use Piaget's descriptions of the accomplishments during the sensorimotor period as the basis of the curriculum. With many of the children it is possible to administer the tasks in the manner described by Uzgiris and Hunt (1975) in their scales of Piagetian sensorimotor development. However, a substantial number of children have physical handicaps that make the conventional means of presenting the tasks unrealistic for assessing the child's development. Consequently, we are attempting to work out alternative response strategies for individual children, particularly in the areas of object permanence, means-end, and causality concepts. In developing the alternative response strategies we are of course setting the requirement that they be behaviors which can be objectively described and agreed upon by two or more individuals independently rating the responses. Development of those alternative responses is frequently a shaping process. For example, initially after hiding an object we would wait for the child's gaze to return to the hiding place and we would then uncover the object. If the child did not look in the direction himself, we would physically prompt him by turning his head in the correct direction and then uncover the object. We would continue the activity on appropriate occasions until the child consistently showed directed gaze as a means of searching for the missing object. Once the strategy of directed looking or *whatever alternative response is selected,* is established, it is possible to present the child with the more complex object permanence problems including the most advanced level of systematic search when the exact location is unknown. In this task the child must simply use his alternate response to tell us to search in each of the possible locations until the object is found.

Sensorimotor Assessment

The sensorimotor assessment that we are using consists of tasks from the Uzgiris-Hunt Instrument for Assessing Infant Psychological Development (1966, 1975). When assessing children who do not have physical or sensory handicaps we have found that the standard administration of the tasks results in an assessment of sensorimotor activities for which inter-rater reliability based upon

percent agreement between two observers was .99 and corrected split-half reliability was .96 (Robinson, Chatelanat, Spritzer, Robertson, & Bricker, 1973).

The sensorimotor scales that we have come to consider especially important and adaptable to modification for our physically handicapped children are the object permanence, means-end, and causality series. Each of these series involves the development of behaviors which we feel are extremely important requisites to the development of communication on the part of the children with whom we are working.

Means-end development. The initial level of means-end development described by Piaget is the repetition of responses that result in the continuation of an event. This is a familiar form of behavior in the three-to-four-month-old infant who engages in a lot of gross motor movement such as flailing of arms and legs, which if done in his crib is likely to result in movement of a toy such as a mobile suspended above the crib. Initial observations would be likely to yield rates of movement roughly equal for both arms or both legs. Before very long, however, the child's responses seem to become more efficient; that is, there is more movement on the part of the toy with less movement on the part of the child. Piaget assumes that at this stage the child's behavior is not intentional in the sense of anticipating the results of his movements but rather that the "systematic responses" are reinforced operants. In the context of this type of experience we can conceptualize the beginnings of a systematic strategy for acting upon the environment to reproduce events. For the normal child this activity consumes an enormous amount of his time during the first 12 to 18 months. For the severely physically handicapped child this experience of manipulating his environment in increasingly complex ways generally does not happen spontaneously. He has little control over his patterns of movement and has great difficulty in repeating a pattern that has been successful. For such children a good part of our early intervention is directed toward trying to take advantage of any possible movements, harnessing them if you will, in an effort to produce the experience of effecting some control over the physical environment. For the child who shows a very low rate and amplitude of arm movement we might begin by attaching a piece of yarn to the child's wrist with the other end tied to metal wind chimes. This arrangement results in a sound and visual event with the slightest movement on the part of the child. Our eventual goal is the same form of differentiated performance in terms of development of an efficient response as seen with the young baby, under whatever prosthetic conditions are necessary for the given child. The second part of the goal is of course a generalized strategy in which we see use of previously developed responses with novel stimuli. Figure 1 illustrates the performance of a severely handicapped child who showed a differentiated means-end strategy after several weeks of experience with the wind chimes situation. Note that initially all of his movement was bilateral movement, but after several weeks he began to show differentiation of the response with increase in unilateral movement.

Causality concepts. The series of developments related to the concept of causality begins in the same manner as the means-end series with systematic repetition of a response which produces an event. Following that point, however, we assess causality by observing the child's reaction to an event that he cannot

2. DIAGNOSIS AND ASSESSMENT

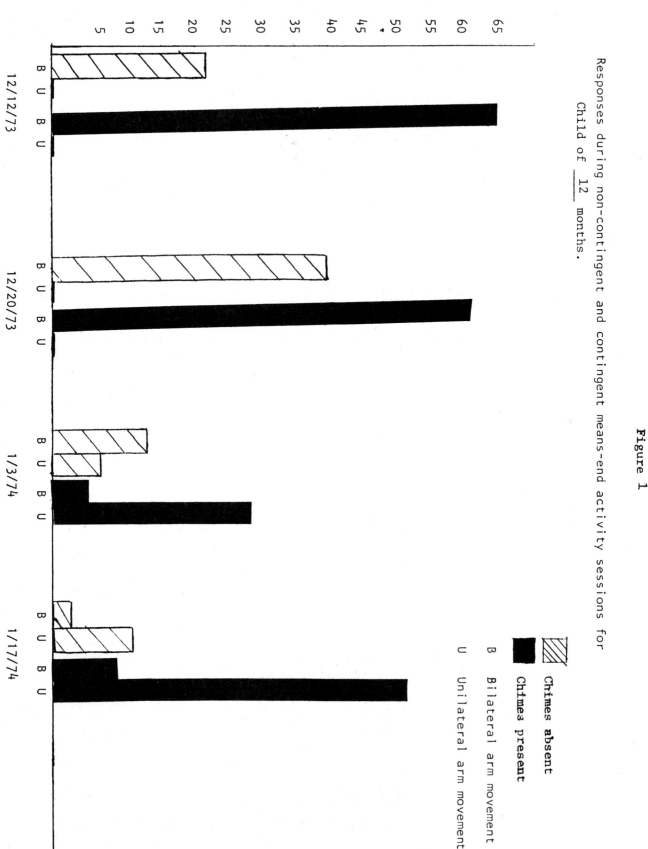

Figure 1

Responses during non-contingent and contingent means-end activity sessions for Child of ___12___ months.

Number of Responses per Minute

Chimes absent

Chimes present

B   Bilateral arm movement

U   Unilateral arm movement

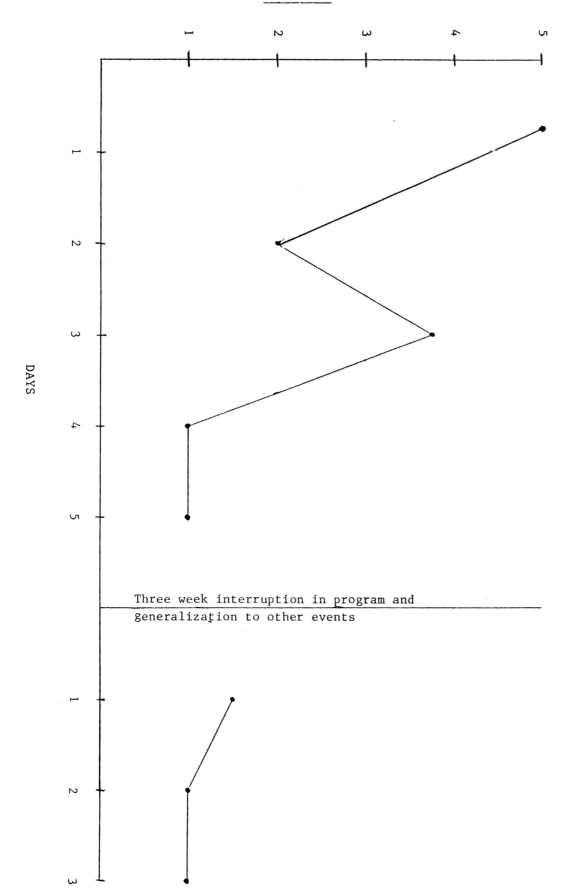

Figure 2: Mean Number of requests by teacher "do you want to bounce?" before child responds with vocalization

2. DIAGNOSIS AND ASSESSMENT

reproduce himself. Again using a young baby (now about 6-7 months of age) as an examp... bounced on his father's lap. ... wiggles and the father interpre... to bounce some more." Witl... beginnings of a gesture system... upon context but is an impo... communication, for it marks th... use a response to make so... produce for himself. We lc... motivation for developing con... means by which we assess th... with a severely handicapped... child responded with a smile... being bounced in the teacher... teaching situation. He bounc... "Tommy, would you like to bc... asked the question five tim... vocalized "Ahh..." The teache... days Tommy was saying "Ahh... you want to bounce?" The c... then interrupted for several weeks. When Tommy returned the teacher again presented the situation. Tommy used his "Ahh" response and also generalized it to other situations such as the swings in the playground.

The next step in this series will be to ask Tommy if he wants to bounce before the teacher bounces him the first time. Following correct performance in that situation he will then be asked if he wants to bounce before he is placed on the teacher's lap. Thus, the contextual cues to the child are gradually reduced in an effort to approximate a gesture system. The system is still dependent upon familiarity with the individual child and his response repertoire but it provides an outline of a series of steps that we might go through to reduce that dependency. During the course of the day many opportunities occur in which the child can be required to use some form of gesture, no matter how idiosyncratic to his response repertoire, in order for those events which are reinforcing, either by their presentation or removal, to occur. As we think of the context in which communication develops for children with normal speech capabilities it is typically that of obtaining something that is positively reinforcing or avoiding or escaping something which is a negative event. We view the type of causality experience described as analogous to early vocal experiences for normal children and, consequently, the description of this type of experience as the motivation for communication.

Of course as the child becomes more capable of producing more explicit gestures, such as bringing his hand to a toy which he cannot activate or, perhaps, pushing your hand with the spoon in it toward his plate of food, we of course require that more explicit gesture whenever it is possible for that event to occur. One essential point to keep in mind when requiring a child to use a "gesture" in order for an event to occur is the necessity for consistency. Once the decision is made, the gesture or an approximation of the gesture should be required at every opportunity. When an opportunity is offered it should be carried through to completion.

Object permanence. The third sensorimotor area that we particularly emphasize with severely physically handicapped children is object permanence. Object permanence is assumed to be a necessary requisite for the development of representational

communication where reference is made to an absent object, person, or event. With whatever communication system is used, spoken words, hand gestures, signs, plastic chips, or pictures, the individual parts of that system are used to represent an object or event that exists or did exist at one time. Presumably when a person uses one of the various communication systems for representation he can do so because an object or event exists for him independent of his sensory contact with it. We have not yet encountered any children who demonstrate communication in the sense of making a request for absent objects, people, or events who do not also demonstrate object permanence.

We have also found efforts in teaching the child an alternative response for demonstrating object permanence, such as directed looking or pointing, to be useful in establishing a strategy for early communication in the context of making choices and getting feedback about those choices. We begin with a situation where an object which we have found to be a reinforcer is covered and the child is asked, "Where is the *cookie?*" When he looks at the cover we uncover the cookie and he gets to eat it. If he does not look we physically prompt him to do so. Once he is consistent in this situation we go to the two-choice situation and he has to look in the correct direction in order to get the object. At this level we begin to ask him to make choices between two objects, a glass of juice or a glass of milk, a cracker or a cookie. He learns the consequences of making a choice as he gets the one at which he directs his gaze. This type of experience which is so much a part of the average toddler's day is frequently not provided for the young physically handicapped child.

The next steps involve presenting increasingly difficult object search situations as outlined in Table 1 and also extending the choice-making situation to a greater variety of objects, not just food, but items of clothing and toys. The next step is to ask the child to use his choice-making strategy (directed looking) to identify an object or event named. Up until this point this strategy has been used with the objects present. When the child is consistent in using this strategy in the presence of the actual object, it is then possible to begin work in a representational context. The child now chooses between two pictures, one of a glass of milk, the other of a glass of juice. We also begin to ask him to indicate his receptive language by selecting a picture of the object or event named. It is when a child has these two strategies that a device such as a communication board becomes feasible. The sensorimotor experiences in the areas described, means-end, causality, and object permanence concepts, serve to provide prerequisite experiences with communication at a less symbolic level.

It is apparent from the paucity of data-based examples that our work in developing sensorimotor curriculum and documenting its efficacy is just beginning. The number of children that we encounter with such severe physical handicaps is fortunately few. We have seen a few of the children go on to use communication boards with considerable success. We are working with several children who seem to be approaching the point where they will soon begin work on representational language. We think that using the sensorimotor assessment provides us with useful descriptions of the kinds of experiences that make up the first two years for the average toddler. By adapting the activities and materials that make up those experiences to the response capabilities of the severely physically handicapped child we no longer have to passively wait until his receptive language is

50

adequate to teach him new concepts or assess those he has already acquired but which we had no way of understanding. By working on the sensorimotor concepts we can try to approximate for the severely handicapped child the average child's experiences of gaining ever increasing control over his physical and social environments.

Table 1

Object Permanence Problem Sequence

Description of Response

1. *Single Visible Displacement with One Screen*
   Removes screen and takes object. Do not credit if child merely removes screen and plays with it.

2. *Single Visible Displacement, Random Alternation Between Two Screens*
   Removes correct screen and obtains object.

3. *Sequential Visible Displacement with Two Screens*
   Searches directly under the last screen.

4. *Invisible Displacement with One Screen*
   Child searches under screen. (May check examiner's hand first.)

5. *Invisible Displacement with Two Screens*
   Searches directly under the correct screen. (May check examiner's hand first.)

6. *Sequential Invisible Displacement With Two Screens*
   Child searches under screens, in order of first to last or directly under last screen.

7. *Sequential Invisible Displacement with Three Screens*
   Child searches under screens, in order of first to last or directly under last screen.

8. *Representation of Sequential Invisible Displacements*
   Child searches systematically from the last screen to the first in reverse order. (Administer this item using the same path as in number 4 but leaving the object under the first screen and continuing hand movements if the child searched consistently under the last screen in number 4.)

Visible displacement — object is visible in examiner's hand as it is placed completely under screen.

Sequential visible displacement — object is visible in examiner's hand as it is placed under first one screen and then the other(s). The object is left under the last screen.

Invisible displacement — object is hidden in examiner's hand and then placed under the screen without letting the child see the object again until the child uncovers it.

Sequential invisible displacement — object is hidden in examiner's hand and examiner moves hand with object under a screen. Child is not permitted to see the object from the time it is covered in examiner's hand until the child uncovers the object.

References

Bruner, J.S. Organization of early skilled action. *Child Development*, 1973, *44*, 1-11.

Hauesserman, E. *Developmental potential of preschool children.* New York: Grune & Stratton, 1958.

Kagan, J. Attention and psychological change in the young child. *Science*, 1970, *170*, 826-832.

Kopp, C.B. *Development of fine motor behaviors: Issues and research.* Paper presented at the Symposium on Aberrant Development in Infancy, Gatlinburg, Tennessee, March 1974.

Kopp, C.B., & Shaperman, J. Cognitive development in the absence of object manipulation during infancy. *Developmental Psychology*, 1973, *9*, 430.

Robinson, C., Chatelanat, G., Spritzer, S., Robertson, M., & Bricker, W. Study of sensorimotor development in delayed and non-delayed children. In *Infant, toddler and preschool research and intervention project report: III.* IMRID Behavioral Science Monograph No. 23. Nashville, Tenn.: John F. Kennedy Center for Research on Education and Human Development, 1973.

Uzgiris, I.C., & Hunt, J. McV. *An instrument for assessing infant psychological development.* Urbana: University of Illinois Press, 1966.

Uzgiris, I.C., & Hunt, J. McV. *Assessment in infancy ordinal scales of psychological development.* Urbana: University of Illinois Press, 1975.

Social Adjustment in More Severely Retarded, Institutionalized Individuals: The Sum of Adjusted Behavior

E. E. BALTHAZAR AND J. L. PHILLIPS

Central Wisconsin Colony and Training School (Madison)

A measure which is used to count kinds of social behavior in more severely mentally retarded residents was described in this study. The measure is an aggregate or sum, and it is referred to as the Sum of Adjusted Behavior. In this study, we determined measures of social adjustment which are useful for obtaining population parameters. Data concerning the relationship between the Sum of Adjusted Behavior and CA to MA, age at time of institutionalization, gender, medical diagnosis, medication, and social behavior were discussed. The relationships between adjustment and adaptive behavior were also defined on the basis of the findings.

In the present investigation, a measure which is used to count certain kinds of social behavior in more severely mentally retarded and less retarded younger institutionalized residents was examined. The component items for the measure were selected from the Balthazar Scales of Adaptive Behavior II, The Scales of Social Adaptation (Balthazar, 1973). Since the measures were used as an aggregate or sum total, they are referred to as the Sum of Adjusted Behavior. Whereas the Balthazar Scales of Adaptive Behavior-II was designed to provide profile scores and target behavior for program development and to establish measures of adaptive behavior, the Sum of Adjusted Behavior served to furnish information regarding certain parameters which relate to particular social factors in general adjustment. The present investigation, then, was intended to identify those parameters which comprise the activity levels, interpersonal behavior, language performance, use of objects, play activities, response to instructions, and level of cooperation among other kinds of behavior and to relate them to other measures which are characteristic of an institutional population.

The Sum of Adjusted Behavior is one of a set of measures which was designed to measure various kinds of behavior in more severely retarded and less retarded younger individuals. One measure has already been reported, i.e., a language index (Naor & Balthazar, 1975). Others, which will be dealt with in a series of independent reports, are: a stereopathy index, an index of socially ambivalent behavior, and a behavioral management index.

Three variables—chronological age (CA), age at institutionalization, and length of institutionalization—taken together can provide data concerning the extent to which the particular environment is contributing to the level of the Sum of Adjusted Behavior. A comparison with other institutional and noninstitutional environments, however, was not possible in the scope of the current study. Instead, the Sum of Adjusted Behavior was examined as it related to such resident characteristics as mental age (MA), social age, functional self-help skills, and indicators of emotional disturbance in a single institutional sample.

Method

Subjects

The sample consisted of 77 ambulatory, severely and profoundly retarded persons, 42 males and 35 females, who had lived in the same midwestern institution for 3 or more years. They ranged in age from 6 to 57 years, with median age of 14.6 years at the time of observation. MA based on the Bayley Infant Intelligence, Wechsler, and Stanford-Binet measures ranged from 3 to 63

"Social Adjustment in More Severely Retarded, Institutionalized Individuals: The Sum of Adjusted Behavior," E.E. Balthazan and J.L. Phillips, *American Journal of Mental Deficiency,* Vol. 80, No. 4, January 1976. © 1976 American Journal of Mental Deficiency.

months (median 16.4 months). Social age, measured by the Vineland Social Maturity Scale, ranged from 9 to 85 months (median 23.8 months). MA and social age were calculated by the institutional staff, and scores used in this study were obtained from the residents' medical records. MA was available for 66 subjects and social age for 56, based on tests during the 5 years prior to observations in which the Balthazar Scales were used.

According to the medical records, a total of 22 different diagnoses of the source of retardation were represented in the sample, of which the two most frequent were Down's syndrome (11) and "mental retardation of unknown origin with functional reaction alone manifest" (13). Only two residents in the sample suffered motor difficulties, and all except one passed a gross hearing test. Thirty-six had some form of physical or neurological disorder. Fifty-nine subjects had no history of seizures, 13 had seizures only in the past, 4 had seizures controlled medically, and 1 had uncontrolled seizures. Medication records, available for 70 subjects, indicated that 23 males and 23 females were receiving some form of psychotropic drugs at the time of observation.

The psychological reports in the residents' medical records furnished categorical descriptions of self-care skills and individual behavioral characteristics. Eating skills were available for 71 subjects, of whom 53 were classed as independent eaters, and only 1 had no self-care eating skills. Of the 61 subjects with dressing skills indicated, 38 could dress themselves with minimal assistance, and 9 were reported to have no self-care dressing skills. Toileting records were available for 57 subjects; 43 were fully toilet-regulated or trained, 5 had accidents, and 9 were reported not to be toilet-regulated.

With respect to behavioral characteristics, the psychological reports identified 16 subjects characterized by aggressive behavior, 9 by hyperactivity, 23 by behavior problems (kicks, screams, bites, tears clothing, temper tantrums), and 15 by inappropriate social behavior (strips, licks peers, eats unedible objects, masturbates). Residents who had no indication of the preceding four behavioral characteristics on their records did not in all probability engage in them frequently enough for staff concern. They were, therefore, coded with residents whose records state that the behavior was not manifest.

A fifth behavioral indicator, peer interaction, was available for 48 subjects. The psychological reports identified 22 as social isolates, 1 as engaging in one-to-one interaction but no group activity, 6 as not interested in ward activities and/or not engaging in meaningful play, and 19 as liking ward activities and enjoying peer interaction.

Procedure

A broad spectrum of social coping behavior was recorded using the Balthazar Scales of Adaptive Behavior, Section II: The Scales of Social Adaptation. In this study, six 10-minute distributed observation sessions were conducted for each subject, and the results of the event-sampling procedure were cumulated over all sessions.

The Balthazar Scales of Adaptive Behavior-II was used as a basis for this study because it is based on standardized methods of direct observation and because the individual subscale items which comprise it span the full spectrum of social coping behavior recorded in direct observational studies of these and similar individuals. The complete scale is comprised of 19 factor scales, including 72 subscale items designed to provide measures of specific and discrete types of social behavior.

The scales and subscale items which were relevant to this investigation are detailed below.[1] The Sum of Adjusted Behavior is defined as the sum of the kinds of behavior listed, across all six 10-minute observation sessions, arbitrarily grouped by quartiles for this analysis. Operational definitions and examples for each of the scales and subscale items are provided in the Balthazar Scales of Adaptive Behavior-II manual (Balthazar, 1973).

In brief, Subscale Items 8 (b, c, d) designate alert activity, investigative curiosity, and passive recreation, respectively, and 8 (e) represents purposeful and specific exploration of the self and self-curiosity. Scales 9 and 10 designate positive approach-response behavior without communication and similar behavior involving nonverbal communication, respectively, and Scale 11 represents appropriate response to danger or bullying. Scales 9, 10, and 11 are categorized in the Balthazar Scales of Adaptive Behavior-II manual as delineating interpersonal behavior. Scales 12 and 13 indicate verbal communication and refer to inarticulate or nonmeaningful speech, a type of prespeech behavior, and to meaningful receptive and expressive verbal behavior. Scale 14 (c, d) refer to handling objects in a fundamental or elementary but meaningful way and to the creative use of objects; and Scales 15 and 16 measure play-

---

[1] These scales are copyrighted by Consulting Psychologists Press, Palo Alto, California, 1973.

2. DIAGNOSIS AND ASSESSMENT

Balthazar Scale of Adaptive Behavior-II

Scale No.	Scale or Subscale Item
8b	Generalized activity
8c	Exploratory, searching activity
8d	Recreational activity
8e	Self-regard
9	Fundamental social behavior: noncommunication
10	Fundamental social behavior: social vocalization and gestures
11	Appropriate response to negative peer contact
12	Nonfunctional, repetitious, or inarticulate verbalization
13	Verbalization
14c	Uses objects appropriately
14d	Creative use of objects
15	Playful contact
16	Play activities
17abc	Responds to instructions
18a	Responds to firmly given instructions
18c	Responds to physical guidance
19	Cooperative contact

ful behavior and game-like activities involving rules, respectively. Subscales 17 (a, b, c) and 18 (a, c) designate compliance to instruction either given verbally or by means of physical guidance; and Scale 19 represents those kinds of behavior involving helping another or actively carrying out a task assignment.

The associations between the Sum of Adjusted Behavior and CA, gender, diagnosis, MA, social age, age at institutionalization, length of institutionalization, and the self-help skills and behavioral characteristics described above were determined. Because the Sum of Adjusted Behavior and most of the other variables are most accurately treated as ordinal variables, Kendall's *tau* was selected for statistical analysis. For estimating the effects of medical diagnosis, the Kruskal-Wallis one-way analysis of variance was employed because no prior rationale existed for ordering diagnoses.

While staff reports of prior behavioral characteristics do not share the standardized validity of the Balthazar Scales of Adaptive Behavior-II, they are used here as rough indicators of continuity of behavior. These reports refer to previously exhibited behavior which is indicative of emotional disturbance in social situations. In the absence of treatment any underlying disturbance would be expected to persist, at least to the extent that those for whom disturbed behavior was recorded in the past had a higher probability of exhibiting disturbances at the time of observation than those not previously so characterized.

Results

In analyzing the data, it can be stated that extremely low scores on the Sum of Ad-

TABLE 2

RELATIONSHIP OF THE SUM OF ADJUSTED BEHAVIOR TO MENTAL AGE (MA), SOCIAL AGE, FUNCTIONAL SKILLS, AND BEHAVIORAL INDICATIONS, CONTROLLING FOR MEDICATION

Characteristic	No medication		With medication	
	τ	p	τ	p
MA	.65[a]	.0005	.16	.13
Social age	.57[a]	.01	.19	.12
Functional skills				
Eating	.35[a]	.02	.09	.21
Dressing	.45[a]	.01	.23	.06
Toileting	.34	.07	.12	.13
Behavioral indications				
Peer interaction	.34	.14	.23	.09
Aggressiveness	−.07	.32	−.14	.09
Hyperactivity	.21	.06	−.02	.44
Behavior problems	−.13	.28	−.15	.18
Inappropriate behavior	−.13	.26	.04	.39

[a] τ significantly greater than zero at α .05.

justed Behavior obtained by persons who are (a) basically inactive, or (b) engaged in predominantly disturbed behavior, or both. At the theoretical high end of the continuum are persons who are extremely active and whose behavior is predominantly socially "adjusted." A high Sum of Adjusted Behavior score is not indicative of the hyperactive individual, because hyperactivity tends to result in a high frequency of inappropriate behavior initiated (behavior not included in the Sum of Adjusted Behavior) coupled with a low frequency of appropriate social responses (Balthazar & Stevens, 1975). For this sample, the Sum of Adjusted Behavior ranged from 0 to 152, with a first quartile of 46, median of 73, and third quartile of 96. The mean was 74.5.

The Sum of Adjusted Behavior was negatively related to age at time of institutionalization ($\tau = -.27, p = .02$), but it was not found to be related to CA or length of institutionalization. It did not differ significantly by gender. The Sum of Adjusted Behavior was higher for subjects with a history of seizures ($\tau = .19, p = .007$), but it was unrelated to medical diagnosis.

The Sum of Adjusted Behavior was directly related to both MA ($\tau = .40, p < .0001$) and social age ($\tau = .34, p = .003$) and to the self-care skills of eating ($\tau = .23, p = .02$), dressing ($\tau = .30, p = .003$), and toileting ($\tau = .18, p = .03$). It was positively related to staff indications of peer interaction ($\tau = .26, p = .02$), and unrelated to indications of aggressiveness, hyperactivity, behavior problems, and inappropriate behavior.

Sixty percent of the sample were receiving some form of medication at the time of observation, the majority receiving tranquilizers, sedatives, or both (Table 1). Most subjects receiving anticonvulsants were receiving additional medication. Because of the complex medication schedules and because of the variety of drugs administered, the present analysis will focus on the simple dichotomy: presence or absence of drug treatment.

There was little doubt that psychotropic medication did have an effect on the Sum of Adjusted Behavior, which was significantly lower for the portion of the sample receiving medication than the remainder ($\tau = -.26, p = .002$). The median value of the Sum of Adjusted Behavior for nonmedicated subjects was 88.0, while the median value for medicated subjects was only 66.5.

Medication also had an effect on the relationship of the Sum of Adjusted Behavior to MA, social age, and the self-care skills but not on the relationship of Sum of Adjusted Behavior to medical record indications of

TABLE 1
MEDICATION USED BY SAMPLE

Medication	Number of subjects[a]
Tranquilizers	
Compazine	2
Mellaril	29
Quide	4
Repoise	2
Serentil	2
Stelazine	6
Thorazine	4
Trilafon	1
Valium	4
Sedatives	
Delmane	1
Doriden	3
Noludor	1
Phenergan	1
Phenobarbital	18
Seconal	1
Anticonvulsants	
Dilantin	8

Note. The variety of psychotropic and other types of medication in use at the time of observation was too great to test the effects of individual drugs.

[a] The total number of subjects receiving medication was 46. Many subjects received more than one drug during observations.

disturbed behavior (see Table 2). With respect to both MA and social age, and all skill indicators except toileting (which was not quite significantly related to the Sum of Adjusted Behavior for the nonmedicated group), controlling for the use of psychotropic and other types of medication yielded a positive relationship in the nonmedicated group only. In contrast, for all disturbed behavior indicators, no significant relationship was found between any indicator and the Sum of Adjusted Behavior in either the medicated or the nonmedicated group.

Discussion

In a strict sense, the present investigation is descriptive of social adjustment in a relatively unstructured environment and is in contrast to an effort to measure specific programs which target adaptive behavior from baseline. With respect to measures of social adjustment itself and to adaptive behavior in regard to more severely mentally retarded individuals, the relationship between scalar measures and program development and measures of adjustment have an important bearing on the matter of definition of adaptation. This is especially true when measures of appropriate adaptive behavior are provided by measures of successful program outcomes which was not done here.

Balthazar and others have stressed scalar measures in mental retardation and program development and in monitoring adaptive be-

2. DIAGNOSIS AND ASSESSMENT

havior in relatively early and in recently published research (Balthazar, 1966, 1971, 1972; Balthazar, Naor, & Sindberg, 1973; Balthazar & Stevens, 1969, 1975; Naor & Balthazar, 1973a, 1973b, 1974, 1975). We are speculating at this time that there may be a distinctive difference between measures of adaptive behavior as such and measures of general adjustment. In common parlance, adjustment seems to represent a homeostatic process in which the organism spontaneously mobilizes its resources in its interactions with the external environment in order to maintain some sort of equilibrium.

Adaptivity, in ordinary usage, is often described as a process of unification as in Webster's (1969) definition, "to fit, to make fit (as for a specific or new use or situation) often by modifying." In physiology, for example, adaptation occurs in reference to definite and discrete stimuli, as in ocular studies of light-dark adaptation. With more severely mentally retarded subjects, however, spontaneous adaptation may not occur, at least appropriately. Such implications may have an important bearing on measuring behavior of severely and profoundly mentally retarded individuals.

Adjustment, then, would seem to represent the current status of the individual in responding to a broad range of stimuli. The term, adaptive, on the other hand, more precisely represents the status of the individual in responding to particular stimuli. Adaptive behavior for the younger or more severely retarded individual, at least, represents systematic changes in distinctive kinds of behavior which are consistent with changes or modifications in discrete stimuli and which are brought about by orderly changes in the environment.

On the other hand, trait characteristics in the individual organism are often outcomes of learning experiences which have been previously established by adaptation. Adaptation, then, represents the learning efforts of the organism in the face of presenting discrete stimuli in a changing external environment and may best be measured on a pre- and posttest basis. Adjustment, however, is indicated in the individual's characteristic mode of spontaneously responding to changes in the environment.

Thus, new modes of adaptation are constantly feeding into adjustment mechanisms. The capability of the organism to maintain regularity in the face of changing conditions is an outgrowth of both its ability to adapt and to adjust using present and previous learning to meet the challenging demands of changing situations.

Our specific aim in designing the present study, then, was to determine a measure of social adjustment which is useful for descriptive purposes and for investigating behavior in specific populations. Even though there may be limitations in the sample presented, and perhaps in the measurements and procedures which have provided the dimensional judgments in this study, such measures, if effective and if sufficiently extended, would act to delineate and identify adjustment in a more severely mentally retarded group and eventually to provide norms for this type of population.

References

Balthazar, E. E. Treatment needs based upon differential diagnosis. *Mental Retardation*, 1966, 4(5), 16-19.

Balthazar, E. E. The assessment of adaptive behavior. In D. A. Primrose (Ed.), *Proceedings of the Second Congress of the International Association for the Scientific Study of Mental Deficiency*. Warsaw: Polish Medical Publishers (Swets & Zeitlinger N.V., The Netherlands, Distributors), 1971.

Balthazar, E. E. Residential programs in adaptive behavior for the emotionally disturbed more severely retarded. *Mental Retardation*, 1972, 10(3), 10-13.

Balthazar, E. E. *The Balthazar Scales of Adaptive Behavior, II: The Scales of Social Adaptation*. Palo Alto, CA.: Consulting Psychologists Press, 1973.

Balthazar, E. E., Naor, E. M., & Sindberg, R. M. *Absence of intervention training programs: Effects upon the severely and profoundly retarded. Part I: Selected cases of emotional and behavioral disturbance*. Madison: Central Wisconsin Colony and Training School Research Department, 1973. (ERIC Document Reproduction Service No. ED 87 150)

Balthazar, E. E., & Stevens, H. A. Scalar techniques for program evaluation with the severely mentally retarded. *Mental Retardation*, 1969, 7(2), 25-28.

Balthazar, E. E., & Stevens, H. A. *The emotionally disturbed mentally retarded: A historical and contemporary perspective*. Englewood Cliffs, NJ: Prentice-Hall, 1975.

Naor, E. M., & Balthazar, E. E. The program planning paradigm: Application to the area of functional independence. *Mental Retardation*, 1973, 11(1), 22-26. (a)

Naor, E. M., & Balthazar, E. E. *Absence of intervention training programs: Effects upon institutionalized retardates. Part II: Selected cases with minimal behavioral disturbance*. Madison: Central Wisconsin Colony and Training School Research Department, 1973. (ERIC Document Reproduction Service No. ED 87 151) (b)

Naor, E. M., & Balthazar, E. E. The effects of a self-help training program upon social coping behaviors. *The British Journal of Mental Subnormality*, 1974, 20(Part 2, No. 39), 69-77.

Naor, E. M., & Balthazar, E. E. Provision of a language index for severely and profoundly retarded individuals. *American Journal of Mental Deficiency*, 1975, 79, 717-725.

Webster's seventh new collegiate dictionary. Springfield, MA: G. & C. Merriam, 1969.

Feeding Assessment and Therapy for the Neurologically Impaired

Paula Schmidt
University of Washington

Abstract. This paper is concerned with a therapeutic approach to problems in feeding children with abnormal muscle tone and poor muscle coordination. Feeding therapy is intended to promote normal sensorimotor experience and maximum independence during feeding, as well as to assist in meeting the basic nutritional requirements of the neurologically impaired child. With regard to the goals of therapy, attention is given to means of assessment, intervention, and treatment. The Eating Assessment Tool is presented as an instrument for measuring progress in feeding behaviors.

The following discussion is focused primarily on children with neuromuscular incoordination and abnormal muscle tone. Much of the information could apply to adult rehabilitation and facilitation of normal feeding in mentally retarded individuals. "Feeding therapy" means more than satisfying the basic requirements of nutrition for growth and health. Feeding therapy means promoting normal sensorimotor experiences within the mouth and the entire body during feeding so that maximum independence can be achieved. Many benefits result from this therapy, including: (a) a more pleasurable mealtime experience for child and parent; (b) elimination of health hazards such as choking or inadequate food intake due to swallowing difficulties; (c) improvement in total body coordination by reducing effort involved and reinforcing physical therapy goals; (d) facilitation of speech through improved oral musculature coordination; and (e) a decrease in feeding behaviors unacceptable to the general public.

Therapy goals are not achieved overnight, especially when the abnormal patterns are well-established from years of reinforcement. However, some changes for the better should be observable very quickly if the treatment program is appropriate.

Background Information

The initial feeding assessment should be done by a physical, occupational, or speech therapist with specialized training in neuromuscular disorders. An assessment of the child's overall skills and limitations is usually done first to determine the influence of pathological or primitive reflexes. An understanding of how gravity, posture, effort, and emotions affect muscle tone is important during the assessment and treatment planning. A good resource on this subject is Finnie (1975).

All professionals and parents who provide care for neurologically impaired children should be familiar with some basic principles. Abnormal muscle tone is the primary cause of feeding problems. It interferes with muscle coordination and with tactile and proprioceptive sensation. Proper muscle coordination is dependent upon accurate proprioceptive and tactile information. We have good reason to aim for normal muscle tone during intervention, so that we can break up the abnormal cycle and start building a positive learning experience.

Abnormal muscle tone occurs in different ways, depending on the location and extent of damage to the central nervous system. The abnormal muscle tone may be expressed in the following ways:

1. Hypotonia (floppy, slow or absent righting, equilibrium, and protective responses, affects the entire body);

2. Hypertonia (stiff, may affect all or only part of the body, when behavior is dominated by lower CNS structures early in infant development the only symptoms may be delayed motor development and low muscle tone; as higher centers are activated, and the CNS disorganization becomes more apparent, increased muscle tone occurs); and

3. Fluctuating muscle tone (simplified classification of several types of cerebral palsy requiring a similar treatment approach, muscle tone fluctuates to various degrees of hypotonia and hypertonia).

Hypertonia occurs in patterns which are influenced by (a) the limb positions in relation to the body, and (b) the body position in relation to gravity. The most important way to inhibit high muscle tone is to avoid the abnormal patterns. The most common patterns in which high muscle tone occurs are as follows:

1. Extensor pattern (extended legs held close together, spine extended, arms pulled back at the shoulders, elbows stuck in flexion or extension, head pushed back; jaw thrust and tongue thrust may also be seen as part of this pattern). Gravity makes this pattern stronger when the child is on his back and less strong when he is upright or lying on his side. Often when this pattern is present, the flexor pattern is also present to some degree.

2. The flexor pattern (legs *may be* flexed, knees apart, spine flexed, arms flexed, hands fisted, head pulled forward; the bite reflex is part of this pattern but may not be present. Gravity makes this pattern stronger when the child is prone and has less influence when the child is upright or lying on his side. The flexor and extensor patterns are reciprocal so it is important not to try to induce one as an antidote for the other — neither one is functional.

3. The asymmetrical tonic neck reflex (face is turned to one side, limbs on that side tend to flex, limbs on the other side tend to extend, the back tends toward curvature, especially if the pattern is consistent towards one side).

A discussion of how to avoid these patterns will be included in the section on "intervention." Muscle tone also increases with effort and emotions (stress, excitement). Therefore it is important to be aware of environmental and emotional factors. Self-feeding might be limited to part of the meal if the effort causes an increase in muscle tone which interferes with muscle coordination.

2. DIAGNOSIS AND ASSESSMENT

Case Finding

The first step is to recognize a problem. When a child has a long history of abnormal feeding patterns, parents may not be concerned about changing them or they may not realize that any change is possible. Patterns which indicate that a feeding assessment is required are:

1. Choking and coughing more than once or twice during each meal.
2. Inability to keep most food and liquid inside the mouth and swallow it.
3. Tendency to bite down hard on the spoon.
4. Intolerance of solid foods beyond the developmental age of 6 to 9 months (inability to chew, choking, tactile sensitivity).
5. Abnormal sitting posture (i.e., head tilted back or to the side, body tilted laterally, etc.).
6. High muscle tone.
7. Great effort expended by parent or child resulting in unpleasant mealtimes.
8. Persistent tongue thrust beyond the age of 6 months (in and out movement of the tongue); usually goes along with inability to chew, choking, and other findings.

Many children will have several of the above mentioned problems or possibly others interfering with food intake. The next step is assessment.

The Assessment

The best place for the first assessment to take place is in the child's home, with one of his parents feeding him small portions of a typical meal. In addition, small portions of food which offer a variety of texture, consistency, and temperature can be offered.

The Eating Assessment Tool (E.A.T.) was developed by this author very recently for the purpose of providing a measurement of progress. I attempted to make it simple, yet comprehensive; I have not used it enough to know how much time it will take to score. After the initial assessment has been done in full, and the focus of treatment selected, it might be most useful to use only part of the test to periodically measure progress in a specific area of concern. The instructions and explanations are important for proper use of the tool.

The following comments follow the outline of the Eating Assessment Tool (Appendix A).

I. It is important to observe the child's posture first. Ask if there is more than one way the child is positioned for eating and which way is most typical. If he is not sitting upright, estimate the angle between horizontal and vertical. If the child does not look symmetrical with the head upright, describe. What kind of physical support is provided (under "adaptations")? Comment also in this section on the child's overall muscle tone.

II. When evaluating oral skills, be aware of which body positions trigger pathological patterns. Also notice differences in how foods of various textures are handled together with the relative difficulty of various types of food. It may be difficult to translate your observations of abnormal feeding behavior into the positive scoring method of this test. You may want to write down your observations of abnormal patterns in detail, perhaps including counts of certain behaviors (i.e., choking or bite reflex or jaw thrust) so that you can compare later test observations in these respects. However, it is still advisable to score the test as written so that you can determine its value as a measure of progress. Ask parents about the child's daily dental hygiene and whether they have located a dentist for their child. Note condition of child's teeth and gums. Dilantin, a common seizure medication, causes swollen gums; good oral hygiene becomes even more important to prevent gum tissue and tooth enamel damage. If the child is taking Dilantin medication, the family should be aware of the need for an increased intake of Vitamin D, the dosage levels to be determined by a physician (Pipes, in press).

III. Assessment of eye-hand coordination as well as total postural control will help determine the practicality of teaching self-feeding or on what level this might begin. If the child can bring the hand to the mouth and maintain grasp on an object once it is put in his hand, he can begin to experience "self-feeding" with long narrow pieces of food such as toast, baby cookies, chicken leg bone (the meat removed gives flavor and teething experience primarily).

Some of the items are subjective and not well-defined; therefore, comments would be especially appropriate. Item number 40 means that most of the food ends up inside the child rather than spread on the table, floor, and clothes. Sticky hands and face are considered acceptable and within my definition of "neat."

IV. Assessment of the feeding behavior and environment will require asking questions of the parents. In addition, however, make your own observations of the emotional tone and interaction pattern between parents and child. Is it stressful? Is mealtime a pleasurable experience for parents and child? Is there any verbal or non-verbal communication and what is the tone? This will require your assuming a non-intrusive role. Ask if the observed behavior is typical or if any differences were perceived.

V. Does the parent perceive problems or desire changes? If not, who does and why? Feeding skills may vary in different situations depending on the excitement level of the environment, the skills of the feeding assistant, hunger, and the anxiety or emotional level of the child.

If the parent does not see the need for change and you do, discuss your concerns and ask permission to start a therapy program without asking for any commitment from the parents until you can convince them that the effort will be worthwhile (this is assuming that you will have daily contact with the child through school). You may want to ask for partial participation, that is, trying your ideas for part of each meal in order to obtain feedback about how successful or non-successful these methods are. When things are not going well at home, another evaluation may be necessary in order to see that instructions are clearly understood and properly used without frustration or discomfort.

The Treatment Plan

Once the assessment is done, how do we determine treatment priorities? The highest priority, it seems to me, should be maintenance of health. This includes reducing incidences of choking and improving quality and quantity of nutritional intake if necessary (see "Foods and Nutrition" section).

The second priority is to improve oral-motor patterns and the third is to promote self-feeding skills. At times the second and third priorities have to be weighed in terms of age; that is, self-feeding may be more important to an older child than chewing without tongue thrust. In these cases one might plan a specific time (all or part of one meal) to work on improving oral-motor patterns and then let the individual self-feed. Adaptations may be helpful in improving self-help skills (to be discussed later).

Keep in mind the normal sequence of motor and oral development so that you work on the more basic skills first. The normal developmental sequence of oral control is: (a) coordination of swallowing and breathing, up and down jaw movements with sucking (tongue moves with jaw), lip closure around nipple during sucking (birth to 2 months); (b) forward and back movement of tongue while sucking (similar to the exaggerated abnormal pattern often seen in older retarded and C.P. persons), the child rejects textures (pushes out of mouth), shows beginning head control, some hands in mouth (2 to 4 months); (c) the child has good head control, opens mouth in anticipation, moves head and mouth towards food, accepts strained, soft foods off spoon without much lip closure, frequently brings fingers and toys to mouth, biting and using tongue to explore (important practice for tongue lateralization to move food in mouth and important for normal sensation) (4 to 6 months); (d) about the time a child learns to sit independently he begins to feed himself finger food (6 to 10 months; starting with total hand grasp of object such as baby toast or cookie); at first the finger food is mouthed and chewed on (usually before the child has teeth) but does not provide much of the child's nutritional intake. As hand coordination improves, a wider variety of foods can be picked up and put in the mouth. Tongue and lip control are also improving with maturation so that lumps can be introduced with only occasional choking occurring (often associated with too much food in the mouth or a mixture of liquid and solid textures). See Appendix B for an example for transition from first foods to table foods.

The normal developmental sequence cannot always be followed with a handicapped child. Head and trunk control are not necessary prerequisites to chewing or self-feeding, but appropriate adaptations must be provided to compensate for lack of those skills. Nor is the ability to lateralize the tongue a prerequisite for the transition to solid foods; just the experience of having solids stimulating his gums (with an adult holding the tongue in place at the back and side of the mouth) will stimulate lateral tongue movement. If a child is unable to get his hands or toys to his mouth to explore, this type of experience (with assistance) should be a part of his pre-feeding program to normalize sensation and stimulate a variety of tongue movements. Recognizing the normal sequence may also be a way to discover a specific gap in a child's development, such as persisting immature tongue movements.

Intervention

Choking, a fairly common problem with severely impaired children, has different causes. The first thing to check is the child's head position in relation to gravity. If food falls to the back of the mouth due to gravity, it is hard to coordinate the breathing-swallowing timing and to control the amount of food ingested with each swallow. (Try eating or drinking while lying on your back.) Secondly, look at the child's head alignment with the body — if the head is tilted back, the airway is open and food can easily go down the wrong tube (try tilting your head back and swallowing; also remember that mouth to mouth resuscitation is done with the head tilted back in order to keep the airway passage to the lungs open). Certain foods cause more choking than others, such as thin liquids versus thick and foods that require a lot of chewing and don't dissolve in saliva such as raw vegetables, peanuts, and meat (see "Foods and Nutrition" section).

When choking does occur, be sure to get the child's head *down before* hitting his back between the shoulder blades so that gravity pulls the food out of the air passage rather than lodging in it more securely. Another method is to hold the individual in front of you, his back against your front, your hands clasped over his diaphragm and pull in suddenly, forcing reserve air out of the lungs to help dislodge the food (assuming that it's too far down to reach or shake out).

Positioning is one of the most important parts of the intervention program. The upright sitting posture is usually best, but may be modified to a slight backward tilt of the chair with head support, if head control is poor. Cut-out foam cushions may be needed to provide trunk or head support. Adaptations to keep a child from sliding out of his chair due to involuntary hip extension include: knee separator, foam wedge under knees, slight (30^0-45^0) backward tilt of the chair, peroneal straps around each leg, a seat-belt, a rolled up towel under the knees (tied to prevent slipping). The feet should be supported. If the child tends to pull his head and arms back (extension pattern) cushions behind the upper arms to keep the arms forward and a cushion behind the head should help. Also applying some pressure to the child's chest while bringing the arms forward helps reduce the influence of the extension pattern. Sometimes a wide belt around the child's upper arms and across the chest is useful in keeping the arms forward.

There are many different ways to hold a baby or very young child during feeding. The child might sit side-ways on the adult's lap; if the adult's legs are held slightly apart the child has less tendency to slip off, because his hips are more flexed. The arms and head can be controlled with one adult arm and the food presented at midline with the other hand. The problem with this method is the tendency to let the child's head slip back too far in relation to the body and to gravity but that can be easily corrected when one is aware of it. Resting the adult's arm on a table often helps. Other feeding positions are discussed in Finnie (1975).

The child should look symmetrical and aligned for optimal functioning and normal muscle tone. If he does not, try to analyze how to change the position.

When the child is floppy, postural muscle tone in the trunk and head can be improved by intermittently giving pressure down

2. DIAGNOSIS AND ASSESSMENT

through the spine via the child's head and shoulders (be sure he is aligned properly).

If the child cannot open and close the jaw voluntarily, or if the jaw opens too widely and sets off other abnormal patterns, jaw control by the adult assistant may be necessary. This is usually done with the index finger and middle finger at the chin if done from the side or back; if the assistant is facing the child, the control is provided with the thumb and bent index finger at the tip of the chin. The only disadvantage with the front approach is the tendency to push the child's head back, out of alignment. See the illustration in Finnie (1975). Often simply correcting abnormal posture can help with jaw control (the tendency to open the jaw too wide with extensor pattern and bite down hard with flexor pattern).

Exaggerated primitive tongue movements (in and out) can be inhibited with jaw control and by placing food to the *side* of the mouth. At first choose foods you can hang on to while the child chews. Placing food to the side of the mouth also works well with small portions of beginning solid foods such as cheese, crackers, cookies, and vienna sausage. Before feeding or intermittently during feeding, stimulate the side of the tongue by pushing firmly or stroking with a tongue blade (expect movement toward the stimulus). A variety of tongue movements is also stimulated when ice chips are placed in the mouth.

Some older children who have exaggerated tongue and jaw movements when drinking liquid from a cup do better with straw drinking and external jaw control. Straw drinking can be taught by using a flexible tube fitted tightly into a flexible plastic bottle so that pressure on the bottle puts fluid in the tube and assures early success. Be aware of the possibility of increased abnormal tongue thrusting; discontinue use of the straw if the oral patterns deteriorate.

If the child has trouble swallowing food once it is in the mouth, try moving the jaw open and closed and waiting for a response, repeating as necessary. If this technique is not successful, some people feel that stroking under the chin (base of tongue) helps. Generally the stimulus for swallowing is pressure on the tongue from food, so pressing down on the tongue with the spoon just before pulling it out will stimulate swallowing (a technique also used to decrease tongue thrusting). Some people suggest that blowing on the face will promote swallowing.

Lip closure can be stimulated in several ways. Tapping around the outside of the lips is one method of "quick stretch" to the muscle. Rubbing ice around the outside of the lips and on the lips as long as tolerated (about 20 seconds; avoid discomfort, watch for clues) before a meal will also stimulate lip closure. Battery operated vibrators are also used. Some people have suggested using lemons or pickles to promote the pucker.

Chewing can be facilitated by helping the up and down jaw movement get started, but never try to facilitate the rotary component of chewing. It's much too subtle and will develop spontaneously when tongue lateralization during chewing is developed. The stimulus of pressure of food on the teeth is the key to the chewing response. Jaw closure can also be stimulated by tapping on the chin.

The rejection of solid foods by the child may be based on primitive protective responses. Very often tactile and proprioceptive sensation is impaired (remember how difficult it is to chew after novocaine?) but can be remedied through graded application of stimulation to the inside of the mouth. Rubbing your finger firmly on the child's gums twice from midline to the back of both sides, top and bottom, allowing time to swallow between each stimulus is a helpful pre-feeding exercise.

An example of gradual transition from mushy foods to solids is seen in Appendix B. It is usually best to introduce new foods and textures in small quantities at the beginning of a meal before offering the easily accepted foods, gradually increasing the amount and variety of new foods. This is *not* going to work with all children. Some children seem to do better with total elimination of "baby" foods when soft solids are first introduced. If a child seems to have a hyperactive gag reflex (stimulation on the front part of the tongue produces a gag response which is supposed to occur only with stimulation way back on the tongue) start reducing the sensitivity by touching firmly with a tongue depressor on the lips, then tip of tongue, slowly working back further on the tongue as it is tolerated, over a period of time. Flexing the head forward as the child starts to gag will usually stop the response. Behavior modification is also often necessary because the gag response usually has elicited a lot of attention from others in the past.

Drooling can be a result of lack of lip closure or jaw closure, poor sucking, low tactile sensation, or mouth breathing. Finnie (1975) suggests that firm pressure between the nose and upper lip be applied periodically throughout the day in order to stimulate mouth closure. Sucking on popsicles or ice chips will improve sensation and the use of tongue and lips. Tapping on the chin or cheeks will facilitate jaw closure. Frequent use of straws may also help. You might also have the child practice breathing through the nose for short periods of time and increase the length of time. Behavior modification procedures are also very helpful in promoting change. Learning to hum songs may be helpful for the child.

If the child tends to push his head back, it is helpful to approach him slowly with the spoon or food and stop short of his mouth, encouraging head movement forward to get the food off the spoon. Try not to lift the handle of the spoon up when pulling it out — rather pull it straight out. Drinking from a cup with a space cut out of the rim at the top as described in Finnie (1975) or drinking with a straw will eliminate the necessity of tilting the head back. A straw that fits inside a baby bottle nipple can be used for babies so that they can sit with head slightly forward holding the bottle down instead of propped up.

Self-feeding can be initiated as soon as the child can handle food in the mouth with normal muscle tone. Interest in food is an important motivational factor. The adult can assist the child by holding his hand or elbow as necessary, withdrawing assistance as the child is able to take over. This can occur for part or all of the meal. If the child has difficulty with voluntary grasp and release, a bread stick or other long, thin food can be placed into his hand. Children often are able to bring a spoon with food to the mouth before they are able to load food onto the spoon so the adult can assist with that. A variety of adaptations can be made or purchased including spoon handles, rimmed plates, non-slip placemats, and a wide variety of cups. The bowl of the spoon should fit into the child's mouth easily. Curved handles are helpful to some children and are designed to be used with only the left or the right hand, depending on the direction of the curve. A simple sandwich holder using a rubber band for tension can make it possible for a child to take several bites before the sandwich needs to be relocated if his own grasp might squeeze the sandwich too hard.

Parent participation is very important; they should be encouraged to share their ideas and observations in a problem-solving team approach. The basic principles affecting muscle tone should be taught at the beginning, so that parents can readily assess which positions and approaches work best for their child. Many of my ideas come from parents who have tried a variety of approaches to see what works best. It is a good idea for everyone involved in feeding the child to use basically the same approach and expectations. Periodically these people should be questioned about how they feel things are going; difficulties can then be corrected early. A solution may be as easy as finding a more comfortable position for the adult, or adding support for the child's posture.

Foods and Nutrition

The parents should list foods that the child likes, dislikes, or has difficulty with. Start therapy with foods the child likes, then introduce new foods, perhaps alternating them. In general, the following guidelines are offered:

Liquids are easier to handle when thickened (buttermilk, thinned yogurt, thinned apple sauce or pudding, milkshakes, gelatin or instant pudding added to liquids for thickening purposes).

Multi-textures such as vegetable soup, apples, watermelon, and grapes that involve handling thin liquid and a solid are most difficult. Also foods that don't dissolve such as raw vegetables, peanuts, popcorn, and meat are most difficult.

Taste, temperature (warm or cold vs. room temperature), and texture stimulate chewing and swallowing. Foods with a crunchy quality that dissolve fairly easily, such as crackers, cookies, breadsticks, dry cereal, and toast strips, give good sensory stimulation and are safe. Other beginning finger foods include: fruit leather, beef jerky, meat cut with the grain in strips, licorice sticks, cheese sticks, and popsicles. Many children enjoy holding a chicken, turkey, or beef bone and gnawing at it.

Many neurologically handicapped children start slowing down in growth rate by 2 years of age (Pipes, in press). This usually has nothing to do with their adequacy of nutrient intake, but rather seems to be related to the neurological damage. If the child's height and weight correspond roughly on the growth grid charts, then there is usually no reason to worry.

There are many questions that arise that only a nutritionist can answer. The areas of concern include: (a) marked discrepancy in height and weight (fat or skinny); (b) limited variety of food intake; (c) unusual family diet; (d) need for supplemental vitamin D when taking Dilantin seizure medication; and (e) restricted diet due to allergies. Other guidelines are listed in Erickson (1976; Chapter 9).

Summary

Feeding therapy promotes normal sensorimotor experience within the mouth and the entire body during feeding so that maximum independence can be eventually achieved. An understanding of how gravity, posture, effort, and emotions affect muscle tone is important during the assessment and treatment planning. Positioning is one of the most important parts of the intervention program, due to the effect this has on muscle tone. The attitude of the child's assistant must be relaxed and friendly and calm to avoid hypertonus related to emotions. The feeding environment should also be assessed in relation to the child's needs. Attention should be directed toward developing normal oral-motor patterns before encouraging self-feeding. The effort of self-feeding often increases muscle tone initially, making oral control less coordinated. More success is likely when the individual has had experience with normal oral-motor sensation.

Feeding therapy is intended to complement and provide carry-over from regularly scheduled physical therapy and occupational therapy. A treatment plan should be based on input from every person who feeds the child, especially parents, and then carried out fairly consistently, with attention to changes in the child's skills which will indicate need for program change. A positive approach is advocated in which the child is praised for his accomplishments (often enough to make him feel good and to recognize his efforts, not so much that it loses its meaning). Breaking tasks down into small steps makes it possible to measure changes more readily in severely handicapped children. The Eating Assessment Tool is designed to measure change while looking for normal developmental skills. Abnormal patterns can be described in the comments section, but are not considered in the score.

Feedback on the E.A.T. and this article would be sincerely appreciated.

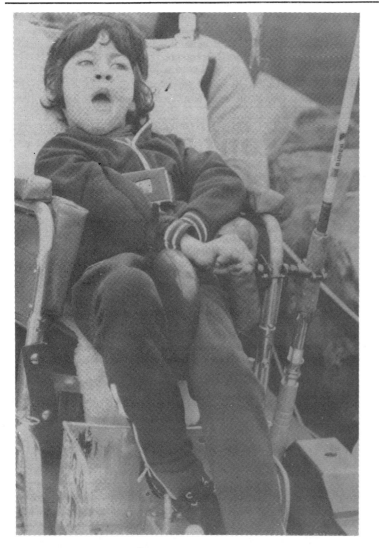

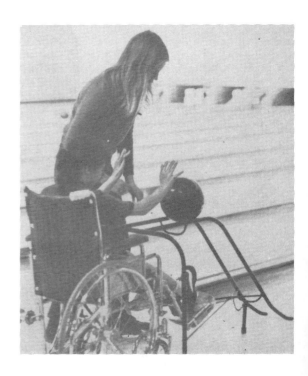

Instruction and Model Programs

Severely and profoundly handicapped students differ greatly from "normal" and "mildly handicapped" students on a number of relevant instructional dimensions (e.g., generalization, retention, imitation, language acquisition, visual skills). Their educational needs are likewise very different. Traditional approaches to training will, in all probability, be of little value or no value. Teachers of the severely and profoundly handicapped will need to delineate and task analyze skills that teachers of less handicapped students assume are operative. We are only now beginning to recognize some of the instructional components necessary for this undertaking.

The task that lies ahead will require the coordination and effort of many professionals. The myriad needs of the severely and profoundly handicapped, with its seemingly never ending parameters, is obviously beyond the expertise of any one profession. Besides special education personnel, speech and language clinicians, psychologists, physical and occupational therapists, behavior modification specialists, researchers and others can contribute to the development of effective programs for the population at hand. The need for an exchange of ideas and information among many disciplines is also paramount.

There is much that we must do. We are only scratching the surface with respect to knowledge and techniques to arrange for successful intervention. Our current curricula efforts for the severely and profoundly handicapped are discontinuous and fragmented. However, we can look forward to success in this endeavor because we now have the technology and professional expertise to effect meaningful levels of behavioral change even in the most handicapped child. A measure of our effectiveness as professionals will be in the ability to provide programs couched in accountability.

The following articles will examine a wide range of instructional strategies for severely and profoundly handicapped children. A public school education for the severely and profoundly handicapped assumes a teaching-learning process will occur. There is an urgent need to identify and disseminate instructional programs and strategies. While a comprehensive curriculum is obviously beyond the scope of this section, the articles were chosen to provide a general frame of reference necessary to understand the complexities of that task.

An alternative pattern of educational/residential care and services for mentally retarded children

Mary Ann Gage
H. D. Fredericks
Victor L. Baldwin
William G. Moore
David Grove

The process of deinstitutionalization requires the development and evaluation of alternative residential facilities within a community. This paper describes two experimental group homes serving moderately and severely handicapped children. The characteristics of the homes, ages and types of children served, and the two staffing patterns used are described. The results of this 2-year study are reported in (1) effects of staffing patterns, (2) results with children, and (3) costs.

This is a report of a study on alternative residences for handicapped children conducted by the staff of the Teaching Research Infant and Child Center, Monmouth, Oregon. The study was partially funded by grants from the Bureau of Education for the Handicapped, #GOO 74-00 475, #OEC 300-74-7994 in conjunction with HCEEP and the severely handicapped model centers.

The alternative residences, two group homes, were developed and operated by Teaching Research staff members to facilitate deinstitutionalization for handicapped children. Both homes function primarily as "halfway houses" in that the ultimate goal for all children placed there is to equip them with the necessary skills and social behaviors to let them be successfully returned to their natural homes or to foster placement within a local community.

DEINSTITUTIONALIZATION

Deinstitutionalization encompasses three interrelated processes: (a) prevention of admission by finding and developing alternative community methods of care and training, (b) return to the community of all residents who have been prepared through programs of habilitation and training to function adequately in appropriate local settings, and (c) establishment and maintenance of a responsive residential environment which protects human and civil rights and which contributes to the expeditious return of the individual to normal community living, whenever possible. (National Association of Superintendents, 1974, pp. 4–5)

Since 1970 advocacy for making this concept of deinstitutionalization a reality, particularly for developmentally disabled and emotionally disturbed children, has been increasing. This advocacy has both humanitarian and practical foundations. First, proponents of human rights have used legislative and legal action to involve federal, state, and local governments in providing to handicapped children the same access to education, humane living conditions, and civil rights that has been previously available only to the nonhandicapped.

Second, many institutions were providing little more than custodial care for the handicapped. Dennis and Sayegh (1956) report the debilitating effects of institutionalization on early development. Turnbull and Turnbull (1975), Vail (1967), Blatt and Kaplan (1967), and White and Wolfensberger (1969) all describe the dehumanizing conditions found in many institutions. As Rowland and Patterson (1972) state,

> Often there has been, on the whole, too little expectation that the individuals committed to the institution's care would return to participate in any meaningful way to the mainstream of society. Low expectations and lack of respect for the dignity of the retarded person have resulted in a continually decreasing repertory of opportunity. (p. 36)

Additional claims were advanced, and to some extent supported by evidence, that long-term residents of large institutions often developed a repertory of "institutional behaviors" that diminished the probability that they would successfully fit into the community. McCormick, Bella, and Zigler (1975) discuss work reviewed by Zigler (1972) which indicates that the behavior of institutionalized persons is influenced by the institutionalization which they experience rather than by their mental retardation per se.

Third, and most important, in the past decade there has been a tremendous growth in knowledge regarding the education of handicapped children. Furthermore, much instruction can now be conducted not only in classrooms but also in homes by parents and others who can be appropriately trained in a relatively short time. This advance in education makes it feasible to explore a variety of types of educational and residential programs for the handicapped that had not seemed possible earlier.

There are dangers in indiscriminantly advocating deinstitutionalization. Not every residential/educational alternative is going to prove equally practical for every handicapped child of any age. In fact, some alternatives may prove no more humane or valid than the institutions they were meant to replace.

According to the National Association of Superintendents of Public Residential Facilities for the Mentally Retarded (1974),

> While the Association advocates without reservation the rights of the retarded to live in the least restrictive environment and to enjoy fully the benefits of a free and open society whenever possible, it does express concern over the manner in which this goal is being realized. First, the quality of community programs and services being offered to the mentally retarded and other developmentally disabled persons in many parts of the country is inadequate. All too often, "community back wards" and "closeting" are being substituted for institutional "warehousing." Neither community nor residential back wards or "closeting" are justified: the rights of the retarded must be respected wherever they reside. In essence, the Association calls attention to the need not only for continued upgrading of residential facilities . . . but also for a greater interest in quality control for developing community programs. (pp. 2–3)

Therefore, an experimental approach to examining possible alternatives seems warranted. This paper describes the examination of one alternative type of residence for handicapped children, that of group homes.

Literature regarding group homes for handicapped children is sparce. Jewett (1973) reports on a home for emotionally disturbed children. O'Connor and Sitkie (1975) conducted a study of 3,582 community facilities for developmentally disabled persons; however, the majority of the population served in these facilities were adults.

PURPOSE OF THIS STUDY

This study has been guided by three major objectives:
1. To document the procedures required to establish and maintain two group home models for children.

3. INSTRUCTION

   2. To examine in depth features of both models, including the two staffing patterns employed, the ages of the children served, and ways in which each model may effect:
      a. Staff personnel,
      b. Consistency of programming,
      c. Progress of children in training programs,
      d. Placement of children in natural or foster homes,
      e. Costs.
   3. To study the feasibility of using the group home facilities and personnel as resources for training both natural and foster parents and others who work or potentially could work with handicapped children either in their home or in a group home.

The parent training is felt to be crucial if these children are to continue to grow and develop satisfactorily in that environment. Browder, Ellis, and Neal (1974) report the need to provide appropriate training for foster parents of handicapped children. Studies conducted with natural parents with handicapped children support the efficacy of parent training in behavioral strategies (Grim, 1974; Longin, Cone, & Longin, 1975; Tymchuk, 1975; Wolf, Risley, Johnston, Harris, & Allen, 1964).

CHARACTERISTICS OF THE HOMES

Both homes were located in the same small community. The two group homes varied primarily in two ways: (a) the ages of children in residence and (b) the patterns by which they were staffed.

Each group home had places for four children, the maximum number who could be accommodated without having excessive life and safety restrictions imposed. In addition, homes serving only four children are not required to comply to special zoning restrictions. It was also felt that this is the optimum number who can be adequately served in the homes with the established staffing patterns.

Residents were transferred to the group home from state institutions or private institutional facilities, or they were admitted from families who were no longer able to maintain them at home. Initially, incoming children were placed in the homes at 3-week intervals. This enabled the staff to evaluate each child in various skill areas and to implement appropriate training programs. This also allowed for a period of adjustment for each child before any additional children entered the home.

Both homes had children with physical, mental, and emotional handicaps, or combinations of these handicaps in varying degrees of severity. Autistic children and those with severe behavior problems were also eligible for placement.

Children served in one home, which was staffed with group home "parents," ranged in age from 5 to 8 years. Children ages 8 through 16 were placed in a home staffed with managers.

Children were not separated by handicapping condition in any residential or educational facility operated by Teaching Research. This heterogeneity does require competent staff members who can cope with almost any training problem or type of impairment. It was important to examine the feasibility of operating group homes whose resident children were representative of a variety of handicapping conditions for several reasons:

   1. Small and rural communities may have only three or four children requiring this type of residential care. However, the probability is high that these children would represent more than one category of handicapping conditions.
   2. Mixing all children provides for flexibility in programming and use of facilities and equipment.
   3. Teaching Research staff members have conducted educational training programs with all types of handicapped children for several years. The performance data from these children indicate that children with a variety of handicaps can be served effectively in the same facility.

When placed in a heterogeneous group, handicapped children learn from one another, play with each other, and socialize together in ways which would not be possible if all children exhibited the same handicaps.

CHILDREN'S TRAINING PROGRAMS

Approximately two to four prescriptive programs were conducted daily with each child in the home environment. This training was conducted by the group home staff and was characterized by:

1. Conducting evaluations concurrently at home and school of each child's performance in basic skill areas: self-help, motor skills, receptive and expressive language, and social behaviors;
2. Identifying specific behavior problems;
3. Establishing baseline data on skill performance and on behavior problems;
4. Prioritizing programs to be conducted with each child;
5. Monitoring performance and record data.

Less formal programs, similar to the kinds of activities likely to occur in most homes, were also conducted. For example, children were expected to learn to do chores, share with other children, and assist with meals. Play activities were designed to involve handicapped children in the same forms of recreation engaged in by nonhandicapped children of approximately the same age.

COORDINATION BETWEEN HOME AND SCHOOL

The handicapped children attended classrooms where each child's programs were individualized, training objectives clearly stipulated, each child's performance carefully monitored, and records of that performance maintained. The children worked on four to six programs in the classroom each day. With the exception of behavior problems, most of the programs conducted with these children were taken from *The Teaching Research Curriculum for Moderately and Severely Handicapped* (Fredericks et al., 1976)

Programs thought to be of highest priority for a child, usually in self-help and language skills, were conducted concurrently in both the home and classroom. After consulting with the group home parent or manager, the classroom instructor was able to send a program home with the child and feel assured that the program would be conducted in the group home, that data on the child's performance would be recorded, and that records on all programs for that child would be returned to the classroom on the next day the child returned to school. This system is known as the *Lunch Box Data System* (Fredericks et al., 1975, pp. 160–163).

The instructional procedures used in the classrooms were almost identical to those used in the homes, and there was extensive and intensive coordination between group home and classroom personnel. The activities of these children in both the group home and classroom were closely monitored by the group home coordinator.

RESULTS

The results of this study are reported in three areas:
1. Documentation of procedures;
2. Effects of staffing patterns upon personnel, programming, progress on training programs, movements of children, and costs;
3. Training conducted in the home with parents and others.

Documentation of Procedures

All processes, procedures, and outcomes in the development of these homes for handicapped children were documented in the form of a book which is now available, *Group Homes for Developmentally Disabled Children,* Gage et al., 1977.

Effects of Staffing Patterns

Two staffing patterns were employed, one with group home parents who resided in the home fulltime and the other with managers who worked in shifts. Before assuming their responsibilities in the group homes, all staff members participated in 2 weeks of extensive training conducted in one of the teaching research classrooms for handicapped children. The group home personnel were instructed in child management and skill acquisition techniques which are consistent with those methods implemented with the children attending the teaching research model

3. INSTRUCTION

classrooms.

Staff Personnel

The couple employed as group home parents reported two major problems: (1) feelings of being burnt out and (2) difficulty in maintaining trained relief staff. The physical and emotional fatigue labeled *burn out* increased in relation to the number of children in the home who lacked basic self-help skills or whose handicaps could only be managed with a great deal of physical assistance from the staff. In order to assure that relief would be available for the group home parents, it was necessary to have three or four trained staff members on call. It was particularly difficult to obtain relief when a child was ill and during extended school or staff vacation periods.

The house parents were able to create an atmosphere more closely resembling a "normal" family environment than the manager model. However, the staff employed as managers did not report the burn-out problems which affected the house parents. They also did not have difficulties in finding relief staff, as they were generally able to relieve each other during times of illness or vacation.

Consistency of Programming

The parent model did have an inherent consistency of treating children. The parents were totally responsible for conducting training programs with the children and the only staff coordination required was with the substitute house parents. Problems associated with coordination were greater in the manager model in that all program had to be closely coordinated between three sets of managers to assure continuity and consistency. This was accomplished by a great deal of conference, discussion, and daily review of data.

Progress of Children in Training Programs

There were no discernable differences in the effectiveness of the two staffing patterns in dealing with the children. The progress demonstrated by the children on individual skill acquisition programs and the remediation of inappropriate behaviors did not indicate any difference. The brevity of this report does not allow us to document the performance of each child while in the home or upon his or her return to the natural home or a foster home. However, a summary of the results with two children, one served in each home, will show the kinds of progress achieved with children who have participated or are now participating in this program.

A 6½-year old mentally retarded boy was placed in the parent model from The Oregon State Hospital and Training Center. Upon entering the program he was unable to dress himself without adult assistance, had no expressive language other than one randomly used syllable, engaged in 6 to 14 prolonged temper tantrums each day, complied with less than 20% of all given commands or directions, and had no appropriate play skills.

In less than 10 months he had acquired sufficient skills to enable him to return to his natural home. He is currently attending a public school special education program. Shortly before he left the program, his command compliance had stabilized at 80% or higher. Temper tantrums were virtually eliminated. He was able to dress himself, play appropriately with toys, and his vocabulary consisted of over 200 words.

An 11-year-old mentally retarded boy was placed in the manager model home from his natural home, where he had attended a public school program for trainable mentally retarded children. Both the classroom teacher and parents stated they were unable to control the child's disruptive behaviors, which included fighting with peers, low compliance with commands, speaking in a loud voice, destroying materials, and being unable to attend to tasks for more than a few seconds.

While in this program, he learned to handle materials appropriately; he no longer fought with peers; he attended to tasks; he complied with 90% of given commands; and he learned to speak in a quiet, pleasant manner. Due to the rapid progress which this child demonstrated in areas of social accommodation to others in both home and school environments, he was able to return to his parents' home after 5 months.

Placement of Children in Natural or Foster Homes

All of the children initially residing in the parent model homes were returned to their natural home or placed in a foster home within less than 1 year of the time they entered the group home. One of the children who resided in the manager model home returned to his natural family after 5 months. A second child is scheduled to return to his family within the next 3 months. The remaining two children, who were more severely impaired, will require group home services for a longer period. However, these children are progressing well, both at school and in the group home.

Child progress data were collected by staff members who conducted follow-up visits to the home and school environments of children who have left the group home. These data indicate that these children are maintaining in both environments the skills they acquired while in the group home.

Costs of the Two Models

The start-up costs for each home, including personnel, furniture and supplies, initial utilities and rent, and home modifications were $6,528.59 for the parent model and $5,056.53 for the manager model. (These costs were incurred in fall and spring of 1974–75). The average monthly costs for maintaining a child in each model is based on the total amount of money spent for the operation of the parent model and the manager model for 1 year. The figures are broken into specific categories and are shown in Table 1.

We have compared the cost for maintaining a child in the largest state hospital and training center in Oregon to the costs for maintaining a child in each group home model. There are, however, two expenses in the institution costs which have not

Table 1 *Average monthly cost*

	Parent Model	Manager Model
Personnel	$1,745	$2,100
Rent and utilities	495	466
Clothing	80	100
*Weekend allowance (Housing parents)	100	—
Food	360	400
Training supplies	50	50
Household supplies	50	50
Recreation	15	50
Transportation	65	150
Total per month budget	$2,960	$3,346
Cost per month/per child	740	836.50

The agency paid for a rest location for the house parents one weekend a month, which allowed them to live in a motel that weekend.

been included in the group home budget: (1) medical expenses and (2) education costs. These costs have been added to the monthly group home figures below. Medical expenses in both homes were comparable, $35.26 and $35.23 monthly. Education costs for all children served in the Teaching Research Infant and Child Center are $127.08.

State Institution for Developmentally Disabled	$918.00 per child/per month
Manager model	902.34 per child/per month
Parent model	998.81 per child/per month

Training Conducted with Parents and Others

The group home facilities and personnel were used for training natural and foster parents of handicapped children. Before a child left the program, both parents were urged to participate in a 5-day training program conducted in the group home. Ten objectives for training were delineated which focus upon child management and methods of teaching and maintaining new behaviors with the child in a home environment. To date, seven natural or foster parents of children residing in the group homes have been trained. Two parents of handicapped children who reside in nearby communities have also been trained. Training is now being implemented with others interested in establishing and maintaining group homes.

3. INSTRUCTION

COMMENTS, POSSIBLE IMPLICATIONS, AND RECOMMENDATIONS

Both models of the group home produced gains in children's skills far beyond those originally anticipated. However, these gains came about not only as a result of the programs conducted in the home, but also because of the close coordination of these programs with school programs. It is therefore axiomatic that a group home for handicapped children must be geographically located close to educational facilities that provide appropriate training programs. Both environments, school and home, must have coordinated individual programs with clearly established objectives. A child's performance in the programs must be systematically monitored with data maintained.

There were advantages and disadvantages to each of the staffing models, and these must be carefully weighed before a group home is established in a community.

The manager model is more expensive to operate; however, these costs may be justified in terms of staff turnover. One implication is that the parent model may not be the model best suited for young children, particularly if the children have no self-help skills or require constant physical assistance. Parent training is critical if the child is to maintain the skills gained in the group home and continue to grow and develop satisfactorily in other areas. The costs for maintaining a child in the manager model home exceed the costs for maintaining a child in the state institution. Any comparative costs, however, must be viewed not only in terms of immediate costs, but also in terms of projected long-term costs, which should be greatly reduced as the handicapped persons gain a degree of independent or semidependent living and work skills.

The results achieved with the children served in these homes, together with movement of these children into natural and foster homes, dictate a serious consideration of the establishment of group homes as an alternative to large institutions.

REFERENCES

Blatt, B., & Kaplan J. *Christmas in purgatory: A photographic essay on mental retardation.* Boston: Allyn and Bacon, 1967.

Browder, A. J., Ellis, L., & Neal, J. Foster homes: Alternative to institutions? *Mental Retardation,* December 1974, *12* (6), 33–36.

Dennis, W., & Sayegh. The effect of supplementary experiences upon the behavioral development of infants in institutions. *Child Development,* 1965, *38,* 81–90.

Fredericks, H. D., Baldwin, V. L., Grove, D. N., Riggs, C., Furey, V., Moore, W. G., Jordan, E., Gage, M. A., Levak, L., Alrick, G., & Wadlow, M. *A data-based classroom for the moderately and severely handicapped.* Monmouth, Ore.: Instructional Development Corporation, 1975.

Fredericks, H. D., Riggs, C., Furey, T., Grove, D., Moore, W. G., McDonnell, J., Jordan, E., Hanson, W., Baldwin, V. L., & Wadlow, M. *The teaching research curriculum for moderately and severely handicapped.* Springfield, Ill.: Charles C Thomas, 1976.

Gage, M. A., Fredericks, H. D., Baldwin, V. L., Grove, D. N., Moore, W. G., Moore, M. G., Riggs, C., Furey, V., Levak, L., Alrick, G., Samples, B., & Macklehan, L. *Teaching research group homes for developmentally disabled children.* Monmouth Ore.: Instructional Development Corporation, 1977.

Jewett, D. R. The group home, a neighborhood-based treatment facility. *Children Today,* May-June 1973, 16–20.

Longin, S. N., Cone, J. D., & Longin, H. E. Training behavior modifiers: Mothers' behavioral and attitudinal changes following general and specific training. *Mental Retardation,* October 1975, *13* (5).

Language Training for the Severely Retarded: Five Years of Behavior Analysis Research

LEE K. SNYDER
THOMAS C. LOVITT
JAMES O. SMITH

LEE K. SNYDER *is a doctoral student and research associate, and* JAMES O. SMITH *is Professor and Chairman of Special Education, George Peabody College, Nashville, Tennessee;* THOMAS C. LOVITT *is Professor of Special Education, the University of Washington, Seattle.*

Abstract: Twenty-three behavior analysis studies which have appeared since 1968 are reviewed and analyzed in terms of (a) target behaviors investigated, (b) research methodologies employed, and (c) implications for classroom or clinical practice and for future research. A majority of the studies cited were found to deal exclusively with expressive language, and many of these investigated the generative property of the language under study. All of the studies involved the use of tangible reinforcers, and most used institutionalized subjects more than 8 years old. Implications are drawn which suggest the need for (a) an increased emphasis on antecedent conditions, (b) consideration of a broad range of reinforcement contingencies, (c) specific attention to variables which effect maintenance and generalization, and (d) investigation of younger subjects in noninstitutional settings.

In the past 20 years, an increasing amount of research has focused on the complex questions related to language development. This trend is reflected in both journals and texts on mental retardation, and has been documented by several thorough reviews of the literature (e.g., Schiefelbusch, 1969; Smith, 1962). Such an emphasis is not surprising in light of the high incidence of language disorders reported among the retarded and considering the central role which language plays in almost every aspect of our daily lives.

Recently, parents, professionals, and legislatures have exerted pressure on the public schools, as well as on state institutions, to provide a meaningful and appropriate education for all handicapped students, including those who are severely retarded. Certainly, language training must play an important part in any such educational program. Behavior analysis researchers have been especially prolific in their response to this new urgency. In the past few years, so many relevant and promising studies have been offered by the behavior analysts, and in such rapid succession, that it has become difficult for the educator to keep abreast of the latest developments in this area. Thus, the need has become apparent for a brief review of the most recent work in this rapidly expanding field of research.

The Focus

The research to be discussed here deals specifically with subjects who have been identified by the investigators as severely retarded, or whose reported levels of functioning and IQ would indicate such a classification. The term "severely mentally retarded," according to the 1973 American

3. INSTRUCTION

Association of Mental Deficiency (AAMD) classification system, refers to persons whose measured intelligence is at least four standard deviations below the mean.

Although adaptive behavior criteria are somewhat more ambiguous, Dunn (1973) suggests that severely retarded individuals "have the ability (1) to walk, toilet, dress and feed themselves; (2) to speak in a very elementary fashion; and (3) to perform simple chores in the home or in a very protective environment" (p. 86). This population has been selected as the focus of concern because (a) for the first time, large numbers of these students are being enrolled in the public schools, requiring new instructional programs and techniques, and (b) it seems at least possible that these students may exhibit qualitatively, as well as quantitatively, distinctive patterns of learning and responding. Therefore, in limiting the focus of this review, it has been decided to exclude the many interesting and exciting language development studies which employed subjects who are "high level retardates" (e.g., McLean, 1970) or extremely disturbed children (e.g., Lovaas, 1968).

Additionally, the scope of this article has been limited to studies of language behavior. Specifically, only those studies dealing with language as meaningful, symbolic communication (both oral and aural) will be considered. Thus, related research in such areas as articulation, audiometry, and motor imitation are not included here.

Finally, this article covers only those studies which have employed a behavior analysis research design. Each of these studies met the following criteria: (a) the behavior under study (the dependent variable) was clearly defined in observable terms; (b) this behavior was directly and precisely measured on a continuous basis with data reported accordingly; and (c) the research analyzed the effects of systematic manipulation of specific environmental factors (the independent variables). There has been an obvious trend in recent educational research toward this methodology. This seems to be a particularly promising approach to the study of language acquisition.

So many studies of this type have appeared in the literature of the past two decades that it would be impossible to discuss all of them here. Therefore, only those studies published since 1968 are included. The 23 studies which were found to meet the above criteria are characterized in Table 1.

The first section of this article will be a summary and comparison of the specific language behaviors investigated in these studies. Several aspects of the research methodologies employed will be considered next. Finally, the implications for classroom or clinical practice, as well as for future research will be discussed.

Target Behaviors (Dependent Variables)

In all of these studies, the behavior under analysis was the subject's performance on specific language tasks. These tasks may be classified along two dimensions—type and level. There are two main types of language: receptive (auditory perception, "input") and expressive (usually vocal production, "output"). Tasks in either of these modes may be at one of three levels—initial acquisition (if the subject lacks prior reception and/or expressive language), appropriate use of language, or, use of correct grammar or syntax.

Another feature which may be incorporated in a study of language development is the generative property of language; that is, the ability to produce and receive "an unlimited number of utterances which share a limited number of regularities" (Lahey, 1973, p. x). This concept is illustrated by the following statement by Twardosz and Baer (1973),

> Several studies have shown that when a child is taught to use specific examples of a grammatical rule, he also produces novel examples of this rule that have never been trained, *i.e.*, the rule is generative, (p. 655).

Elsewhere, this phenomenon is referred to as "generalization to untrained stimuli" (p. 660). It has been suggested by Baer and Guess (1973) that, "So conceptualized, these rules of morphological grammar appear equivalent to the behavioral concept of response class" (p. 498). This suggestion, that "generative" and "response class" may actually be equivalent concepts, seems supportable in light of the definition of a response class as "a set of responses so organized that an operation applied to a relatively small subset of their members produces similar results in other members as well" (Garcia, Guess, & Byrnes, 1973, p. 299). Therefore, in the present discussion, those studies which dealt with the generalization of responses to untrained stimuli, or with the formation of a linguistic response class, are all considered analyses of the generative property of the language behavior under investigation.

Receptive Language

Only three of the studies under consideration dealt exclusively with receptive language. Two of these dealt with initial acquisition of the ability to receive (i.e., respond to) verbal instructions (Whitman, Zakaras, & Chardos, 1971; Striefel & Wetherby, 1973). The generative property of this ability was assessed in both studies, with very different results. In the earlier study (Whitman, et al.), the subjects learned to respond correctly to 11 specific verbal commands and generalized this ability to a set of 11 similar, but untrained, instructions. However, Striefel and Wetherby (1973), working with an older and more severely retarded subject, found no generalization to similar instructions, or even to variations of the same 20 instructions which had been successfully trained.

Baer and Guess (1971) assessed the effects of training the receptive discrimination of comparative and superlative forms of adjectives (concepts of which had been previously trained as opposites). All three of their subjects learned to point correctly to pictures representing the superlative and comparative forms of specific adjectives and generalized this ability to similar, but untrained, adjectives.

Expressive Language

Seventeen studies focused exclusively on the modification of expressive language, and nine of these were concerned with the initial acquisition of the ability to imitate and produce specific words or phonemic elements. Four studies (Sloane, Johnston, & Harris, 1968; Kircher, Pear, & Martin, 1971; Stewart, 1972; Jeffrey, 1972) simply demonstrated the effectiveness of operant conditioning in developing and maintaining verbal responses to specific stimuli (e.g., pictures or adult model). The work of Peine, Gregersen, & Sloane, (1970) and Lawrence (1971) was similar in nature, but additionally demonstrated successful manipulation of spontaneous speech through contingent reinforcement. The generative nature of imitative vocal responses was investigated by Garcia, Baer, & Firestone (1971) and by Schroeder and Baer (1972). In both these studies, subjects who had been operantly trained to imitate specific types of motor and vocal responses generalized this ability to the imitation of topographically similar, but untrained, responses. Griffiths and Craighead (1972) successfully trained a specific response class (pronunciation of 10 words with the initial phoneme /l/) which generalized across three different types of stimuli (all evoking the same 10 words), but not across two different settings.

The appropriate use of language was successfully manipulated through contingent reinforcement in three studies. Barton (1972) increased the amount of social speech (verbalization directed toward others) in four severely retarded women. In 1970, Barton reported the success of operant training techniques in increasing the number of appropriate responses made to magazine pictures by an 11 year old institutionalized boy. However, she found that this behavior did not generalize to similar, but untrained,

tasks. In contrast, Twardosz and Baer (1973) succeeded in training two institutionalized adolescents to ask a specific class of questions ("What letter?") in one setting, and found that this did generalize to similar stimuli within the same setting.

Five studies in recent years dealt with the operant training of grammar or syntax in expressive language. Guess, Sailor, Rutherford, & Baer (1968), Sailor (1971) and Garcia, et al. (1973) successfully trained subjects to correctly use singular and plural forms of nouns and, through the use of probes and experimental reversals, clearly demonstrated the generative nature of these learnings. Similarly, Schumaker and Sherman (1970) trained three subjects to produce verbs of the appropriate tense (past or present progressive) in response to verbal stimuli, and demonstrated the generation of appropriate tense use in untrained verbs. Baer and Guess (1973) reported successfully teaching four severely retarded adolescents to produce noun suffixes ("_er" and "_ist") and generalize this skill to untrained words.

Receptive and Expressive Language

Finally, three studies analyzed both receptive and expressive language behaviors. MacAulay (1968) reported on her work with 11 severely retarded students, between the ages of 9 and 15, at the Rainier State School in Buckley, Washington. These studies were discussed rather informally in an article intended to give an overview of the procedures employed, and no complete list of the specific behaviors was provided. However, the data which were presented demonstrated successful operant training of vocabulary reception ("point to the ____"), phoneme production, and morpheme production in response to verbal, pictorial, and, in some cases, written stimuli.

Two more studies dealing with pluralization (Guess, 1969; Guess and Baer, 1973) explored the interrelationships, in terms of generalization, between receptive and expressive training. The earlier study demonstrated that successful training to discriminate receptively between the singular and plural forms of a noun did not generalize to the production of the appropriate form of that noun. In the followup study, four subjects were trained to receptively discriminate one class of plurals and expressively use another class. Probes revealed no generalization across modes.

Research Methodology

Subjects and Settings

The 23 studies discussed here involved a total of 64 subjects. With very few exceptions,

Author/date	Intervention Techniques					
	Target behavior		Antecedent events	Consequent events		Research design employed
	Type	Level		Reinforcement	Nonreinforcement	
Guess, Sailor, Rutherford, & Baer (1968)	Expressive [a]	Grammar, Syntax		Primary		Reversal of contingency
MacAulay (1968)	Receptive, Expressive	Initial Acquisition [b]	Shaping/fading; Modeling	Token		
Sloane, Johnston, & Harris (1968)	Expressive	Initial Acquisition [b]	Shaping/fading; Modeling	Primary	Time out	Noncontingent reinforcement
Guess (1969)	Receptive, Expressive	Grammar, Syntax		Token		Reversal of contingency
Schumaker & Sherman (1970)	Expressive [a]	Grammar, Syntax	Modeling [c]	Token	Time out	Multiple baseline
Barton (1970)	Expressive [a]	Appropriate Usage		Primary	Time out	Reversal of contingency
Peine, Gregersen & Sloane (1970)	Expressive	Initial Acquisition [b]		Token [d]		Reversal of contingency
Garcia, Baer, & Firestone (1971)	Expressive [a]	Initial Acquisition [b]	Shaping/fading; Modeling	Primary		Multiple baseline
Baer & Guess (1971)	Receptive [a]	Grammar Syntax		Token	Time out	Multiple baseline
Kircher, Pear, & Martin (1971)	Expressive	Initial Acquisition [b]	Modeling	Token	Time out	
Whitman, Zakaras, & Chardos (1971)	Receptive [a]	Initial Acquisition [b]	Shaping/fading	Primary		A-B-A design
Sailor (1971)	Expressive [a]	Grammar, Syntax	Modeling	Primary		Multiple baseline
Lawrence (1971)	Expressive	Initial Acquisition [b]		Primary [d]	Time out	A-B-A design; Pretest/ posttest
Stewart (1972)	Expressive	Initial Acquisition [b]	Modeling	Primary		
Jeffrey (1972)	Expressive	Initial Acquisition [b]	Shaping/fading; Modeling	Primary		
Schroder & Baer (1972)	Expressive [a]	Initial Acquisition [b]	Shaping/fading; [c] Modeling	Primary		
Barton (1972)	Expressive	Appropriate Usage		Primary/token		
Griffiths & Craighead (1972)	Expressive	Initial Acquisition [b]	Modeling	Token		Multiple baseline
Garcia, Guess, & Byrnes (1972)	Expressive [a]	Grammar, Syntax	Modeling	Primary		Reversal of contingency
Guess & Baer (1973)	Receptive, Expressive	Grammar, Syntax		Token		
Twardosz & Baer (1973)	Expressive [a]	Appropriate Usage	Shaping/fading; [b] leling	Token		Multiple baseline
Striefel & Wetherby (1973)	Receptive [a]	Initial Acquisition [b]	Shaping/fading	Primary		
Baer & Guess (1973)	Expressive [a]	Grammar, Syntax	Modeling	Primary/token		Reversal of contingency

[a] Study included analysis of generative property of specific language behavior trained.
[b] Initial acquisition of specific words or phonemic elements.
[c] Optional. Used only if other interventions failed to elicit desired response.
[d] Systematically paired with social reinforcement.

TABLE 1 — Characteristics of 23 Behavior Analysis Studies of Language Training for the Severely Retarded

these subjects had either been officially diagnosed as severely retarded, according to the AAMD classification system, or could be so classified on the basis of their reported functioning and IQ. Four of the studies, employing a total of 9 subjects, involved children under 8 years of age. Fifteen subjects, in 7 different studies, were over 14 years of age. The remaining 36 subjects, involved in 15 of the studies, were all between the ages of 8 and 13. (Several studies employed subjects of widely varying ages and so were counted twice in these figures.)

Nineteen studies, involving 52 of the subjects, were conducted within residential institutions for the retarded. Only 5 studies, involving 12 children, were carried out in noninstitutional settings. These included one public school, one preschool, one day care center, and two clinics.

Intervention Techniques
(Independent Variables)

Most of these studies involved more than one independent variable. Without exception, all of the studies included the use of some tangible reinforcement (12 using primaries and 11 using tokens) for desired verbal behavior. In two studies, the relative effectiveness of different reinforcers was assessed. Lawrence (1971) found that the use of social reinforcement, alone or paired with a consumable primary, was more effective with three adolescents than the use of the consumable alone. In a study with four retarded women, Barton (1972) found that token reinforcement produced dramatically greater increases in verbal behavior than did primary reinforcement.

Several of the studies placed the subject(s) on a continuous or fixed ratio schedule of reinforcement only until the verbal behavior attained a predetermined criterion level (Sloane, et al., 1968; Guess, 1969; Garcia, et al., 1971; Baer & Guess, 1971; Sailor, 1971; Schroeder & Baer, 1972; Garcia, et al., 1973; Guess & Baer, 1973; Twardosz & Baer, 1973). The behavior was then placed on a variable ratio schedule (VR) of reinforcement (usually VR 2 or VR 3) to facilitate the interjection of nonreinforced probes designed to assess generalization of learning.

In many of the studies, a time out contingency (ranging from 10 to 30 seconds in most cases) was arranged for incorrect responses or nonattending behavior (Sloane et al., 1968; Schumaker & Sherman, 1970; Barton, 1970; Baer & Guess, 1971; Kircher et al., 1971; Lawrence, 1971). No evidence is provided in any of these studies to support the effectiveness of this technique, and one might question its appropriateness with this population. As Lawrence (1971) has observed, time

out from reinforcement is the usual state of affairs for most institutional residents. In fact, Kircher et al. (1971) demonstrated the relative ineffectiveness of time out, as contrasted with contingent mild shocks, in decreasing inappropriate behavior.

In 11 of these studies, antecedent modeling of desired responses was provided. Usually, if this failed to elicit the correct imitation or verbalization, the response was shaped through reinforcement of increasing approximations as physical prompts were gradually faded out. In two studies (Whitman, et al., 1971; Striefel & Wetherby, 1973), this process of shaping and fading was the central intervention technique under study.

The relative effectiveness of two different training procedures on generalization to untrained response types was assessed by Schroeder and Baer (1972) in their study of vocal imitation. Two subjects were taught to verbally imitate groups of three words (through modeling and shaping) with two alternating procedures: In one condition, each of the three words would be trained to criterion before the next was introduced; in the second condition, the three words would be trained concurrently until all three had reached criterion. The two procedures were equally effective in producing correct imitations of the words being trained. However, generalization to probe items was significantly greater following concurrent training.

In 7 studies, contingent reinforcement of responses was the only intervention employed. In these studies, no antecedent events preceded the presentation of the stimulus to which the subject(s) responded (Guess et al., 1968; Guess, 1969; Barton, 1970; Peine et al., 1970; Baer & Guess, 1971; Barton, 1972; Guess & Baer, 1973).

Experimental Control

Several research designs were employed in these 23 studies, the complexity of which probably reflects the complexity of the language behaviors being investigated. Behavior analysis researchers commonly use an A-B-A design (baseline—intervention—return to baseline) to demonstrate the effectiveness of their interventions. However, in most of the studies reported here, such a design was either not practical or not desirable.

The method of reversing contingencies was employed by several of these investigators and involves the switch of contingent reinforcement to a previously unreinforced, and usually incorrect, response after the correct response has been successfully trained. In the studies which used this design, reestablishment of the normal contingencies for correct responding consistently succeeded in reinsti-

3. INSTRUCTION

tuting the previously established patterns of correct responding. In a multiple baseline design, experimental control is demonstrated through successive application of the intervention to two or more subjects, behaviors or settings. As the intervention is applied to each, a change in the pattern of responses is interpreted as indication of the effectiveness of the technique employed.

Implications

Suggestions for Classroom and Clinical Practice

In the past five years, a large amount of behavior analysis research has appeared dealing with the language development of severely retarded subjects. Perhaps the most striking implication to be drawn from all these studies is that it is definitely possible to improve the language skills of severely retarded children and adults through the application of systematic instructional techniques and reinforcement contingencies. However, for the teacher or clinician who is applying such behavior management techniques, some more specific inferences can be made.

In order for a response to be reinforced, it must first exist in the student's repertoire. This is an obvious fact, but one we can easily forget in our enthusiasm for behavior modification. In several of the studies discussed here, the investigators found it necessary to develop a systematic shaping procedure in order to initially establish the desired behaviors. The use of modeling and physical prompting, which could be gradually faded out as the behavior came under reinforcement control, was reported as a successful approach in several of these studies.

Several implications for the scheduling of consequent events can be drawn from the research reviewed here. The selection of effective reinforcers is certainly one critical component in a program designed to strengthen or extend a desired behavior once it has been initially acquired. While we frequently assume that primary reinforcers are the most potent, the study by Barton (1972) demonstrated that tokens were significantly more effective than primary reinforcers in modifying the social speech of the four severely retarded women included in that study. In selecting a reinforcer for any one student, the teacher or clinician should experiment with a wide variety of reinforcers—both primary and secondary—to determine which is most reinforcing for that particular person. Similarly if a time out procedure is to be used effectively, it must take the form of time out from a truly reinforcing reinforcement, not just time out from the activity or attention.

The conflicting findings regarding generalization which were reported in these studies indicate clearly that we should not expect generalization to occur automatically. The practice of gradually fading from a one to one to a variable ratio schedule of reinforcement, employed in many of these investigations, may prove to be a useful practice for the clinician or teacher who wishes to promote generalization across settings, as well as maintenance over time. Although it may be possible to reinforce a desired response every time it occurs, in a clinical or classroom setting, this behavior will disappear if it is not reinforced when it occurs in other settings. If the behavior is placed on an intermittent schedule, it will be more resistant to the inevitable instances of nonreinforcement in uncontrolled situations.

One potential means for fostering generalization to new responses is indicated by the findings of Schroeder and Baer (1972). In their study, generalization was found to be greater after several words had been trained concurrently, as opposed to a sequential teaching procedure. Certainly, this would be an easy technique to apply in both clinical and classroom settings and one with which the teacher or clinician may wish to experiment.

Directions for Future Research

From the results of the studies discussed here, it would seem that the possibility of modifying the language behavior of severely retarded subjects through the use of operant procedures has been clearly established. Far from exhausting the need for research in this area, however, these studies have revealed many unanswered questions which call for further investigation.

Certainly, there is a need to extend the range of ages and settings involved in future language training research. With the current trend towards early screening and intervention for handicapped children, more studies involving severely retarded subjects under the age of seven would be relevant. Similarly, as the move towards deinstitutionalization progresses, we look increasingly towards research conducted in public school, group home, foster home, and natural home environments.

It is somewhat surprising that every study discussed here involved the use of some tangible reinforcement. It would seem worthwhile to investigate the possible application of purely social reinforcement in the form of contingent praise or physical contact (e.g., hugging, patting). As has been noted earlier, this type of reinforcement has all too often been lacking in the environments of institutionalized subjects. It seems possible that this might provide a source of very potent reinforcement. Similarly, the effects of different antecedent events, without any elaborate reinforcement contingencies, would seem to merit investigation. Certainly, in studies of language *acquisition*, the efficiency of waiting for the subject to emit a desired response, which has not yet been mastered, and then reinforcing it, may be questioned. Although most studies have employed antecedent strategies as a "last resort," it is hoped that future investigators will focus more direct attention on these antecedent instructional interventions.

It should be noted that only a few of the studies described here have reported data on either maintenance over time or generalization of learned responses to new settings. Since the reason for training language skills is to have those skills applied in the subject's daily living, it is hoped that future investigators will analyze intervention strategies employed in training or modifying specific language behaviors in order to identify those variables which are most effective in promoting maintenance. Similarly, analyses of data obtained through the systematic manipulation of antecedent or consequent events are needed to determine the efficacy of different intervention strategies in terms of response generalization—both to untrained responses *and* to new settings.

The 23 studies which have been discussed here represent an exciting avenue of research which holds great promise for the severely retarded individual. As future investigators find answers to the many new and difficult questions raised by the present studies, we may hope to see this promise realized and the door of two-way communication finally opened to those who have been shut out for so long.

References

American Association of Mental Deficiency, *Manual on Terminology and Classification in Mental Retardation: 1973 Revision.* Washington DC: Author, 1973.

Baer, D. M., & Guess, D. Receptive training of adjectival inflections in mental retardates. *Journal of Applied Behavior Analysis,* 1971, *4,* 129-139.

Baer, D. M., & Guess, D. Teaching productive noun suffixes to severely retarded children. *American Journal of Mental Deficiency,* 1973, *77,* 498-505.

Barton, E. S. Inappropriate speech in a severely retarded child: A case study in language conditioning and generalization. *Journal of Applied Behavior Analysis,* 1970, *3,* 299-307.

Barton, E. S. Operant conditioning of social speech in the severely subnormal and the use of different reinforcers. *British Journal of Social and Clinical Psychology,* 1972, *11,* 387-396.

Dunn, L. M. (Ed.) *Exceptional Children in the*

Guess, D., & Baer, D. M. An analysis of individual differences in generalization between receptive and productive language in retarded children. *Journal of Applied Behavior Analysis,* 1973, *6,* 311-329.

Guess, D., Sailor, W., Rutherford, G., & Baer, D. M. An experimental analysis of linguistic development: The productive use of the plural morpheme. *Journal of Applied Behavior Analysis,* 1968, *1,* 297-306.

Jeffrey, D. B. Increase and maintenance of verbal behavior of a mentally retarded child. *Mental Retardation,* 1972, *10(2),* 35-39

Kircher, A. S., Pear, J. J., & Martin, G. L. Shock as punishment in a picture-naming task with retarded children. *Journal of Applied Behavior Analysis,* 1971, *4,* 227-233.

Lahey, B. B. (Ed.) *The Modification of Language Behavior.* Springfield IL: Charles C Thomas, 1973.

Lawrence, J. A. A comparison of operant methodologies relative to language development in the institutionalized mentally retarded. Boston University School of Education, 1971, *Dissertation Abstracts International,* 1971, *32A,* 1943-1944.

Lovaas, I. A program for the establishment of speech in psychotic children. In H. N. Sloane and B. MacAulay (Eds.), *Operant Procedures in Remedial Speech and Language Training.* Boston: Houghton-Mifflin, 1968.

MacAulay, B. D. A program for teaching speech and beginning reading to non-verbal retardates. In H. N. Sloane, Jr., and B. MacAulay (Eds.), *Operant*

Peine, H. A., Gregersen, G. F., & Sloane, H., Jr. A program to increase vocabulary and spontaneous verbal behavior. *Mental Retardation,* 1970, *8(2),* 38-44.

Sailor, W. Reinforcement and generalization of productive plural allomorphs in two retarded children. *Journal of Applied Behavior Analysis,* 1971, *4,* 305-310.

Schiefelbusch, R. L. Language functions of retarded children. *Folia Phoniatricia,* 1969, *21(2),* 129-144.

Schroeder, G. R., & Baer, D. M. Effects of concurrent and serial training on generalized vocal imitation in retarded children. *Developmental Psychology,* 1972, *6,* 293-301.

Schumaker, J., & Sherman, J. A. Training generative verb usage by imitation and reinforcement procedures. *Journal of Applied Behavior Analysis,* 1970, *3,* 273-287.

Sloane, H. N., Jr., Johnston, M. K. & Harris, F. R. Remedial procedures for teaching verbal behavior to speech deficient and defective young children. In H. N. Sloane, Jr., and B. MacAulay (Eds.), *Operant Procedures in Remedial Speech and Language Training.* Boston: Houghton-Mifflin, 1968.

Twardosz, S., & Baer, D. M. Training two severely retarded adolescents to ask questions. *Journal of Applied Behavior Analysis,* 1973, *6,* 655-661.

Whitman, T. L., Zakaras, M., & Chardos, S. Effects of reinforcement and guidance procedures on instruction-following behavior of severely retarded children. *Journal of Applied Behavior Analysis,* 1971, *4,* 283-290.

Language Programming for the Severely Handicapped

Ken G. Jens, Ken Belmore,

Jane Belmore

Ken Jens is Associate Professor, Department of Special Education, and Head of the Special Education Unit, Division for Disorders of Development and Learning, University of North Carolina, Chapel Hill; formerly Associate Professor, Department of Special Education, Georgia State University, Atlanta. Ken Belmore and Jane Belmore are teachers in the Madison Public Schools, Madison, Wisconsin.

LANGUAGE PROGRAMMING FOR THE SEVERELY HANDICAPPED

Currently, one of the most popular but least adequately dealt with aspects of special education is that portion which deals with the education of the severely and profoundly handicapped. Recently, pressure has been put upon educators to acknowledge and respond to litigations which have arisen on behalf of handicapped persons and to develop reasonable public school educational programs for them. Cases such as the *Pennsylvania Association for Retarded Children* v. *Commonwealth of Pennsylvania* (1972), *LeBanks* v. *Spears* (1973), and *Mills* v. *Board of Education of the District of Columbia* (1972) have given clear indication that handicapped children of any kind should not be excluded from provision of an education suited to their individual needs. While some of these cases were clearly decided on behalf of *all* children excluded from public education because of handicapping conditions of any sort, there is even stronger support for providing services to the severely and profoundly handicapped. *Wyatt* v. *Stickney* (1972) and *New York Association for Retarded Children* v. *Rockefeller* (1973) demonstrated clearly that states are also expected to realize their obligation to provide educational services to institutionalized handicapped youngsters regardless whose wards they might be. Probably most important, however, is that set of decisions provided in *Wolf* v. *Legislature of the State of Utah* (1969), *Doe* v. *Board of Education of School Directors of Milwaukee* (1970), *McMillan* v. *Board of Education* (1970), *Reid* v. *Board of Education* (1971), etc., which reaffirmed the fact that our individual state constitutions and laws *guarantee an education to all children.*

One might ask, "Why all the sudden concern regarding the education of the severely and profoundly handicapped?" The answer should be obvious. Despite the fact that educators have been aware of their legal responsibilities regarding the education of all children, they have assumed the right to exclude those who are difficult to educate or whom they could show were extremely expensive to educate. In fact, there are still

"Language Programming for the Severely Handicapped," Ken G. Jens, Ken Belmore, and Jane Belmore, *Focus on Exceptional Children,* Vol. 8, No. 3, May 1976. © 1976 Love Publishing.

school systems that exclude children who do not have "adequate" language for communication, "adequate" self-help skills, or who have not yet reached a given mental age level, such as six years. The absurdity of this is very much apparent when one considers the basic function that schools can and should be assuming with regard to the development of language and communication skills as well as self-care skills for this population of children. In fact, development in these areas, among others, will certainly enhance the apparent mental functioning of even severely handicapped youngsters.

What does this mean for those of us working in the public schools? Obviously, it means that we can no longer rationalize our exclusion of any handicapped children from public school programs regardless of the severity of their handicap. It means that we can no longer exclude children because we "don't know how to teach them" or "do not have adequate facilities" for teaching them. Rather, it is implied that we should be using all of the information available to us to program for them in the most efficient manner possible.

This article was written explicitly for the classroom teacher who is faced with the responsibility of educating the severely mentally handicapped youngster or who is anticipating the imminent arrival of such youngsters in his or her classroom. We have attempted to provide information regarding specific but generalizable procedures which can be used in developing language skills as teachers identify problems of concern with severely handicapped youngsters.

There are numerous reasons why language programming is an essential curriculum area for severely handicapped students. The following statements are suggested as some of the more cogent arguments supporting language training.

1. The majority of severely handicapped students have been labeled deficient in speech, language, and overall communication skills. Jordan (1967) found these deficiencies in 40 to 79 percent of the population studied. The number of specific deficiencies was reported to increase with the degree of retardation.

2. Normal environmental conditions similar to those under which most children develop language skills do not lead to corresponding language growth in the severely handicapped. The effects of parent and/or peer modeling are minimal. There are numerous research articles suggesting that severely and profoundly handicapped students acquire language in developmental stages similar to nonhandicapped children but not under the same normal environmental conditions.

3. Much recent work has suggested that longitudinal, well-planned programs for teaching language skills to severely and profoundly handicapped students can be effective (Baer & Guess, 1971; Bricker & Bricker,

1970; Guess, Sailor, Rutherford & Baer, 1968; Lovaas, 1968).

4. In addition to the intrinsic value of improved or new language skills, language behaviors are essential prerequisites to the development of skills in most other curricular areas for severely and profoundly handicapped students (i.e., many self-help skills, vocational skills, and functional academic skills).

5. The potential for language development in severely handicapped children has not been determined to date. It is very likely that as our ability for language training improves, long-term gains in language development will be demonstrated in some severely handicapped students that exceed those currently thought possible.

6. Language, in addition to being a prerequisite to other essential skills, is one of the most prominent factors separating severely handicapped persons from nonhandicapped persons. Appearances, motor skills, and academic abilities are of lesser import when integration of severely handicapped persons with nonhandicapped persons into some areas of normal societal living is seriously considered.

If some of the above arguments constitute justifiable reasons for teaching language skills to severely handicapped students, then it follows that teachers must have a frame of reference from which they can design and implement language training programs. Thus, the following outline is suggested as one scheme for organizing the components of language instruction for severely handicapped students.

1. *Specific skills essential for persons who teach language to severely handicapped students*

    a. What skills does the teacher need?

    b. Which of these skills does the teacher currently possess?

2. *Strategies for the analysis of available language training programs*

    a. What language training programs are available?

    b. How can a teacher efficiently evaluate available programs?

    c. Which facets of a program are relevant to the current teacher/student situation?

3. *Determination of a classroom model appropriate for meeting current student needs*

    a. Content

        (1) What skills should be taught?

        (2) Why should these skills be taught?

    b. Method

        (1) How can skills best be taught?

3. INSTRUCTION

       (2)   What materials will be needed?

    c. Evaluation

       (1)   How is success determined?

       (2)   What are the alternatives if success is not achieved?

       (3)   What are the next steps if success is achieved?

The remainder of this article will attempt to provide functional information that may be used to facilitate the teaching of language by addressing each of these items. In addition, an exemplary segment of a language training program is provided.

SPECIFIC SKILLS ESSENTIAL FOR PERSONS WHO TEACH LANGUAGE TO SEVERELY HANDICAPPED STUDENTS

Severely handicapped students are often dramatically different, if only in degree, from mildly handicapped or nonhandicapped students; teaching this population does require teachers equipped with unique competencies (Brown & York, 1974). The importance of these teacher competencies is directly related to the degree of disability presented in the student population. Thus, the more severely handicapped the student, the more well developed a teacher's competencies need to be. Competencies necessary for language instruction overlap considerably with the basic skills necessary to teach anything to severely handicapped students. Minimally, teachers must become competent and comfortable with the use of teaching techniques and strategies including modeling/imitation, reinforcement, shaping, prompting, fading, extinction, stimulus control, and generalization training. An operational definition of each of these techniques and examples of their use in language training are given in Figure 1. Further information regarding their use can be found in texts by Reese (1966), Whaley and Malott (1968), Bandura (1969), Sulzer and Mayer (1972), and Miller (1975) to mention just a few.

Teacher competencies necessary for language training obviously go beyond the basic behavioral techniques delineated in Figure 1. Skills which are necessary in designing the instructional situation prior to direct instruction include (1) the ability to task analyze segments of language, and (2) the ability to develop an instructional program in a sequence appropriate to the task analysis derived. These two skills are essential for teachers of severely handicapped students. It is the ability to specify what responses a student should make, and in what sequence the responses should be made, that determines the adequacy of the curriculum for language programming with this population. Hopefully, the example of one segment of a language program presented at the end of this article will suggest a means of task analyzing a set of language skills and a method of building an instructional

program based on that analysis.

In addition to task analysis and instructional sequencing skills, further considerations vital to the instructional situation include the selection of appropriate materials and the arrangement of the classroom environment. The classroom arrangement should provide for control and presentation of antecedent stimuli as well as delivery of reinforcement for learning on a planned basis. Provisions should also be made for ongoing and end-product assessment.

The following also are appropriate for teacher consideration.

1. Importance of integrating language programming into other curricular areas

2. Necessity of communicating methods of instruction to parents, teachers, and other persons in the students' immediate environment

3. Availability of existing program and research information regarding language training for severely handicapped students

What are the alternatives for teachers who do not have all of the skills delineated? It is unlikely that many teachers have mastered all of the aforementioned competencies. The important point is that teachers should thoroughly and objectively assess their competencies in terms of strengths and weaknesses. In doing so, one is likely to find that he or she has competencies in most areas, but may need skill refinement in one area, such as planning language development programs for specific students. One reason for this is that there are so few commercially prepared packages designed for teaching language to severely handicapped students. Thus, the brunt of planning frequently falls on the classroom teacher. Detailed examples of task analyses and instructional program development appropriate for use with the severely handicapped are available (Brown, Scheuerman, Cartwright & York, 1973; Brown & Sontag, 1972; Brown, Williams & Crowner, 1974).

STRATEGIES FOR THE ANALYSIS OF AVAILABLE LANGUAGE TRAINING PROGRAMS

No attempt will be made to provide an analysis of language programs previously used with severely handicapped students within this article. A concise summary of information in this area has been provided by Snyder, Lovitt, and Smith (1975). Published studies and programs vary across several important dimensions beyond the skill areas taught. As previously mentioned, the ability to analyze studies and programs is highly desirable for teachers beginning language instruction with severely handicapped students. Figure 2 is offered to provide assistance in the analysis of programs along several dimensions related specifically to classroom situations.

The dimensions outlined in Figure 2 may be used as a

Figure 1
BEHAVIORAL PROCEDURES FOR USE IN TEACHING*

Procedure	Definition		Example/Use
1. Reinforcement (Positive)	1. The process of increasing or maintaining behavior through the presentation of a stimulus contingent upon the emission of the behavior	Use: 1. Ex: 1.	Positive reinforcement may be used whenever the teacher desires to teach a new behavior, to increase a behavior already in the child's repertoire, or to maintain a behavior. To determine appropriate positive reinforcer, teacher may present an assortment and observe child in a free-choice situation.
a. Primary	2. Primary reinforcement has the effect of maintaining or perpetuating life	Use: 2. Ex: 2.	Primary reinforcement should be used in the early stages of teaching and for children who do not respond to other forms of reinforcement. When child emits desired sound, teacher delivers food (candy, cereal, etc.).
b. Secondary	3. Secondary reinforcement has effectiveness because of prior systematic association with primary reinforcement	Use: 3. Ex: 3.	Secondary reinforcement may be used with many children for whom primary reinforcement is not necessary. Praise, or physical approval (hug, pat), should always be given when primary reinforcement is used in order to establish these as secondary reinforcers. When child emits desired phoneme, teacher delivers pat on back and verbal praise.
2. Modeling/ Imitation	4. A procedure which occurs when the desired behavior is demonstrated, then copied by the student	Use: 4. Ex: 4.	Imitation may be used when the child does not have the desired behavior in his repertoire but does have the skills necessary to perform the behavior, or some approximation of it. Teacher emits desired response and reinforces the child for repeating it.
3. Shaping	5. A procedure through which new behaviors are developed. The systematic reinforcement of successive approximations toward the behavioral goal.	Use: 5. Ex: 5.	Shaping is used when the child does not have the skills to perform the desired terminal behavior. Teacher reinforces "b," "ba," "ball" in sequence when teaching the word "ball."
4. Prompting	6. A procedure through which extra discriminative stimuli are provided during the learning of a new behavior	Use: 6a. Ex: 6a. Use: 6b. Ex: 6b.	Prompting is used when a child needs additional cues. In the case of a child who has no language, physical prompts may be necessary. Teacher holds child's lips together to facilitate emission of "buh" sound. For a child who has language, verbal prompts may be used. Teacher shows ball and says, "It's a ball. Tell me what it is."
5. Fading	7. The gradual removal of discriminative stimuli such as cues and prompts	Use: 7. Ex: 7.	Fading is used when a teacher perceives that prompts are no longer necessary. Teacher puts fingers increasingly gently on child's lips while child emits "buh" sound or teacher shows ball and says, "Tell me what it is."
6. Stimulus Control	8. A procedure for discrimination training during which reinforcement is provided for responses to the presence of a certain stimulus and not for responses in the presence of other stimuli	Use: 8. Ex: 8.	Stimulus control is used when the teacher wishes to be sure that the child will apply his words only under appropriate circumstances. Teacher reinforces the word "ball" only when a ball is presented to the child.
7. Generalization	9. A process which occurs when the student responds to different stimuli in a similar manner.	Use: 9. Ex: 9.	The teacher programs for generalization when she wants to be sure that the word the child has learned will be used appropriately for all members of a class of stimuli. Child says "ball" when various balls or pictures of balls are presented.
8. Extinction	10. The reduction or elimination of a conditioned response by withholding reinforcement for that response	Use: 10. Ex: 10.	Extinction may be used when the child makes sounds other than those desired—for example, babbling, mumbling screaming. Teacher does not reinforce the emission of extraneous sounds.

*This is a minimal list of procedures which teachers should be able to use.

3. INSTRUCTION

guide in determining which aspects of a published language program are appropriate for particular students in a classroom setting. Different facets of one or more published programs may be combined, with modifications if they appear warranted, to form a basis for language training programs in these situations.

Reviewing several language programs prior to selecting elements of any for use is generally necessary since the range of language differences presented by students is frequently quite extreme and the content of various language programs varies considerably. Some language programs have focused on very early stages of development (Garcia, Baer, & Firestone, 1971; Jeffrey, 1972; MacAuley, 1968; Peine, Gregersen & Sloane, 1970; Schroder & Baer, 1972; Sloane, Johnston & Harris, 1968; Stewart, 1972) while others have emphasized the development of higher level expressive and receptive skills in severely handicapped populations (Baer & Guess, 1973; Barcia, Guess & Byrnes, 1972; Barton, 1970; Guess et al.,; Schumaker & Sherman, 1970; Twardosz & Baer, 1973). It is extremely important that teachers avail themselves of opportunities to become familiar with language training programs available commercially and those suggested in the professional literature.

DETERMINATION OF A CLASSROOM MODEL APPROPRIATE FOR MEETING CURRENT STUDENT NEEDS

One of the most difficult questions for a teacher to answer is, "What did I teach Johnny, Susie, and Billy today?" In order to answer such a question it is imperative that teachers avail themselves of some form of feedback/decision making system. One of the most frequently mentioned systems for this purpose is the Test-Teach-Test model (Chalfant, Kirk & Jensen, 1968). In fact, teachers have been encouraged to use this and similar models with the implication that the use of such a model will surely bring success to their classroom. Unfortunately, the problems involved in providing success in teaching severely handicapped or, for that matter, any students are somewhat more complex. Certainly, such a model is basic when considering that teachers must have available a working model which allows them to make decisions about what they are doing on a day-to-day basis. The problem is, the aforementioned model is generally not discreet enough, as such, to be of much value in making decisions about *what* should be taught. Especially when one is concerned with the ultimate behavior to be attained by severely handicapped students, the need for logical sequencing of behaviors to be learned becomes critical. Immediately then, one is forced to expand his feedback/decision making system so that it includes at least the following questions.

1. What do I want to teach?
2. Why do I want to teach that skill or concept?
3. How can I teach it?
4. What materials will I need?

5. How can I know if I am succeeding?
6. If I am not succeeding, what do I do?
7. If I succeed, what do I do next?

What Do I Want to Teach?

When teachers ask the question, "What do I want to teach?" they are really asking, "What do I want the student to be able to do that he could not do in the past?" (Brown & York, 1974, p. 6). Teachers have become accustomed to looking for the "what" or content of instruction in curriculum guides or other written resources which they assume can be presented to them by someone who has overall responsibility for educational programming for the youngsters they teach. Unfortunately, this is not the case. While a few curriculum guides are available, most of them do not provide reasonable guidelines which classroom teachers can use in making curricular decisions regarding individual students for whom they must program. There are exceptions to this, of course. Bricker and Bricker (1970) and Sailor, Guess, and Baer (1973), for example, have provided language programs which are both well-developed and sequenced in a manner which contributes significantly to providing an answer to the question, "What do I want to teach?" The following guidelines may be of further assistance in selecting specific content for inclusion in a language training program.

1. *What objects does the child come in contact with most frequently during his daily activities?* Certain objects such as balls, spoons, cups, etc., may provide more naturally reinforcing interactions than other objects because they are functionally useful to the child. Initially, labels for objects that can be manipulated for some purpose should be considered when selecting vocabulary content for language training.

2. *Which people does the child interact with most frequently?* Names, as labels for people of importance to the child, should be considered as target vocabulary content. The ability to label people is reinforced by the natural response of the person hearing his name. The child's own name is always a primary target for receptive and expressive language training.

3. *What words and phrases does he hear most often in his instructional programs?* Selection of key instructional words—such as *put, go, sit, stand,* etc.—that will become components of functional directions will facilitate functioning in both the educational and community environments. Other instructional terms—such as selected adjectives, adverbs, prepositions, and color words—should be taught as they become useful and meaningful to the child or as their use is occasioned in other instructional settings. Initially, stress may be placed on receptive language abilities, but expressive use of

Figure 2
DIMENSIONS FOR CONSIDERATION IN REVIEWING EXISTING LANGUAGE PROGRAMS

1. What are relevant characteristics of the population receiving training?
   a. CA; MA; IQ scores; visible anomalies
   b. Institutionalized or noninstitutionalized population
   c. History of previous language training
   d. Entering language skills
      (1)   Receptive skills
      (2)   Expressive skills
      (3)   Gestural skills

2. What specific language functions were taught?
   a. Expressive vs. receptive training
   b. Form of communication
      (1)   Verbal
      (2)   Gestural (hand signs)
      (3)   Combined verbal and gestural
      (4)   Other

3. What resulting language improvements occurred?
   a. Long- vs. short-term results
   b. Follow-up data after training

4. What methods were used for training language?
   a. Imitation training
      (1)   Motor training, initially
      (2)   Verbal training, initially
   b. Shaping; priming, fading, other operant techniques
   c. Principal technique employed

5. What was the teacher/student ratio?
   a. Individualized vs. group instruction
   b. Number of students taught within instructional setting

6. What specific materials were used?
   a. Classroom materials
   b. Special apparatus (reinforcement desk, etc.)
   c. Reinforcers

7. What skills did the language instructors possess?
   a. Psychologist or trained behavior analyst
   b. Classroom teacher
   c. Classroom aide
   d. Aides employed by institution
   e. Combination of personnel

8. Was there data supporting generalization of language skills?
   a. Generalization within instructional setting
   b. Generalization outside instructional setting
   c. Spontaneous generalization vs. elicited generalization

9. How long did the program take?
   a. Overall time period for program
   b. Length of teaching sessions
   c. Number of sessions per week

10. What modifications will be necessary to adapt this program for classroom use?
    a. Planning time required
    b. Professional assistance required
    c. Specific modifications necessary, i.e., material changes; group instruction feasibility

3. INSTRUCTION

words and phrases should also be taught as soon as possible.

4. *What words or phrases are commonly used in the child's home?* Coordination with the parents is necessary to choose words and phrases for language training that can be used at home and at school. This provides the child with as many opportunities as possible for repeated practice and reinforcement of newly acquired language.

5. *What verbal responses will the child be asked to make most often in his environment?* Selection of words and phrases that will facilitate the child's interaction with his environment is essential. Words that enable him to express his needs—such as *play, eat, go, outside*—provide him with vehicles for self-initiated behavior and appropriate interaction with other people in his environment.

6. *What are the long-range goals for the individual student?* The long-range plans for a given child will be determined by teachers, parents, and concerned others. His ultimate station in life should be considered when selecting content for language training, focusing on words and phrases that will be useful given his probable life style and future environment.

To answer these questions, it becomes obvious that a teacher must assess not only a student's language abilities but also his language environment and what this language environment expects from the student.

The principle goals of student assessment should be to pinpoint that skill range within which language training should begin and to specify the direction in which instruction should proceed. There are numerous methods of accurately assessing student performance within a language program. The following sequence represents one possible method.

1. Select a developmental scale that is complete enough to yield a repertoire of language related behaviors of a severely handicapped student. Since there are several developmental scales in this area—Developmental Pinpoints (Cohen, Gross & Haring, 1975), the TARC Assessment System (Sailor & Mix, 1975)—a teacher could save time and effort by employing a published material rather than developing his/her own.

2. Utilize such a scale to assess developmental, expressive, and receptive language abilities of each student.

3. Combine developmental language information with an assessment of the student's language environment for the purpose of generating a complete picture of student's current language needs.

Why Do I Want to Teach That Skill or Concept?

The second question a teacher must ask herself as part of any teaching-learning program is "Why do I want to teach that skill or concept?" In the opinion of the authors, there are really only two legitimate answers to this question: (1) the skill or concept that one is about to teach is a prerequisite skill or concept for another useful behavior which it is intended to teach later; or (2) the skill or concept being taught has immediate usefulness for the student by either increasing his potential for meaningful interactions with others or providing him with increased ability to function independently. If, as we set about outlining what we will teach to given youngsters, we cannot fit our rationale for teaching given skills or concepts into either of these, we must indeed ask ourselves, "Why do I want to teach that skill or concept?"

How Can I Teach It?

Having decided what should be taught, the teacher must now answer the question, "How can I teach it?" This is probably the most difficult question a teacher has to answer. Teachers look back forlornly to the methods' courses they took as part of their university programs for the answer—and, most frequently, they do not find it. The answer is not to be found solely in the selection of materials as is often implied via the suggestion that a teacher try yet another language program if he or she has not been successful with one or more already. Rather, we must learn to make use of empirical knowledge available to us regarding *how* children learn. Several teaching procedures which when mastered would provide a teacher with basic techniques and strategies for implementing of language programming have been delineated in Figure 1.

What Materials Will I Need?

Having settled on what you will teach and how you will go about the teaching function, it becomes necessary to ask oneself, "What materials will I need?" There are a good number of language development and/or training programs available for use with normal, culturally distinct and mildly handicapped populations. The Peabody Language Development Kits (Dunn, Horton & Smith, 1967) and the Distar Language Program (Englemann, 1969) are primary examples of such programs.

Fewer programs have been designed specifically for teaching language to severely handicapped populations —those youngsters who may enter an educational program with little or no functional language whatsoever. Among those which have recently become available are *A Language Program for the Nonlanguage Child* (Gray & Ryan, 1973), *Language Acquisition Program for the Severely Retarded* (Kent, 1974), and the *Non-Speech Language Initiation Program* (Carrier & Peak, 1975). The development of materials for use in teaching this population is currently of high priority, and a good deal is being produced. The American Association for the Education of the Severely and Profoundly Handicapped provides an information dissemination service to its members which is extremely invaluable and which teachers could readily use to stay abreast of the development of new materials in this area.

Given that materials for use with the severely handicapped are currently difficult to locate and obtain, it is extremely important that teachers of this population develop their ability to (1) use task analysis to delineate the responses their students should regularly be making, and then (2) determine what stimuli should occasion the occurrence of those responses. These stimuli, the items in the environment to which students should respond, must then become the materials for our teaching programs.

How Can I Know If I'm Succeeding?

When each of the aforementioned questions has been dealt with and a teaching program is under way, the need for feedback becomes obvious. Critical decisions need to be made regarding the effectiveness of the strategies and materials which have been employed. Data must be obtained for the purpose of determining whether or not one is making progress toward the accomplishment of given objectives. The critical question confronting teachers now becomes, "What should I record?" The answer to this question is related directly to the objectives set forth when originally asking the question, "What do I want to teach?" Before we can measure any behavior we must have defined it operationally, i.e., in observable and quantifiable terms. Having done this, one has several options.

1. If trials are held constant from one teaching session to the next, "number correct" is an adequate measure. It constitutes one of the easiest ways to determine whether or not a student is making progress in a teaching/learning program. This method of assessment is problematical though in that, if data is to be compared from day to day on a meaningful basis, the number of trials occurring when teaching a given behavior must be held constant from day to day. For example, if one is working on the teaching of an object name such as *table*, a teacher might ask a student to "point to the *table*," "touch the *table*," or "put the _____ on the *table*," but the number of trials afforded students would have to be the same in all teaching situations, i.e., 10 trials per session. If this is not done, differences appearing from day to day may well be a function of the number of opportunities (trials) afforded a youngster while teaching a given concept of action. Examples of teaching programs for severely handicapped students which have utilized this type of measurement can be found in the papers compiled by Brown and Sontag (1972) and Brown, Scheuerman, Cartwright, and York (1973).

2. A second option available to teachers is to record the percentage of correct responses made by students per session. This type of measurement is preferrable to using number of correct and incorrect responses for each session. When using percentage of correct responses as a dependent teaching variable, the length of the teaching sessions or number of trials offered on a given day are not intrinsically important. There is a potential hazard inherent in recording the percentage of correct responses per session though. If the number of trials is not held constant from one session to the next, a student may be making more errors per session while showing higher percentages of correct responses, i.e., with 10 problems, 90% correct indicates 9 correct and 1 wrong response; with 30 problems, 90% correct indicates 27 correct and 3 wrong responses—an actual increase in both correct and incorrect responses. Examples of the use of percent of correct responses as a measure of learning are provided by Barton (1970) and Garcia, Guess, and Byrnes (1973).

3. Rate of correct responding can be recorded for each teaching session (number of correct responses divided by the time taken to emit them). Rate measures, while being somewhat more difficult for teachers to work with initially, provide the most meaningful kind of data for analyzing student learning. All responses are appropriate or inappropriate, despite their accuracy, in relation to a measure of time. A student may, for example, be able to respond verbally to simple questions; but if he does not do so within time limits which make his behavior socially acceptable, it will not be perceived as adequate. Once verbal responses are learned, they must be regulated in terms of rate so as to be acceptable in appropriate social circumstances. Examples of this type of recording have been provided by Freschi (1974) and numerous others.

If I Am Not Succeeding, What Do I Do?
If I Succeed, What Do I Do Next?

One of the obvious benefits resulting from the collection of data while teaching is that the data collected tells us immediately whether or not we are making progress toward the achievement of our objectives. The appropriate interpretation of data is often difficult though. When working with severely handicapped youngsters, we sometimes lose our objectivity and tend toward evaluation of our teaching programs on the basis of our own involvement or effort. This is reflected in statements such as "Gee, the _____ language program works great with these kids!" or "That imitation/modeling procedure sure seems to be working well!" which are frequently made without reference to student data. Freschi (1974) has provided examples of data reflecting several problems which frequently occur in the teaching/learning situation along with interpretive ideas and suggestions for solving them. In general, if a student is not making reasonable progress toward the criterion established for a given objective, teachers should consider the alternatives shown in Figure 3 as possible courses of action.

3. INSTRUCTION

Figure 3
AN INSTRUCTIONAL FLOW CHART FOR USE WITH SEVERELY HANDICAPPED STUDENTS

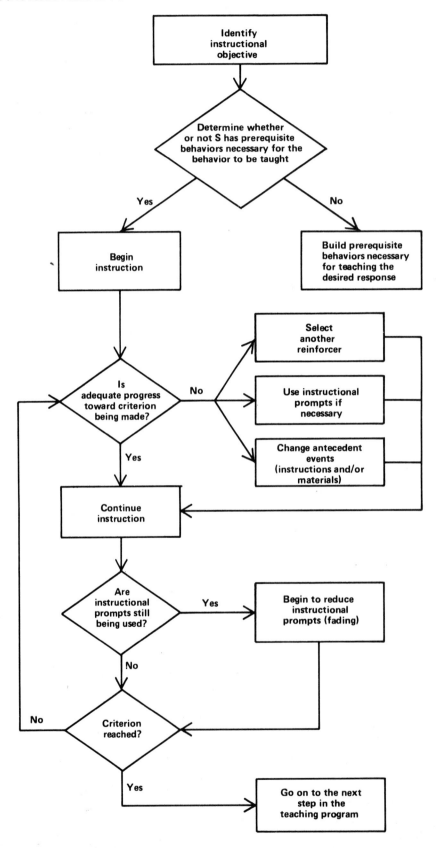

SEGMENT FROM A
LANGUAGE TRAINING PROGRAM

In an effort to make the suggestions within this article concrete and of greater application in the classroom, the following example of one segment of a language training program is offered. This example is presented in the order of questions that were raised relative to the development of a classroom teaching model. Obviously, this set of language skills was selected, and a corresponding program was designed, for a particular group of students. The program's application to other severely handicapped students may or may not be appropriate. The segment represents one phase of receptive language training which deals specifically with the understanding of words that denote a time and place sequence. It was developed for a group of five severely handicapped students in a public school classroom based on the following assessment procedures.

1. Developmental language skills were assessed using Developmental Pinpoints (Cohen, Gross & Haring, 1975). Specific areas assessed included students' responses to verbal requests. It was found that the students could respond to some one-component verbal directions but not to those involving *first*, *next*, and *last*.

2. An assessment of the language environments of the students showed that most would be in self-contained special education classes integrated in a regular elementary school for at least 3 or 4 more years. Thus the students would need to respond to the "language of school instruction" which includes the functional use of language concepts involving *first, next, last*.

1. What Skills Should Be Taught?

The instructional program outlined here is an attempt to provide direct and systematic instruction in a receptive language skill: understanding a selected word sequence denoting time and position in space. The word sequence chosen for instruction is *first/next/last*. The major or terminal objective of this program is stated as follows:

Given a teacher direction or statement that includes the word sequence *first, next, last, S* will touch or label an object, person or pictured event that designates each position according to time (auditory cue) and/or position in space (visual cue).[2]

---

2. The objective here is not necessarily performance of each specific task (although that measurement across cues, tasks, and settings will be used for evaluation) but rather the ability to act appropriately upon word sequence cues. For example, in the bead stringing task the objective is not that the child string beads, but that he show comprehension of the language cues.

A task analysis approach such as that suggested by Batemen (1971) was used to delineate and sequence specific content objectives.

TASK ANALYSIS

Objective I: Teaching the word sequence *first, next, last* with time (auditory cue) and position in space (visual cue) presented concurrently. Given a set of objects, people, or pictured events and an auditory cue (verbal explanation of position) containing the word sequence first, next, and last, *S* will touch or label the *first, next,* and *last* positions when the position in space (visual cue) is given concurrent with the auditory cue.

Part 1: Given a set of 3 beads of different colors and a verbal explanation, *S* will respond correctly to *T* cue, "Touch the one that is *first (next, last)."*

Step 1: Given 1 bead on a string, *S* will touch *first* position after verbal explanation.

Step 2: Given 3 beads on a string and a verbal explanation, *S* will touch the one in the *first* position.

Step 3: Given 3 beads of different color on a string and a verbal explanation, *S* will touch the one in *next* position.

Step 4: ...*S* will touch *first* and *next*.

Step 5: ...*S* will touch *last*.

Step 6: ...*S* will touch *first, next* and/or *last*.

Part 2: Given 3 objects and a verbal explanation, *S* will label or touch the one in each position *first, next,* and/or *last* when auditory and visual cues are concurrent.

Step 1: *S* will respond to the cue, "Touch the one that is *first."*

Step 2: *S* will touch the one that is *next*.

Step 3: *S* will touch the one that is *last*.

Step 4: *S* will touch the one that is *first, next,* and/or *last*.

Part 3: Given 3 people in a line one behind the other and a verbal explanation, *S* will touch or label the person in each position *first, next, last* when auditory and visual cues are concurrent.

Step 1: *S* will touch the person in *first* position.

Step 2: *S* will touch the person in *next* position.

Step 3: *S* will touch the person in *last* position.

Step 4: *S* will touch the person in *first, next,*

3. INSTRUCTION

and/or *last* position.

Part 4: Given 3 pictures each representing a daily event or activity and a verbal explanation, *S* will touch or label the event in each position *first, next,* and/or *last* when auditory cue is concurrent with visual cue.

Step 1: *S* will touch the event that is *first.*

Step 2: *S* will touch the event that is *next.*

Step 3: *S* will touch the event that is *last.*

Step 4: *S* will touch the event that is *first, next,* and/or *last.*

Part 5: Given 3 beads, objects, people, or pictured events *without* verbal explanation, *S* will touch or label the bead, object, person, or event in each position *first, next,* or *last* upon *T* cue.

Step 1: Part 1, step 6 repeated without verbal explanation.

Step 2: Part 2, step 4 repeated without verbal explanation.

Step 3: Part 3, step 4 repeated without verbal explanation.

Step 4: Part 4, step 4 repeated without verbal explanation.

Objective II: Teaching *first, next,* and *last* when time (auditory cue) is not concurrent with spatial order (visual cue).

Given 3 objects, people, or pictured events presented in varied or ordered positions in space, *S* will respond correctly to teacher cue, "Touch the one that is *first (next* and/or *last)."*

Part 1: Given 3 objects and verbal explanation, *S* will touch or label the object presented *first, next,* and/or *last* in explanation upon *T* cue.

Step 1: *S* will touch object presented *first* in verbal explanation.

Step 2: *S* will touch object presented *next* in verbal explanation.

Step 3: *S* will touch object presented *last* in verbal explanation.

Step 4: *S* will touch object presented *first, next,* or *last* in verbal explanation.

Part 2: Given 3 people in a line and a verbal explanation, *S* will touch the person whose name was presented *first, next,* and/or *last* in the explanation upon *T* cue.

Step 1: *S* will touch person presented *first.*

Step 2: *S* will touch person presented *next.*

Step 3: *S* will touch person presented *last.*

Step 4: *S* will touch person presented *first, next,* and/or *last.*

Part 3: Given 3 pictured events or activities in varied order *S* will correctly touch the event that occurs *first, next,* and/or *last* upon *T* cue.

Step 1: *S* will touch the event that occurs *first.*

Step 2: *S* will touch the event that occurs *next.*

Step 3: *S* will touch the event that occurs *last.*

Step 4: *S* will touch the event that occurs *first, next,* and/or *last.*

2. Why Should These Skills Be Taught?

It is crucial that severely handicapped students be given as many methods as possible for ordering incoming verbal and nonverbal information. This specific word sequence was chosen because (1) it is frequently used in teacher directions, (2) it is useful in making directions clearer for students, (3) it can make instruction more efficient, and (4) it provides a framework for expanded instruction in time and/or position of objects in space. Severely handicapped students entering a regular public school building will need to be able to respond to many commands involving the terms *first, next, last.* For example, "Line up first." "You're next." "Who's next?" and "Raise your hand first." are frequently heard statements.

3. How Can Skills Best Be Taught?
What Materials Will Be Needed?

The methodology for teaching these or any skills will vary somewhat according to individual teacher training and student differences. Nevertheless, the strategies presented are typical of those necessary when working with persons presenting severe language deficiencies. Specific methods are given for teaching each step of the task analysis.

Objective I: Teaching *first, next, last* with time (auditory cue) and position in space (visual cue) presented concurrently.

Part I: Beads
Instructional Arrangement: Ss are seated across table from *T*

Materials: Beads of various colors and a string

Prerequisites: Color discrimination

Teaching Procedure:

Step 1: Teacher strings one bead as she says,

"First is the (red) one. *S's name,* touch the one that is *first."* If *S* responds correctly, he is reinforced and *T* removes bead, picks a different colored bead, strings it and says, *"First* is the (green) one." *T* continues with each *S* until criterion is reached.

Criterion:	5 correct responses out of 5 trials
Correction Procedures:	1. Present cue again. 2. Model, then present cue. 3. Model, prime, present cue until response is correct, then reinforce.

Step 2: Teacher strings three beads of different colors. *T* says, *"First* is the (red) one." (*T* strings 2 more beads but does not give verbal explanation.) *"S's name,* touch the one that is *first."* Repeat for each *S* until criterion is met.

Criterion:	Same as Step 1
Correction:	Same as Step 1

Step 3: Teacher repeats stringing operation as in Step 2 saying, *"First* is the (red) one, *next* is the (green) one." (*T* strings last bead but does not give verbal explanation.) If *S* responds correctly, *T* removes beads and strings 3 beads of different colors repeating verbal explanation until criterion is met for each *S.* For incorrect responses, *T* begins correction procedure.

Criterion:	Same as Step 1
Correction:	Same as Step 1

Step 4: *T* strings beads as in Step 3 saying, "*First* is the (green) one, *next* is the (red) one." (*T* strings last bead but does not give verbal explanation.) *"S's name,* touch the one that is *first."* *T* waits for *S* response. If correct, *T* says, "Touch the one that is *next."* *S* is reinforced for correct responses. If response is incorrect after *first* cue, *T* repeats verbal explanation and presents cue again. If response is again incorrect, *T* begins correction procedure.

Criterion:	5/5 correct responses to both cues in one session
Correction:	Same as Part 1

Step 5: Teacher strings beads as in Step 4 saying, *"First* is the (red) one, *next* is the (green) one, *last* is the (blue) one. *S's name,* touch the one that is *last."* *S* is reinforced for correct response. If incorrect, *T* repeats first two components of verbal explanation and says, "Touch the one that is *last."* If response is again incorrect, *T* begins correction procedure.

Criterion:	Same as Step 1
Correction:	Same as Step 1

Step 6: *T* strings beads as in Step 5 and gives verbal explanation, *"First* is the (red) one, *next* is the (blue) one, *last* is the (green) one. *S's name,* touch the one that is *first."* *T* waits for response. If correct, *T* repeats verbal explanation and says, *"S's name,* touch the one that is *last."* Cues are then varied.

Criterion:	Same as Step 1
Correction:	Same as Step 1 or move back to previous step for repeated trials

Steps 1 through 6 would now be repeated with the additional requirement that students actually place beads on a string in response to teacher verbal cues, i.e., *"First,* put the red one on the string. *Next,* put the green one on the string. Put the blue one on *last."*

4. How Is Success Determined? What Alternatives Are Available If Success Is Not Achieved?

In this program success is determined by an ongoing evaluation of whether or not students achieve given criterion levels set for mastery of the steps necessary to reach each objective. Thus, when a student reaches the criterion set for one step, he progresses to the next step. However, if the student does not succeed in reaching criterion, the teacher institutes a correction procedure and continues teaching until criterion is met.

5. What Are the Next Steps If Success Is Achieved?

One major advantage of using a task analysis approach such as the one presented here is that it provides a method of predetermining the sequence in which content objectives will be taught. As the student masters each objective, the teacher moves to instruction on the next objective in the task analysis. In the example given in this article, when the student masters Step 6 of Objective I, Part 1, the teacher prepares to teach Step 1, Objective I, Part 2 (teaching the same skills with varying cues) which is the next step in the task analysis.

Ultimately, a student who is taught this entire segment of a language program should acquire functional understanding of the words *first, next,* and *last* across varying cues, events, objects, and places. The teacher's next responsibility would be to see that this newly acquired skill is integrated into other curricular areas. Thus, the student should be using his understanding of *first, next,* and *last* in the development of math, self-help, and home-living skills to mention just a few. At the same time a reassessment of the student's language needs, considered in conjunction with available program information, will dictate new levels of language learning toward which one should strive.

3. INSTRUCTION

CONCLUSION

Providing a meaningful educational program for severely handicapped students is an extremely complex process. Despite concerted efforts in this area, there are very few resources available to the classroom teachers who are responsible for educating these children at this time. This article presents an admittedly simplistic compilation of ideas and suggestions which it is hoped will be of some immediate usefulness to classroom teachers. Existing programs were not dealt with adequately, but it is hoped that teachers will avail themselves of the references provided for the purpose of pursuing more information regarding programs which seem appropriate to their use.

It seems obvious that we should be striving to establish a continuum of logical and functional language skills for the purpose of teaching them to severely handicapped students. It is imperative that our long- and short-term goals and objectives be specified and taught in a manner which does contribute to the maximum development of language skills over a period of time. As this is being done, we should also give consideration to the way in which given students will probably ultimately communicate. While the development of verbal language should be our goal for this population, whenever feasible, we should not lose sight of the fact that gestural communication and the use of various types of communication boards can also facilitate the communicative abilities of this population significantly at times. Whatever the specific nature of the language program being used, we must constantly be reminded to ask ourselves, "Are there modifications in language performance being observed?" and "Are new language behaviors being acquired within reasonable periods of time?" These questions are in effect the parameters which we must use to determine the effectiveness of our teaching programs.

It is also important that we integrate the results of our language training into the overall curriculum for the youngsters we teach. A critical question which we will consistently have to ask ourselves is, "Is the student using what he learns in the structured classroom situation in other places and situations and with other people? The overall worth of what we do with these youngsters will be determined by whether or not their interaction with their environment is improved immediately and, more importantly, for the future.

REFERENCES

Baer, D. M., & Guess, D. Receptive training of adjectival inflections in mental retardates. *Journal of Applied Behavior Analysis*, 1971, *4*, 129-139.

Baer, D. M., & Guess, D. Teaching productive noun suffixes to severely retarded children. *American Journal of Mental Deficiency*, 1973, *77*, 498-505.

Bandura, A. *Principles of behavior modification.* New York: Holt, Rinehart & Winston, 1969.

Barton, E. S. Inappropriate speech in a severely retarded child: A case study in language conditioning and generalization. *Journal of Applied Behavior Analysis*, 1970, *3*, 299-307.

Barton, E. S. Operant conditioning of social speech in the severely subnormal and the use of different reinforcers. *British Journal of Social & Clinical Psychology*, 1972, *11*, 387-396.

Bateman, B. *The essentials of teaching.* San Rafael, CA: Dimensions Publishing, 1971.

Bricker, W. A., & Bricker, D. D. A program of language training for the severely language handicapped child. *Exceptional Children,* 1970, *37*, 101-111.

Bricker, W. A., & Bricker, D. D. Assessment and modification of verbal imitation with low-functioning retarded children. *Journal of Speech and Hearing Research*, 1972, *15*, 690-698.

Brown, L., Scheuerman, N., Cartwright, S., & York, R. The design and implementation of an empirically based instructional program for severely handicapped students: Toward the rejection of the exclusion principle. Part III. Madison Public Schools, Madison, Wisconsin, 1973.

Brown, L., & Sontag, E. Toward the development and implementation of an empirically based public school program for trainable mentally retarded and severely emotionally disturbed students. Part II. Madison Public Schools, Madison, Wisconsin, 1972.

Brown, L. Williams, W. & Crowner, T. A collection of papers and programs related to public school services for severely handicapped students. Volume 4. Madison, WI: Madison Public Schools, 1974.

Brown, L., & York, R. Developing programs for severely handicapped students: Teacher training and classroom instruction. *Focus on Exceptional Children*, 1974, *6*(2).

Carrier, J. K. & Peak, T. *Non-speech language initiation program.* Lawrence, KS: H & H Enterprises, 1975.

Sign Language For the SMR and PMR

Toni Richardson

Author: TONI RICHARDSON, M.A., Co-Ordinator, Gestural Language Program, Southbury Training School, Southbury, Connecticut.

While progress continues in the development of techniques for educating and training the severely and profoundly retarded, the area of communication development has remained one of many difficulties and disappointments. These difficulties in teaching speech as the mode of communication were so apparent in the spring of 1972 at Southbury Training School, that several teachers, an audiologist and a psychologist jointly decided to explore an alternative approach to communication known as sign language.

While a prevalent though not always accepted means of communicating in the deaf world, sign language was receiving more favorable attention in the field of deaf education and was coming into discussion and into experimental use with the retarded (Larson, 1971; Levett, 1969, 1971; Bricker, 1972). After evaluating the limited amount of published information then available and after visiting an existing program at the Mansfield Training School in Mansfield, Connecticut, the teachers, psychologist and audiologist formed a team which proposed what has now become the sign language program at Southbury.

Program

Nine severely or profoundly retarded residents of the training school who were enrolled in half-day education programs were selected for the initial classes. Five of these first nine students were physically limited. Selection was made on the basis of their lack of ability to express language (the five physically handicapped) and on the lack of ability to receive or express in spite of hearing ability (the four nonhandicapped).

A 100-word vocabulary was selected. At the end of the first year, significant progress had been made by all nine students ranging from development of an expressive vocabulary of over 400 words by one of the physically handicapped to the development of a receptive vocabulary of 20 words by one of the nonhandicapped students.

At the beginning of the second year of the program the enrollment was increased to 23, with some students displaying emotional problems, some diagnosed as autistic. Using the basic approach of introducing signs as they become relevant to tasks being performed in the classroom and demanding production only after the student demonstrated an understanding of the sign and the physical ability and willingness to imitate it, progress was achieved by over 75% of the students in comprehension and in expression.

References

Bricker, D.D. Imitative Sign Training as a facilitator of word-association with low-functioning children. *American Journal of Mental Deficiency* 1972, **76**(5), 509-516.

Goehl, H. & Shaffer, T.R. The alinquistic child. *Mental Retardation,* 1974, **12**(2), 3-6.

Larson, T. Communication for the nonverbal child. *Academic Therapy,* 1971, **6**(3), 305-312.

Levett, L. M. A method of communication for non-speaking, severely subnormal children. *British Journal of Disorders of Communication,* 1969.

Levett, L. M. A method of communication for non-speaking, severely subnormal children – Trial results. *British Journal of Disorders of Communication,* 1971.

"Sign Language for the SMR and PMR," Toni Richardson, *Mental Retardation*, Vol. 13, No. 3, June 1975. © 1975 American Association of Mental Deficiency, Washington, D.C.

91

Classrooms for the Autistic Child

WAYNE SAGE

Once it seemed hopeless to send autistic children to school. Now a pioneering group in California is finding that these children can learn in a public classroom. And, in turn, they can teach us a lot about themselves.

Wayne Sage is a contributing editor to HUMAN BEHAVIOR.

There is one type of child that does not belong in school, his parents have always been told. His presence would be useless, even dangerous, said educators, administrators, social workers and most psychologists. But a small vanguard of autistic children seem to have proved the experts wrong.

The mere suggestion of enrolling an autistic child in a public elementary school would be enough to terrorize most principals. No kid gets kicked out of school these days for being slow to learn. Special classes for the retarded and the emotionally disturbed absorb those who cannot keep up with their peers. But once the word *autism* is written on a child's folder, he is viewed as little more than a dangerous vegetable, and until recently not even special education programs, public or private, would touch him.

The autistic child was thought dangerous because he is often self-destructive and sometimes does not confine his assaults to his own body. He may bite, kick, scratch, throw things at or urinate on any therapist who comes near. He was considered impossible to teach because of his self-stimulatory behavior, compulsive but mindless babbling, rocking, running, flailing of the arms or perhaps just obsessional study of his own fingers. In California, classes for the "educationally handicapped" are required to have at least 12 students

recognizing letters

to a classroom. Even one autistic child in such a setting would bring all instruction to a screeching halt.

Schools for the retarded and the emotionally disturbed are probably not the place for the autistic, anyway. They are often not retarded and the evidence is mounting that they

are not emotionally disturbed (see "Autism's Child," HB, Feb. 1974). Revolutionary laboratory and clinical studies are discovering that they can be both tamed and taught, and the parents of the last children to be fenced out of the schoolyard are demanding that they be let in at last.

"We're going to win. No doubt about it," Dr. Harvey Lapin said last year, referring to a class-action suit filed by parents of autistic children against the state of California. Dr. Lapin, a dentist and the father of an autistic child, was then president of the Los Angeles chapter of the National Society for Autistic Children. Along with the California Association for the Retarded, the organization argued that every child has a constitutional right to an education regardless of his or her handicap.

"Probably the state will capitulate," said Dr. Lapin. "By the time they [the state] know they're going to court, the kids will have all we're suing for." According to Tom Gilhool, a law professor at the University of Southern California who acted as advisor to the suit, such battles are building legal standards throughout the country. Several mass lawsuits grew out of the California movement. Parental activism reached an all-time high when the mothers and fathers of autistic children demanded to be heard in news articles, on television and radio programs and through aggressive legislative lobbying efforts. All of a sudden, autistic children were in the classroom.

In California, education for autistic children is now mandated. Pioneering efforts there seem to have established that such kids do indeed belong in school.

"I knew that if I could put together an expert in language and an expert in behavior modification, I'd have

something fantastic," says Florence Needels. Looking like the personification of compassionate determination, Needels is the project director of a program that is educating autistic children at three elementary schools in Southern California: Mark Twain Elementary School in Lawndale; Foster Elementary School in Bellflower; and Lassen Elementary School in Sepulveda.

Her Ph.D. language expert is Rookie Hirsch; the behavioral consultant is Alexander Tymchuk, an assistant professor of psychology at UCLA. The program that the three of them have put together is fantastic, to say the least. Four months after the program's inception, two of their autistic girls were working their way through standard reading and arithmetic manuals used in special education courses and even in regular elementary school classrooms. And one three-year-old autistic boy was reading.

When Mark Twain set aside three of its classrooms for the autistic in September 1974, the 20 prospective students were rated according to what services they might presently qualify for. Top priority went to "those who didn't have anything," Tymchuk remarks, "so we ended up with the worst." Community reaction was uncertain; backlash from the parents of normal children had already driven the program from one site while it was still in the planning stages. At Mark Twain, the atmosphere proved more accepting.

Even the worst autistic children have proven responsive to the controversial but undeniably effective punishment techniques developed in research laboratories. But transfer-

Students learn to make eye contact and kiss their playmates.

A tot does without lunch and is ignored after refusing the balanced meal.

3. INSTRUCTION

ring such methods to a public school system was a trick the Mark Twain team knew would not be easy.

To most laymen, mere mention of the words *behavior modification* still conjures up images of sadistic assistants chasing screaming children with electric cattle prods. "There is just no way I could bring an electric cattle prod in here," says Needels. Even punishment and reward systems are not trusted by the general public. "It's like living in the Dark Ages," says one of the school's specialists. "They think teachers don't care. They do. They care desperately. But you can spend all day saying 'quit' [to an autistic child] with no effect. It's only when they [traditional teachers] see you save that time with 10 minutes of a highly structured program that their minds change."

"The proper use of punishment is a very important part of our program," Needels emphasizes. But instructors at Mark Twain have been able to establish control of tantrums and self-stimulation without electric shocks or corporal punishment. Yet those in charge have realized that the elimination, not just the reduction, of self-stimulating behavior is usually essential if learning is to begin. The only way to accomplish this is through operant conditioning. The responses of each child are carefully studied. Treatment is then prescribed for each, to be put into effect immediately when such behavior begins. In no case does the teacher decide what the punishment should be.

In some instances, a child's prescription called for a "startle response"—loud shouts of "no!" coupled with slaps on the table. The program is so finely tuned to each child's needs that there are three levels of "no!" that can be prescribed. The first is a simple spoken "no." The second is a loud, angry "no!" The third is the startle "no!" The prescriptions are written by consensus agreement at weekly staff meetings where each child's program is reviewed and possible alternatives for handling him are argued from every angle. "Anyone who says he knows how to handle autistic children, I feel funny around," says Needels. "We're finding out that some things work with many of the children and we usually try those first, but you never really know. There has to be a way of shifting."

So far, one of the three levels of "no" has proved successful with every child in the program. However,

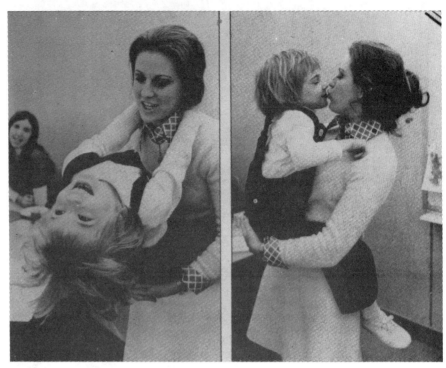

A therapist encourages a student to give affection and enjoy healthy play (above). Behavior therapy elicits direct eye contact and silence (at right).

"there is something about self-stimulation that is so perpetuating that when you insist on eliminating it they often slip over into a tantrum," Needels explains. "All my teachers have had their tetanus shots."

When the self-destructive behavior begins, the major weapon is isolation. The children are "trained to the wall." The teacher restrains the child, but she must not hold or console him. Either would only reinforce self-destruction. The teacher turns the child to the wall and spreads his arms out against it so that he cannot self-stimulate. Through conditioning, the wall thus becomes aversive and can be used to ward off the child's bouts with his own body. At first, screens were erected on each side of the child to block outside stimuli. Such screens are common in public school special education programs, according to Needels. "But our kids would knock over the screen onto another kid and go after the teacher to bite her."

For the extremely self-destructive child, hefty "time-out boxes" were constructed from wooden two-by-fours with open tops. The compartments were thickly padded and lined with black oilcloth so that the child could not bang his head against the walls or otherwise hurt himself once the door was tightly closed. Seven children's prescriptions called for these boxes. Although the huge struc-

tures still loom in two of the classrooms, the teachers have become so skilled at controlling such behavior, the boxes have not been used in over eight months. The program is limited to children two to nine years old. After that age, it is impossible for a single teacher to physically restrain a self-destructive autistic child.

When the simple "no" becomes enough to halt self-stimulation, the child is taught the prerequisites to instruction. Beginning with simple commands such as "sit down," "hands down" and "look at me," from here, his attention span is built and extended as his teacher rewards him with bites of his favorite food when he establishes eye contact with her.

A sampling of scenes at Mark Twain illustrates the success of inching from Point A to Point B.

"This is our biter, screamer, kicker, holy terror," says Needels, pointing out a beautiful little blonde girl. The girl looks around and smiles sheepishly. Needels goes over and puts her arm around the child. The girl nuzzles her face into her supervisor's neck. "Looks like I'm going to get a good loving this time and not a big bite," Needels remarks, still hoping she's right, and then turns the child back to face her teacher. "More work time now and then we'll love," Needels tells her.

In another part of the room, a boy

of four sits shivering as he fights to keep the tears in his eyes from falling down his face. His toddler-size chair has been pushed away from the table where his teacher sits ignoring him. Once the simple "no" has become enough to halt self-stimulation, if a child slides back into self-stimulation too often for instruction to proceed, he is removed from his desk and seated alone. He must bring himself under control before the teacher will attend to him. "He must learn self-control, not just manipulation," Needels explains, if the program is to have meaning.

In another room, a research assistant sits day after day in front of a boy of about five. "No, quiet," the therapist says and puts his hand to the child's lips. As soon as he takes his hand away, the child starts to babble in the monotone that blocks out the child's efforts at concentration. "No, quiet," the therapist says again and puts his hand over the child's mouth. "No, quiet . . . no, quiet . . . no, quiet. . . ." He continues the procedure again and again. Another research assistant seated beside him hits a stopwatch every time the therapist's hand is removed and records the time interval, continually only two or three seconds, before the child begins to babble. If the boy does remain quiet for even a few seconds, he is patted affectionately and told, "Good boy," but then as the babbling starts again, the therapist covers the child's mouth with his hand and insists on quiet. The procedure goes on and on. If over several days the data show that the babbling is beginning to extinguish, the procedure continues. If not, a new prescription will be written until one is found that works.

What will work, from token economics to sign language, is the overriding criterion for the methods that are used with each child. Those treatments that have no objectively discernible effect, such as psychoanalysis, are not considered appropriate for a public school program. "We don't worry about what caused it, whether it was organic or some psychological trauma. We just take in the kid as he comes and try to do something with him," says Needels.

Once self-stimulation and self-destruction are under control, the major goal is the development of useful language. But that stage often can be reached only through a tremendous number of minute steps. Not only can some children not associate or even

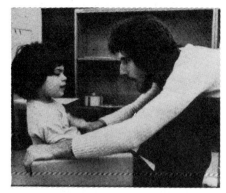

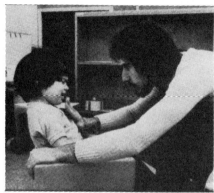

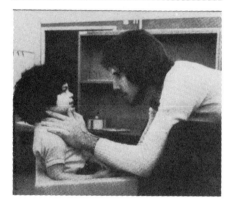

pronounce words, they sometimes do not have the cognitive skills that will allow them to benefit from language instruction.

Most theorists believe a child first organizes his world without language. He then learns to impose words upon it. Only after this receptive stage does he begin to use words symbolically to communicate with others. In order to draw an autistic child first into the receptive stage, his teacher seats him at a table before three objects, such as a toy chair, a doll and an apple. He is rewarded with bites of food when he picks up one of the objects and then when he hands it to the therapist. Once the command "Give me " is understood, the therapist will say, "Give me chair " or "Give me apple." If the child makes the correct response, he is rewarded with another bite of food and patted affectionately.

He thus learns to impose words on the objects, and the foundation of his receptive vocabulary is laid. Later, he will need to repeat the words himself. For some children, language must be built from the basics up, beginning with only vowel sounds, then going on to consonants and consonant blends and then to whole words. For others, symbolic gestures must be taught to communicate with the child until verbal language can be built.

The cognitive processes that allow even this instruction may be absent. If so, they must also be built. Simple concepts such as same versus different are developed by asking the child to match colored blocks to squares of the same color drawn on paper. And if the child is ever to read, he must be able to associate two dimensional representations with the three dimensional objects he is learning to name.

One characteristic of the autistic child is that he keeps experiencing every learning situation as though it were happening for the first time. Full color photographs are taken, for example, of the actual apple and toy chair to be used. The pictures are placed on the bottom of each compartment of an open box. The child is asked to put each object into the space where its picture lies. Photos of the same apple to be presented to the child must be taken because the child does not yet understand the concept of "appleness." That is, although he may learn to match the apple with its own photo, he may not be able to understand that the photo of a different apple is also an apple. As such generalization is taught, the cognitive processes are being built that will hopefully enable him eventually to use words meaningfully.

Although language is the key to higher learning, for the autistic, education also must include the basics of how to live. Some of the children were not even toilet trained at the beginning of the year. Instruction in buttoning and unbuttoning clothes, pushing and pulling doors and washing hands are all part of the curriculum at Mark Twain. At lunch time, eating a meal according to ordinary human custom is taught. The autistic are known for their bizarre eating habits—insisting on one brand of salami, for example, or living on Kentucky Fried Chicken only. In order to normalize their diets, children first are given food they ordinarily would not accept. The foods they like are used as rewards for eating. Here again the

3. INSTRUCTION

obstacles to learning can be surmounted only by the teacher with supreme patience and skill. One boy sat nearly in tears as he sucked uselessly at a section of an orange, stuffing it sideways in his mouth and then spitting it out in his hand to try again. His teacher turned the section so as to bring only the edge of the morsel between his teeth and then nudged his jaw upward saying "bite." As his teeth finally went into the orange, he got the idea and continued to chew happily.

When their delicate attention spans begin to wane, the children are taken outside to learn to play. Each child's instructor accompanies him onto the grounds and structures his activities into the standard children's games such as riding a tricycle or throwing and catching a ball. As soon as the child has learned to play alone, he is taught to play alongside another child and, eventually, to play with him. Although, generally, the autistic children are kept completely separate from the regular school children, occasionally a normal child is brought in to play with the more advanced autistic children, to serve as a model. The regular kids consider it a treat to go over to play wtih the autistic children and compete with one another for the privilege of doing so. Recently, an integration program has gotten underway. A youngster from the regular classes at Mark Twain comes over and gets his friend from the classrooms for the autistic and takes him to lunch in the school cafeteria or to other school activities.

For the more advanced kids, a physical therapist is brought in for coordination exercises, which sometimes take the form of a game of Simon Says. "Simon says touch your left elbow," intones the therapist. Two of the verbal girls can now exchange places with the teacher in this game. "Simon says touch your head to your foot," says one autistic girl, and the therapist strains to obey.

Those social and emotional aspects of life that most of us experience without conscious effort must be taught to the autistic. They are nudged into camaraderie with one another, and the emotional coldness that supposedly marks them all begins to disappear. One teacher lifted an autistic boy from his desk to find herself caught in a joyful bear hug with his arms around her neck and his legs

Sensory exercises spur maturity in the autistic child (at left). In the rear is an isolation box for the very self-destructive—unused for many months. When attention wanes, it's time for a game of ball outside (above).

around her waist. "This is the autistic child who does not show love and affection," she said weakly.

One night a week, parents of the Mark Twain autistic children can attend workshops in behavior modification that will help them to extend their children's education into the home. With programs such as the one at Mark Twain, home life for the family of the autistic child is at last beginning to normalize. The state of California has closed down large numbers of its mental hospitals and therefore has tacitly taken the position that psychotic kids should be kept at home. Most experts agree that the home is the only place where autistic children, as well, can possibly progress. Yet by providing no community services or public school programs, the state forces parents into a Catch 22 situation—they have been forced to institutionalize their children, although it is cheaper to keep them at home where most parents and the state would prefer them.

But then the benevolence of neither the state nor society as a whole is to be thanked for the Mark Twain program, according to Dr. Lapin. "Society couldn't give a good flying fuck what happens to autistic kids," he says. "The handicapped are the most discriminated-against group in America. Hell, they don't even have civil rights." Certainly, the Mark Twain program has disproved any argument that autistic children cannot benefit from education. Probably other programs like the one in California can

no longer be denied.

A few months after the program started, all of the autistic children at Mark Twain, their families and the project staff gathered for a potluck dinner to celebrate the program's successes thus far. The autistic kids took their seats at the table alongside their families and showed off their new social skills. "They were beautiful," says Needels proudly.

Afterward, Tymchuk gathered with the students' healthy siblings for a discussion of what it's like to be the brother or sister of an autistic child. Home life for the families is at last beginning to normalize. "We're very lucky to have a very good, very emotionally strong group of parents," Needels declares. "Some of the husbands and wives haven't been out for an evening alone together since the birth of their autistic child. Of course," she adds, "there was no getting a baby-sitter." Now that the kids are more manageable, that should change. A program for the summers and holidays has made state and county recreational facilities available to the autistic for the first time.

Parents of autistic children from across the country write in, some of them willing to move to California and live there for a year to establish residence in the hope of getting their children into a public school. Others have taken to activism in their own areas. "Hell, every child is deserving of an education," says one parent. "They can't lose."

Take a Giant Step to Independent Living

Adaptive Toothbrushing

RALPH H. SAUNDERS, JR.

Ralph H. Saunders, Jr., is a resident in clinical dentistry, School of Medicine and Dentistry, University of Rochester, New York.

Children with multiple handicaps and retardation ranging from moderate to severe can be taught a protocol for brushing their teeth when a few pieces of simple equipment are constructed and provided for them. Instruction and guidance in the proper methods for care and use of equipment are provided by the teacher and may be supplemented by a dentist or dental hygienist. The techniques are reinforced daily by the teacher, as severely handicapped children take a giant step toward independent living skills.

CHOOSING AND ADAPTING THE RIGHT TOOTHBRUSH

Many types of toothbrushes are available that vary in size, design, bristle hardness, length, and arrangement. It may be best to start all children with a soft brush, which is less likely to produce acute trauma to oral tissues, until the child's ability to manipulate the brush can be observed. The size necessary can probably be determined by simple observation of the child's hand and mouth, but some trial and error may be necessary.

The proper diameter of the brush handle should be selected next. If the child can close his hand completely and has little or no limitation of movement, no adjustment may be necessary. If a larger handle is required, the proper size can be determined by adding modeling clay, crinkled foil, or Styrofoam plastic until the proper size is reached.

To make the buildups more permanent, bicycle handle grips in the proper size are especially successful. Fill the grip with a fairly thick mix of plaster of paris by shaking and tapping against the side of the table. Insert the brush handle into the plaster, but be careful to leave enough of the bristle end exposed so that the child can reach the back teeth.

Another useful buildup is a wooden handle to which the brush is attached with screws. The handle is at an angle of approximately 20 degrees to the long axis of the brush. The angle permits the child to reach many teeth with less refined movements. This attachment is easily made in a school workshop. A third possibility is to pierce a small (2¼ inch diameter) rubber ball with an ice pick and then with the brush handle.

The next step is to determine whether the child can retain the brush in his hand throughout the brushing procedure. If not, fasten elastics to the brush to pass across the child's hand and help him hold the brush firmly. Strips of elastic ½ inch in width work well and are available from any dry goods store. Care must be used in selecting the proper length as severely retarded children may not be able to tell you if elastics are too tight. Two grooves are cut completely around brush handles at areas selected for attachment with a small triangular file. The elastics are then tied at each end in the grooves with monofilament fishing leader line available from any sporting goods department. To fasten elastics to the built-up brushes, grooves are cut in the rubber handles and elastics are attached to wooden handles with small tacks.

GETTING READY

To maintain optimum cleanliness, the toothbrushes must have covers. A satisfactory type is the Oral B Toothbrush Travel Case, available from a drugstore. The case covers only the bristle end and is especially good for the built-up brushes. The cover stays closed by means of two small snap tabs, which may be reduced in height with a nail file or razor blade for the child with weakened pull or grasp.

Store the brushes in a rack that is easily cleaned and readily available to handicapped children. A convenient type is made from pressed board with Formica covering on one side. The racks are built with a wide stance to prevent tipping and have widely spaced slots for easy access. Temporary storage can be half-pint milk cartons opened completely and rinsed well.

An important part of the toothbrushing procedure is the child's selection of his own brush. To aid in identification, affix labels to handles, covers, and slots in the rack. To further simplify identification, brush covers may be coded with brightly colored tape.

LOOK, I CAN DO IT!

The child who is to brush comes to the sink and washes his hands. He pours a cup of water to be ready for rinsing. He selects the brush from the rack, removes the cover, and sets it aside. The brush is moistened to make it ready for paste. The teacher or aide instructs the child to begin brushing.

There are several methods for brushing. Glickman (1972) noted that thoroughness rather than technique is the important factor in determining the effectiveness of brushing. Spilke (1974) found that in most cases a scrub technique with a soft brush is highly effective. The method selected may be based, at least in part, on motions easiest for the child to perform. When the child finishes, the observer should see that the brush is well rinsed.

Observe the child closely during the entire procedure and help him with those

3. INSTRUCTION

parts that are difficult for him. Attempt to gradually but steadily decrease the amount of aid given so the child will learn to become as independent as possible.

. . . AND I DID!

In actual practice, one class of seven trainable students and two classes of severely retarded children with multiple handicaps were observed over a period of 10 weeks.

Greatest improvement was seen in the trainable class in which all but one of the students learned the entire procedure, and significant improvement was seen in the other groups.

Based on observations, it appears that toothbrushing can be thoroughly learned by trainable mentally retarded students and learned to a significant degree even by students with severe retardation. Any such learning will help increase an individual's personal maintenance. It seems

to follow, moreover, that a positive experience in this activity will permit easier learning in other areas and that toothbrushing, therefore, might be a step in the process of learning increased independent living skills.

REFERENCES

Glickman, I. Clinical periodontology (4th. ed.) Philadelphia: W.B. Saunders Co., 1972
Spilke, H. The dentist and the mentally retarded. New York State Dental Journal, 1974, 40, 214.

A Rapid Method of Teaching Profoundly Retarded Persons to Dress by a Reinforcement - Guidance Method

Nathan H. Azrin
Ruth M. Schaeffer
Michael D. Wesolowski

ABSTRACT. Dressing and undressing is a major problem for the adult profoundly retarded person. A new program was developed that included lengthy and intensive training sessions, a forward sequence of steps rather than backward chaining, graduated and intermittent manual guidance, continuous talking and praising, graduated sized clothing, and an emphasis on reinforcers natural to dressing. The seven profoundly retarded adults who received the dressing training learned to dress and undress themselves in an average of 12 hours distributed over 3 or 4 training days.

Introduction

Normal non-retarded children learn to dress with no special training, but profoundly retarded persons often have not learned the minimal dressing skills even as adults.

Behavior modification programs, such as Bensberg's (1965) early efforts, had offered hope that profoundly retarded persons could be taught to dress. Although these new procedures appeared effective for higher level persons, the evidence has been that little or no success occurs for the profoundly retarded. Minge and Ball (1967), in training six profoundly retarded girls for 30 training hours, found some improvement in undressing but virtually no improvement in dressing. Horner (1970) provided dressing training to 83 severely and profoundly retarded persons and found that about one-third could not be trained. The others required an average of 70 sessions. Ball, Seric and Payne (1971) found only slight improvement in the dressing skills of retarded boys after 90 days of training. Watson (1972) estimated that 8 to 12 months would be required to teach the profoundly retarded. In summary, the evidence indicates that the new behavior modification procedures have been of value, but have not been substantially successful in teaching dressing to the profoundly retarded, even after many months of training.

Several reinforcement procedures for teaching dressing skills have been described in detail and in overall rationale (Bensberg, Colwell & Cassell, 1965; Breland, 1965; Minge & Ball, 1967; Bensberg & Slominski, 1965; Ball, Seric & Payne, 1971; Horner, 1970; Watson, 1972). Almost all of these reports have the following procedures in common: Food snacks or praise serve as the reinforcers; reinforcement is given at the completion of the act of taking off or putting on a specific garment; an instruction is given to start each trial for a given garment; "backward chaining" is used for each garment whereby the instructor himself puts on or takes off the garment almost entirely, allowing the student to complete only the final portion; the student learns to deal with one article of clothing before proceeding to the next; finally, the instructor fades out the instructions and the reinforcers. Brief training sessions of about 15 minutes duration are used over a period of many weeks or months.

The present study designed and evaluated a new program for teaching dressing and undressing and incorporated the following principal characteristics:

1. Instead of backward chaining, the method used a forward sequence in which the student participated fully in the initial, as well as in the final, components of the dressing actions.

2. Instead of trials involving only one article of clothing, the entire dressing or undressing sequence was used.

3. Instead of a single sized garment, the program used larger sizes initially.

4. Instead of using snacks and praise exclusively, the program used reinforcers intrinsic to dressing and undressing, and also used praise and stroking on a near-continuous basis rather than only at response completion.

5. At the start of training, instructions were given nearly continuously rather than only at the beginning of a trial.

"A Rapid Method of Teaching Profoundly Retarded Persons to Dress by a Reinforcement-Guidance Method," Nathan H. Azrin, Ruth M. Schaeffer, and Michael D. Wesolowski, *Mental Retardation*, Vol. 14, No. 6, December 1976. © 1976 American Association of Mental Deficiency, Washington, D.C.

3. INSTRUCTION

6. Manual guidance, which has been noted only incidentally as a teaching method, was used as a major component.

7. The program incorporated provisions for fading out this assistance by a Graduated Guidance and Intermittent Guidance feature.

8. Training was made more intensive by increasing the duration of each session of two to three hours and providing two sessions per day.

9. To reduce confusion of the student, dressing was taught separately from undressing.

10. To increase initial success, the undressing, which was easier, was taught before dressing.

11. The objective was to teach dressing to the profoundly retarded within a few days and in a very enjoyable atmosphere.

Method

Students. All residents in a state residential center for retarded persons were considered for training. Of the 20 residents who were unable to dress, even after instruction and slight assistance, seven were selected for training. Twelve residents, were not included because they had physical problems which prevented them from dressing entirely without assistance. One other resident was excluded who was so passive as to require total feeding by the employees. The seven students had an average age of 31 years of which an average of 25 years was spent institutionalized. Three were male and four female. None had functional speech. They had an average Social Age of 1.6 years as measured by the Vineland Social Maturity Scale (1965) and an average Mental Age of less than 1.5 years as measured by the Merrill-Palmer Scale of Mental Tests (1965). Four students exhibited substantial behavioral stereotypy.

Dressing-Undressing Test. Prior to training, each student was given a standard test on at least two occasions to assure that the student could not dress. This same test was readministered at the start of each training day and at the end of training to provide a standardized measure of progress.

Identification and use of reinforcers. The attendants were interviewed to determine what was reinforcing for each student. To the extent possible, all of the reinforcers for a student were given for correct responses during training. The reinforcers which required substantial time, such as going for a walk, playing, being with a preferred employee, showering, napping, etc., were given only at the completion of each dressing-undressing sequence. The more discrete, short-duration reinforcers, such as snack items, were given after each garment was put on or removed. The non-interrupting types of reinforcers, such as praise and back-stroking were given virtually continually while the student was engaged in garment removal or dressing.

Positioning. The student was seated in a chair with a back support to eliminate unsteadiness while standing.

Both hands used. The student was taught to use both hands in handling each garment thereby reducing interfering actions by an unutilized hand.

Type of garment. Five types of garments were used: underpants, shoes, socks, pants, and shirt. All were the slip-on type with no laces, buttons,

zippers, belts or snaps to make success more attainable.

Clothing size approximation. For each garment, the student began with a garment which was two sizes too large. When the student required no more than touch assistance, the trainer used the next smaller size, thereby making success more likely at the start.

Entire Sequence. The student first learned to undress, removing the shoes, then the socks, pants, underpants, and finally, the more difficult shirt. The trainers themselves dressed the student for the next undressing trial. The student then undressed himself. After the student learned to undress, dressing training began, and the student dressed as well as undressed.

Forward sequence of steps. The student learned to put on (or take off) a garment using the normal forward sequence whereby one usually dresses rather than the interrupted and step-by-step backward chaining procedure.

Session length. The intensive reinforcement procedure permitted sessions of 3 hours duration in spite of the otherwise short attention span.

Use of student's name. If the student was not paying attention, the instruction was preceded by calling his name and if necessary directing his head toward the task.

Reason for reinforcement. The student was given an explanation each time he received reinforcement and regularly shown a mirror and praised for his appearance.

General vs. specific instruction. Instruction proceeded from the most general, i.e., "Get dressed," to more structured and specific, i.e., "Pull up your socks," to allow the student the opportunity to follow the more general instruction if he could do so.

Nature of the prompts and sequence. The first instruction for each garment was simply verbal. If a few seconds passed with no action, the trainer pointed at or touched the garment. After a few seconds, the instruction was repeated and the trainer molded the student's hands around the garment. If the student still was not participating, the trainer then described each movement the student was to make as he guided the hands through the necessary motion. The instructions were very specific. This procedure provided multisensory information: verbal, visual, auditory and tactual.

Delayed manual guidance for passive learners. Once a student demonstrated that he could deal with a particular garment without manual guidance, further guidance was delayed on subsequent trials. The instruction and pointing was repeated about every 10 seconds for one minute before manual guidance was used again. This procedure was needed for passive students who otherwise awaited the instructor's guidance.

Multiple trainers. Two trainers were present during the first training session and thereafter until the student could be easily managed by one. Both trainers provided praise, stroking and manual guidance, but only one trainer provided verbal instructions.

Graduated guidance. Gentle manual guidance was used with all students in the early stages of training. The trainer's hands were molded around the student's hands but not touching the article of clothing. A student who resisted guidance was never forced and guidance began again when the student was relaxed. The trainer's touch was lightened as the student began to respond more on his own. An instruction was never given unless the trainer was close enough to manually guide if necessary.

Intermittent guidance. Near the end of training, the trainer did not maintain touch contact all the time, rather he lightly and momentarily touched the student's hands only when he was not responding on his own or when he had difficulty.

Verbal praise and stroking. Whenever the student followed an instruction, the trainers provided praise and stroking but discontinued when the student resisted guidance (when graduated guidance was employed) or made no effort to follow the instructions (when intermittent guidance was employed). Praise and stroking began again when the student made an effort.

Intensive training on one garment. If a student experienced difficulty with only one or two garments, intensive training on only those garments began. Several trials of this intensive training were alternated with the complete sequence in order to keep the intensive training within the context of total dressing-undressing.

Results

All seven students learned to dress and undress themselves. The criterion for learning was that the student put on each of the five garments without assistance upon an initial instruction to put the garment on and, when instructed to take the garment off, remove each of five garments also without assistance. Figure 1 shows the percentage of students who reached this learning criterion as a function of training time. The fastest learner required only four training hours (less than one training day) whereas the two slowest learners both required 20 training hours (equal to four training days). The average time required was 12 hours. The median time (indicated by the 50% value of the ordinate in the Figure) was about 10 training hours, equivalent to two training days for the average student.

Prior to training, the students averaged only 7% successful attempts at handling each garment on the standard test and 10% success on the second test prior to training. At the end of training the students averaged 90% success on the same test.

Illustrative Case Study

Sid was nonverbal, 27 years old, and had been institutionalized since he was 5 years old. He was not toilet-trained. He could feed himself with a spoon but was messy. During his free time Sid normally sat on his bed with his legs drawn under his body. He was withdrawn and resistive and did not respond to ongoing activities. The attendants indicated that Sid liked sweet snacks, resting in bed, walking and playing outside.

At first it was necessary for the trainer to mold his hands around Sid's in order for him to undress, and Sid frequently became rigid during guidance. For example, one trainer said, "Sid, take off your pants." No response. The trainer repeated the

instruction and touched Sid's pants. No response. The trainer repeated the instruction and placed Sid's hands around the waistband of the pants. No

FIGURE 1

Per cent of students trained to criterion as a function of training time.

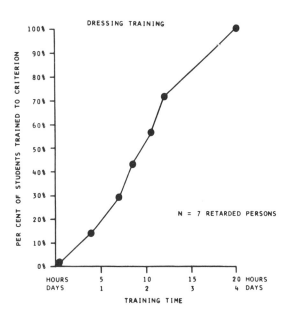

response. The trainer said, "Take off your pants", then, with his hands molded around Sid's, said "Push them down to your knees." "Good, you're pushing them down!" "Now push them to your feet." "Good you're pushing them!" "Get your foot out." When Sid became relaxed the trainer again molded his hands around Sid's and the back stroking began. When Sid had taken his foot out of the pants leg, the trainer praised him. While Sid was eating his snack, the trainers stroked his back and praised him.

When Sid was completely undressed, he enjoyed resting in bed for 5 minutes after which the trainers dressed him. Gradually, Sid began to do more of the undressing independently, and the trainer needed only touch Sid's hands lightly. Sid never resisted this touch guidance.

After Sid was removing all of his clothing in his normal size, dressing training began. When Sid had put on his clothes, the trainers told him "Sid, you're all dressed; now you can go outside and play." While Sid and the trainers were walking through Sid's living area they stopped an attendant and said, "Fred, doesn't Sid look great? He's all dressed and he did it practically all by himself!" Fred agreed and said, "Sid, you look so nice! You've put all your clothes on!" while he patted Sid on the back.

After Sid had been playing for a few minutes, he and the trainers went back to his room where he undressed and rested for a few minutes. Each time the sequence was repeated, Sid dressed and undressed more independently.

After a total of 10 hours of training, Sid had put on his pants and underpants with the trainer

3. INSTRUCTION

instructing and pointing at the pants. Consequently, instead of molding Sid's hands, the trainer repeated the instruction and pointed at the pants every 10 seconds. After the instructions had been repeated 3 times, Sid picked them up without guidance and put them on.

Sid needed only a touch occasionally to dress. When the trainer said, "Sid, put on your shirt," Sid began to pick up his shirt and the trainers praised Sid. After Sid had put the shirt over his head, he stopped. The trainer said "Put your arm in," then pointed at the sleeve and stopped praising. After 2 seconds, the trainer lightly touched Sid's elbow, whereupon Sid pushed his arm through the sleeve and the trainers praised him.

After 12 hours of training, Sid, for the first time in his life, took off all of his clothes when asked to undress and put on all of his clothes when asked to dress. Other staff members were understandably surprised and praised him a great deal when he got undressed and dressed himself again to go outside for a walk. In order to maintain Sid's skills, the attendants needed only to touch his hands occasionally when he was dressing or undressing and to praise him when he was finished.

Discussion

The dressing program achieved the objective of rapidly teaching all of the profoundly retarded adults to dress and undress themselves in simple garments without the need for assistance. All seven students achieved mastery. The average time required for mastery was about two training days, each day including five hours of training. A standard test of dressing skills showed less than 10% mastery when administered before training. These results show that mastery was not attributable to simple testing and retesting. The same test showed almost total mastery after training. The applicability of the program to retarded persons with very low levels of development is evidenced by the extremely low level of functioning possessed by the present study: The students had an average mental age equivalency of one and one-half years and yet averaged 31 years of age in actuality. The present method taught retarded persons who had an IQ as low as 10, long institutionalization up to 41 years, had failed previous efforts, had extensive behavioral stereotypies, had no speech, and no other self-care skills.

The applicability of the present method to children cannot be estimated directly from the results presented thus far, since only adults were included in this formal study. An informal attempt to use this method with two profoundly retarded children was most encouraging but indicated that some slight changes in procedure would be desirable. First, the snack treats may not be as useful as reinforcers for children as they are for adults because of the greater prevalence of "food-finikiness" of children. On the other hand, praise, hugging, and back-stroking seemed more effective with the children. A second difference is the greater likelihood of temper tantrums among children. The solution for this problem was to provide the child with a brief period of required relaxation on a chair until the child had become calm. A third difference was the greater desire for activity by the children. This problem was solved by using various play activities as the reinforcer for the child at the end of each dressing sequence, and by reducing or eliminating the bed rest that had been scheduled as a reinforcer for most adults at the end of the undressing sequence. With additional simple changes of the same type, the present methods seem potentially as applicable to young retarded children as has been found true for adults.

Physical disability seems to present the major obstacle to general applicability of the present method to the profoundly retarded person since physical disabilities are so frequently associated with this extreme degree of retardation. In the present study, 12 persons had a physical limitation that made it impossible for them to put on, or take off, the garments without assistance. They were excluded from the study since the results would have had to be reported in a manner that was individually related to the specific nature of each physical disability. Yet, for many of these profoundly retarded persons with physical disability, some degree of mastery of learning to dress and undress many of the garments could have been achieved, especially if some assistance were given.

In previous studies, rapid success has been achieved in teaching profoundly retarded persons to toilet themselves (Azrin & Foxx, 1971; Foxx & Azrin, 1973), to stop bedwetting (Azrin, Sneed & Foxx, 1973), to stop self-stimulation (Azrin, Kaplin & Foxx, 1973), to stop self-injury (Azrin, Gottlieb, Hughart, Wesolowski, & Rahn, 1975), to discontinue aggressive disruptive behaviors (Foxx & Azrin, 1972; Webster & Azrin, 1973) and to eat properly (Azrin & Armstrong, 1973). The present method provides a similarly rapid and effective training program to teach profoundly retarded persons to dress themselves.

References

Azrin, N. H. & Armstrong, P. M. The "mini-meal"—A method for teaching eating skills to the profoundly retarded. *Mental Retardation*, 1973, 11 (1), 9-11.

Azrin, N. H. & Foxx, R. M. A rapid method of toilet training the institutionalized retarded. *Journal of Applied Behavior Analysis*, 1971, 4 (2), 89-99.

Azrin, N. H., Gottlieb, L., Hughart, L., Wesolowski, M. D., & Rahn, T. Eliminating self-injurious behavior by educative procedures. *Behaviour Research and Therapy*, 1975, 13 (2/3), 101-111.

Azrin, N. H., Kaplan, S. J. & Foxx, R. M. Autism reversal: Eliminating stereotyped self-stimulation of retarded individuals. *American Journal of Mental Deficiency*, 1973, 78 (3), 241-248.

Azrin, N. H., Sneed, T. J. & Foxx, R. N. Dry-bed training: Rapid elimination of childhood enuresis. *Behavior Research and Therapy* 1974, 12 (3), 147-156.

Ball, T. S., Seric, K. & Payne, L. E. Long-term retention of self-help skill training in the profoundly retarded. *American Journal of Mental Deficiency, 1971,* 76 (3) 378-382

Bensberg, G. J. *Teaching the mentally retarded: A handbook for ward personnel.* Atlanta, Georgia: Southern Regional Education Board, 1965.

Bensberg, G. J., Colwell, C. N. & Cassel, R. H. Teaching the profoundly retarded self-help activities by behavior shaping techniques. *American Journal of Mental Deficiencyy*, 1965, 69 (5) 674-679.

Bensberg, G. J. & Slominski, A. Helping the retarded learn self-care. In G. J. Bensberg (Ed.), *Teaching the mentally retarded: A handbook for ward personnel.* Atlanta, Georgia: Sourthern Regional Education Board, 1965.

Breland, M. Application of method. In G. J. Bensberg (Ed.), *Teaching the mentally retarded: A handbook for ward personnel.* Atlanta, Georgia: Southern Regional Education Board, 1965.

Foxx, R. M. & Azrin, N. H. Restitution: A method of eliminating aggressive-disruptive behavior of retarded and brain damaged patients. *Behaviour Research and Therapy*, 1972, 10 (1), 15-27.

Foxx, R. M. & Azrin, N. H. *Toilet training the retarded: A rapid program for day and nighttime independent toileting*. Champaign, Illinois, REsearch Press, 1973.

Horner, R. D. *Detailed progress report: Behavior modification program to develop self-help skills*. Final report. Wheat Ridge, Colorado: State Home and Training School, June 1968 to June 1970.

Merrill-Palmer Scale of Mental Tests. Beverly Hills, California: Western Psychological Service, 1965.

Minge, M. R. & Ball, T. S. Teaching of self-help skills to profoundly retarded patients. *American Journal of Mental Deficiency*, 1967, 71 (5), 864-868.

Vineland Social Maturity Scale. Circle Pines, Minnesota: American Guidance Service, 1965.

Watson, L. S. *How to use behavior modification with mentally retarded and autistic children: Programs for administrators, teachers, parents and nurses*. Libertyville, Illinois: Behavior Modification Technology, Inc., 1972.

Webster, D. R. & Azrin, N. H. Required relaxation: A method of inhibiting agitative-disruptive behavior of retardates. *Behaviour Research and Therapy*, 1973, 11 (1), 67-78.

Developing an Instructional Sequence for Teaching a Self-Help Skill

Educational Materials

EUGENE EDGAR
JENNIFER MASER
DEBORAH DEUTSCH SMITH
NORRIS G. HARING

Most teachers of handicapped children become frustrated by their inability to obtain sufficient quantity of commercially available instructional materials which provide systematic procedures for teaching basic life skills. Therefore, in addition to performing typical classroom duties, teachers develop their own instructional materials and techniques to meet the needs of individual pupils. Valuable time could be saved and perhaps more effective teaching strategies developed if validated effective instructional materials were available.

Model Development

A prototypic model for preparing instructional materials was developed (Smith, Smith, & Haring, 1974) at the Experimental Education Unit (College of Education, and Child Development and Mental Retardation Center, University of Washington). This model offers developers of educational materials, either commercial agencies or individual educators, a detailed set of procedures or a process to follow in creating instructional sequences. The programs which result from this process teach specific skills in minimal time with minimal error by student or teacher.

The Prototypic Model: Components

To clarify the following brief discussion of this model, we will use as an example one instructional program developed through this process—the Shoe Tie Program (Smith, Smith, & Haring, 1974). [For a more detailed description of the prototypic model see Smith, Smith & Edgar, 1976].

Prerequisite knowledge. Before writing the instructional sequence, the programer must have or acquire both the skill to be taught, in this case shoe tying, and basic programing techniques. Techniques such as cueing, fading, chaining, modeling, and overlearning are important aspects of developing instructional frames for errorless learning.

Primary decisions. The programer must specify the *exact* skill to be taught. In this example, shoe tying is the specific skill and terminal objective of the proposed instructional sequence.

The second decision concerns the intended audience or target population for whom the program is to be written. The Shoe Tie Program was designed for any individual who can pinch, pull against tension, and imitate or model the actions of others (these are "entry behaviors").

Lattice format. Once these decisions are made, the programer completes a task analysis of the skill and displays it in lattice format. A lattice is a graphic display of a skill analysis which facilitates communication about the target skill and its component steps. [For a more detailed discussion of lattice development see Smith,

"Developing an Instructional Sequence for Teaching a Self-Help Skill," Eugene Edgar, Jennifer Maser, Deborah Deutsch Smith, and Norris G. Haring, *Education and Training of the Mentally Retarded*, Vol. 12, No. 1, February 1977. © 1977 Council for Exceptional Children Division of Mental Retardation.

Smith and Edgar, 1976]. Figure 1 is the lattice for the Shoe Tie Program.

Pretest. Using the lattice, the programer develops a pretest to assess whether the student can perform either the target skill or the entry behaviors the programer believes are necessary for mastering that skill. Those children who on the pretest demonstrate mastery of the target skill are excluded from program validation process as are those who do not possess the required entry skills. The pretest also is used to determine differential placement in the program as all children may not need to begin the sequence at the first lesson. Test items, therefore, are constructed for each component of the target skill, including the entry behaviors (e.g., pinch, pull against tension, and imitate or model the actions of others).

Program format. Next, the programer selects the specific format: many options exist, such as a series of worksheets which do not require teacher assistance, or structured lessons administered by the teacher. The Shoe Tie Program was developed for one-to-one teaching. Since this is an expensive educational procedure, the program was designed to be administered by adult volun-teers, paraprofessionals, teachers, or peer volunteers.

Initial Field Testing of the Shoe Tie Program

Initial fieldtest population. The first group of students to receive the instructional sequence is selected after the pretest is administered to a group of potential learners. Since programers need to know whether the entire lesson sequence is effective, only those who possess all the entry behaviors, but none of the skills taught from the first lesson onward are selected.

Phase 1. During the first phase of initial fieldtesting, the programer concurrently develops, tests, and refines each lesson and the accompanying inexpensive instructional aids, until the entire program package is complete. The only teaching aid developed for the Shoe Tie Program was a simple device used to teach pinching and pulling a shoelace.

The sequence. Although more than one lesson may be required to teach any given component of the target skill (the enroute behaviors), the aim of the lesson sequence is to move the student progressively closer to the target skill. After the

FIGURE 1. Lattice for SHOES TIED

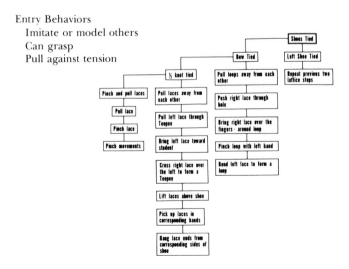

D. D. Smith, J. O. Smith, & E. Edgar. Research and application of instructional materials development. In N. G. Haring & L. Brown (Eds.), *Teaching the severely handicapped: A yearly publication of the American Association for the Education of the Severely/Profoundly Handicapped*, Vol. 1. New York: Grune & Stratton, 1976. Reprinted with permission.

3. INSTRUCTION

first lesson is written, it is tested on one or two students. When we reached this phase of developing the Shoe Tie Program, if more than 10 percent of error occurred on any lesson, the lesson was rewritten and retested. The second lesson was then written and tested. Once again, if errors exceeded the 10 percent criterion, the lesson was rewritten and retested. These procedures were repeated until all of the lessons were written and fieldtested on a small group of students. The lesson sequence which resulted from this process is shown in Table 1.

Phase 2. The second phase of initial fieldtesting is initiated when the entire sequence is developed, but not yet tested as a whole. This situation occurs because of the considerable amount of rewriting that normally occurs in the first phase of initial fieldtesting. Therefore, the entire program is tested on a small scale, and it is useful if the testing is performed by one or two of the program writer's colleagues in order to ensure unbiased feedback. This testing of the program by individuals who were not directly involved in its writing provides the programer with data on the clarity of the material. Feedback from these administrators enables the programer to rewrite any teacher directions which prove to be ambiguous or incomplete.

Six children at the Experimental Education Unit were selected for this second phase of initial fieldtesting of the Shoe Tie Program. All possessed only the entry skills specified in the pretest; and, therefore, were not differentially placed in the program at advanced levels. The entire sequence was tested to ensure that most error in fact had been eliminated in the previous fieldtest stage. Four of the six students chosen for the second fieldtest were enrolled in the Down's Syndrome Kindergarten. The fifth student was an 8-year-old moderately retarded boy, and the sixth student was an 18-year-old severely emotionally disturbed young man.

Results. One of the kindergarten students successfully completed the entire Shoe Tie Program in 21 sessions. After 44 sessions, the most severely handicapped 5-year-old student completed all but the last lesson. The other two kindergarten students failed to complete the program due to absenteeism and/or uncooperative behavior. The 8-year-old student completed the entire lesson sequence in 11 sessions, and the 18-year-old student learned to tie his shoes in 7 sessions. These fieldtest data indicated that the sequence enabled the children to master the terminal behavior with a minimum amount of error; hence the program was ready for secondary fieldtesting. If substantial error had occurred during the second phase of initial fieldtesting, the program would have been rewritten and retested, as was the case with several other programs.

Secondary Fieldtesting

Once the instructional program is written and successfully fieldtested with a limited number of subjects, the sequence is ready for more extensive fieldtesting. Multiple packages of the instructional program are produced. The teachers' manuals are edited, typed, duplicated (at least 50 copies), and bound. If supplemental materials such as teaching aids and student workbooks are used in the program, they must also be produced in sufficient quantity for the secondary fieldtest population.

Rationale. Additional fieldtesting is required for several reasons. First, it is important for more children to be included in the fieldtest population. This number need not exceed 50 youngsters, but should be more than the 5 to 10 students who participated in the initial fieldtest stage. Additional data are needed to validate the instructional sequence and to determine whether error pileup occurred because of unclear instructional frames.

Second, wider fieldtesting yields information about teacher-induced error. In the initial stage of fieldtesting the Shoe Tie program, the instructional programer and those familiar with his procedures tested the program. Because of the "in-house" nature of the initial fieldtesting, elements of the directions may have been omitted or written unclearly. Instructional programers frequently use jargon familiar only to themselves and their colleagues. This jargon could mislead or confuse the classroom teacher and could result in new student error.

Before an instructional program is ready for full-scale dissemination, those parts of the lesson sequence which caused teacher error should be isolated. By analyzing children's data and feedback from teachers using the program, the programer can locate problem areas. For instance, if numerous errors now occur in sections which were error-free in the initial fieldtesting, it is probable that teachers do not understand the directions. In some cases, error pileup occurs for one teacher and not for another. This kind of inconsistency will appear in children's data, indicating ambiguous or incomplete teacher directions. Often, however, student data fail to indicate some ambiguities which do in fact exist. For example, a teacher may not understand the directions in one section, but if he or she nevertheless teaches the section appropriately, the children's data will not indicate a need for rewriting. For that reason, it is important to collect this second kind of feedback: information from those using the program. Through direct communication, the programer can identify ambiguities which may exist in any part of the program package. *Whenever ambiguity or error occurs, the instructional programer has an obligation to rewrite the affected sections.*

Secondary Fieldtesting of the Shoe Tie Program

For the Shoe Tie Program, 24 special education teachers were contacted and 18 indicated a willingness to fieldtest the program with 32 of their students. All of these students had learning problems arising from conditions such as severe retardation and moderate developmental lags with considerable behavioral disorders. The students were well past the age when shoe tying is expected to occur in normal children and had experienced numerous failures in attempting to learn basic self-help skills. One teacher commented about a pupil: "If this child, who has very low academic abilities, can successfully complete this program, I feel almost anyone would be successful."

Results. After 45 instructional days, 12 teachers reported data on 25 students. Of those 25 students, 12 successfully completed the program (Table 1). The range of instructional days needed to meet criterion was 10 to 36 with a median of 19 days. Three additional students (two who did not have laced shoes and one confined to a wheelchair) completed Lesson 9, which required that they be able to tie the model shoe. Thus, 15 of 25 students successfully learned to tie shoes. The remaining 10 students experienced various problems with the program. One student's poor visual acuity impaired his performance. He was removed from the program until he could be provided with appropriate corrective lenses. Three other students (the poorest performers) had excessive behavioral problems that could not be controlled by their teachers. One child made no progress after Lesson 4; several others were frequently absent.

We analyzed each frame of the program to determine if we needed to rewrite any sections. "Pushes lace through hole" in objectives 14 and 18 were the only obvious problem areas in the program (Table 2).

We considered a reasonable criterion to be 3 days per lesson, and using this criterion, we found that these two objective checks in Lessons 5 and 6 appeared to be problematic. But by Lesson 7, this same objective (22, "pushes lace through hole") no longer produced a high frequency of error. The final Shoe Tie Program contained a warning to teachers that this skill appeared to be the most difficult to learn. The teachers were encouraged to give their students extra practice on this skill and to use tangible reinforcers if necessary.

Teachers' comments. From the follow-up questionnaire sent to all participating teachers, the only suggestion consistently made by the majority of teachers concerned the verbal instructions to the student. In order to determine whether these instructions were appropriate and helpful for the children, the secondary fieldtest administrators were asked to give the instructions *exactly as stated in the lessons.* The majority of teachers felt the instructions were cumbersome and in some cases difficult to follow while working with a child. The teachers wanted the lesson sequence to remain the same but with simplified instructions for the student and more leeway for modifying the lesson plan to suit individual children. Therefore, the revised program encouraged teachers to alter the verbal directions at their discretion and to provide extra assistance as needed; however, the lessons remained essentially unchanged.

Final Fieldtesting of the Shoe Tie Program

During the last phase of instructional materials development, enough program packages were produced to conduct final fieldtesting with another 25 to 30 students. The procedures used in secondary fieldtesting were repeated in order to validate the entire program, including all of the revisions. Final fieldtesting ensures that revisions based on secondary fieldtest data actually reduce student and teacher error.

Results. After a maximum of 25 instructional days, 9 administrators reported data on 25 students in the Shoe Tie Program. These students ranged from 6 to 21 years of age and were labeled from mildly retarded to severely handicapped. Of these 25 students, 9 successfully completed the program (Table 3). The range of instructional days needed to complete the program was 3 to 15, with a median of 8 days. Two additional children completed Lesson 9, which requires that they tie the model shoe. Thus, 11 of 25 students successfully learned to tie shoes (Table 4). Two other students left school before completing the program, two were still working on the

3. INSTRUCTION

TABLE 1
Results of secondary fieldtesting—shoe tie program

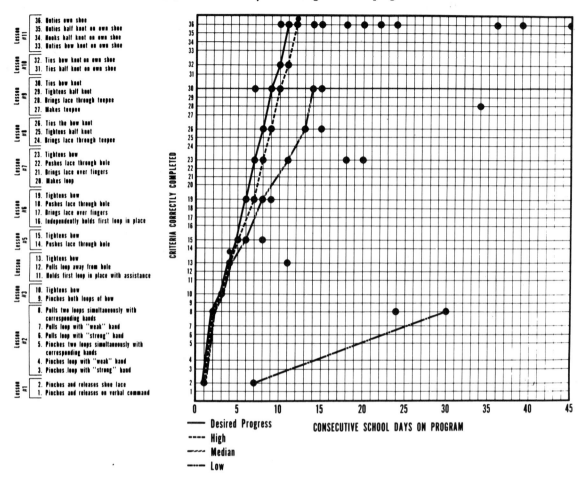

D. D. Smith, J. O. Smith, & E. Edgar. Research and application of instructional materials development. In N. G. Haring & L. Brown (Eds.), *Teaching the severely handicapped: A yearly publication of the American Association for the Education of the Severely/Profoundly Handicapped*, Vol. 1. New York: Grune & Stratton, 1976. Reprinted with permission.

program when the school year ended, and two failed the pretest for the program. The remaining 8 students who failed to learn to tie shoes were reported to have lost interest in learning to tie their shoes.

We analyzed each frame of the program to determine whether we would need to rewrite any sections. Using the criterion that more than three days per lesson indicated problem frames, we found that objectives 11 (holds first loop in place with assistance) and 12 (pulls loop away from hole) were the only problem frames. Five students required more than 3 days to acquire these skills. Interestingly, objectives 14 and 18, which caused substantial student error during secondary fieldtesting, did not cause excessive errors during final fieldtesting. When the data from both secondary and final fieldtesting are combined (Tables 2 and

4), there do not appear to be any problem lessons.

Comments. The data from the follow-up questionnaires received from the final field-test administrators indicated that the teachers felt comfortable with the added freedom permitted in their verbal instructions to the students. Additionally, the administrators expressed general satisfaction with the program and a desire to continue to use it with other children.

Two general comments about the final fieldtest are appropriate. First, what many administrators called "behavior problems" or "uncooperative behavior" were the most consistent reasons for pupils' not completing the program successfully. The pretest does not measure this aspect of pupil readiness and the materials do not provide the teacher with special means to motivate or

TABLE 2
Number of instructional days per student per criterion test

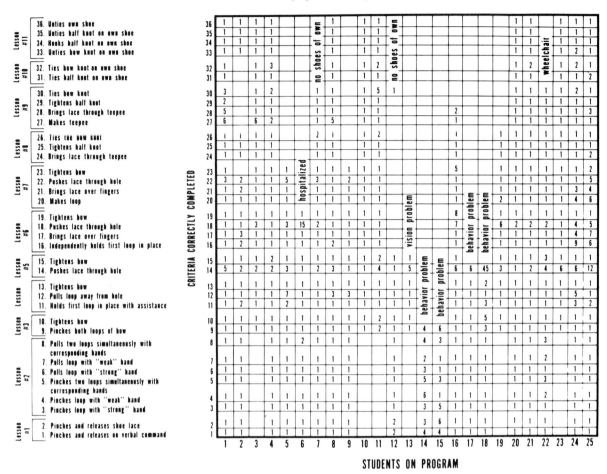

D. D. Smith, J. O. Smith, & E. Edgar. Research and application of instructional materials development. In N. G. Haring & L. Brown (Eds.), *Teaching the severely handicapped: A yearly publication of the American Association for the Education of the Severely/Profoundly Handicapped*, Vol. 1. New York: Grune & Stratton, 1976. Reprinted with permission.

control noncompliant pupils. As with all instructional techniques, the teacher maintains primary responsibility for insuring pupil compliance. Second, the materials appear to be well sequenced and appropriate for a wide range of pupils. For individuals who possess the entry skills, the Shoe Tie Program is an efficient method for teaching the skill of shoe tying.

Conclusions

To summarize: the specific skill taught by the instructional sequence we have discussed was selected and analyzed carefully so each step in acquiring the skill was identified and sequenced precisely, and the emerging program was fieldtested three times. The final phase of such an endeavor for any instructional programer is to deter-

mine the most appropriate means (e.g., federally sponsored clearing houses and commercial publishers) for disseminating the fully developed and verified instructional program.

Recently, many writers have commented on the lack of accountable instructional materials commercially available to teachers of the handicapped (e.g., Bliel, 1975; Meuser, 1973; Harmes, 1973). Several provided suggestions for upgrading instructional materials (Bliel, 1975; Latham, 1974). While some tend to place the burden of change on the consumers (e.g., Bliel, 1975), other writers assert that consumers (teachers) have little interest in fieldtesting materials (e.g., Latham, 1974).

Meuser (1973) called for instructional programs which: (a) describe characteristics of a specific target population, (b) state

3. INSTRUCTION

TABLE 3
Results of final fieldtesting—shoe tie program

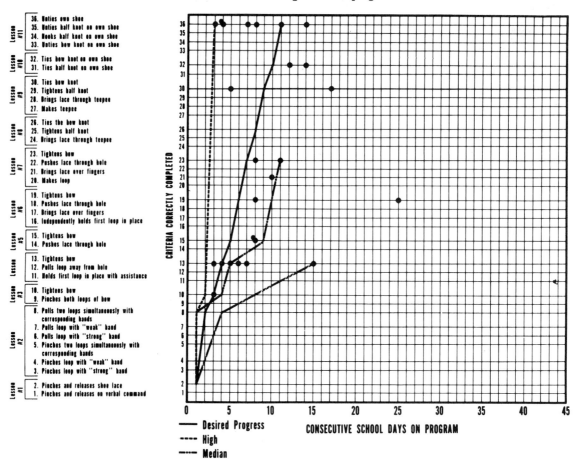

behavioral objectives precisely, (c) describe the procedures and techniques required for achieving the objectives, and (d) specify program management requirements. We would add that the programer needs to collect data to support the contention that the procedures are in fact effective with the target population when they are used by teachers. Additionally, we feel that materials need to be developed to meet the stated needs of teachers in the field.

The prototypic model for developing instructional materials, as described in this paper, is one systematic approach that provides hard data on the effectiveness of any given instructional material before it is placed on the open market.

Certainly these procedures are only one method of evaluating instructional materials. The National Center on Educational Media and Materials for the Handicapped in Columbus, Ohio is engaged in a massive, nationwide material evaluation procedure. Regional Learning Resource Centers and commercial publishers (Bliel, 1975) are also attempting to systematically evaluate materials. Until a set of common evaluation procedures is developed and adopted, many diverse procedures must continue to be used. Educational materials developed through procedures described in this paper ensure student skill acquisition and teacher ability to use the materials effectively and efficiently. Initial, secondary, and final fieldtesting provide specific child performance data; and secondary and final fieldtest data yield information on teachers' ability to use the materials appropriately.

There is no question that the process derived from this model is costly and time consuming. There is also no question that handicapped children, and teachers of these children, deserve well prepared instructional materials. In our experience, teachers in the field were very willing to aid in testing materials and programs—they assumed a large share of the responsibility in the

TABLE 4
Final fieldtest—shoe tie program. Number of instructional days per student per criterion test

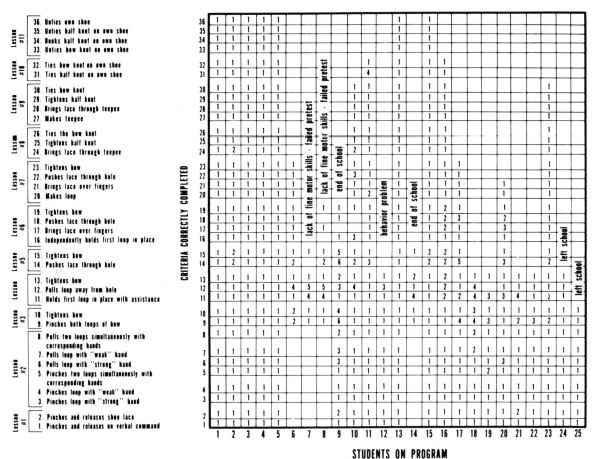

overall development of these instructional materials. At the market place, publishers of instructional materials must also assume some responsibility to handicapped children by telling consumers exactly how reliable their materials are.

We encourage teachers to be discriminating in selecting instructional materials. We encourage publishers to be discriminating in producing and advertising their materials. To our way of thinking, it hardly seems fair to compound the learning difficulties of a handicapped child, or the instructional challenge of his/her teacher, by producing materials that are incomplete, vague, poorly organized, or otherwise hampered. Such situations prevent us from providing an optimal educational opportunity for all handicapped children.

References

Bliel, G. Evaluating educational materials. *Journal of Learning Disabilities*, 1975, *8*, 19–26.

Harmes, H. M. Given a program: A new model of instructional research. *Educational Technology*, 1973, *8* (10), 23–25.

Latham, G. Measuring teacher responses to instructional materials. *Educational Technology*, 1974, *14* (12), 11–15.

Meuser, D. Building programs to meet evaluation design criteria. *Educational Technology*, 1973, *8* (10), 21–23.

Smith, D. D., Smith, J. O., & Edgar, E. A prototypic model for developing instructional materials for the severely handicapped. In N. G. Haring & L. Brown (Eds.), *Teaching the severely handicapped: A yearly publication of the American Association for the Education of the Severely/Profoundly Handicapped*, Vol. 1, New York: Grune & Stratton, 1976.

Evaluation of Self-Help Habit Training of the Profoundly Retarded

Cecil N. Colwell

Eileen Richards

Ronald B. McCarver

Norman R. Ellis

ABSTRACT. The training program at Columbia State School, Louisiana, a new short-term residential facility for intensive self-help training for the severely and profoundly retarded (CA, 4 to 16 years), was investigated. The first 47 children admitted made significant and substantial gains in dressing, feeding, toileting, and mental age (average stay, 7.1 months). Preliminary data regarding the extent to which certain children will benefit from self-help habit training are also presented.

THE TREND TO INSTITUTIONALIZE only the more severely retarded child has been evident for some years and is likely to become even more pronounced. Indeed, it seems likely that within a decade, institutional populations will consist mainly of the profoundly and severely retarded, perhaps with some from the moderate range with special problems. These and other signs point to the introduction of "transient institutions" serving several purposes, a major one being to provide a regimen of intensive training for the child.

Whether the institutions of this new age are for long-term or short-term training and care, the need for and focus on self-help habit training will quicken. Undoubtedly, some of the severely retarded will continue to spend their days within the protective environment of an institution, and their adaptation within this setting will be appreciably improved if they learn and maintain a repetoire of basic self-help skills. The need for training the transient resident is just as, if not more, compelling. Indeed, successful training procedures can lead to more effective adaptation within a community setting, thereby reducing the need for long-term institutional care.

Some research and much casual observation suggests that the effectiveness of training with children at the severely and profoundly retarded level is quite variable. In the main, the usual training regimen of the home has failed. In some instances, home training may have been intensive and enduring, carried out by informed and conscientious parents. Other children may have failed to develop skills because of a lack of training. Thus, a child's presenting behavioral inadequacies may be due to variations in the amount and effectiveness of previous training, interacting with variations in neurological integrity of the individual. Even though it has been said that the behavior of all children can be improved with training, the amount that a given child's behavior can be improved is of central importance. Can his behavior be modified to the extent that an aspect of his adjustment is substantially altered? Ideally, one could argue for training which yields reliable changes in any behavioral aspect, irrespective of whether or not those changes are of significance in adaptation. However, in view of limited resources, there is a need to focus on training procedures that yield substantive behavioral modification. Moreover, there is a clear need to focus on those areas of behavior most likely to improve substantially with training. This requires instructors to reliably and validly assess the results of training, and to predict with some accuracy those who are most likely to benefit from a particular type of training.

Few studies have attempted to measure the toileting, dressing, and feeding behaviors of the retarded child. Two scales, the Pinecrest Behavior Meters (PBM), (Cassel, Cassel, & Milford, 1967) and the Adaptive Behavior Scales (ABS), (Nihira, Foster, Shellhaas, & Leland, 1969) include items which purport to measure these skills. The consistency of agreement between two raters hearing the same information is reflected in reliabilities ranging from .85 to 1.00 for the different subareas of the PBM. Interrater reliability of the ABS was .86 for independent functioning, a category including these self-care skills. Validity studies are lacking for the PBM, but several studies of the ABS suggest its possible use in placement of the retarded into appropriate programs and its use in evaluation of operant conditioning programs for developing self-help skills.

"Evaluation of Self-Help Habit Training of the Profoundly Retarded," Cecil N. Colwell, Eileen Richards, Ronald B. McCarver, and Norman R. Ellis, *Mental Retardation*, Vol. 11, No. 3, June 1973. © 1973 American Association of Mental Deficiency, Washington, D.C.

Method

Training Program

The training program was carried out at Columbia State School (La.), a new short-term residential institution for profoundly and severely retarded children of CA 4 to 16 years. Children are accepted for periods of 2 to 12 months; the average stay for the initial 47 children was 7.1 months. The capacity of the institution is 32 residents, who are housed in two 16-bed units with each unit subdivided into subunits (bedrooms) of 4 beds each. Training in self-help skills is about a 15-hour-per-day regimen of intensive training and structural play carried out in the living quarters, the dining room, the playground and the training center. The training center consists of self-help motor skills and communication skills training rooms. These are adjacent to an observation room from which all training rooms can be viewed. In the training center, the children are rotated from motor training to self-help training, to communication training and outside play in groups of eight over a 6-hour period. Usually, the training is based upon operant procedures using positive, tangible rewards (candies, cookies, soda, etc.) which are faded out and replaced with social praise as training progresses. The present goal is to bring behavior in three main areas (toileting, feeding, and dressing) under verbal control. Somewhat less emphasis is placed upon motor skills, play activity and communication skills. A closed-circuit TV system provides the opportunity to observe and communicate with all areas in the school. This system is now being used to bring behavior in the various areas under verbal control without the physical presence of the trainer. All of the training in the school is carried out by non-professional personnel.

Measurement of Behavior Change

The focus of the present report is on the measurement and prediction of behavioral changes in three basic self-help areas—dressing, feeding, and toileting. Checklist type scales were developed at Columbia to measure performance along each of these dimensions. The items on each scale are arranged from simple to more complex skills. This arrangement parallels the course of the training regimen.

Dressing. The scale consists of 27 items ranging from taking off shirt, shorts, long pants, to putting on these items and including buttoning, zipping, hooking, snapping, lacing, buckling, etc. The items are weighted on an intuitive basis as to whether fine or gross movement is involved, one or two hands, the time required to complete the task, the number of steps involved in teaching, and number of discriminations required of the child. The scale is administered by a trainer (subprofessional) and then scored by a psychologist.

Feeding. The feeding scale consists of a checklist of 20 items arranged in steps indicating the extent to which a child is able to drink from a glass, use a spoon,

TABLE 1

	IQ	CA	Time in Institution
Mean	16.1	108 mo.	7.1 mo.
S.D.	8.3	32.4	2.8
Range	5–40	48–184	3–13

DESCRIPTIVE STATISTICS OF IQ, CA, AND PERIOD OF INSTITUTIONALIZATION FOR THE CHILDREN

fork, and knife. In addition, it evaluates the appropriateness of eating behavior, e.g., does he drink all of his milk? Does he use the appropriate instrument for a given food? A weighting procedure similar to the dressing scale is used.

Toileting. The toileting scale consists of 23 items which describe "daytime wetting," "nighttime wetting," and "soiling." Again, a trainer administers the scale and a psychologist computes the score.

Results

To date, 47 children have been admitted to the institution. Of these, 24 have been discharged. Table 1 presents some statistics on these children at the time of admission, along with data on the period of institutionalization. There were 20 white males, 10 white females, 10 negro males, and 7 negro females. Twelve residents were judged to be from middle class families, 35 from the lower class with 10 of these from deprived families.

Measurement of Behavior Change

The dressing scale reliability was determined in two ways. In one, two raters independently observed the same behavior, i.e., both the A and B raters observed each child dressing and undressing. The second approach had raters A and B rate each child on different days, i.e., each judged different samples of behaviors. Both approaches yield a pearson product-moment correlation coefficient of .99. The n in the first assessment was 27 and that in the second, 30. For feeding, the correlation based on different behavior samples, i.e., using the second method, was .95 (N = 27). A replication (N = 30) of this procedure yielded an r of .97. A similar procedure yielded an r of .96 (N = 27) for toileting behavior, and a replication, .96 (N = 30).

Behavioral changes over the training period

The children were evaluated on dressing, feeding, and toileting skills at admission and again at discharge, or to the present, i.e., after intervals ranging from 3 to 12 months. Mental age scores were obtained from the Cattell Infant Intelligence Scale (Cattell, 1940). The Revised Stanford Binet Intelligence Scale, Form L-M was used with those 8 children whose MA exceeded

3. INSTRUCTION

TABLE 2

DESCRIPTIVE STATISTICS AND t VALUES COMPARING PRE- AND POSTTEST PERFORMANCE ON FOUR DEPENDENT VARIABLES

	Mental Age Months		Dressing		Feeding		Toileting	
	Pre	Post	Pre	Post	Pre	Post	Pre	Post
X	16.7	20.1	37.3	79.1	11.3	18.6	6.0	10.1
S.D.	6.2	7.4	44.8	55.9	9.0	9.1	4.7	4.7
Range	7–32	9–41	0–156	0–194	0–38	2–40	2–18	3–18
t	5.41*		8.11*		6.32*		6.08*	

* p.<001, df=46

2 years. Table 2 presents the results of these pre- and post-measures, along with mental age changes over the period of institutionalization. Table 3 shows the number of children showing gain or loss in MA, dressing, feeding, or toileting skills.

A raw score of 37 in dressing (possible 218) suggests a level where the child can take off (on command) his t-shirt, short or long pants, shoes and socks and possibly his coat. He is beginning to learn to put on his t-shirt. A child who has a score of 79 can dress and undress when each of the items are called by name. The child has yet to learn to zip, button, buckle, lace, etc.

A feeding score of 11 (possible 40) gives the child credit for chewing his food, drinking from a glass neatly, using a spoon, though messy, and knowing to eat bread with his hands. If he has 18 points, he is typically able to do all of the above neatly, and in addition, use a fork efficiently. The child has yet to learn to use the spoon and fork correctly with the appropriate foods, and to drink, with the meal, rather than all at once.

The toileting level 6 (possible 18) describes a child who will go to the bathroom area on command, but who needs help with his clothes. He does have accidents. When the child has reached level 10, he is scheduled, i.e., he goes on command, needs no help with his clothes, and has few, if any, accidents.

The mental age gain deserves further attention, and these are presented in Figure 1 which shows each child's mental gain in relation to the expected gain and period of instructionalization. The expected gain is determined on the basis of IQ and period of institutionalization. Children with lower expected gain are retained in the training program longer than those with higher potential. The correlation between actual gain and length of institutionalization is .65. This results from the fact that children are discharged when it is judged that they are no longer benefiting from the program.

Prediction of Behavioral Change Over the Training Period

In order to compute pearson product-moment correlations, the raw scores on the three scales, along with MA, were converted to t distributions (X = 50, S.D. = 10). The pretest self-help scale scores along with CA, IQ, MA, and a total which was a simple average of MA, dressing skills, feeding skills, and toileting skills, along with a rating (5-point scale) of the extent to which the parents were involved with and concerned about the child, were subjected to a multiple correlation analysis. Neither sex nor race was considered in this analysis, since statistical tests demonstrated that neither was associated with any of the other variables. Table 4 presents the main results of the multiple regression analyses. The n for these analyses was 42.

TABLE 3

THE NUMBER OF CHILDREN SHOWING GAIN, LOSS, OR NO CHANGE BETWEEN THE PRE- AND POSTTEST

	Mental Age	Dressing	Feeding	Toileting
Gain	42	44	36	33
No Gain	0	3*	6	8**
Loss	5	0	5	3

* 1 subjects were on the "floor" on the pre- and posttests.
** 1 subjects were at the "ceiling" on the pre- and posttests.

TABLE 4

SUMMARY OF THE MULTIPLE CORRELATION ANALYSES

Predicting Gain in	Variables Used	r
Mental age	CA, PI, MA, DS, FS, TOT	.552
Dressing skills	CA, IQ, PI, MA, DS, FS, TS, TOT	.596
Toileting skills	IQ, PI, MA, TS, TOT	.708
Feeding skills	IQ, PI, DS, FS, TS	.510

CA—chronological age   DS—dressing skills
PI—parental involvement   FS—feeding skills
MA—mental age   TS—toileting skills
TOT—single average of MA, DS, FS, TS

FIGURE 1
BAR GRAPH SHOWING MENTAL AGE GAIN IN COMPARISON TO EXPECTED GAIN FOR THE INDIVIDUAL CHILDREN

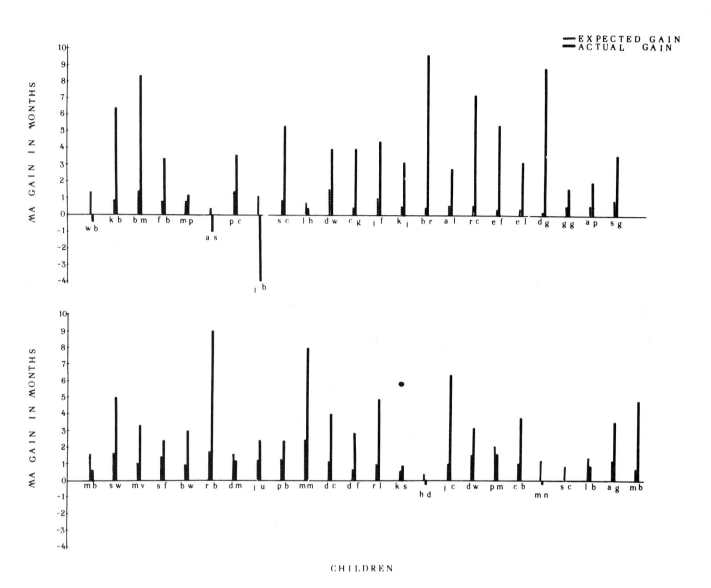

The Use of Operant Techniques in Teaching Severely Retarded Clients Work Habits

SHLOMO KATZ
JOEL GOLDBERG
ESTHER SHURKA

Abstract: Four severely retarded clients who had never adapted to the work requirements of a sheltered workshop underwent a special training program based on operant conditioning techniques. Because of the low intellectual level of the subjects, and the general complexity of the work tasks available in the workshop, it was decided to first teach them the general principle of a job, using a simpler work task. The model task was broken down into four stages and taught in isolation from the other clients in the workshop. Each stage was taught in gradual steps with concrete reinforcements for successful responses. Once the model task was mastered, a work task from the workshop was introduced. After the subjects mastered this task, they were returned to the workshop where they continued to receive reinforcements. Three of the four subjects successfully completed the training and are currently achieving an acceptable productivity level in the workshop.

The use of operant techniques has opened up many new possibilities of treatment for the severely retarded who previously were assumed to be beyond help. Watson (1967), in a review of the use of operant techniques, has shown that operant techniques have been successfully used in institutions to develop self help and social skills in severely and profoundly retarded children. The skills developed were self feeding, self dressing and grooming, toilet training, social interaction and play. Smolov (1971) provides an extensive review of the effective use of operant techniques for the modification of self injurious behavior. The use of the technique in teaching severely retarded work skills has been reviewed by Gold (1973).

As in developing self help skills, the emphasis in workshops is on the acquisition of new behaviors, rather than on the modification of existing rates of behavior. While a number of studies has been carried out, Crossen, Youngberg and White (1970);

Gold (1973), Gold and Barclay (1973) in the area of teaching the severely retarded work skills, generally the literature on methods of improving acquisition of new behaviors in workshops is fairly sparse.

Purpose

The purpose of this study was to investigate the use of a successive approximation technique in teaching severely retarded clients vocational tasks in a sheltered workshop. The study was aimed at those clients generally below the intellectual level of the general client population and who have never adjusted to the work requirements of the workshop. These are clients who, because of lack of institutional space or parental refusal to institutionalize, are placed in the workshop but spend most of their time sitting around doing nothing and generally making a nuisance of themselves. These kind of clients are found in most sheltered workshops in

"The Use of Operant Techniques in Teaching Severely Retarded Clients Work Habits," Shlomo Katz, Joel Goldberg, and Esther Shurka, *Education and Training of the Mentally Retarded*, Vol. 12, No. 1, February 1977. © 1977 Council for Exceptional Children Division of Mental Retardation.

TABLE 1

Description of Each Subject

Subject	C.A.	M.A.	Sex	Behavior Profile
A	27 years	3 years	Male	Has been in workshop for a year. Non-verbal, but understands when spoken to. When angry makes loud noises. Eats continuously and often wets his pants. Spends his day sitting, passively watching the other clients at work. No contact with others.
B	20 years	2 years	Female	New immigrant. Has been in workshop for a year. Completely non-verbal and does not understand Hebrew, but does understand Persian. She is partially blind, has no contact with others and has no behavior problems. Passes the time sitting around and gazing into space.
C	19 years	2? years	Female	Although says a few words, her verbal understanding is low. She is able to relate to others and has one friend, an older female client. She has been in the workshop for over two years, but has never been productive.
D	25 years	—	Male	Although he has been in the workshop for five years, they have never succeeded in getting him to work or break his social isolation. He spends his day wandering around, picking up papers which he then places in his mouth and eats. There is no contact with anyone in the workshop. Completely non-verbal.

Israel and help with these problems would be of value to the personnel and the workshop. All previous attempts to teach vocational skills to these subjects had failed and they were considered to be nonproductive workers and non-trainable.

Method

Subjects

Four subjects, two males and two females, were selected on the basis of their limited productivity in the workshop. A description of each subject is given in Table 1.

Description of the Workshop

Generally, the workshop caters to moderately and mildly retarded clients with an IQ range between 35 and 60, on the WISC and Stanford Binet Scales. However, due to the reasons given in the purpose,

there are a number of severely retarded who have been placed in the workshop. The workshop provides sheltered employment and social and educational experiences. Most of the work is subcontracting jobs, assembling of manufactured goods, mainly in the electrical field. The clients work for most of the day, with a number of hours devoted to academic skills. In addition, a social club functions after work and all are free to attend.

Procedure

A successive approximation procedure was set up with different types of candy, chocolate and popcorn as the reinforcements. These were varied so as to provide a maximum range of type of reinforcer and to prevent satiation of a specific reinforcer.

The work task selected was the screwing of three small screws into three holes with a screwdriver into an electric plug. This

3. INSTRUCTION

task is one of the regular subcontracting items supplied to the workshop. As the task was fairly complicated for their level, it was decided to first teach them the general principles of the task, i.e., parts discrimination, correct hand use and screwing, using a simpler model. The model chosen was a large bolt with a nut, and the task required was similar to the target behavior, i.e., picking up a nut and screwing it onto the bolt. It was anticipated that once they had mastered this task, the skills learned would then be generalized to the actual work task, and it would then be easier to teach them the prescribed work task.

The subjects were separated from the rest of the clients and underwent the training individually in a secluded room with a minimum of interference.

First Stage — Learning with Model Task

The model task was broken down into four component steps: (1) pick up nut from box of nuts with left hand; (2) pick up screw with thumb and forefinger of right hand; (2) simultaneously pick up nut and screw with respective hand, and (4) simultaneously pick up nut and bolt and screw nut on bolt.

In the first step the subject was trained to pick out and raise a nut with his left hand. The task was demonstrated by the investigator, and the subject urged to attempt the task. Every correct attempt was reinforced by giving the subject one of the candy reinforcers. This was carried on until 10 consecutively correct responses were achieved.

The second step procedure was the same, learning to pick up the screw with the thumb and forefinger and then to replace it in the box. Every correct response was reinforced until 10 consecutively correct responses were achieved.

In the third step the subject was taught to lift the nut and bolt simultaneously from the respective boxes and to replace them. A reinforcement was immediately presented. This was carried on until 10 consecutively correct responses were achieved.

In the final step the subject was required to lift the nut and bolt simultaneously

and to screw the nut onto the bolt. Every correct response was reinforced and the activity was terminated after 10 consecutively correct responses.

Generally it took two to three days, with 15 to 20 minute sessions to achieve the required performance for each component step. Thus, 10 to 12 days were required to master the training task for all the subjects. The training was carried out by a research assistant and not by the regular staff.

Once the subjects had mastered the model task, they were now exposed to the actual work task.

Second Stage — Work Task Electric Plug Assembly

The second stage was also initially carried out individually. A pile of plugs and a box of screws were placed before each subject. The experimenter then demonstrated how to lift up one screw with the left hand and a plug with the right hand, then placing the screw into position and then, with a screwdriver, screwing the screw into position. After this demonstration the subjects were prompted to attempt and were reinforced with candy for every screw correctly placed and screwed in. Each subject received a daily hour long session for six days to master the task. The criterion for having mastered the task was an average of four completed plugs.

Once having mastered the task in isolation, they were returned to the general workshop where they began to work a full day. In the workshop they were reinforced with candy for every plug completed during the entire day, for a period of six days, i.e., one work week.

At the beginning of the following work week, that is, 22 days after initiation of the training, the concrete reinforcers were gradually removed and replaced by verbal reinforcers. The verbal reinforcers consisted of phrases like "very good," "good show," "nice," etc. The reinforcement schedule for this period was as follows: For one week, every one correct plug received a verbal reinforcement and for every three plugs, a concrete reinforcer. During the following week, they received a verbal reinforcement for every three correct plugs and a concrete reinforcer for every five correct plugs. This schedule was carried on for two weeks, after which it was changed to verbal for every 10 correct and concrete for every 15 correct. A week later reinforcement was limited to only verbal reinforcement, dispersed at random during the course of a work day. During this stage the regular staff of the workshop also began to dispense verbal reinforcers. Up to now the reinforcement had been given by the research assistant only.

At this stage the subjects went on a ten day vacation. On their return the reinforcers were reactivated and they received a verbal reinforcement for every correct plug and a concrete reinforcer for every three correct plugs, for a period of three days, after which the reinforcers were terminated.

Third Stage—Follow-Up

The subjects carried on working in the workshop without the presence of the investigator under normal workshop conditions for another 50 days. There were no reinforcements other than the usual verbal reinforcers dispensed to all clients. Measurement of performance was carried out for three successive days at the beginning of the period and then one day a week over the next four weeks.

Results

Results of Model Task

Although four subjects were initially selected, one of the four refused to cooperate and insisted on continuing with his old behavior pattern of picking up and eating papers. Thus, the results relate to the three subjects who cooperated.

The results of this period are presented in Figure 1. As can be seen from the figure, all three subjects learned the model task in a total of 10 days.

Generally there were very few problems with the model task. Subject A, because of his insistence on putting the bolts in his mouth, which made them slippery and thus difficult to handle, had some problems initially but once this problem was eliminated by negative reinforcement, it went smoothly. Subject B had problems because of her poor eyesight, but once she was taught to use touch instead of sight, she mastered the task. Having to use touch only affected her speed of performance which is reflected in the results. The third subject, C, displayed initial problems of concentration, but using a time out technique (removing her from the room) this behavior was soon eliminated.

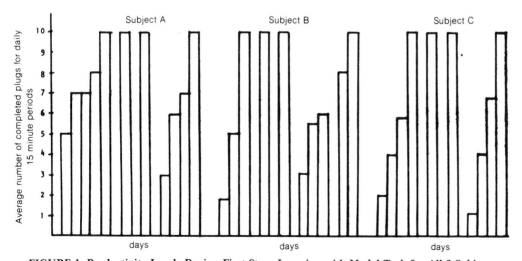

FIGURE 1. Productivity Levels During First Stage Learning with Model Task for All 3 Subjects

3. INSTRUCTION

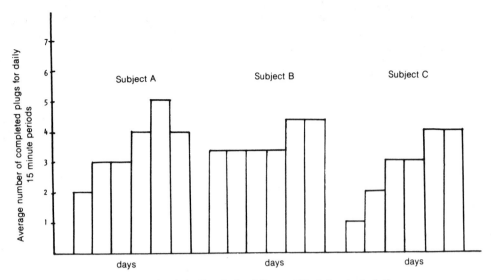

FIGURE 2. Productivity Levels for 6 Days of Training in Isolation on Assembly of Electrical Plug for All 3 Subjects

Results of Work Task

In this stage the procedure was divided into two substages. The first stage consisted of individual training sessions alone with the experimenter for a period of six days. The results are presented in Figure 2.

All three subjects were able to achieve an average of four or five completed plugs for 15 minute periods during the first six days.

The subjects were then returned to the workshop with the other clients. Their individual performance is presented in Figures 3, 4 and 5. The results cover 30 days of production and are presented in average productivity over a 15 minute period.

The return to the workshop did not affect subject A, and his productivity remained stable, gradually increasing over the 30 day period, with minor fluctuations. The reduction of reinforcements, and the change from concrete to verbal reinforcements did not have any effect on his performance. Towards the end of the period he was averaging 10 completed plugs for

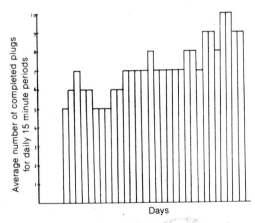

FIGURE 3. Subject A's Productivity Levels Over 30 Days on Assembly of Electrical Plugs in Workshop

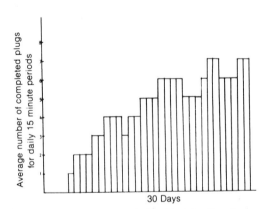

FIGURE 4. Subject B's Productivity Levels Over 30 Days on Assembly of Electrical Plugs in Workshop

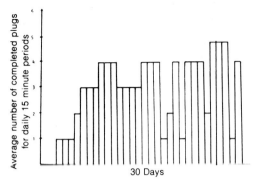

FIGURE 5. Subject C's Productivity Levels
Over 30 Days on Assembly of Electrical
Plugs in Workshop

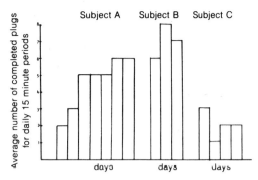

FIGURE 6. Productivity Levels During
Follow Up Period for All 3 Subjects

15 periods, which was very comparable to the norms of the workshop.

The results for Subject B are presented in Figure 4.

The return to the workshop had an effect on Subject B and her productivity fell off. With time, however, it increased and at the end of the period she was averaging between six and eight completed plugs for 15 minute periods. For this subject the concrete reinforcers were of little significance, even at the beginning, and so no reduction in productivity was anticipated once concrete reinforcers were removed.

The results for subject C are presented in Figure 5.

Subject C also had problems on her return to the workshop and her productivity fell off. With time, however, her productivity increased, but was inconsistent. She was in constant need of supervision, especially to prevent undesirable behavior, such as talking to others, etc.

Results of Follow-Up Period

The subjects were followed-up and their performance measured. During this period there were no verbal or concrete reinforcers.

The results are presented in Figure 6.

Subject A's performance was measured for seven days; three days at the beginning of the follow-up and one day a week for an additional four weeks. His productivity fell off initially but over the period of time it improved. However, it never reached the same level as during the reinforcement period. The complete reduction of reinforcement seems to have affected his production. Subject B's productivity was measured for three days only, as she became ill and was removed from the workshop. During the three days there was no decline in productivity. For this subject, concrete reinforcement did not appear to be effective and she seemed to be motivated more by intrinsic motivation, working and being busy, than by extrinsic reinforcement.

Subject C's performance was measured over four days. Her performance dropped and continued to decline. It appears that for this subject the reinforcement, especially the verbal reinforcement, was important as it also provided close supervision in the workshop and the verbal reinforcement appeared to facilitate work performance.

Discussion

Three out of four subjects were taught to work during the study and continued to work during the subsequent follow-up. The fourth subject refused to cooperate, and insisted on continuing his old behavior pattern of picking up and eating papers. Perhaps with this client a reinforcement schedule procedure might have been set up to eliminate the negative behavior prior to the work procedure. However, it was assumed that the negative behavior was far too deeply ingrained and the training schedule could not compete with it.

As the experimenters were interested in the learning of new behavior, the typical

3. INSTRUCTION

ABAB design, Sidman (1960) was not applicable, and therefore it is difficult to draw conclusions as to which of the environmental consequences were of importance in modifying the behavior. This weakens the conclusions that can be drawn from the study, but does, however, indicate the usefulness of the method in at least teaching the clients to work. It should be stressed that all prior attempts to get them to work have failed. It would appear that the method of individual supervision and the use of the successive approximation technique has the best results. It is doubtful that we would have succeeded had the subjects remained in the workshop during the initial training period. Removal from the workshop was an important environmental consequence, and the subsequent personal attention and praise appears to have been more important than the concrete reinforcers. Further support for this hypothesis was found when the subjects returned to the general workshop. Their productivity dropped off in spite of the fact that they continued to receive concrete reinforcement. The subsequent gradual removal of the reinforcers did not have any marked effect on the production.

The fact that they were working in the company of the other clients appears to be reinforcement for production. While prior to the study they were socially isolated, both from the rest of the clients and the workshop staff, they now were part of the work cycle and used the fact of their working as a means to social interaction. Their productive behavior tended now to increase social interaction and personal status. They now received a work card, salary and were regarded as members of the work group.

The study has demonstrated that it is possible to teach severely retarded (IQ less than 30) work skills and enable them to achieve an acceptable level of production and find their place in the workshop. However, more research is needed to study improved training techniques and in more clearly estimating the effects of environmental control. This study suggests the value of developing reinforcement programs to achieve higher standards of performance, both social and work, in the mentally retarded.

References

Bandura, A. *Principles of behavior modification.* New York: Holt, Rinehart & Winston, 1969.

Crosson, J. E., Youngberg, C. D. & White, O. R. Transenvironmental programming: An experimental approach to the rehabilitation of the retarded. In: H. J. Prehn (Ed.) *Rehabilitation research in mental retardation.* Rehabilitation Research and Training Center in Mental Retardation, University of Oregon, Eugene, 1970, Monograph 2, 19–34.

Gold, M. W. Research on the vocational habilitation of the retarded, the present, the future. In: Ellis (Ed.) *International review of research in mental retardation.* Vol. 6, New York: Academic Press.

Gold, M. W. & Barclay, C. R. The effects of verbal labels on the acquisition and retention of a complex assembly task. *The Training School Bulletin,* 1973, **70,** 38–42.

Sidman, M. *Tactics of scientific research.* New York: Basic Books, 1960.

Smolov, S. R. Use of operant techniques for the modification of self-injurious behavior. *American Journal of Mental Deficiency,* 1971, **76,** *3,* 295–305.

Watson, L. S. Application of operant conditioning techniques to institutionalized severely and profoundly retarded children. *Mental Retardation Abstracts,* **4,** 1967.

This investigation was supported by the Bar-Ilan University Research Fund.

Teaching the Unteachables

JOHN FLEISCHMAN

A group of caring people in Oregon are proving that the profoundly retarded can learn to lead happy and useful lives. Yet the mind of the retardate is full of the human mystery. How does one survive and another fail?

John Fleischman is an assistant editor of HUMAN BEHAVIOR.

In Oregon's Willamette Valley, rain is what falls with very little interruption from November to May. If this is October, the drizzle frosting the windshield can't be rain. Some locals put on hats for the autumn storm clouds scudding east into the Cascades, but the army surplus ponchos, the rubberized trousers, the L.L. Bean's moosehunting shoes are held in reserve. In the fall, moss gathers strength on the northern exposures.

Picking up the McKenzie River highway heading northeast out of Eugene, Dan Close is trying to reconstruct a dry July Sunday last summer when a year's work almost died on a highway bridge 48 miles up into the Cascades. Close was then the director of a new group home in Eugene for 10 severely and profoundly retarded adults. He had been off that Sunday climbing Three Sisters Mountain while three of his weekend staff had taken the "folks" for a carefully planned hike along the McKenzie River. The folks were becoming accomplished walkers. Graduating from walks around town, the group-home residents were taken hiking at least every other weekend, usually along logging roads or major trails. The week

before, a staff member had driven up to the tiny town of McKenzie Bridge to alert the rangers and to scout the trail.

It was a flawless summer day—so clear that when Close reached Three Sisters' summit he could see the snowy top of Mount Rainier to the north and, faintly but unmistakably, Mount Shasta over 200 miles south. He took color slides to prove it.

Tired from the day's climb, yet still exhilarated by the view, Close drove home along the river road—unaware that two of his folks had walked away from the hike. In the long July daylight, it was still bright when Close crossed the river above the little village of McKenzie Bridge and continued down the twisting valley towards home. He didn't know that less than two hours before, one of the missing residents had been struck and killed on the bridge itself by a woman motorist who told police that the man had lunged out into the roadway in front of her. When Close reached home, the phone was ringing. John Collier was dead, and Jim Clay had disappeared into the rugged woods.

Jim Clay was a strong, healthy 30-year-old with a measurable IQ below 20. He had almost no language and was wearing no coat. At about the same time that John Collier was run down on the highway bridge, Jim was spotted not very far away on the other side of the river. Crossing the McKenzie on a ramshackle log bridge, Jim encountered a local boy. The boy spoke to him, and Jim became frightened and bolted up a power-line break. The boy's father called the ranger station to report that his son had seen a strange man who looked to be on drugs.

By morning, Close was on his way back up the river road for the first of a dozen runs that July to join a search force of rangers, deputy sheriffs, group-

home staffers, state police and volunteers backed by helicopters and light planes. A nearly equal force of television camerapersons and reporters—as well as the curious—turned up to watch the operation. The news media were very helpful, Close says, by emphasizing that Jim was not dangerous but only hungry and frightened. In their zeal to be of assistance, the people of McKenzie Bridge phoned in every report of an overturned garbage can or mysterious thump in the night. These false reports turned the search away from the rough hills and back towards the village.

Seven days after Jim disappeared, a man hiking up to his remote cabin spotted Jim standing in the cabin's doorway holding a jug of water. The man ran for help, and when the group-home staff came back with him, they found Jim sitting up in bed with his clothes neatly folded at the foot. He was 30 pounds lighter, spotlessly clean and very hungry.

In October, the mountains are black walls of thick fir and pine; the rainclouds, white dragons snuffling eastward up the narrow valley. The tires hiss on the asphalt. "I used to think these were the ugliest hills in the world," Close says, staring off into the wet wilderness, "because I thought Jim was up there." Close remembers the police conducting the hunt with thoroughness, gallons of coffee and the idea that Jim was "escaping." It was the only way they could conceptualize Jim's elusive behavior. As misconceptions go, it was very minor. But while the search continued, there was an unspoken fear in the minds of Close and the others connected with the group home—the fear of much larger misconceptions.

"People think the greatest risk in group homes is the risk of death," says Close. They had had a death. But while the search for Jim continued, the reality of John's loss didn't have time to sink in. But what if Jim was never found or was found dead? If the police saw Jim as an escapee, would the public see the group-home staff as delinquent custodians? What were two such helpless men doing hiking around in a wilderness area? Surely the severely and profoundly retarded had to be protected from themselves and the outside world.

A death seemed a disastrous way to introduce the public to a novel treatment for the severely and profoundly retarded. The very label makes professionals wince. The severely and profoundly retarded are those with IQs below 35, the bottom limit of the trainable mentally retarded (TMR) category. That sounds splendid except that it is very difficult to accurately measure an IQ below 50. The subjects have little or no language, and often cannot hold a pencil in a way that could possibly be construed as functional. Behavioral-inventory tests are the only way to measure their IQ. You find out if the subjects can eat with a fork. Do they wash behind their ears? Can the men close their own flies? Are they toilet trained?

The severely and profoundly retarded don't do very well on these kinds of tests, either. Which may explain why most of the severely retarded, especially the adults, are stored in institutions where attendants close their flies, cut their food, wash behind their ears and clean them up when they forget their toilet training. These custodial institutions are filled with severely retarded adults because their natural parents wear out or die or are told to do the "best thing" or throw up their hands in despair once the impact of their child's condition sinks in. Also children, even retarded children, are cute. Children are symbols of hope, but a 20-year-old man with three days of stubble and an IQ estimated below 20 looks neither cute nor hopeful.

"The adult severely and profoundly retarded population is not in the forefront of the public consciousness. The attitude is 'Let's get the children and prevent them from ending up like this,'" says Close. "They've lived in institutions all their lives. They're those retarded people you've heard about. Maybe you've seen one on the street with his mother, but you've never thought about them." In institutions and nursing homes, the severely and profoundly retarded exist out of sight and out of mind. "This group has been kissed off," says Close.

The group Close talks about is larger than we like to think. A 1972 HEW

"They've lived in institutions all their lives. They are those retarded people you've heard about. This group of people has been kissed off."

study shows that there were 200,000 mentally retarded Americans of all ages and levels in institutions. Dr. Richard Eyman, a demographic researcher at Pacific State Hospital in Pomona, California, has looked at it more closely. His studies have shown that in a hypothetical community of 100,000, there are 25 profoundly retarded adults (measurable IQ below 20) and 100 severely retarded adults (measurable IQ below 35). He points out that these figures can be extrapolated for the nation as a whole, giving a figure of 275,000 severely and profoundly retarded Americans.

A 1970 study conducted by Eyman in Riverside, California, showed that the severely and profoundly retarded have a "well over 80 percent" probability of being committed to an institution at some point in their lives. In particular, the profoundly retarded are likely to be institutionalized—a probability of 95 percent. "The place you are going to find the profoundly retarded is in an institution," says Eyman. "There are not many homes that can stand up to that kind of thing."

The Eugene home wanted to try. The idea of group homes for the handicapped and the retarded has been around for years. But as far as Close or any of the others involved in the Eugene home could discover, it had never actually been attempted with this class of retarded adults. The low level of the subjects' intelligence, combined with their adult strength and size, had discouraged this kind of treatment.

The problem with a group home is what to do with the residents during the day. Retarded children can be sent off to special schools. Moderately retarded adults can work in sheltered workshops. But here was a group seemingly too old to educate or too slow to work. Still, the last 10 years have seen

a revolution in the behavioral sciences that seemed to promise both a solution to the daytime problem and the means to operate a group home for so difficult a population.

Tom Bellamy, a young doctoral candidate in special education at the University of Oregon, started a workshop for severely and profoundly retarded adults in Eugene. He adapted some of the techniques pioneered by Marc Gold, whose work at the University of Illinois had opened up the whole field of vocational training for the severely retarded. Through a method called task analysis and sequential training technique, Gold divided the assembly of a 15-piece bicycle brake into its smallest discriminations and successfully taught the steps to a group of 64 moderately and severely retarded individuals in sheltered workshops. Gold had opened the door to useful and commercially valuable work for the retarded.

Bellamy set up a shop to subcontract the assembly of electronic subunits. Bellamy's severely and profoundly retarded workers were able to put together a 52-piece cam switch actuator at a rate close to industry standard and with quality equal to or higher than that of industry. Bellamy's first workers lived at home, but there simply weren't enough uninstitutionalized potential subjects living in Eugene to give his program a meaningful sample. The population Bellamy wanted was living outside town at the state hospital, Fairview.

Meanwhile, Dan Close was working with Gold in Chicago. Initially, Close worked with severely and profoundly retarded adults at Camarillo (California) State Hospital as a psychology undergraduate at California Lutheran College. Pursuing a master's degree at Idaho State University in Pocatello, he became involved with a sheltered workshop for TMR adolescents and adults. Marc Gold was consultant to the project; and the first time Close heard him speak, he knew this man was onto something. Gold invited him to Chicago to run the research on a vocational-skill training experiment. Close says flatly of Gold, "He taught me everything I know."

Close had become interested in the community-living approach; and when he heard about the proposed Eugene group home, he came out to Oregon to join Bellamy.

Bellamy found a sponsor through the Alvord-Taylor Homes, a nonprofit organization operating a group home for the mildly retarded and another as a respite care center in Eugene. Through the state Mental Health Division, he found money and access to the patients at Fairview.

In the fall of 1974, Close drove out to Fairview for an initial look at his future residents. He knew what institutions were like, but he was momentarily overwhelmed by the scene. Fairview is an excellent institution of its kind with a cooperative director backed up by a progressive state mental health establishment. Still, the first encounter unnerved Close. "They looked bizarre," he recalls. "You go out to a state hospital, and you'll find people sitting around in white shirts and pants and bowl haircuts. Some with shoes, some barefoot, some with snot running down their faces. I thought there was no way we were going to be able to work with these people."

Institutions teach institutional behavior. Stereotypical institutional behavior for the mentally retarded is head banging, floor searching, hand rubbing and throwing tantrums. After 20 years in institutions, the patients often curl into a permanently stooped posture, the shoulder blades half-folded around the chest. Sitting aimlessly in wards, the retarded become addicted to self-stimulation, or "self-stim" as it is called—crotch rubbing, earhole grinding and endless rocking back and forth. The line between the symptoms of the retardation itself and the institutional stereotype is blurred.

The journey from the institution to the normal world is a cultural ocean as frightening and as wide as the one many Europeans crossed seeking a New World. Close likes the metaphor: "Our people are like that—immigrants from another land. They don't understand our language, and their culture is the culture of the institution."

In a ward of endless rockers and

"Our people are like new immigrants from another land. They just don't understand our language, and their culture is that of the institution."

shriveled men, Dan Close found 27-year-old John Collier sitting immobile in front of a TV set. John hated to move, and he had discovered that if he parked himself in front of a TV, no one would disturb him. But Dan Close had plans to disturb him. "The thing about John was that he acted as if he knew nothing, but then he would come out with things like counting to 10," he explained.

For his generation, John's case was unusual. The cause of his retardation was unknown, and it was only after he started school that he was given the dread label of mentally retarded. He lived with his parents until he was 19, when the strain of caring for and supervising him every minute became too great. But even after he was committed to a state institution for the retarded, his family stayed in contact—coming to visit, sending presents and asking about his living conditions. Most of the severely and profoundly retarded John's age were committed early, and their families lost touch with them. "It becomes pretty unrewarding to visit a child who is unresponsive," says Close.

Because of his parents' attention and his relatively short period of institutionalization, John had the most going for himself of the eight chosen in the fall of 1974 for the new group home. John was selected by the toss of a coin from a group of 17 retarded adults at Fairview Hospital and Training Center outside Eugene. The "target" population was made up of those patients who were over 18, able to walk and use a spoon and who tested out as "severely or profoundly retarded." Because of the funding through the Oregon Mental Health Division, the target group had to have been committed from Eugene or the surrounding Lane County. Eight were arbitrarily picked for the group home, and nine people remained at Fairview as a control group. Subse-

quently, two more residents were added to the home, but they remained outside the "experiment."

Less than a year before his death, John Collier emigrated to a new world. He was in the first group brought to the electric-blue house at 670-16th Street, the group home that would much later be called the John Collier House.

*   *   *

A few minutes before nine, they straggle up 16th Street on their way to work. There is no mistaking the six women and four men. Some walk fast, intent on their goal. Others shuffle, looking lost to the world. Louie, the "Big L," lopes along in great strides, then stops to survey the scene, then bounces forward again. Jim, clad in a bright yellow windbreaker, brings up the rear. His hand is clenched just in front of his eyes, his fingers working up and down like a trumpet player's. When the front of the group reaches Alder Street, Jim screws his eyes tight and waits, his fingers marking time.

At every corner, Jay Buckley, who has taken over after Close went back to school to get his doctorate, puts the folks through the street-crossing program one at a time. Buckley takes Alice's hand and points down the street. "Car's close," says Jay. "Car's close," says Alice. She tracks the car with her outstretched finger as it speeds past. "Car's far away," Jay says. "Car's far away," she repeats. Under his direction, she tracks both directions and then steps off on her own. In ones and twos, the group repeats the corner drill.

Alder Street borders the University of Oregon campus. On the far side, the folks turn right and follow a sidewalk past the tennis courts and up a small rise to the new special-education building where the workshop is located. The university is a hotbed of behaviorism, where the first tenet is "Show me the data." The special-ed building was designed for data collection. A darkened gallery runs above the classrooms. Beveled one-way windows look down into the workshop. Directional microphones are positioned in the ceiling. Perched on hard metal stools, "coders" sit in the shadows watching the scene below. Disembodied voices from the wall speakers echo in the gallery. A beeper sounds every 10 seconds, and the coders dutifully mark down on special sheets what their subject is doing at that moment—looking around, "self-stim," attending to directions, working and so on.

Graphed and computerized, the results are empirical, tangible and comparable. Can "self-stim" be decreased in X? Code the behavior and find out its exact rate of occurrence. Design a program to change the behavior. Code the subject's behavior during the correction program and afterward. Then compare the numbers. Has there been a change? Is the program effective? Behavioral science marches on to the beep of a 10-second timer.

The workshop is an ordinary-looking classroom furnished with evenly spaced trapezoidal tables. Each table has a row of shallow bins and the necessary forms and tools for the task. The folks manufacture cable trusses, plugs and switches for oscilloscopes. The key to the workshop is task analysis. A job is broken down into its tiniest steps, and the necessary discriminations are plotted. Then the job is taught tidbit by tidbit, and the worker is reinforced every step of the way.

Assembling a switch becomes a series of small discriminations and simple operations. Take one piece out of a bin. Fit it in a wooden form. Place the second piece on top. Screw the two together. Lay the unit on a marked card. Repeat the process until the card is filled. Call for a supervisor to count the units and check the quality. Start another card.

Louie has been institutionalized for 34 of his 38 years. His hair is long and lank, and he has grown a full beard that, at first glance, gives him a vaguely sinister air. It is a false impression. Louie fits the first piece into the form. He studies the result with melancholic concentration; then he snatches the second piece and slaps it carelessly into place. The workshop surpervisor squats at his elbow. She puts the second piece back into the bin. "Fix it, Louie," she says.

His frustration boils over, his arms jerking back at his head, the forearms

locked at the wrists. "Fix it, Louie," she says. His locked arms slowly uncoil. He snaps up the returned piece and slaps it back. She puts it back. "Fix it, Louie." His arms fly up again, his head twisting backward. Suddenly he pulls his arms down again and quickly fits the piece correctly. "All right, Louie," she congratulates, "all right, Louie.

Very nice." He races through the card, assembling the units with spasmodic intensity. He jerks his head away and throws one arm up in triumph.

"Hey, Louie, you've got your one hand up." She comes over to inspect the card, poking the pieces to make sure they are screwed tightly. Satisfied, she offers Louie a penny, an immediate reward for the job. "Let's trade," she suggests. Louie studies the coin. "What did you get, Louie?" she asks. "What did you get?" "Penny," says the bearded man in the softest of voices. "Way to go, Louie, way to go." He slips his reward into a plastic cup taped to his workbench and starts another card.

The pennies are the basis of a token economy to reinforce correct behavior. Besides pennies, everyone earns a flat piece rate. Some exceed minimum wage because of high productivity. But for many, paychecks and even tokens are too remote. They work for the constant verbal and social reinforcements the supervisors lavish on them.

Barry is on the token economy. All day he works at his station screwing plugs together, shaking them at his ear and tapping them against his face to insure they are tight. The pennies mount up. At 4 p.m., he grasps his money tightly in his fist and goes to the "store," a table spread with small plastic boxes of raisins and cookies. The boxes are arranged by price, and he walks up and down the row, deciding. He settles on a box of animal crackers, which he takes to a table and opens with great care. Satisfied, Barry munches his day's earnings.

The house on 16th Street comes alive when the folks come home. Sam, the house mongrel, barks like crazy. Mark heads straight for the stereo, stuffs "The Who" into the machine, and Friday night is off and running. Soon there are dancers in the living room and vegetable choppers in the kitchen, where Jeanne Bell is patching together a dinner without a stove, since the old one gave up the ghost that morning. Jay Buckley is out in the driveway wrestling a donated replacement off a pickup truck.

Jeanne started out as an elementary school teacher and then became inter-

ested in "exceptional" children. Together with Dan Close, she helped to set up the group home. When Close left, she stayed on to work with Jay. They are supposed to work a roughly normal Monday-through-Friday week. When stoves burn out, or other problems mount, the week becomes longer.

Two other staff members come in first thing in the morning, and two more after dinner. There is also a different weekend staff. The night manager is the only staff member who lives in, in a room in the basement. The group home also has a stream of volunteers and practicing students from the university.

"At first, we hired a man to stay up all night. We didn't have any idea what would happen," Jeanne remembers. "But it turned out that they sleep like anybody else."

The folks do most of the work—the cooking, the laundry, the housecleaning, the dishwashing, the yard work, the table setting and emptying the garbage cans. They feed the pets and make the beds—just like in a real home.

Barry is methodically slicing up apples for a salad while a staff member half-watches him and half-watches two sandwichmakers. One of the sandwichmakers has changed her clothes twice since she came home from work. Changing your clothes when you want is an example of the distance between the institution and 670-16th Street. Jeanne says, "In an institution, they slept in a large room. There was another room where their clothes were kept locked up. But when they came here, suddenly they had bedrooms, dressers and drawers with clothes in them."

The house on 16th Street is not just a bunch of nice people being nice to retarded people. The ideology of the group home is behaviorist, and the methodology is thumbtacked to the pantry wall. The wall is covered with programs for problems great and small —to get Bonnie to say certain sounds, to teach shoe tying, to toilet train Alice. For example:

Name: Barry. (Desired) Behavior: Keeping his clothes to himself. Objective: Barry will tell Louie to take off any article of clothing that is rightfully Barry's.
If Louie has Barry's clothing—
(1) Get Barry, point at Louie and at the article of clothing, say, "Barry, Louie has your ——— on."
(2) Nudge Barry and get him involved.

"Many of the folks had no idea how to show elementary affection. It's hard to believe, but some of them didn't know how to hug and kiss."

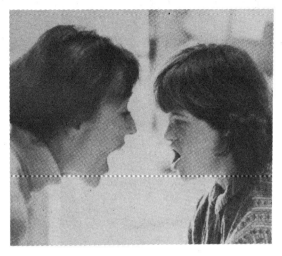

(3) Tell Barry to tell Louie, "Hey take my pants, etc., off."
(4) Wait for Barry's verbalization.
(5) Then tell Louie to take off Barry's article of clothing.
Note: This is especially important for you morning folks.

Another part of the group home's behaviorist approach is the use of systematic coding observations to generate data for the experiment and also to analyze specific behavior problems.

When Louie first came from Fairview, he spent hours on his hands and knees searching the floor. The behavior showed up on the community-living observations as a form of "self-stim" because of the way Louie rubbed the carpet with his fingers. A program was written up to "overcorrect" the searching. Anytime a staff member found Louie searching, Louie was made to wash his hands and was then given paper to scribble on. Now Louie collects pencils like a magnet. He scribbles intently and then stops to study the circles. Then he returns to scribbling.

The Friday night excitement is heightened by the news that Alice is going out to dinner with Bob Johnson. Bob is a severely retarded young man from a foster-care home. Alice, who is 10 years older chronologically but his equal mentally, is beside herself with anticipation. "You're going out to dinner with Bob Johnson?" asks Jeanne. "Bob Johnson," blushes Alice, tucking her chin under.

Just as the group sits down to dinner, Bob arrives. Bob is delighted to be there, delighted to be going out to dinner, delighted to be going out with Alice and delighted to see Jeanne. He shakes everybody's hand. Along with two staffers, they are off to Mama's Truckstop. Bob is slipped a few bucks to pay for the outing and with much hand-shaking and at least two complete sets of farewells, the couple sets out.

Jeanne seems almost as delighted as Bob. Sex has never been a problem, she says. Quite the contrary, many of the residents have little idea how to show even elementary affection. "It's hard to believe, but some of them don't know how to hug and kiss." Hugging and kissing are an unofficial priority. There is no program on the pantry wall, but the staff teaches it, anyway.

Eating is a big part of the official program. Institutions don't spend a great deal of time on table manners; they don't even teach chewing. Since institutional food is soft and bland, the patients only have to master the spoon. The severely and profoundly retarded often choke on foods such as apples that require chewing. Louie is a chronic choker. He eats with the same wild abandon with which he walks. Once he was surprised stealing a potato from the kitchen. He jammed the whole thing down his throat and was nearly asphyxiated.

Eight residents sit at the main table while two others work on eating programs with Jay at the small "training table." Jeanne presides at the main table. "Isn't everyone sitting up straight? Isn't Sally sitting up straight? Good, Sally, really good." Sally beams from her seat. In institutions, the patients slump at the table, their noses in their plates, shoveling the food into their mouths. In the group home, everyone sits up straight to eat. After a few meals spent reinforcing the residents, staffers find themselves eating with the carriage of ballet dancers.

Louie eyes an extra sandwich. "Would you like another sandwich, Louie?" Jeanne asks, offering him the plate. He picks up a half and takes one small bite. "Good chewing," says Jeanne. "Isn't everyone sitting up straight?" Every-

one, staff included, is sitting bolt upright.

Saturday morning, staff member Tama Levine sets out for the local Y with five of the folks. Underlying the group home's philosophy is the principle of normalization; retarded people should lead as normal a life as possible in the least restrictive setting. The folks go bowling. They go to movies and to concerts. Three nights a week, the folks study rudimentary arithmetic, handwriting and reading at a local school. Normal people go to baseball games, so the folks go see Eugene's minor league Emeralds. Whether they understand the rules is not important; they cheer from beginning to end.

Normal people like to work out, and so do the folks. They play a unique brand of basketball. Jan, who is 24 and suffers from Down's syndrome, can barely manage the ball. She seems frozen; yet slowly she coils her body for a two-handed cradle shot straight from the knees. Jim has a different approach: shouldering the ball one-handedly, he advances on the basket with one eye screwed shut, his free hand working its continual trumpet-playing routine. At 15 feet, he pops the ball through the hoop with the assurance of Wilt Chamberlain. He squeezes both eyes shut in delight.

Tama puts the group through calisthenics. Down's people are incredibly limber. Jan drops easily into a full leg split, then tucks both legs behind her head. Then they all jog around the gym. Barry, who is the state champion in the Special Olympics 50-yard dash, leads the way, squealing in a high voice, his left hand raised over his head.

It is too late for a swim, but Tama takes them down to the weight-lifting room. As the group enters, the lifters look up in amazement. Tama soon gets everyone lifting something, and the body builders go back to the serious business at hand. Fifteen minutes later, the folks have blended into the strange rituals of weight lifting. Jim kneels before an iron bar connected through a pulley to a stack of iron discs. As he pulls, his face continues its perpetual grimacing. Next to him, a weight lifter staggers under an immense barbell resting on a foam-rubber backpad. The lifter's face is contorted with strain as his buddy shouts encouragement:

"Work it, work the weight." Tama urges Jim on: "Pull, Jim, pull. All right, Jim. All right." Jim lets the pulley down with a clang. He shakes his wrists wildly. "All right, Jim. Way to go," says Tama.

3. INSTRUCTION

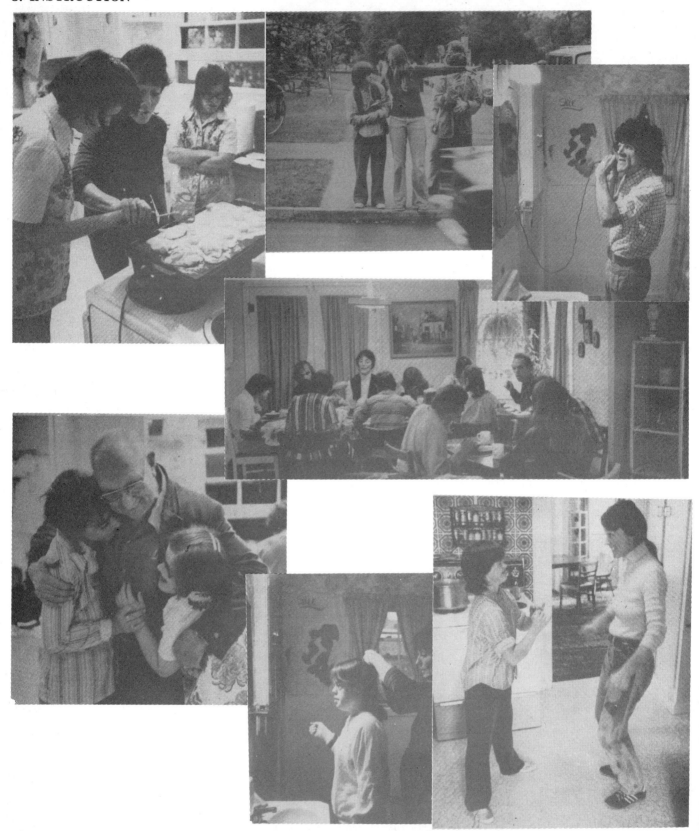

Having spent most of their lives stored in various state hospitals, 10 severely and profoundly retarded adults now have their own home. It's a place (clockwise from lower left) where one can stand at the front window watching for the paperboy, and where codirector Jeanne Bell can share a hug with a visiting father and his stepdaughter. Bell and the staff teach such basic how-tos of living as frying an egg, crossing a street, shaving, tripping the light fantastic in the kitchen, amateur hairstyling and minding one's table manners at dinner.

Prevocational Training of the Severely Retarded Using Task Analysis[1]

William P. Friedenberg
Andrew S. Martin

Authors: WILLIAM P. FRIEDENBERG, M.S. (Syracuse University), currently completing work for his Ph.D. in clinical psychology at Texas Tech University, Lubbock and is also a research assistant at the Research and Training Center in Mental Retardation, Texas Tech University; ANDREW S. MARTIN, Ph.D. (University of Connecticut), a research scientist at the Research and Training Center in Mental Retardation, P.O. Box 4510, Texas Tech University, Lubbock, Texas 79409.

ABSTRACT. Two severely retarded students were trained on a task requiring multiple, multidimensional discrimination. Two procedures for accomplishing the task were subjected to task analysis and training procedures for each devised. Each student was trained on both a hand and machine procedure for stapling labels on plastic bags. Subsequent production tests suggested that tangible reinforcement may be a necessary ingredient in maintaining low-error performance with an inherently non-reinforcing task. Recommendations are made for in-depth analysis of tasks prior to setting up training programs.

Prevocational programs for the mentally retarded are designed to evaluate and train potential workers in basic skills. Gold (1973b) shows that intelligence tests, manual dexterity tests, and work sample tasks are of limited usefulness in predicting work performance. An actual work assignment is preferred because it can develop valuable skills in the client while it is being used for evaluation.

Crosson (1969) set the standard for extending behavioral techniques to sheltered workshop settings through his use of task analysis and intensification of cues by the trainer. In this training procedure, "the trainer demonstrates each of the component behaviors in the proper sequence and prompts the trainee to immediately model the behavior. This can be accomplished by verbal or gestured command although it is occasionally necessary to mold the response by physically guiding the trainee through an appropriate topography" (p. 815). Other researchers have since added evidence that laboratory techniques can be used with success in the real life setting of the workshop (Zimmerman, Stuckey, Garlick, & Miller, 1969; Gold, 1972; Gold, 1973a; Brown, Bellamy, & Sontag, 1971).

The current study applied task analysis procedures to train students in the prevocational area of a sheltered workshop. Gold's thesis (1973a) that pay or praise in some form are not the only reinforcers available for work was tested using a task with different reinforcing properties from that used by Gold. The assumption that retarded students would require more training time and have lower subsequent production rates using a "complicated" piece of equipment than they would with standard techniques was also investigated.

Participants. Patrick, a 21-year-old severely retarded male (IQ = 30) and Tommy, a 30-year-old male with a measured IQ of 36 were assigned to the prevocational area of the workshop since neither was judged to be ready for work in the sheltered workshop.

Setting. The state school where the study took place is a residential facility for the mentally retarded. The school has a sheltered workshop of the extended care type and a newly instituted pre-vocational training area.

Training Task. The workshop presently has several contracts involving production of goods for local businesses. One such contract consists of the bagging, labeling, and displaying of spices for sale in grocery stores. Stapling labels onto plastic bags filled with garlic bulbs was chosen as a training task since the skills involved were applicable to other workshop jobs.

Task Analysis. The task of putting a label on a plastic bag filled with two garlic bulbs was analyzed for economy and ease of physical movement using task analysis procedures adapted from Gold (1975). The task was first method-analyzed to establish the method or methods which would

3. INSTRUCTION

be easiest to learn or teach. Two alternatives were designated—stapling by hand and stapling using a foot-operated machine (See Figure 1). This machine required coordinated use of eyes, hands, and feet in a sequence unfamiliar to the trainees. Based on the fact that the machine required more effort from the student and more input from the instructor, it would not appear at first glance to be the method of choice. Content analysis was used to break the two tasks into teachable units. The steps for hand and machine stapling are presented in Table 1. Finally, process analysis determined the format and type of feedback used in training. Following a procedure developed for use with housekeeping tasks (Brown, Bellamy & Sontag, 1971), four levels of instruction were used: nonpunitive indication of error, verbal direction, modeling, and priming.

FIGURE 1

Foot-operated stapling machine

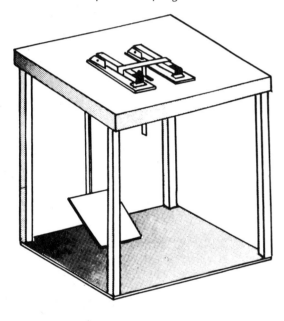

General Procedure. Each student was trained to staple labels onto bags using one of the two methods, machine or hand, for approximately 20 minutes each day. This period was lengthened to allow a block of 10 trials in progress to be completed. After the student met the criterion of 20 consecutive trials without error, he was tested for production in three 20-minute sessions. During these test sessions, the student was told to work as fast as he could and staple as many labels as possible for 20 minutes. When the production test was completed, each student was trained using the alternate production method. Three production test sessions followed to test speed and accuracy using the second stapling method. A production test session using the hand method was given between the 1st and 2nd machine production sessions for Patrick, and a machine session was given between the 2nd and 3rd sessions for Tommy. These interpolated trials were used to test for practice effects.

Training. The trainer began by physically modeling the steps necessary to obtain a completed product while stating verbally the operations he was performing according to the task analysis. He then told the student to try the task. An inability to complete a step correctly was dealt with first

TABLE 1

Steps in Machine and Hand Stapling
from Task Analysis

LABEL STAPLING — MACHINE

1. Pick up one label with one hand.
2. Place the label in front of you (face down with the open end of the flap facing you).
3. Retrieve a bag of garlic from the tray, with both hands, holding only the corners of the open end.
4. Insert the mouth of the garlic bag into the "v" shaped space made by the raised flap of the label.
5. Hold the bag in place with the thumbs.
6. Now press the flap down (over the mouth of the bag) with the forefingers.
7. Carefully put your thumb on the flap also and press down.
8. Now remove your forefingers and carefully pick up the bag without moving your thumb.
9. Insert under the stapler and staple by depressing the pedal.
10. Place the labeled bag in a tray.

LABEL STAPLING — HAND

1. Pick up one label with one hand.
2. Place the label in front of you (face down with the open end of the flap facing you).
3. Retrieve a bag of garlic from the tray, with both hands, holding only the corners of the open end.
4. Insert the mouth of the garlic bag into the "v" shaped space made by the elevated bag.
5. Hold the bag in place with the thumbs.
6. Now press the flap down (over the mouth of the bag) with the forefingers.
7. Carefully put your thumb on the flap also and press down.
8. Now remove your forefingers and carefully pick up the bag without moving your thumb.
9. Insert under the stapler, carefully letting go of assembly on side of label to be stapled first.
10. Using free hand, hit or push down on stapler.
11. Push label over, keeping assembly under stapler.
12. Grasp with free hand, letting go with other hand.
13. Position and staple other side of label.
14. Place labeled bag in a tray.

by a non-punitive indication of error ("Try it another way"). If this had no effect, a verbal direction was given such as "hold the bag tightly." If the verbal instruction did not result in the performer correcting his error, a physical cue was given in the form of the step being modeled by the trainer with accompanying verbal instructions. The fourth level of correction (priming) consisted of manipulating the boy's hands to help him complete the step correctly. No tangible reinforcement was given. The experimentor tried as much as possible not to make eye contact or provide other social reinforcement since the student's constant checking with the trainer to see if he is correct can easily disrupt learning (Gold, 1973c).

Production Test. When criterion was reached, three production test sessions of 20 minutes each were given. In these sessions. the student was encouraged to complete as many units as he could with no corrections made by the trainer. Earlier experience had indicated that production rates were not easily maintained without any reinforcement so non-contingent verbal reward was included in this stage. This consisted of dramatic exhortations to try hard and work quickly, and praise of current performance. The verbal reinforcement was not tied to specific performance of the student at that moment.

Results

Figures 2 and 3 show the number of errors and the number of completely correct products made for each block of 10 trials during training for both procedures. Patrick took only two sessions or approximately 40 minutes to meet the criterion of 20 consecutively correct responses using the hand stapling procedure. He quickly went from 10 step

FIGURE 2

Number of substep errors and completely correct products produced per block of ten trials during training.

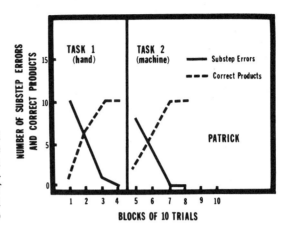

FIGURE 3

Number of substep errors and completely correct products produced per block of ten trials during training.

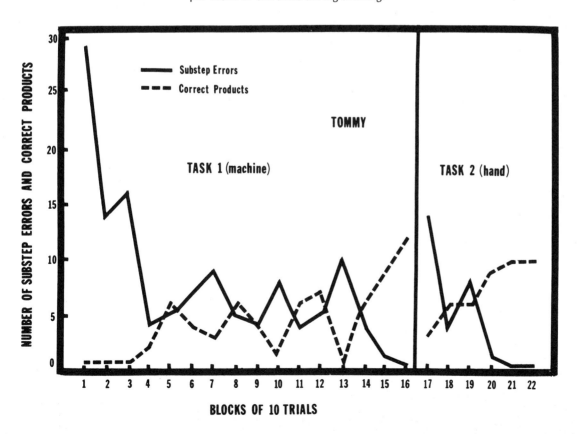

3. INSTRUCTION

errors per 10 products to zero errors. The transfer of training to the second method can be seen in lower initial step errors, higher initial number of completely correct products, and shorter training time (approximately 20 minutes for the machine training). Tommy took longer to learn the machine procedure than Patrick took to learn the hand procedure. His total training time over 6 days was, however, less than 2 hours (107 minutes). He started with lower overall performance characteristics than did Patrick, reached a plateau for several sessions, then quickly reached criterion within one day's session. This fast rise to criterion after a period of plateau performance has been described by Zeaman and House (1963) for visual discrimination learning in retardates. Transfer was accomplished (lower step errors and more correct products), with complete training taking place in 2 days (60 trials) on hand stapling.

Table 2 shows the relative numbers of completely correct products and unacceptable products for each test session, and the mean performance on these two measures for both students.

Patrick produced an average of 21 correct products by hand with an average of 9.5 unacceptable. This represents an average unacceptable rate of 31%. When tested after being trained on machine stapling, he produced an average 20 correct with an average 7.34 unacceptable. This yields an unacceptable product rate of 27% —an improvement of 4% for machine over hand stapling. Tommy produced 31.75 correct and 6.5 unacceptable by machine with an unacceptable product rate of 17%. His performance after being trained to staple by hand shows 29 correct and an average 6.0 unacceptable for an error rate of 17%—the same as for machine stapling. No apparent differences are seen between interpolated and original test session production rates, thus indicating that the second stapling technique results were not enhanced by practice effects.

In test sessions the average number correct produced by both students was 26.7 by machine and 24.4 by hand. For both the average number of unacceptable products was 6.85 by machine and 8.0 by hand, representing an unacceptable product rate of 20% and 25% respectively.

TABLE 2

Mean Production in Test Sessions on
Machine and Hand Stapling

	MACHINE					HAND				
	Sessions					*Sessions*				
	1	2	3	4	$\bar{X}$	1	2	3	4	$\bar{X}$
TOMMY										
Number Correct	31	30	33	33*	31.74	30	20	37		29.0
Unacceptable	6	7	8	5	6.5	6	8	4		6.0
PATRICK										
Number Correct	23	10	27		20.0	22	28	8	26*	21.0
Unacceptable	10	10	2		7.34	6	6	13	13	9.5
Machine Correct	$\bar{X}$ = 26.7					Hand Correct	$\bar{X}$ = 24.4			
Machine Unacceptable	$\bar{X}$ = 6.85					Hand Unacceptable	$\bar{X}$ = 8.0			

*Interpolated trials — using alternate method

Discussion

In addition to showing that training was successfully completed for both students within a very short period of time, the results tend to favor machine stapling slightly over hand stapling in number produced, unacceptable products, and error rate. One of the aims of this study was to see if possible increased training time on machine stapling would be offset by improved performance. Although no conclusions can be drawn from such a small sample, the results at least indicate that one should consider possible gains in the long run production obtainable by investing in a longer initial training period, and the fact that quality may deteriorate less over time due to the standardization provided by the machine. In addition, the trainer should not be overly apprehensive about the use of work aids that seem complicated but which are contributory to increased production. A careful study of potential work aids and training methods to teach use of these aids should be made before assuming a simpler method is preferable.

Concerning the high unacceptable rate seen in production after errorless performance had previously been reached in training, the possibility that the criterion was too low for assurance of complete learning or that over-learning should have been instituted to insure retention is discounted. The criterion for acquisition used in the present study (20 consecutive correct trials) is considerably higher than that used in other studies. In addition, Gold (1972) found no positive effect of over-learning on retention rates. A more likely explanation is that the inherent interest in the task (Gold, 1972; Gold, 1973a) and social reinforcement was not strong enough in the present study to maintain performance at a high level. The present task is a fairly difficult one, and unlike the bicycle brake used by Gold, the discriminations necessary for successful completion of this task are multiple and multidimensional rather than simple 2-choice discriminations. The fine motor coordination necessary for holding a thin plastic bag and stapling a label is substantial. There are many possible errors in such fine work and any lack of precision would result in an unacceptable product. Once the task had been learned, the inherent reinforcement value of the task may have been low compared to that of longer-cycle assembly tasks with an impressive "mechanical" look. Lack of interest may have caused attention lapses, resulting in small errors. Thus, either tangible rewards (Logan, Kinsinger, Shelton, & Brown, 1971), tokens (Zimmerman, Stuckey, Garlick, & Miller, 1969), competition (Huddle, 1967), or more explicit social reinforcement (Logan, Kinsinger, Shelton, & Brown, 1971) are probably necessary to maintain performance. Both students were aware that workers in the sheltered workshop were paid for their work. One finished his first performance trial by asking the trainer for payment. Although Gold's (1973a) students received no response-contingent reinforcement, they still received their regular workshop pay.

References

Brown, L., Bellamy, T., & Sontag, L. (Eds.) The development and implementation of a public school prevocational training program for trainable retarded and severely emotionally disturbed children: Progress report part I. Unpublished manuscript, Madison Public Schools, Madison, Wisconsin, 1971.

Crosson, J. E. A technique for programming sheltered workshop environments for training severely retarded workers. *American Journal of Mental Deficiency*, 1969, 73(5), 814-818.

Gold, M. W. Factors affecting production by the retarded: Base rate. *Mental Retardation*, 1973, 11(6), 41-45(a).

Gold, M. W. Research on the vocational habilitation of the retarded: The present, the future. In N. R. Ellis (Ed.), *International review of research in mental retardation*, (Vol. 6). New York: Academic Press, 1973 (b).

Gold, M. W. Stimulus factors in skill training of retarded adolescents on a complex assembly task: Acquisition, transfer and retention. *American Journal of Mental Deficiency*, 1972, 76(4), 517-526.

Gold, M. W. Utilization of task analysis and task complexity in training. Paper presented at Training Techniques and Approaches for the Mentally Retarded, Research and Training Center in Mental Retardation, Texas Tech University, Lubbock, Texas, May, 1975.

Huddle, D. D. Work performance of trainable adults as influenced by competition, cooperation, and monetary reward. *American Journal of Mental Deficiency*, 1967, 72(2), 198-211.

Logan, D. L., Kinsinger, J., Shelton, G., & Brown, J. The use of multiple reinforcers in a rehabilitation setting. *Mental Retardation*, 1971, 9(3), 3-6.

Zeaman, D. & House, B. J. The role of attention in retardate discrimination learning. In N. R. Ellis (Ed.), *Handbook of mental deficiency*. New York: McGraw-Hill, 1963.

Zimmerman, J., Stuckey, T., Garlick, R., & Miller, M. Effects of token reinforcement on productivity in multiply handicapped clients in a sheltered workshop. *Rehabilitation Literature*, 1969, 30, 34-41.

Acknowledgments

The authors wish to express their appreciation to Mr. Jerry L. Morris for his assistance in designing and building the stapling apparatus, Dr. Carol K. Sigelman and Dr. Robert W. Flexer for their editorial assistance, and Ms. Jan Chapman for her help in preparing the manuscript.

Reinforcement of Cooperation between Profoundly Retarded Adults

MARY STENNING SAMARAS
Chula Vista, California

THOMAS S. BALL
Pacific-Neuropsychiatric
Institute Research Group

An experimental approach to the development and maintenance of cooperation responses in profoundly retarded institutionalized male adults was evaluated in this study. A single-subject reversal design was used for the major experiment which involved automatic recording of cooperative responses. Within a relatively short period, 7 dyads learned independent operation of the cooperation machine. During the first reinforcement period, a high and fairly stable rate of cooperative responding occurred which decreased markedly after several extinction sessions and immediately recovered when reinforcements were reinstituted. The operation of such machines by profoundly retarded subjects resulted in increased social interaction beyond purely mechanistic behavior.

In recent years the former pessimistic attitude toward the learning abilities of profoundly retarded persons has given way to an increasing recognition that they have considerable learning potential. A number of researchers have demonstrated the efficacy of operant conditioning in teaching profoundly retarded persons self-help skills (Bensberg, Colwell, & Cassell, 1965; Kartye, 1971; Kimbrell, Luckey, Batbuto, & Love, 1967; Minge & Ball, 1967). Yet little attention has been given to the fact that most profoundly retarded individuals lack even the most rudimentary forms of cooperative behavior (Hollis, 1965).

A method for developing human cooperation by means of a machine which required two persons to operate it was first published by Peters and Murphree (1954). The unique feature of their lever-pulling apparatus, which was used with schizophrenic adults, was that it permitted isolation of a cooperative response which was easily measurable. The fallibility of

interpreting observed responses was avoided by use of an automatic recorder.

In a review of cooperation procedures, Hake and Vukelich (1972) pointed out that in all the studies in which cooperatively operated devices have been used, two essential elements were involved in the cooperative act: (a) the reinforcers of each individual were at least partly dependent upon the response of the other individual and (b) an equitable division of responses and reinforcers was possible. In studies by Hollis (1966), Madsen and Conner (1973), and Hake and Vukelich (1973), retarded individuals served as subjects in cooperation experiments. However, no similar study has been done exclusively using profoundly retarded subjects. The purpose of this study, therefore, was to investigate the development and maintenance of cooperative behavior in profoundly retarded adults with an apparatus similar to that used by Azrin and Lindsley (1956) in a study of nonretarded children. In a pilot study (Samaras & Ball, Note 1), five out of ten severely and profoundly retarded boys, 10 to 17 years of age, learned to operate this machine with a peer within a relatively short training period.

Three main questions were posed for this

This report was based in part on the senior author's doctoral dissertation of the same title submitted to the School of Education, University of Southern California. This research was supported in part by NICHD Grant No. HD-04612 and the General Research Support Grant No. RR-05632.

study: (a) Within a relatively short period, can pairs of profoundly retarded adults be trained to emit cooperative responses consisting of simultaneous button pressing? (b) If cooperation can be developed, can it be maintained and eliminated solely by the presentation or nonpresentation of a reinforcing stimulus following each cooperative response? (c) Does the shaping of cooperative responses result in an enhanced social interaction between the retarded adults which goes beyond the specific simultaneous button-pressing response?

Method

Subjects

Twenty-eight subjects were selected at random from a single adult male ward at Pacific State Hospital from among those who accepted an M & M when it was offered to them on the playground or in the dayroom. Five individuals were reserved for use as naive subjects, receiving no training in the use of the cooperation machine. The age range of the subjects was 19 to 49 years, with a mean of 30. Their Kuhlman—Binet IQs ranged from 6 to 18, with only 4 exceeding 14. All had been institutionalized for 9 or more years. Their average period of institutionalization was 19 years. Ten subjects had controlled epilepsy, and only a few of the 28 participants were not taking some type of tranquilizing drug daily. Two subjects had Down's syndrome, and others had various physical disabilities. However, all subjects were sighted, hearing, and ambulatory. Each subject had sufficient motor control to pick up an M & M and put it into his mouth without assistance. Twenty-two subjects were nonverbal, 4 had very limited speech, and 2 occasionally spoke in simple sentences.

Apparatus and Design

All experimental sessions were held in a sideroom with floor dimensions of 2.4 × 3.3 m. The electronic assembly, controls, and automatic counters were housed in a metal cabinet 1.8 m high, 1.2 m wide, and .6 m deep. Two translucent white plastic buttons, 3.8 cm in diameter, which lighted when pressed simultaneously, were located on the front of the cabinet 79.5 cm apart and 104 cm above the floor. A 1.9 cm circle of felt was glued to the center of each button. A Davis Universal Feeder dispensed reinforcement into a feeder tray 13.5 cm high, 14 cm wide, and 13 cm located exactly between the buttons. A 61 × 91 cm divider of 1 cm thick plexiglass could be attached to the front of the machine, separating the buttons but allowing access to the reinforcements from either side through a 7.5 × 20.5 cm opening adjacent to the feeder tray.

A single-subject reversal design was used for the major experiment in which dyads operated the cooperation machine. During reinforcement periods two M & Ms fell into the feeder tray whenever the buttons were simultaneously pressed for 3 or more seconds. Several additional experimental procedures were later carried out, including the pairing of each dyad member with a naive subject.

Procedure

Preliminary training. Each subject was randomly assigned to a right or a left button position which he retained throughout the experiment. The experimenter used one hand to guide the subject's hand or to cue him with gestures such as pointing to or tapping his button. The physical assistance and cuing were gradually faded out as the subject learned to perform independently.

Whenever a cooperative response occurred, two M & M candies fell into the feeder tray, but the subject was allowed to take only one M & M while the experimenter took the other. The experimenter allowed the subject to be first to take an M & M about one-half of the time. During this, and only this training phase, the room's fluorescent lights were turned off so that when the buttons were pressed simultaneously they lighted up very noticeably.

During the initial training session, the duration of simultaneous button pressing required for a cooperative response was 3 seconds. If five or more independent cooperative responses were not made by the subject during this session, the duration dial was set for immediate reinforcement during the following session. When five or more independent cooperative responses occurred at this setting, the dial was set so that 1.8 seconds of simultaneous pressing was required. As soon as five or more noncued cooperative responses occurred within a session, the remaining sessions were held with a 3-second duration of simultaneous button pressing required before M & Ms were dispensed.

To meet the criterion for performing with the experimenter, the subject had to begin operating the machine within 30 seconds of entering the experimental room, and at least 10 cooperative responses with at least a 3-second duration had to occur within a 10-minute session without cuing by the experimenter. When a subject reached the feeder tray first, he had to take one M & M and leave the other for the experimenter. Subjects who did not meet these criteria within 25 sessions were discontinued.

Both preliminary and dyad training sessions lasted 7 to 10 minutes. At least 1 hour had elapsed since a subject had eaten a meal. Once training had been initiated, one session per day was usually given.

3. INSTRUCTION

Dyad training. Each subject who learned to operate the machine with the experimenter was paired with another subject. A subject who had been trained to push the left button was paired with a subject who had been trained to push the right button. If the dyad began operating the machine independently within 15 seconds of entering the experimental room and continued to do so for a total of 5 minutes while the experimenter remained outside the room, experimenter-assisted training was considered unnecessary, and the subjects were considered to have completed the first session of the first reinforcement period.

Dyads who failed to meet the above standards during the first session received training in operating the machine together. If a dyad who began to operate the machine independently within the first 15 seconds discontinued doing so for approximately 2 minutes, the experimenter entered the room and continued the session as a training session. During dyad training the experimenter stood between and slightly behind the subjects so that either subject could be guided or cued simultaneously with the other, when necessary, to push the appropriate button or retrieve an M & M.

The criterion for operating the machine cooperatively was reached when a dyad operated it for 5 minutes upon entering the experimental room while the experimenter remained outside the room observing through a peephole. At least 10 cooperative responses of 3 seconds or longer had to occur during the 5 minutes, and both subjects had to have taken one or more M & Ms. Dyads who did not reach this criterion within 20 sessions were discontinued. However, when it seemed likely that 1 subject in an unsuccessful dyad would operate the machine successfully, he was paired with another subject and dyad training with the new partner was undertaken, unless the new dyad operated the machine independently without training.

Major Experiment

During the first reinforcement period, two M & Ms were delivered automatically each time a cooperative response occurred. A minimum of 12 reinforcement sessions was given each dyad. If performance fluctuated considerably within this period, additional reinforcement sessions were held until a fairly stable rate of responding was established.

The cooperative responses were not reinforced during the extinction period. This period was extended until the number of cooperative responses during a session fell markedly below the average number achieved during the last 4 sessions of the first reinforcement period and remained at a low rate for 4 consecutive sessions.

Cooperative responses were reinforced in the second reinforcement period as in the first reinforcement period. This reinforcement period was continued until a relatively high and stable rate of cooperative responding was maintained for at least four consecutive sessions.

Supplementary Experiments

Three brief additional investigations were conducted as follows:

1. Within a few days of the close of the second reinforcement period, each member of the seven dyads was paired with a naive subject in a 5-minute session in which the trained subject and naive subject were left alone in the experimental room. The experimenter observed the behavior of both subjects through a peephole. Any dyad member who operated the machine by pushing both buttons himself was paired with the same naive subject for another 5-minute session. In this session the plexiglass divider was attached to the machine.

2. Between 1 and 2 months after the pairing with a naive subject, 1 5-minute session was held with each of the seven trained dyads, and the number of cooperative responses was recorded.

3. With one dyad, after the above session was held, a session was given in which only one M & M was delivered for each cooperative response. Since 1 subject took all of the M & Ms and the other subject quickly stopped operating the machine, the experimenter decided to determine whether it would be possible to train the subjects in this dyad to take turns taking the one M & M. Each member of this dyad received individual training until each subject alternated taking an M & M with the experimenter, without cuing, for a 5-minute period. The dyad was then re-formed and its members trained to alternate with each other in taking the M & M. These training sessions were continued until the subjects achieved perfect alternation for 5 minutes, first with the experimenter in the room and then with the experimenter observing from outside the room.

Results

Of the 23 subjects who were given preliminary training with the experimenter, 19 met the criterion performance within 25 sessions and were retained for dyad training. Only 1 of the 23 subjects required no training to learn to push the button. In this case the subject immediately imitated the experimenter's movements. Of the 4 subjects who were dropped, 2 were excluded after only a few sessions due to unmanageable behavior. One was severely self-destructive. The other sat on the floor repeatedly in the experimental room and thus was physically unmanageable. The other 2 subjects simply failed to meet criterion. One learned to push the button

SAMARAS AND BALL

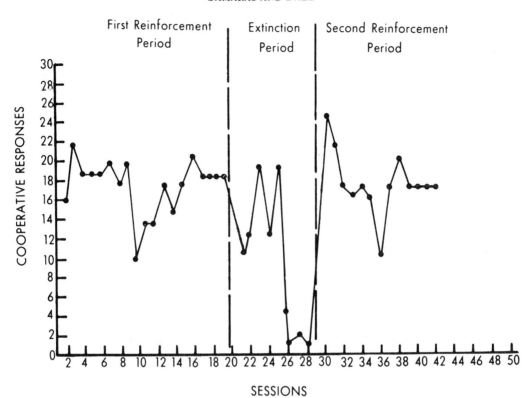

FIGURE 1. Cooperative-response data: Dyad 1.

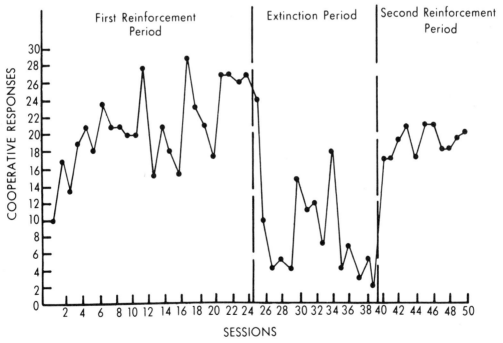

FIGURE 2. Cooperative-response data: Dyad 2.

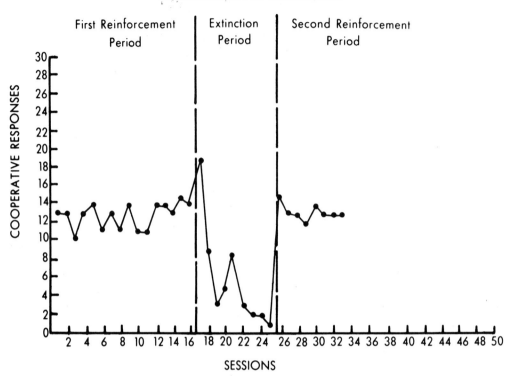

FIGURE 3. Cooperative-response data: Dyad 3.

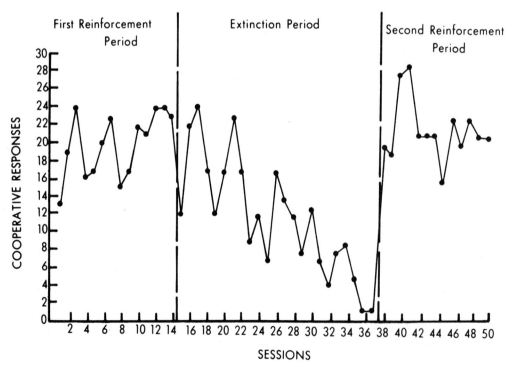

FIGURE 4. Cooperative-response data: Dyad 4.

SAMARAS AND BALL

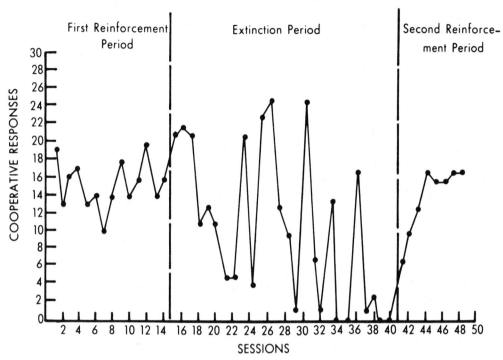

FIGURE 5. Cooperative-response data: Dyad 5.

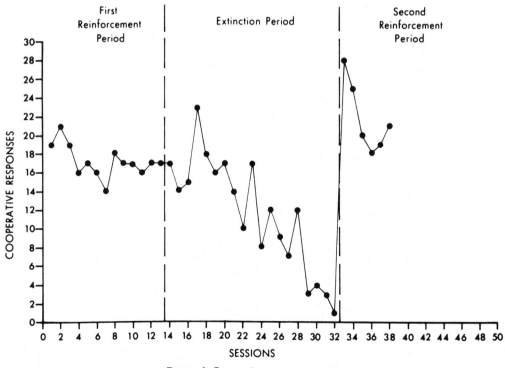

FIGURE 6. Cooperative-response data: Dyad 6.

3. INSTRUCTION

without cuing but would not take M & Ms independently. The other subject learned to take one M & M when two fell into the tray and to put his hand on the button without cuing but did not learn to exert the slight pressure necessary for a cooperative response. The IQ of both of these subjects was 9. The other 18 subjects learned to operate the machine with the experimenter in an average of 10 training sessions. Their IQs ranged from 8 to 16. Almost all of the subjects initially required complete physical guidance for both button pushing and M & M retrieval. However, by the close of the second training session, only a light touch on the arm or pointing by the experimenter was necessary for cuing most of the subjects.

During the dyad-training phase of the study, the experimenter worked consecutively with pairs of subjects. Four original pairings produced dyads later employed in the major experiment. However, 2 subjects from other dyads were dropped after several sessions, 1 because of frequent home visits of several days duration, the other because of the severe psychotic episode. Three other subjects failed to meet the criterion for independent operation within 20 training sessions because each required cuing. Their IQs were 9, 11, and 18. Since they did not require such cuing, the more successful partners of the 3 subjects who failed were provided with new partners. These three reconstituted dyads were then subjected to the regular dyad training procedure.

One dyad required 4 training sessions and a second required 7 sessions in order to reach the criterion set for dyad training. Five of the dyads met the criterion in the first session without experimenter assistance. Two of these dyads were formed by the second pairing of one of the subjects as previously described.

The IQ range of the 14 subjects (seven dyads) who were retained for the major experiment was 8 to 16. Figures 1 through 7 indicate that all seven dyads achieved a high and fairly stable rate of cooperative responding during the first reinforcement period, a marked decrease in responding during the extinction period, and immediate or almost immediate reacquisition of a high rate of responding when reinforcement was reinstituted. The marked decrease of cooperative responding during extinction and the immediacy of its recovery at the beginning of the second reinforcement period left no doubt that the maintenance of the response was contingent upon the M & M reinforcements. The results of the three phases of the major experiment, in general, paralleled those of Azrin and Lindsley (1956) in the reinforcement of cooperation between non-retarded children.

As in the Azrin and Lindsley study, con-siderable variation in the rate of cooperative responding was observed during extinction. Spontaneous recovery after a marked decline in rate was common. So also was the temporary rise in performance which sometimes occurs during extinction (Reynolds, 1968). Specifically, during 1 or more sessions of the extinction period, cooperative responding of Dyads 3, 5, 6, and 7 exceeded that of any session in the reinforcement period.

Supplementary Experiments

During the pairing with naive subjects, some of the experienced subjects demonstrated unexpected problem-solving behavior. Although the procedure had never been demonstrated to them, 7 of the experienced subjects simply pressed both buttons simultaneously. When the plexiglass divider was used, 2 subjects actually attempted to enlist the naive subject's cooperation by leading him over to one of the buttons. Two other experienced subjects almost succeeded in reaching both buttons by putting an arm through the opening in the divider. One tall subject stood on tiptoe and somehow managed to push both buttons at once. None of the naive subjects made any attempt to operate the machine or to take M & Ms that fell into the feeder tray.

Much self-stimulatory behavior such as body rocking and head shaking was observed in several trained subjects during the extinction period and in the pairing with naive subjects but was rarely observed during reinforcement periods. This finding suggests that the performance of a rewarding activity is largely incompatible with self-stimulatory behavior, a fact previously noted by Azrin, Kaplan, and Foxx (1973) and others.

In every dyad session held between 1 and 2 months after the close of the major experiment, cooperative responding began immediately. It is evident that once learned, the cooperative response was well retained. However, in one dyad, 1 member attempted to leave the room several times but was pulled back to the machine by his partner and cooperative operation was resumed.

The dyad which was trained to take turns in taking the reinforcer when only one M & M was delivered after each cooperative response, learned to do so in 11 5-minute dyad-training sessions preceded by 20 individual training sessions with the experimenter for 1 subject and 23 sessions for the other.

All subjects in the major experiment were involved in a human interaction that went beyond the mechanistic button-pressing performance since some form of sharing took place in each dyad. One dyad spontaneously worked out a system of each member's alternately taking the two M & Ms most of the time rather than taking one each as they had been taught. Generalization of the sharing response was evinced when three dyads cooperated during the first dyad pairing without being cued by the experimenter and later when 1 trained subject shared M & Ms with a naive subject. Another trained subject first pulled the naive subject toward one button and then guided his hand toward it. After a moment the trained subject pushed the naive one away and operated the machine by himself. One subject walked over to the naive subject twice during the session and put an M & M into his mouth.

Friendly touching and gesturing by a number of subjects was observed as the experiment progressed. Generalization of the increased social interaction in the experimental room was not, however, observed in the ward setting. This finding parallels the results of a study of cooperative responses in pairs of schizophrenic children (Hingtgen, Sanders, & DeMyer, 1965).

Despite a lack of spontaneous generalization to other settings, there is no reason why a portable apparatus such as the present one could not be moved to such settings for specific generalization training. Furthermore, the principle of the cooperation machine could be adapted to standardized playground equipment thereby providing cooperation training in a more natural recreational context.

T. S. B.
Neuropsychiatric Institute —
Pacific State Hospital Research Group
P. O. Box 100-R
Pomona, CA 91766

Reference Note

1. Samaras, M. S., & Ball, T. S. *The reinforcement of cooperation between profoundly retarded children.* Paper presented at the 26th annual convention of the California State Psychological Association, Oakland, January 1973.

References

Azrin, N. H., Kaplan, S. J., & Foxx. R. M. Autism reversal: Eliminating stereotyped self-stimulation of retarded individuals. *American Journal of Mental Deficiency,* 1973, 78, 241–248.
Bensberg, G. J., Colwell, C. M., & Cassell, R. H. Teaching the profoundly retarded self-help skill activities by behavior shaping techniques. *American Journal of Mental Deficiency,* 1965, 69, 674–679.
Hake, D. F., & Vukelich, R. A classification and review of cooperation procedures. *Journal of the Experimental Analysis of Behavior,* 1972, 18, 333–343.
Kimbrell, D. L., Luckey, R. E., Batbuto, P. F., & Love, J. G. Operation dry pants: An intensive habit training program for severely and profoundly retarded. *Mental Retardation,* 1967, 5(2), 32–36.
Madsen, M. C., & Connor, C. Cooperative and competitive behavior of retarded and nonretarded children at two ages. *Child Development,* 1973, 44, 175–178.
Peters, H. N., & Murphree, O. D. A cooperative multiple-choice apparatus. *Science,* 1954, 119, 189–191.
Reynolds, G. S. *A primer of operant conditioning.* Springfield, IL: Scott, Foresman, 1968.

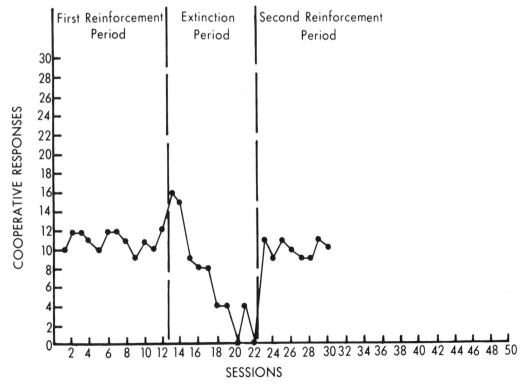

FIGURE 7. Cooperative-response data: Dyad 7.

Selection of Play Materials for the Severely Handicapped: A A Continuing Dilemma

PAUL WEHMAN

PAUL H. WEHMAN *is a Doctoral Candidate and Research Assistant, Department of Studies in Behavioral Disabilities, University of Wisconsin, Madison.*

The choice of appropriate toys and play materials is an important consideration when initiating leisure time programs for the severely and profoundly handicapped. Inasmuch as severely retarded individuals engage in limited symbolic activity, they lack the fantasy play exhibited by many normal children. Hence, the role of selecting play materials for the severely handicapped takes on added meaning. Only with novel, diverse, and reinforcing toys commensurate with an individual's mental age and functioning level can play activity lead to development across many dimensions of behavior.

Several difficulties result from the commercial market's poor selection of toys for severely handicapped persons. The initial problem lies in the fragility of many toys and their failure to hold up over time. Older retarded children, adolescents, and adults are physically too strong for the materials, and the toys break easily. Secondly, many manufactured toys are designed to facilitate symbolic or imaginative play-skills that elude most severely handicapped persons. Furthermore, it is questionable how normalizing pulling a baby buggy around the room or playing with blocks is for retarded adolescents or adults. Yet, this is a problem faced by many recreation practitioners who lack large gymnasium or field facilities.

The difficulties inherent in providing play materials consistent with individual behavior and learning characteristics of the severely handicapped can be summarized as follows:

1. Little research is available to document the type of toys, materials, and equipment that are most effective in eliciting play behavior from the mentally retarded at different age and functioning levels.
2. Toy manufacturers do not typically design play materials for severely and profoundly retarded persons. Consequently, selection must come from nonretarded preschooler's preferences, or toys must be made and adapted.

One research strategy that has been successfully used by special educators is studying normal children's behavior and attempting to apply the findings to the problems of exceptional children. It was decided to approach the play materials dilemma for severely handicapped individuals in a similar way. Research with nonretarded infants and preschoolers relative to preferences for different toys and materials was closely examined. Recommendations and guidelines were then advanced for selecting optimal play materials for severely and profoundly retarded persons.

Research with Nonretarded Preschoolers

There has been considerable effort directed to identifying optimal play materials and the stimulus attributes of toys used by nonretarded infants and young children. Research in the field should also be examined to determine which materials might be effective in promoting play activity for the severely and profoundly handicapped.

McCall (1974) has identified several stimulus characteristics found to differentially influence the exploratory activity of nine, twelve, and fifteen-month-old infants when selecting play objects. These attributes were configural complexity, sound potential, and plasticity. Configural complexity refers to objects that possess various contours and edges. Sound potential characteristics are found in objects that make noise or sounds when acted upon. Objects with plasticity are those that are malleable, such as clay.

It was found that objects with these stimulus characteristics influenced duration of play and

"Selection of Play Materials for the Severely Handicapped: A Continuing Dilemma," Paul Wehman, *Education and Training of the Mentally Retarded*, Vol. 11, No. 1, February 1976. © 1976 Council for Exceptional Children Division of Mental Retardation.

decreased response latencies in infants of all three age groups. Materials with sound potential and plasticity were discovered to be more effective than those with configural complexity, and objects which possessed a combination of attributes were the most successful in inducing exploratory activity.

Similar research with two-year-olds indicate the role information conflict, or stimulus ambiguity, plays in the novelty of different materials (Nunnally & Lemond, 1973). These writers observe that novelty is a stimulus characteristic which is heavily influenced by the child's previous history. Each object presented is only as novel as the relative amount of exposure the child has had to it at an earlier time, Bijou (1975) also concurs with this notion, and in an operant analysis of play behavior, suggests two primary setting factors involved in eliciting exploratory activity in young children:

1. In the absence of more powerful appetitive (primary) reinforcers, ecological reinforcers such as objects or materials eliciting sounds or bright colors may lead to heightened exploratory behavior.
2. When an individual is deprived of ecological reinforcers (toys) for an extended period of time, exploratory activity should increase when the reinforcers are reintroduced.

In order to avoid satiation of play materials and to maintain toy novelty and attractiveness, it is wise not to continually present the same materials. It may be advisable for a teacher to verbally prompt or suggest that a child try a toy used infrequently. Such an enforced sampling procedure has been successful in encouraging preschoolers to broaden their range of play materials (Quilitch, Christopherson, Risley, 1972).

Toy Preference Research

Several studies have examined the toy preference of young children during free play sessions (Hamad, Herbert-Jackson, & Risley, 1975: Hulson, 1930; Quilitch, et. al., 1972). While Hulson's findings are dated, they are still cogent to this discussion. Several relevant dependent variables were studied in relation to the play and social behavior of 10 four-year old children of normal intellectual functioning. Blocks and sand were found to have a high preference value for this nonretarded four-year-old population.

In a more specific analysis of toy preferences, Quilitch and his associates (1972) studied toy selections of 73 children between the ages of one and ten. A combined total of 9545 child-minutes of play was observed with 25 toys and play materials, all of which were available at less than $5.00 apiece. Suction cup dart games, Lincoln

Logs, a water color set, and colored blocks were among the materials played with for the longest duration. These materials also were played with the most frequently by the largest number of children.

In a related study, toy preferences of nonretarded preschoolers were rank ordered by using duration data as an index of preference (Hamad, et. al., 1975). In this report, 92 commercially available toys were evaluated. Unfortunately, neither the toys used in this study or the Quilitch, et. al. (1972) report are described in terms of their stimulus characteristics. This makes it extremely difficult to assess how applicable the toys might be to the play skill development of severely handicapped persons.

Research has also been completed with preschoolers to evaluate whether certain play materials differentially influence the level of social interaction among peers. (Quilitch & Risley, 1973). Specifically, toys such as checkers or pick-up sticks were found to be useful in developing social play, whereas materials such as clay were more likely to lead to isolative play. Similar results with blocks and clay have also been reported in early research with nursery school children (Updegraff & Herbst, 1934; Van Alstyne, 1932).

The implications of the child development and experimental child psychology research on play materials and toys cannot be fully realized until:

a. special educators become fully aware of the literature and sensitive to its potential applicability with the retarded.
b. applied researchers begin to systematically attempt replications of this research with retarded individuals at commensurate mental ages.

Also, there are limitations to applying these findings to severely and profoundly handicapped adolescents and adults who have infant-level mental ages.

Toward a Taxonomy of Play Materials

It may be useful to think of toys and play materials as being classified in separate functional groups. For example, it has been repeatedly observed that a primary purpose of play is to develop collateral skills in areas of physical development, language, fine motor skills, and socialization. If a logical toy classificatory scheme could be conceptualized, it might be possible to program certain behavioral areas by developing play skills that are monitored by a specific category of play materials. Thus, children with specific deficit areas could receive specially designed recreation programs aimed at alleviating a certain deficit.

One possible taxonomy of play materials has been advanced in early childhood research from the University of Chicago (Kawin, 1934). In Table 1 the groupings which Kawin suggests are displayed as a means of functionally separating different play materials. This classificatory scheme has no empirical support, although it might be a fruitful area for future investigation. It should be clear that this taxonomy has applicability for *all* functioning levels of mentally retarded persons.

Play Materials for Severely Retarded Pre-Schoolers

On the basis of the previously discussed research and consistent with a model of normalization, it would appear that many of the conclusions drawn from child development studies of exploratory activity and social behavior should have potential value in helping severely retarded preschoolers gain play skills. The practitioner faced with developing play behaviors in the retarded preschooler must initially assess the present level of play activity exhibited by the child. A profoundly retarded infant or toddler who displays little sensory responsiveness or exploration might benefit from McCall's (1974) object preference research. Objects that elicit visual change or are constantly changing in color are additional materials that might be valuable in evoking exploratory play.

A general rule for programming play for severely and profoundly handicapped infants and preschoolers can be stated as follows: Whenever possible, program exploratory play activity that is consistent with the developmental norm. However, objects can be presented more frequently and social or tangible reinforcers may be required initially to encourage such activity.

Play Materials for School-Age Children

For the severely and profoundly retarded child, play materials must be selected that can function both as toys for play and tasks for learning academic and preacademic skills. One of the biggest problems faced by classroom teachers in

TABLE 1

A Taxonomy of Play Materials

Group 1	*Toys for the Infant*	
	Purpose:	to increase sensory awareness and exploratory activity
	Examples:	rattles, spoons, or any bright colored objects with multiple sounds.
Group 2	*Toys for the Development of Strength*	
	Purpose:	promote physical development and growth
	Examples:	push-pull toys, wagons, balls, jump ropes, skates
Group 3	*Toys for Constructive and Creative Play*	
	Purpose:	develop low level creative abilities
	Examples:	building logs, paper construction, tinker toys
Group 4	*Toys for Dramatic and Imitative Play*	
	Purpose:	promote cooperative behavior, sharing, and socialization skills
	Examples:	table games, group games
Group 6	*Toys for Artistic Development*	
	Purpose:	provide introduction to music and the arts
	Examples:	musical intruments, weaving looms, sewing boards
Group 7	*Toys that Stimulate Knowledge and Aid in School Activity*	
	Purpose:	to serve as a facilitator of academic skills and to provide novel tasks
	Examples:	simple puzzles, object lotto games, spelling boards
Group 8	*Hobbies and Special Interests*	
	Purpose:	promote self-initiated activity which may be of educational value
	Examples:	wood carving, photography, animal care

teaching functional academics such as reading and computational skills to severely handicapped children is utilizing tasks that are novel and fun for the student. Toys and games are educational materials that can lead to greater enrichment of classroom programs.

If the school-age child has sufficiently developed exploratory play behavior as a preschooler, the focus should move to social interaction skills. This would suggest involvement in group games and activities. Table games are one means of promoting social behavior, although they may have to be adapted. For example, most simple table games involve rolling dice or spinning a spinner in order to determine forward movement. Usually, there are instances or options where a player can "jump" another piece, lose a turn, or go backward. These alternatives are often confusing to the severely handicapped child and can be deleted. The best table games include the following characteristics:

a. easily modified
b. brightly colored and attractive
d. durable (not made of cardboard)
d. large and easy to handle pieces

No specific statement is made here to support certain commercial toys that are especially effective in promoting cooperative play for the severely and profoundly handicapped student. This is largely because, based on present research available with severely handicapped children, few reliable predictions can be made. However, the practitioner should adhere to the following guidelines in selecting toys to develop recreation programs for the severely handicapped.

1. Do the materials meet general criteria of reactivity as opposed to nonreactivity?

2. Do the materials meet general criteria of logically leading to social interaction, or does the teacher have to "force" social play initially?
3. Has the teacher systematically evaluated toys and games that other researchers have found effective in promoting different categories of play relative to nonretarded children?

Leisure Time Materials for Adolescents and Adults

It is especially difficult to identify appropriate materials for severely and profoundly handicapped adults. As mentioned earlier, the severely retarded adult functions at an extremely low developmental level yet may be physically mature. Most toys and materials are not durable enough for extended use by severely handicapped adults. Play materials are required that can help the adolescent or adult gain exploratory play, social play, and game skills at a level more consistent with chronological age norms.

Unfortunately, virtually no published research is available to address this problem. Most recreation programs seem to be directed at children and early-age adolescents, and many other leisure time programs found in institutions consist largely of arts and crafts activities. However, it appears that certain types of materials and equipment emphasizing gross motor skills could meet the recreational needs of severely and profoundly retarded adults. These materials might include:

medicine balls
large rubber balls
different size scooters
trampolines
basketball and baskets
old tires
balance beams
mats
shuffleboard
open-ended barrels
stationary exercise cycles
ropes for tug-of-war
playground equipment

Materials are required that are not only durable, but can be readily adapted for a variety of activities. An adaptive physical education program could meet exploratory play, social play, and group game play needs for severely handicapped adults, and it might be the direction in which therapeutic recreation practicioners should go. Program planning could be guided according to developmental norms of fine or gross motor skills.

Use of Natural Environment for Play

Up to this point, the focus has been on selecting or adapting appropriate materials to facilitate acquiring a functional play skill repertoire and different behavior dimensions. What has not been discussed is the tremendous utility of everyday surroundings for promoting play and leisure time skills.

For example, during the winter season, playing in the snow and making a snowman are skills that the severely handicapped person should be given an opportunity to learn. Tree climbing, hiking, piling up leaves, and playing in a river or lake are other possibilities of learning to play in the natural environment. In addition to being an excellent way to learn about the environment and different seasons, playing outside is also more consistent with fostering normalization and integration with nonretarded peers in the community.

Future Research Directions

Future investigation by special educators seems clearly warranted in developing more appropriate play materials. Basic research may be required with mentally retarded subjects in order to replicate and validate the object preference studies completed with nonretarded youngsters. In the same vein, it may be useful to scrutinize commercial toys according to their stimulus characteristics and attempt predictions as to the activity level and social behavior they will evoke.

Optimally, it would also appear that empirically validating a toy taxonomy could be of value in programming different behavioral areas. In this way, a more systematic selection of toys and materials could be made in arranging leisure time activities.

Clearly, a more appropriate array of toys for the severely handicapped needs to be offered by toy manufacturers (Wehman, in press). In the writer's experience, blocks, sand, checkers, and a number of the other play materials popular with nonretarded preschoolers, fail to evoke a great deal of play activity with the severely and profoundly retarded. Research is required to document which type of materials, adapted or otherwise, are most useful in developing the play skills of the severely handicapped.

References

Bijou, S.W. Symposium: Functional analysis of complex behavior in children. Paper presented at Society for Research in Child Development. April, 1975.

Hamad, C., Herbert-Jackson, E., & Risley, T. The selection of toys as the basis for maximizing appropriate play behaviors in children. Paper presented at American Psychological Association, Chicago, 1975.

Hulson, E.L. An analysis of free play of ten four-year-old children through consecutive observations. *Journal of Juvenile Research*, 1930, 14, 188-208.

Kawin, E. The function of toys in relation to child development. *Childhood Education*, December, 1934, 122-124.

Teacher Training

Changing attitudes, recent legislation and landmark court decisions have forced special educators and the general populace to re-examine the services the severely and profoundly handicapped are receiving. The field of public education now has the responsibility to provide an education for these individuals. The initiation of these educational services should provide tremendous growth for this population who in the past were just receiving "care" in institutions.

Who is competent to educate these individuals who have been considered, until recently, custodial? Who should determine which competencies a teacher of the severely and profoundly handicapped should have? Hopefully, representatives from teacher training institutions, state and local agencies, parents and advocates would develop coordinated procedures to outline and establish specific guidelines for the training of personnel in this emerging field. This collaborative network should also monitor the effectiveness of ongoing programs.

We are really in the early stages of our knowledge about the education of the severely and profoundly handicapped. At this time there is a need for productive research and dissemination of information about how these individuals can be educated most efficiently with emphasis on curriculum development being paramount. Research and Development Centers at some of our major universities should be concentrating a major portion of their energies for this purpose.

Another problem may be found in our teacher training institutions. Who is to instruct the teacher trainer? Many junior and even senior faculty members have never had direct experience with the severely and profoundly handicapped. Therefore, we find a need for colleges and universities to seek and find competent individuals to fill this void through a coordinated effort so that trainees will receive extensive field experience to supplement classroom instruction. Innovative ideas such as the "educateur concept", which has been found successful in Europe, might be initiated in the United States.

Educators of the severely and profoundly handicapped must have highly specialized skills. These professionals need a basic understanding in the physical, social, emotional and developmental skills required by this population. Colleges and universities face the new challenge in helping trainees acquire these competencies.

The readings in the volume will address some of these issues. An emphasis on interdisciplinary teamwork is stressed along with suggested crucial changes in programs at institutions of higher education.

Training Teachers for the Severely and Profoundly Handicapped: A New Frontier

SUSAN STAINBACK
WILLIAM STAINBACK
STEVEN MAURER

Abstract: Due to recent litigation and legislation, there will be an influx of severely and profoundly handicapped individuals into community based public education programs. As a result, teachers who possess the knowledge and skill to foster the growth of these individuals will be needed. The onus of responsibility is on the universities to prepare competent teachers. This article examines the basic components that will have to be integrated into the existing structures of teacher training programs to adequately prepare teachers of the severely and profoundly handicapped.

SUSAN STAINBACK *is Assistant Professor,* WILLIAM STAINBACK *is Associate Professor, and* STEVEN MAURER *is Graduate Assistant, Special Education Division, University of Northern Iowa, Cedar Falls, Iowa. The preparation of this paper was supported in part by HEW Special Project Grant No. 451AH50558.*

The severely and profoundly handicapped consist of a group of individuals who until recently could generally be found on the back wards of large state institutions. They were frequently found in cribs responding very little to the limited stimuli present. Sontag, Burke and York (1973) describe these children as those who self mutilate, regurgitate, ruminate, aggress towards others, display stereopathics (rocking, handwaving), manifest durable and intense temper tantrums, have serious seizures, and/or have extremely brittle medical existences. Included are those who do not suck, swallow or chew, imitate, ambulate, speak, see, toilet themselves, respond to simple verbal commands and/or those who do possess multiple handicaps. They have been labeled untrainable, profoundly retarded, seriously disturbed, multiply handicapped, crib cases and custodial.

It was not until behaviorists (Bensburg, Colwell & Cassel, 1965; Fuller, 1949; Rice & McDaniel, 1966) began conducting research with this population that the learning potential of the severely and profoundly handicapped was recognized. While the necessary initial research was being conducted, parents of these individuals began lobbying through such strong parent groups as the National Association for Retarded Citizens (NARC). They worked to gain for their children educational and training opportunities to enable them to develop their full potential. This parental pressure resulted in several major court decisions (e.g. Pennsylvania Association for Retarded Children v. The Commonwealth of Pennsylvania, 1972) that have expanded public educational services to include the severely and profoundly handicapped.

Along with this emphasis on the right to education for these individuals, the "deinstitutionalization philosophy" has evolved which postulates that equal education for this group should come under the jurisdiction of public education. It is noted that education is the job of public educational agencies, not of social services in an institutional setting. As a result of this philosophy, court decisions, and parental pressures, laws have been passed in many states (Education Commission of the States, 1972) that place the responsibility on the public schools for the education and training of the severely and profoundly handicapped.

Other events have signaled a growing commitment to the education of this group.

1. In March/April, 1975, the NARC held a national training meeting on the education of the severely and profoundly retarded,
2. A new American Association for the Education of the Severely and Profoundly Handicapped has been formed (Haring, 1975a)
3. The Bureau of Education for the Handicapped has cited as one of its top priorities the education of the severely and profoundly handicapped (Martin, 1975).

The Need for Trained Teachers

As the focus changes from custodial care to education and training for the severely and profoundly handicapped, highly trained teachers will be needed in public education.

> Here the onus of responsibility rests on teacher training institutions to design and implement teacher education programs specifically aimed at preparing persons to further develop multiply handicapped, severely retarded children. (Smith & Arkans, 1974, p. 501).

The number of trained teachers needed will be substantial, especially if one accepts a teacher/student ratio of no more than 1:5. This ratio is tenable when the learning, behavioral, and physical characteristics of the severely and profoundly handicapped are considered.

When estimating the number of teachers needed, the necessity of early intervention should be considered also. Even the more profoundly handicapped preschooler has the potential for learning, among other things, visual and auditory awareness, motor control of the head and trunk, and a rudimentary understanding of vocabulary. It should also be noted that early intervention can prevent the development of abnormal body structure from prolonged periods of bed rest (Luckey & Addison, 1974). In many cases early correct body positioning can prevent physical deformities frequently found in older handicapped individuals (Robinault, 1973).

On the other end of the life continuum, continued education and training during adulthood is imperative to maintain and expand the skills of work productivity and daily existence. It has been recently demonstrated that the markedly handicapped can learn to participate in work activities (Gold, 1973) previously thought beyond their capabilities.

In essence, a teacher/student ratio of 1:5 and the necessity of life long intervention will require that institutions of higher education train teachers competent to aid the growth of severely and profoundly handicapped individuals. In addition, it should be noted that (a) recent medical advances are keeping many children with serious handicaps alive who would otherwise not have lived, and (b) today there is virtually a void of trained teachers of the severely and profoundly handicapped.

Training Requirements

Universities have focused their teacher training in special education toward the mildly and, in some cases, the moderately handicapped. The potential special education teacher has received more diagnostic techniques and remediation approaches than the regular classroom teacher. With few exceptions, the basic techniques and materials presented teachers of the mildly handicapped and teachers of so called "normal" students have been the same with changes mainly of emphasis.

The functioning level of the severely and profoundly handicapped will require a wide deviation from what has been the mainstay in university teacher training. The following is a discussion of the training needs of prospective teachers of the severely and profoundly handicapped to provide an impetus for critical evaluation of the content of some elements necessary in teacher training. Discussed here are: (a) diagnostic evaluation, (d) curriculum, (c) methodology, (d) interdisciplinary team work, (e) field experience, (f) parent training, and (g) prosthetic aids.

Diagnostic Evaluation

The standard diagnostic and evaluation tools presently employed with the mildly handicapped such as readiness and achievement tests will generally be of little use to teachers of the severely and profoundly handicapped. Even the social maturity tests at the preschool level are frequently too high and/or have too large a gap between skills to accurately assess the functioning level of many severely or

4. TEACHER TRAINING

profoundly handicapped individuals for training purposes.

Due to the infantile functioning level of some of these individuals and the small achievement increments made over time, it is imperative that teachers of the severely and profoundly handicapped have a thorough working knowledge of human growth and development patterns from birth through beginning preschool as well as the basic readiness and early academic learning process. A high degree of insight into child development during the infancy stage such as visual tracking, responding to stimuli, lifting head, reaching for objects, grasping objects and turning over is needed since it is within this range of functioning that teachers will find many of the severely and profoundly handicapped.

These diagnostic evaluation needs require going beyond the present educational literature. Teachers must become aware of the psychological and medical information concerning infancy and early childhood development. Developmental instruments such as the Gesell Developmental Schedules (1947), the Cattell Infant Intelligence Scale (1940), the Bayley Infant Scales of Development (1969), the Denver Developmental Screening Test (1970), and the Piagetian based Albert Einstein Scale of Sensory-Motor Intelligence (Corman & Escaloma, 1969) will need to be closely examined. Most teachers are not aware of, for example, the developmental sequence for evaluating and/or teaching such skills as ambulation.

It is obvious that educational diagnosis and evaluation as we know it for the mildly handicapped and normal student will need modification for teachers of the severely and profoundly handicapped. It should be noted that a few special educators and psychologists (Balthazar, 1971; Sailor & Mix, 1975) have already begun developing diagnostic and evaluation instruments for the severely and profoundly handicapped.

Curriculum

As in all educational situations, the goal of the curriculum for the severely and profoundly handicapped is to move each individual to higher levels in the developmental sequence. The major differences relate to the range of the developmental functioning levels of concern. In the education of mildly handicapped and normal students, the major focus is on readiness for and achievement in reading, writing, arithmetic and social skills. With the severely and profoundly handicapped the curricular emphasis is on response to environmental stimulation, head and trunk balance, sucking, swallowing and chewing, grasping, movement of body parts, vocaliza-

tions, and at higher levels, imitation, language acquisition, self feeding, ambulation, dressing skills, toilet training, social/recreational behaviors and functional academic skills. Vocational skills, as with any individual, are important. When individuals reach this level, the bagging of golf tees, stapling packages, or more complex tasks such as the assembly of 14 piece bicycle brakes (Gold, 1973) are a few of the possible additions to the curriculum.

The curricular needs are widely divergent from the mildly handicapped or normal child. Despite the newness of this area, ideas and materials for curricular development are becoming available (Ball, 1971; Meyers, Sinco & Stalma, 1973.)

Methodology

Presently educators and psychologists are finding that the behavior modification methodology is very effective with the moderately and severely handicapped (Haring & Phillips, 1972) with many implications for teaching the most profoundly handicapped.

When classroom teachers have used behavior modification, the stress has been on the manipulation of stimuli that occur after the response to increase or decrease the intensity, duration, or frequency of responses.

With the severely and profoundly handicapped, teachers must continue to apply reinforcement principles. They will need only to become more sophisticated. The concepts of reinforcement sampling, discrimination training, generalization, stimulus control, shaping, backward chaining, contingent aversive stimulation, prompting, fading, modeling, etc. will have to not only be understood, but also incorporated into daily teaching sessions. In addition, the manipulation of antecedent stimuli will be essential. With the severely and profoundly handicapped, responses will not only have to be shaped but elicited. The teacher who waits for the emission of a particular response in order to apply reinforcement principles will waste much precious learning time. Also, knowledge of the most efficient methods for modifying behavior is imperative in controlling severe management problems. Finger chewing, head-banging, aggressing toward others, and feces throwing can quickly and totally disrupt classroom learning.

The precise measurement of behavior will take on new importance. Progress with the severely and profoundly handicapped may not always be easily recognizable. The morale of the teacher as well as plans for the next teaching session will depend upon correct identification of progress.

Perhaps the most important skill that teachers must have is the ability to task analyze behavior. It has been found that breaking down tasks into small sequential steps enhances the speed and quality of response acquisition in the severely and profoundly handicapped (Brown, 1973).

Interdisciplinary Teamwork

The importance of interdisciplinary teamwork becomes evident when the daily life of the severely and profoundly handicapped is examined. Many severely and profoundly handicapped individuals live an extremely brittle medical existence. They frequently are under the supervision of medical staff; sometimes gaining nourishment through tubes, urinating through catheters and/or living with reduced spasmodic seizures by continuous medication. (These children will challenge the literal meaning of "zero reject." Here we are referring to community-based education in hospital wards or schools as well as special classes, special schools, and residential centers.)

Due to multiple handicaps, the activities of these individuals must be carefully considered by physicians as well as by physical and/or occupational therapists in terms of strenuousness, bone and muscular involvement, and body positioning. Misunderstanding or overlooking an individual's needs may cause irreparable damage. In addition, these individuals may suffer from partial or total blindness, deafness, and/or paralysis which further complicates the communication process to which opthalmologists, audiologists, and speech clinicians can contribute their expertise. No one person can be expected to possess all the expertise required to facilitate the development of a profoundly retarded child who is also blind, deaf, and/or cerebral palsied.

Some supportive and ancillary personnel may be unfamiliar with the characteristics of the severely and profoundly handicapped. The school counselor, assistant principal or itinerant art teacher, for example, may never before have worked with children who eat their crayons, self mutilate, stare at their left hand for hours, and/or indiscriminately wail throughout the day (Sontag, et al., 1973).

Receiving medications is a frequent occurrence with the severely and profoundly handicapped. A child who is alert and responsive one day may be docile and unresponsive the next. In their teacher training sequence, teachers will need to be made aware of the reasons certain drugs are administered and their side effects.

These and other aspects will have a bearing on how the teacher works with such individuals. The teacher will be required to design an educational program, but not be the sole contributor. The element of interdisciplinary teamwork is mandatory.

Because of this need for teamwork, it is important that teachers be trained to communicate efficiently and effectively with other disciplines. Courses in speech acquisition and psychology will be needed. Exposure to clinical syndromes and the medical aspects of physically handicapping conditions will also enhance the teacher's ability to communicate.

Finally, it is imperative that teachers be thoroughly aware of their own and other team members' roles. They must know their particular areas of competency as well as the competencies possessed by other professionals and be able to conduct their duties in terms of them.

Extensive Field Experience

Teachers of the severely and profoundly handicapped will be faced with a population previously considered untrainable. Gains may be slight and tediously slow in coming. This combined with the precise skill application required to effect gains emphasizes the need for immediate feedback and support while actually working with children.

Field experiences will permit prospective teachers to determine if they have the abilities and attitudes required. The enhanced precision required in the teaching process will be too difficult for some; the development of appropriate attitudes will be impossible for others. For example, an attitude that permits *normal* risk taking is essential. As for any child, the severely and profoundly handicapped must be allowed to experience pleasure from self discovery even at the risk of minor bumps and bruises. Field experience can assist prospective teachers in developing attitudes that will avoid overprotection.

A teacher training program which includes curriculum, methodology, and field experience may help us avoid some of the pitfalls experienced in the earlier training of teachers for the mildly and moderately handicapped (e.g. knowledge of definitions and characteristics, but no teaching skills). Hopefully, we can reduce the frequency of the first teaching day syndrome: "I know the definitions and characteristics, but what do I do?"

Parent Training

With the severely and profoundly handicapped the training of parents and/or parent surrogates by the teacher is an important factor. Without the necessary information and support, home care will be beyond the abilities and tolerance level of many parents.

Since the teacher is most closely involved in the overall daily planning and training he/she will be called upon to provide information and support to the parents or parent surrogates. With strong lines of communication between the school and home, a consistent and comprehensive 24 hour program can be devised and implemented.

In order for teachers to assume the role of parent trainers, they must become knowledgeable in several areas. This constitutes another component not previously emphasized in many teacher training programs. A few of the specific competencies needed by teachers to be effective in parent or parent surrogate training include:

1. Explaining student abilities and progress to help parents overcome the problems of under or over protection and inappropriate expectations (either too high or too low);
2. Training parents to deal with explosive, stereotype, self stimulative behaviors as well as appropriate motor responding and verbalization behaviors. This, of course, will make home living a more realistic alternative for the handicapped child, siblings and parents;
3. Being a source of information concerning community resources that can provide health care, social interaction, recreation, etc. This will also include knowledge concerning foster and group home alternatives for parents who are unable to cope with their handicapped child within the existing family structure;
4. Providing parents with knowledge of sources of special clothing and equipment that can aid in easing home care problems and encourage greater independence and self care;
5. Training parents in lifting, carrying, and positioning the nonambulatory;
6. Training parents in techniques for fostering sensory awareness, motor development, communication, eating, toileting, bathing and dressing, etc.
7. Explaining the importance of having the nonambulatory child up and correctly positioned for part of each day in a chair, even if strapped in, rather than flat on his back in a crib or bed. (In addition to enhancing motor development, the child can see and respond to stimuli in his environment other than the ceiling.)

Use of Prosthetic Aids

In order to successfully deal with the severely and profoundly handicapped population, teachers must be well versed in the use of modification tools such as prosthetic aids. A prosthetic aid is a device used to modify an individual or environment so a previously handicapping condition can be bypassed or eliminated in a given set of situations. Smith and Neisworth (1975) list five broad categories of prosthetic devices. These are locomotion, life support, personal grooming and hygiene, communication, and household aids.

It can be observed from these categories that the use of prosthetic aids can permeate almost every phase of life from breathing to brushing teeth to recreation.

Due to the high incidence of multiple handicapping conditions in the severe and profound population, many of them use one if not several prosthetic devices in their daily lives. Teachers of these children will find themselves in classrooms with such items as creepers, walkers, standing tables, cut out trays, splints, motorized beds, wheelchairs, built up and/or modified spoons, knives, and forks. In addition, special prosthetic devices will be used in getting some of these individuals to and from school (e.g. adjustable base lifter). Teachers, when helping children load or unload from the transportation vehicle, will need to be familiar with these devices in order to avoid possible accidents. Potential teachers of the severely and profoundly handicapped should be provided the opportunity to acquire a strong working knowledge of prosthetic aids. They should know how to use and maintain the devices so maximum efficiency and effectiveness can be achieved in the classroom setting.

New devices are being designed to help modify the results of the handicaps of blindness, deafness, paralysis, and voice, muscular, and bone aberrations. As research, development, and use of these devices continues, the need for teachers to become familiar with them will increase.

Source of Expertise

We have discussed why and in what areas teachers of the severely and profoundly handicapped should be trained. Now the question is where will the universities get the expertise to train prospective teachers of the severely and profoundly handicapped?

Educators are rapidly gaining the legal right to provide education and training for the severely and profoundly handicapped. With or without this expertise, public schools will establish classes for the most profoundly handicapped. Colleges and universities will begin training teachers. We will accomplish the task of providing education and training for the severely and profoundly handicapped. However, if we are to do the most efficient and effective job, we must recognize our current lack of knowledge of training procedures and begin to correct it.

The recent work of Blatt and Garfunkel (1973), Bricker (1972), Brown (1973), Gold (1973), Haring (1975), Hayden (1975), Lent (1975), Sailor and Mix (1975), Tawney (1974), and others should serve as prime sources of reference for the identification of materials, techniques, and procedures found effective for training the severely and profoundly handicapped. In addition, the excellent work of prominent institution personnel (Azrin & Foxx, 1971; Bensburg, et al., 1965; Gardner, Brust & Watson, 1971; Luckey, Watson & Musick, 1968; Watson, 1967) should be closely examined.

This focus on available expertise does not minimize the need for further research and study to update and expand what is currently known. It is only to insure that these relatively early efforts are not ignored.

Although we are for the most part inexperienced in dealing with the severely and profoundly handicapped, public education does provide real advantages for this population. Through public education the severely and profoundly handicapped will receive, by the nature of the organizational arrangement, a considerable increase in environmental stimulation by such aspects as living in a community setting, being transported to and from school, and exposure to many normal activities throughout the day. For example, the simple act of being transported back and forth to school provides a wide array of experiences (e.g. active and/or passive interaction with people). It is this involvement in ordinary daily living (normalization), not our current expertise, that largely justifies community based public school education for the severely and profoundly handicapped.

Conclusions

Laws and court decisions have been and are being enacted that will mandate a right to education for the severely and profoundly handicapped.

> The right to education, if it is implemented, will bring into our special education orbit those children and adolescents who were not previously considered to have the necessary academic potential or even to be capable of acquiring the basic life skills for community living or who are not of the traditionally prescribed age for education. Many special educators never before saw them . . . They were invisible. (Goldberg &Lippman, 1974, p. 331).

Few teachers are trained to teach these children and few professors of special education are prepared to instruct teachers in educating the severely and profoundly handicapped. This is not to say we cannot do the job. We can and should. However, careful planning will have to occur, if we are to meet this new challenge.

Although laws are being passed to insure public school education for the severely and profoundly handicapped, little money is being appropriated for personnel training. This, of course, enhances the risk of repeating the same mistake made when we first began

trying to meet the needs of the less markedly handicapped in regard to the use of ill prepared and unprepared teachers. Because of the pressure to provide special services to the mildly and moderately handicapped, many teachers were not prepared for their jobs. Unfortunately, some handicapped children have suffered, as well as the overall reputation of special education. Although some states are just beginning to overcome the critical lack of trained and certified personnel for the mildly and in some instances the moderately handicapped, we will be faced with new demands for trained personnel for the severely and profoundly handicapped.

Unless adequate support is forthcoming for personnel training, classrooms for the severely and profoundly handicapped are likely to be staffed by untrained teachers. If this happens, these children may fail to progress in an educational environment. This could happen if untrained teachers establish babysitting centers or a watered down curriculum. The severely and profoundly handicapped do not need this kind of educational programing. They need well planned and designed programs developed by rigorously trained special education teachers.

References

Azrin, N. H., & Foxx, R. M. A rapid method of toilet training the institutionalized retarded. *Journal of Applied Behavior Analysis*, 1971, 4(2), 89-99.

Ball, T. (Ed.). *A guide for the instruction and training of the profoundly retarded and severely multi-handicapped child.* Santa Cruz CA: Santa Cruz County Board of Education, 1971.

Balthazar, E. E. *Balthazar scales of adaptive behavior for the profoundly and severely mentally retarded.* Champaign IL: Research Press, 1971.

Cattell, P. *The measurement of intelligence of infants and young children.* New York: Psychological Corporation, 1940.

Corman, H. H. & Escalona, S. K. Stages of sensorimotor development: A replication study.

Education commission of the states. *Handicapped Children's Education Program Newsletter,* 1972, 1, 3.

Frankenburg, W. K., Dobbs, J. B. & Fandal, A. *The revised Denver developmental screening test manual.* Denver: University of Colorado Press, 1970.

Goldberg, I., & Lippman, L. Plato had a word for it. *Exceptional Children,* 1974, 40, 325-334.

Haring, N. G. Personal communication, May 2, 1975.

Haring, N. G. *Curriculum development for the severely and profoundly retarded students.* Presented at the National Training Meeting on the Education of the Severely and Profoundly Mentally Retarded, April, 1975.

Luckey, R. E., Watson, C. M., & Musick, J. K. Aversive conditioning as a means of inhibiting vomiting and remination. *American Journal of Mental Deficiency,* 1968, 73(1), 139-142.

FOCUS . . . Model Inservice Workshop

DAY	SESSION
ONE	Communication and the Development Process
TWO	Communication and the Learning Process
THREE	Communication and Motor Development
FOUR	Adaptive Teaching Methods and Equipment for the Motorically Impaired
FIVE	Communication and Sensory Input
SIX	Adaptive Teaching Methods and Equipment for the Sensory Impaired
SEVEN	Psycholinguistics and Education
EIGHT	Principles and Techniques of Providing Language Input and Stimulation
NINE	Principles of Teaching and Learning Manual Language
TEN	Instruction in Manual Language
ELEVEN	Instruction in Manual Language
TWELVE	Alternative Communication Methods
THIRTEEN	Communication and Cognitive Development
FOURTEEN	Think Games
FIFTEEN	Communication and Social Growth
SIXTEEN	Parent Training and Family Involvement
SEVENTEEN	Model Programs and Resources
EIGHTEEN	Summary, Synthesis and Review

*Stimulating Functional Communication: Diagnosing and Evaluating Potential Capabilities of Severely Handicapped Children

OUTCOMES
1. Use developmental sequences in linguistic and related non-linguistic areas along with behavioral obervations of severely handicapped children to formulate developmental baselines for the planning of communication programs.
2. Utilize techniques of task analysis to plan communication programs of comparing their behavioral observations to developmental sequences established for normal children.
3. Prepare accurate and periodic written observations of communication related behavior for inclusion in long range language assessment and program evaluation.
4. Work cooperatively with fellow school personnel and the families of the severely handicapped children in their classroom/school.
5. Demonstrate knowledge of the interrelationship between communication development and sensory, social and motor development.
6. Demonstrate basic skills in the instruction and use of manual language..
7. Demonstrate knowledge of a variety of communication alternatives, specialized methods, materials and equipment for stimulating and developing functional communication.
8. Implement communication programs for their children using resource information, materials, skills and knowledge gained through participation in this institute.
9. Design and implement a "training program in their respective schools for the parents and/or staff members concerned with the education of the severely handicapped children in their classroom/school.

*This workshop was developed and directed by Irving Newman, Assistant Professor and Coordinator of the Mental Retardation Program, Southern Connecticut State College. It was co-sponsored by the Connecticut Special Education Resource Center and Southern Connecticut State College.

Interdisciplinary and Transdisciplinary Teamwork

PERSKE

Beyond the Ordinary	*"It doesn't do anyone any good to have a physical therapist walk into a classroom and take a child out for a short time to work with him elsewhere and then bring him back. That kind of mobility training should go on in the classroom where the child needs to be mobile. Head control and positioning are very necessary in the classroom, so it's best that this training go on there, as well. The teacher needs to be the central person who coordinates and sets priorities for all the skills. She even needs to manage the physician. That's quite a role reversal."[64]*

Alignment With Many Disciplines The day when special education teachers can work effectively in a vacuum is over.	THE NEED FOR PROFESSIONALS FROM MANY DISCIPLINES to work with the handicapped has been advocated for years, but never has this need been as critical as it is in educating the severely and profoundly handicapped. Because of the complexities of these children, their heterogeneity, their multiple handicaps, and their age ranges, effective programming for them must be based on a cooperative effort by a variety of experts.[65] As we become more competent, we tend to align ourselves more closely with basic medicine, physiological phychology, the social sciences, those in bioengineering, and other therapies and sciences. If our handicapped students are to be served well, then we must not only be able to par-

"Interdisciplinary and Transdisciplinary Teamwork," *Beyond the Ordinary – Toward the Development of Standards – Criteria,* edited by Robert Perske and Judy Smith, *AAESPH Review,* Seattle, Washington, 1977. © 1977 AAESPH Review.

ticipate coherently with these professions, but we must also win our authority with them and be prepared to take a coordinating and managerial role in organizing their contributions into integrated programs that will be of the maximum benefit to the severely and profoundly handicapped.

The Multidisciplinary Team

The teacher receives isolated and perhaps conflicting recommendations that may be impossible to carry out.

THE TRADITIONAL PRACTICE of professional teamwork has been the medical model's multidisciplinary approach, in which the child is seen by a number of professionals at different times, usually away from the classroom. The professionals involved seldom communicate, collaborate, or make common agreements, nor does the teacher have major input. The teacher is, rather, the receiver of many recommendations, usually in writing, that may represent conflicting views, but which the teacher is expected to interpret and carry out. Parallel to this is the practice of removing a student from the classroom for evaluation or therapy, without involving the educator in the process, and without sharing the rationale and procedures by which the educator might complement the work of the specialist.

"I had a trainee who was having people come into her classroom and remove children for special services elsewhere. I let her know that she had a problem to solve. How she solved it would demonstrate her level of functioning as a team manager. She saw the need to become an advocate for her children and to put a stop to this sort of educational kidnapping. Her first plea was that those representing the disciplines necessary for a particular child would meet with her and plan the program together. Her second plea was to have the physical therapist come into the classroom and work with the child there. She lost on the first one, but she finally convinced the physical therapist to function in the classroom. On the basis of the energy invested, I felt that the trainee was competent, after considering how scattered the rest of the specialists were."[66]

The Interdisciplinary Team

Lacking experience with the child's day-to-day classroom functioning, the team may make recommendations that are more ideal than practical.

THE INTERDISCIPLINARY APPROACH, on the other hand, does bring the team together, thus reducing the fragmentations of findings. As a group, the team focuses on one child's functioning, shares its findings, and develops an individualized educational plan. However, the educator's role may be minimal, and team recommendations may be more ideal than practical because they are based on isolated views of the child, not on his day-to-day functioning in the classroom.

". . . team members often end their responsibilities by only making recommendations. Actual implementation is not considered and is dismissed as not being a part of their responsibility. Implementation then falls to the person often the least able to carry it out because of lack of power, the classroom teacher."[67]

The Transdisciplinary Team

Other disciplines offer consultative backup.

THE TRANSDISCIPLINARY TEAM[68] arrangement seeks to correct some of the weaknesses of the other approaches. Within this team, one or a few people are responsible for direct contact with the child, and the teacher is one of them. The composition of the team depends upon the specific needs of the child and will include any type of professional whose expertise is needed in planning for a particular student.

To implement the plans of the team, role release permits that training and authorization to carry out a particular specialty function can be given to others: to the teacher, to a paraprofessional, or to a parent. Direct care is thus handled by those persons who are closest to the child and who work with the child most regularly, while the team offers consultative backup.

"The only model I've ever been comfortable with has been the transdisciplinary model. A case I'm thinking of was one in which two adults interacted with the children. Everyone else was channeled through them. These were a teacher and a cottage parent. When push came to shove, the cottage parent would prevail. Both of them became extremely skillful in carrying out procedures from many different disciplines represented on a team. Also, the team members for a particular child comprised only disciplines needed by that child. This means that one team might have eight or nine people on it, while another might have only three."[69]

This approach has been translated into an integrated therapy model which advocates four basic approaches:[70]

- Functioning should be assessed in the student's natural environment. Valid assessment cannot be achieved by a person who is unfamiliar with the student and lacks stimulus control.
- Clusters of skills, not isolated developmental skills, should be taught, in that it often requires many months to teach a severely handicapped student an isolated skill.
- Therapy should be incorporated continuously and naturally into a student's daily activities. Skills taught in short episodes once or twice a week will not result in significant gains.
- Skills should be taught in the student's natural environments, with a variety of instructional materials, persons, and cues. Skills taught in one environment by one therapist, using one set of instructional materials, will not necessarily generalize to the student's natural environments.

4. TEACHER TRAINING

"We favor a self-contained, integrated model, rather than an isolated model. We would have the people from other disciplines doing what they do in the classroom, training the teachers or at least including the teacher as part of the educational process, and becoming a consultant more than a hands-on therapist for the handicapped. We do foster the idea of a team, but it's a team of consultants to the teacher. The teacher is the hub and focus of the activity, whatever the therapy. The teacher has the responsibility for the educational processes, and other people are advising, recommending programs, and teaching the teacher to be able to do the things that they can do. There are, of course, some activities that only a physical therapist can do with a child, but these are done within the context of the classroom. We recommend that a child never be removed from the classroom for an educational activity, with the exception of high school and career training classes."[71]

Educational Synthesizer

Trainees must be prepared to become the hub of activity generated by a number of other disciplines.

THE CENTRAL ROLE FOR WHICH WE MUST PREPARE PROFESSIONALS to work with many disciplines may be termed the role of the educational synthesizer, e.g., one who can draw relevant information from a variety of sources and then incorporate it into daily intervention procedures for children. Consequently, an educational synthesizer is any interventionist who:

Seeks appropriate information or techniques from professionals in other disciplines;

Applies such information or techniques to develop effective intervention strategies;

Implements such strategies in order to remediate problems (e.g., ensuring special diets for children with allergies, monitoring seizure activity) or to facilitate the acquisition of new skills (e.g., implementing muscle relaxing activities or special language training procedures)."[72]

"The educational synthesizer needs skills in acquiring, organizing, evaluating, and implementing (in a practical sense) inputs from disciplines that either are not or cannot be included as daily, integral parts of an intervention program. The educational synthesizer becomes the pivotal force in the overall educational program by seeking and coordinating the necessary resources to produce growth and change in the severely impaired child."[73]

The development of the various competencies necessary to bring the education professional to this focus of team activities requires a number of learning experiences.

"Trainees must develop skill in coordinating many different disciplines. They must have a working knowledge of the other disciplines with whom they work. They must know the principles that guide the communication specialist and various other therapists. They must learn the vital psychology of coordination. They must be capable of being interdisciplinary or transdisciplinary. This means they may carry out specific functions that a physical therapist may do, or, on the other hand, they may develop instructional programs that other persons will carry out in their stead."[74]

Professional preparation programs should offer practical opportunities for trainees to gain competencies in team functioning and management, and comprehensive coursework leading to the requisite knowledge competencies. For example:

Competencies.
To successfully complete this course of study, the student must be able to:

- Describe the roles of the various disciplines in serving the various categories of severely and profoundly handicapped individuals, i.e., the deaf-blind, the severely and profoundly retarded, the severely disturbed, the severely physically handicapped, and infants, in terms of the purposes, methods, and techniques. These disciplines include: medicine, nursing, physical therapy, occupational therapy, social work, speech therapy, audiology, behavioral psychology, psychometry, clinical psychology, psychiatry, dentistry, recreation, nutrition.

- Serve as an effective member of an interdisciplinary team.

- Define and describe the essential features of the interdisciplinary model, transdisciplinary model, and multidisciplinary model.

- Meet the expectations that each discipline has of the effective teacher, including:

  Referring individual students and/or their parents to the appropriate discipline, as required.

  Conducting specialized programs and implementing specific procedures in the classroom setting that are prescribed by professionals from other disciplines.

Communicating educational information regarding individual students to members of other disciplines.[75]

Trainees are expected to gain academic knowledge to prepare them for team leadership. Then many trainees are placed on a functioning team, perhaps beginning immediately as team manager but remaining under the clinical supervision of the trainer until he feels that the trainee has achieved the required competency.

The trainee also needs to develop a special skill in bringing parents into team interaction as much as possible. The writing of the individualized educational plan should, in fact, begin with parent input. Moreover, the trainee should become skilled in effective group communication.

"These are refined skills the educator will be needing. In some cases, educators have found themselves working by themselves because they committed a few social errors. Others, because of the interactions they have used, have found themselves working very happily with several other disciplines."[76]

"There are some courses in the School of Business that deal purely with getting the most efficient output possible from the manpower at hand. To be sure, it is impersonal, but they know how to get measured results. Too often, in all of our human services courses, we tend to get softhearted for others around us. That's nice, but I think the handicapped child tends to lose when this happens. We have to take the interests of that child so much to heart that the rest of us keep our own egos and feelings out of the way. The name of this game is his measured change, and that comes before anything else. I think the School of Business could help us at this point to be that kind of efficient manager."[77]

Finally, training institutions need to find ways of recruiting members of other disciplines into training programs that prepare educational professionals. As nurses and therapists become educators, as well, the education of the severely and profoundly handicapped will gain new stature and will offer the maximum in comprehensive service.

[64] Wilcox, B. Telephone communication: conference call. February 9, 1977.
[65] Hart, V. The use of many disciplines with the severely and profoundly handicapped. In E. Sontag, J. Smith, & N. Certo (Eds.). *Educational programming for the severely and profoundly handicapped.* Reston, Virginia: Division on Mental Retardation of the Council for Exceptional Children, 1977.
[66] Edgar, E. In conversation, Random House, New York City. January 6, 1977.
[67] Hart, V. The use of many disciplines with the severely and profoundly handicapped. In E. Sontag, J. Smith, & N. Certo (Eds.). *Educational programming for the severely and profoundly handicapped.* Reston, Virginia: Division on Mental Retardation of the Council for Exceptional Children, 1977 (p. 392).
[68] Hutchinson, D.A. A model for transdisciplinary staff development. In *A nationally organized collaborative program for the provision of comprehensive services to atypical infants and their families* (Technical report No. 8). New York: United Cerebral Palsy Associations, 1974.
[69] Larsen, L. Telephone communication: conference call. February 10, 1977.
[70] Sternat, J., Messina, R., Nietupski, J., Lyon, S., & Brown, L. Occupational and physical therapy services for severely handicapped students. Toward a naturalized public school service delivery model. In E. Sontag, J. Smith, & N. Certo (Eds.). *Educational programming for the severely and profoundly handicapped.* Reston, Virginia: Division on Mental Retardation of the Council for Exceptional Children, 1977.
[71] Sailor, W. Telephone communication: conference call. February 14, 1977.
[72] Bricker, D. Educational synthesizer. In M.A. Thomas (Ed.). *Hey! Don't forget about me: Education's investment in the severely, profoundly, and multiply handicapped.* Reston, Virginia: Council for Exceptional Children, 1976 (p. 88).
[73] Bricker, D. Educational synthesizer. In M.A. Thomas (Ed.). *Hey! Don't forget about me: Education's investment in the severely, profoundly, and multiply handicapped.* Reston, Virginia: Council for Exceptional Children, 1976 (p. 88).
[74] Haring, N.G. In conversation, Random House, New York City. January 6, 1977.
[75] Proposed degree programs in severe and profound handicapping conditions. Baltimore: Johns Hopkins University, The Evening and Summer Session, Division of Education, January 1977 (p. 24-25).
[76] Haring, N.G. In conversation, Random House, New York City. January 6, 1977.
[77] Crowner, T. In conversation, Random House, New York City. January 6, 1977.

The Responsibilities of
Training Programs and Institutions

Beyond the Ordinary

The training program and the institution of higher education have responsibilities to the trainee, the trainer, the community and state, to many professions, and to society. The training program must ensure a network of collaborative interfaces and relationships, judicious recruitment of trainees, the development and implementation of a well rounded competency-based curriculum, and continuing responsibility to the practitioner in the field. In guaranteeing that training programs are fully supported and integrated, the institution must furnish the services and facilities required for the preparation of these particular professionals, and should use its unique resources to bring about progress and change, not only in behalf of handicapped individuals, but in the interest of society as a whole. In short, our institutions of higher education would ideally make a moral, as well as a financial, commitment to the education of the severely and profoundly handicapped — and to improving the quality of American life.

Special Implications

Training programs must develop unusually close ties with a number of interfacing professional and societal communities.

WE HAVE RECENTLY SEEN A DEMAND FOR TEACHERS who must in many ways have new dimensions of skill and high levels of unique competencies. Teaching severely and profoundly handicapped children and youth presents problems of education and management that extend beyond any that the discipline of special education has heretofore faced.

Programs for the preparation of teachers generally bear the responsibility of coordinating teacher trainers, trainees, the facilities of the physical plant, and the many facets involved in the processes of personnel training. Although these are the responsibilities of all good programs of professional preparation, they have special implications for those seeking to provide the variety of well trained personnel currently in demand for the education of the severly and profoundly handicapped.

First, it is incumbent upon departments of special education to work cooperatively and collectively with other disciplines and professions within the institution of higher learning. When education, physical and occupational therapy, nursing, pediatrics, speech and hearing, social work, and other related disciplines share expertise, conduct interdisciplinary classes, and work together to provide comprehensive practical experiences, students in all areas of special education benefit. Most especially for trainees working with the severely handicapped, a basic knowledge of the philosophies and procedures of the ancillary professions is essential to the development of their abilities to plan and carry out effective programs. Further, when training programs relate productively to such professions as architecture and bioengineering, they pave the way for the planning and development that must be undertaken to assure the probability of community living to severely and profoundly handicapped persons.

> Interdisciplinary cooperation in the education of the severely and profoundly handicapped is not only a matter of classroom programming. Teamwork on all professional levels is our primary guarantee that the educational progress of these individuals will culminate in their integration within their communities.

The program must also maintain working relationships with similar programs of professional preparation across the country. This will enable all programs to remain well informed on the latest research and teaching methods being employed with the severely handicapped, and to pass this knowledge on to trainees. Moreover, it will enable programs and professionals to move together in the research and development activities that are crucial to our evolving technology. Thus, a strong research component is vital to each personnel preparation program in order that personnel may be in the forefront of innovative teaching strategies and technologies that will serve the severely and profoundly handicapped. Research requires information on retrieval services, full access to appropriate reference materials, and a population of pupils for study available in the surrounding community.

Also of exceeding importance to the program are a number of strong ties with that surrounding community. This should include collaboration with local branches of such organizations as the National Association for Retarded Citizens, the Council for Exceptional Children, and the National Association for the Education of Young Children which can offer material assistance and expertise to programs preparing teachers of the handicapped. Community agencies and services such as group homes and sheltered workshops can serve as training grounds and as examples to trainees of eventual community placements for the children they will be teaching. These same services and agencies also benefit from the support and cooperation of training programs.

Equally necessary is close contact with state and local education agencies and with the State Division of Social Work and Health Services, the Vocational Rehabilitation Department, the Developmental Disabilities Council, and other agencies and organizations that have total or partial focus on service to the handicapped. Work with these groups will not only lead to greater coordination of programming, but will also expand learning opportunities for program staff and trainees. In addition, state grants for training can be valuable sources of funds for programs preparing teachers of the severely and profoundly handicapped.

Federal funding through grants and contracts, so necessary for research, demonstration, and training, makes it imperative that the program have contacts with the various divisions of the Bureau of Education for the Handicapped, with other bureaus of the U.S. Office of Education, and with various offices of the Department of Health, Education, and Welfare. Ties with federal agencies also enable programs to remain up to date on pending legislation and on the rules and regulations governing their areas of interest.

Selective Recruitment

The most able, most talented, and most dedicated should be encouraged to enter this area of special education.

THE SELECTION OF STUDENTS to enter programs is of major concern. The program must attract and seek the best possible applicants, those new to the teaching profession and those already engaged in teaching. Trainees should be chosen on the basis of personal interviews, career goals statements, demonstrated academic ability, personal recommendations, and manifest interest and desire to serve the severely and profoundly handicapped. Although past experience in teaching should be given weight, those who have never taught should not be dismissed from consideration, inasmuch as diverse backgrounds are desirable. Students with degrees in the humanities and social sciences should be encouraged to enter training. Those applicants who have never before taught handicapped children should be expected to participate in a classroom for severely involved pupils so that admissions faculty can observe and evaluate their responses to such children.

Entering students should immediately be given a clear understanding of the progression they will follow toward their degree and certification. From the very first quarter of training, they should know the competencies that will be expected of them upon graduation, and how to attain these competencies. To provide trainers and trainees with feedback on individual progress, all trainees

4. TEACHER TRAINING

should be evaluated several times during the course of training. Periodic evaluation will also make possible the modification of training components that may not be conducive to the development of teacher competencies.

The program should include or interrelate to programs of study for trainees preparing to become paraprofessionals, teachers of the severely handicapped, master teachers, consulting or itinerant teachers, and teacher trainers.

Competency-Based Curriculum

The program must offer opportunities for the development of the traditional and special competencies required for teaching the severely and profoundly handicapped.

PROGRAMS DESIGNED TO PREPARE PROFESSIONALS for work with the severely and profoundly handicapped must offer coursework and practical experiences that will make it possible for trainees to become competent in behavioral technology and systematic instruction, the teaching of basic life skills, interdisciplinary teamwork, diverse work with parents, and coordination of programs across communities. Moreover, they must also provide for the attainment of the competencies generally required of special educators. To fulfill this responsibility, programs should include at least the following curriculum areas:[140]

1. History of special education, with emphasis on the history of treatment of the severely and profoundly handicapped.
2. The right-to-education movement, including legislation, litigation, and their social context.
3. Interdisciplinary communication and teamwork.
4. Parent training, counseling, and collaboration
5. Utilization of local, state, and national resources
6. Development of community-based services
7. Administration
8. Classroom organization
9. Public speaking and writing
10. Inservice training
11. Normal child development
12. Exceptional child development
13. Medical basics
14. Handling health problems
15. Prosthetic strategies
16. Assessment
17. Applied behavioral analysis
    a. Rationale and definitions
    b. Research overview
       (1) General research emphasis
       (2) Behavioral research emphasis
    c. Instructional procedures
       (1) Arranging antecedent events
       (2) Behavioral slicing procedures
       (3) Arranging consequent events
    d. Functional analysis
       (1) Pinpointing behaviors
       (2) Selecting appropriate measurement systems
       (3) Reliability and validity issues
       (4) Selecting devices to collect data
       (5) Charting basics
       (6) Isolating critical variables
       (7) Data collection and charting
       (8) Data decisions
       (9) Procedures of applied behavioral analysis
18. Considerations for curriculum development
    a. Instructional objectives
    b. Curricular constructs
    c. Task analysis
    d. General sequencing concerns
    e. Commercial materials
    f. General issues in curriculum development
19. Curricula for the severely and profoundly handicapped
    a. Motor skill development
    b. Sensory or perceptual development

    c. Communication
    d. Socialization
    e. Recreation and leisure
    f. Preacademic and academic skill development
    g. Vocational education
    h. Affective education
    i. Independent living skills
       (1) Self-help
       (2) Domestic maintenance
       (3) Community living skills
       (4) Sex education

Continuing Responsibility for Graduates

Programs should provide follow-up, support, and continuing education.

TRAINEES MUST HAVE SOME ASSURANCE OF JOB PLACEMENT after graduation. The program should contain a strong placement component that will assist all graduates in finding employment in appropriate schools. To ensure that compentencies remain valid, evaluation of trainees should continue for up to three years after graduation and placement. Graduates, in turn, should feel free to return to the institution of higher education to continue their studies, to take refresher courses, to seek assistance in matters of research or teaching, and to upgrade skills if their competencies have not remained at an acceptable level.

The success of trainees after graduation and entry into the role of practitioners must be considered a reflection of the quality of the program that produced them. To supply the best personnel for the education of the severely and profoundly handicapped, programs must be well rounded and strong in the areas of research, training, and demonstration. They must actively recruit the best teachers and potential teachers and then provide these individuals with a logical learning sequence that will lead to established competencies. In doing so, the program may foster and nurture a reputation for outstanding training of personnel.

The Institution of Higher Education

The commitment of the administration will underlie the excellence of the program and the dedication of staff and trainees.

THE AGENCY OR INSTITUTION THAT UNDERWRITES TRAINING PROGRAMS must demonstrate competencies, just as trainees, trainers, and training programs are expected to demonstrate competencies. Without appropriate facilities and resources, no training program can ever truly offer students a first-rate education, nor can professors implement their most effective methods and approaches.

A fundamental necessity is a strong commitment to the education of the severely and profoundly handicapped on the part of the administration of the institution of higher education. This kind of administrative support is essential for the provision of adequate facilities, for assistance in securing grants and contracts for research and training, and for obtaining comprehensive computer and library services. The commitment of the administration will also underlie, in more subtle ways, the excellence of the training program and the dedication of staff and trainees.

> The single most important prerequisite for all professionals working with the severely and profoundly handicapped is the belief that all individuals can learn. The belief, shared by the administration of the institution of higher learning, that the education of these people is very worthwhile indeed, will become the foundation on which the success of the professional preparation program will rest.

The Financial Commitment

Personnel preparation of high quality requires the support of demonstration centers, research activities, and dissemination programs.

THE PROVISION OF THE NECESSARY SERVICES, FACILITIES, AND PERSONNEL to prepare professionals to work with the severely and profoundly handicapped will require a considerable expenditure. Although a fundamental requirement is that of classrooms equipped with adequate, up-to-date visual and media aids, much more is essential if trainees are to gain all the skills they will need. A demonstration center is also necessary. Classrooms should be established for children with such handicaps as severe or profound mental retardation, severe emotional disturbance, deafness and other hearing impairments, blindness and other visual disabilities, multiple handicaps, orthopedic handicaps, and other severe impairments. Infant intervention, early childhood education, and pre-vocational training classrooms should also be included. Each classroom must be supplied with the appropriate furnishings, appliances, materials, equipment, adaptive and prosthetic devices, and environmental attributes conducive to the remediation of handicapping conditions and to the education of severely and profoundly handicapped children.

The training institution must also provide those services that will facilitate research by professors in the field of education for the severely and profoundly handicapped, and which will guide trainees in gaining research skills. Accessible computer equipment is necessary for analysis of data collected from research studies. Library resources must be adequate, with appropriate reference works, up-to-date collections of books, selections of journals in the field of special education and related disciplines such as nursing, pediatrics, social work, occupational and physical therapy, speech and hearing. The library system should also have an operable loan program with other institutions of higher education, as well as a computer terminal for searches through ERIC, *Medline,* and *Exceptional Child Abstracts.* Other necessary library resourses include a film collection and a loan system for securing films for multi-media training, a government documents center, and a copy center for duplicating materials.

The institution must also provide the resources and services that staff members need to disseminate information on their programs and products they develop. On the simplest level, these necessities include secretarial and other support services, typewriters and business machines, duplicating and photocopy equipment, postage, long-distance telephone service, and travel funds. On a more sophisticated level, the institution should provide such resources as: a university press; assistance with the design, editing, and packaging of materials and program descriptions; assistance with field testing; the services of a university public information office; and funding for the development of audio-visuals and other media to complement presentations and workshops.

The Moral Commitment

Universities should channel collective knowledge and action to create major positive changes in American society.

LARGE UNIVERSITIES HAVE THE CAPACITY, not only to allocate appropriate funding in support of professional preparation programs, but also to elicit the cooperation and coordination of the many colleges and divisions within their confines. They have the power to convene a university-wide committee that draws on the technology of bioengineers, architectural engineers, urban planners, medicine, and health science affairs. In this manner, universities can take a strategic and central role in long-range planning for community, state, and national development.

It is necessary to do more than pass legislation in order to secure human rights for individuals, and to improve the quality of life for all people. Our major institutions, most predominantly our colleges and universities, possess the unique combinations of talent, resources, and knowledge to get these jobs done. Their potential lies far beyond their capacities to offer higher education. Their overriding responsibility is to become institutions dedicated to positive changes in society, to become sources of thoughtful reasoning, careful planning, and deliberate action in solving universal problems.

This, then, should be the moral commitment of the institution of higher education: to direct the capacities and resources within its jurisdiction not only to the education of individuals, but to constructive collaboration among disciplines and professionals and to the risk and commitment of using collective knowledge and action to create major positive changes in American society.

"On the campus itself, the majority of students and faculty, still hesitant about the new teaching and learning models (and the risks and burdens of taking responsibility for their own education), must be challenged to join in the creation of truly democratic educational institutions. This is nothing less than a call to make . . . all of our nation's colleges and universities the focus of an ongoing search for possible, probable, and preferable futures." [141]

---

[140] Burke, P.J., & Cohen, M. The quest for competence in serving the severely/profoundly handicapped: A critical analysis of personnel preparation programs. In E. Sontag, J. Smith, & N. Certo (Eds.) *Educational programming for the severely and profoundly handicapped.* Reston, Virginia: Division on Mental Retardation of the Council for Exceptional Children, 1977.

[141] Werdell, P. Futurism and the reform of higher education. In A. Tofler (Ed.). *Learning for tomorrow: The role of the future in education.* New York: Random House, Inc., 1974, pp. 281-282.

Teacher Education

KATHLEEN KOPLIK

A Survey of Cooperative Education Programs Between Institutions of Higher Education and Residential Facilities for the Mentally Retarded

In recent years, some special educators have shown increased interest in the struggle of institutional education facilities to expand their services and increase their impact. One area which seems to offer promise is the area of cooperative programs and projects which might be developed between residential facilities for the retarded, and colleges and universities offering teacher training in special education (Younie, 1965; Batarseh & Cicenia, 1972; Davis, 1972; Crosby, 1972).

The Accreditation Council for Facilities for the Mentally Retarded (1971) has recognized that there exists a need to promote the professional growth of institutional educators and to foster cooperation between residential facilities and colleges and universities. Specifically, the Council called for increased opportunities for internships, student teaching and practicum experiences, and the development of ongoing programs designed to promote the professional growth of educators.

With the growing feeling that educators should become involved to a greater extent with all retardates, regardless of level of functioning, many workers have made suggestions as to the types of programs which would seem to be valid for the retarded at various levels. Davis (1972) urged teachers to view contacts with the institutionalized as true potential learning situations, to make concerted efforts to collect good baseline data, to observe and study residents' behaviors, to use evaluation and measurement instruments, and to attempt to teach individuals to attend to specific tasks.

The Accreditation Council for Facilities for the Mentally Retarded (1971) stated:

> The principle that learning begins at birth *shall* be recognized, and the expertise of early childhood educators *shall* be integrated into the interdisciplinary evaluation and programming for residents (p. 49).

Institutions desiring accreditation by this Council will have to implement the Council's recommendations that there be written educational objectives for each resident, and that these objectives be stated in behavioral terms which permit the progress of the individual to be assessed. If institutions are to expand their educational services, increase their effectiveness, and comply with the guidelines established by the Council, it seems that institutional educators will, in many cases, need to turn to other professionals in the field for assistance in training teachers and establishing meaningful programs for residents.

It was the purpose of this study to determine and describe the number and kinds of cooperative educational programs which presently exist between colleges and universities offering teacher training programs in the education of the mentally retarded, and residential facilities for the retarded in seven mid-western states. The study also attempted to survey the attitudes of special educators in college/university and in institu-

"A Survey of Cooperative Education Programs Between Institutions of Higher Education and Residential Facilities for the Mentally Retarded," Kathleen Koplik, *Education and Training of the Mentally Retarded*, Vol. 11, No. 4, December 1976. © 1976 Council of Exceptional Children Division of Mental Retardation.

4. TEACHER TRAINING

tional settings, regarding cooperative education programs.

Method

Instruments

To obtain the necessary information about cooperative education programs now in existence, a thirty item questionnaire was developed and mailed to the heads of education departments at all residential facilities for the retarded in the seven state area; a parallel questionnaire was mailed to heads of special education departments at all colleges and universities in the seven state area, offering special education courses for teachers of the mentally retarded.

To obtain the necessary information concerning the attitudes of special educators toward cooperative education programs, a twelve item attitude scale was developed and mailed to all educators included in the survey.

Sample

The sample surveyed was comprised of 34 residential facilities and 37 colleges and universities from the states of Iowa, Kansas, Minnesota, Missouri, Nebraska, North Dakota, and South Dakota. Names and addresses of the residential facilities were obtained through the *Directory of State and Local Resources for the Mentally Retarded*, published by the Department of Health, Education and Welfare. The names of colleges and universities offering special education programs were obtained from the 1973 *College Blue Book*, and from *Special Education Careers: Programs for Professional Training in Special Education*, a booklet published by the Department of Health, Education and Welfare.

Analysis of the Data

As the completed questionnaires were received, responses were counted on a tabulated sheet. Totals and percentages were computed to provide a descriptive analysis of the data. Additional comments and explanations were read and analyzed for general trends.

To test the null hypothesis that there would be no significant difference in responses toward cooperative education programs between institutional educators and college/university special educators, the t-test of significance was applied to each of the twelve items on the attitude scale. The .05 level of significance was used as the probability level for significance.

Results and Discussion

Questionnaire

Replies to the cooperative education program questionnaire were received from 23 of the 34 institutions contacted, and from 26 of the 37 colleges and universities. Responses were grouped under the following four headings: Institutional Teacher Training, Student and Student Teacher Training, Utilization of Consulting Services and Instructional Materials, and Development of Cooperative Education Programs.

Slightly more than half of the institutions (58%) and colleges/universities (51%), reported maintaining some type of cooperative education programs with the education department of some facility for the retarded. These programs include: institutional teacher training, student teacher training, utilization of consulting services and instructional materials, and the establishment of training programs for institutionalized retardates.

Institutional Teacher Training

Slightly more than half of the institutions surveyed reported that their teachers can arrange time during the work day to take college courses, yet all who responded indicated that some of their teachers had obtained some college credit during the past year. Teachers at institutions which allow released time for college course work tended to participate in such course work more frequently than did teachers at institutions which do not allow teachers to take courses during the work day. It appears that while prohibiting teachers from taking college classes during the work day does not prevent them from doing course work on their own time, allowing them to do course work during the work day serves as an incentive to teachers to seek further training.

In responding to questions concerning the types of certification available through their special education training programs, and the types of courses available to teachers of the retarded, the majority of college/university respondents reported that their schools offer certification in the teaching of the educable mentally retarded. A large number indicated that they offer training leading to certification for teachers of the trainable mentally retarded, but few colleges or universities reported offering any course or courses designed for the teacher of the institutionalized mentally retarded. The data reported by college/university educators support the findings of other researchers who have indicated that there do not exist in the universities, programs suited to the adequate training of competent institutional teachers (Lerner, 1957; Younie, 1965; Davis, 1972).

It also appears that colleges and universities are slightly more willing to extend college credit to institutional teachers for courses offered at an institution but originated by a college or university, than for courses both originated at and presented by an institution. This finding is not surprising since a review of the literature revealed only a single case of an institution originating and presenting a teacher training program for which several colleges extended credit (Batarseh & Cicenia, 1972). There seems to be a need for the development of more cooperative teacher training programs, particularly programs which can be offered at the institutional facility so that teachers of the severely and profoundly retarded may develop the skills and competencies which many workers feel they lack (Lerner, 1957; Roos, 1970; Crosby, 1972).

Student and Student Teacher Training

The most frequent area of cooperation between institutions and colleges/universities is the establishment of field trips. The majority of respondents from both groups reported that field trips to institutions are frequently used in the training of students. However, the majority of college/university respondents noted that a group tends to make only one visit to a given institution, whereas the institutional respondents perceive more frequent visits by the same group. The data reported by college/university respondents support the position of Davis (1972) that a special education student's exposure to the severely and profoundly retarded usually consists of a single tour of a single institution.

The second most common area of cooperation between institutions and colleges/uni-

versities is in the establishment of practicum sites. Of the 20 institutions responding, 14 (70%) indicated that they serve as practicum sites for special education students. Nineteen (76%) of the 25 colleges and universities reported that they place some of their student teachers or practicum students at institutions for the retarded. (See Table 1).

Still fewer respondents reported cooperating on educational programs other than student teaching. It would seem that to establish such programs would require more interest and initiative on the part of both participants than would the two more common types of program previously discussed.

The smallest amount of cooperation was reported by both groups to exist in the area of teacher training programs whether originated by the college/university or by the institution. If institutions and colleges/universities are to establish effective cooperative education programs, educators might well examine the types of programs which presently exist and consider this apparent tendency to cooperate only in those areas which require little formal involvement and loose commitments.

Utilization of Consulting Services and Instructional Materials

The data suggested that institutional educators are unaware of or do not make use of the apparent availability of college/university professional consultants. The discrepancy in the data reported by the two groups seems to indicate that there may be a lack of communication between institutional educators and college/university educators on this subject. It is possible that college/university educators assume that their professionals are available upon request to institutions or other educational facilities which need their services, while institutional educators may

TABLE 1

Institutions and Colleges/Universities Participating in Five Phases of Professional Training

Types of Programs	Institutions		Colleges/Universities	
	Number	Percentage	Number	Percentage
Institution originated and presented teacher training courses receiving college credit	6	31	7	28
University originated teacher training courses presented at institutions, receiving college credit	8	40	11	44
Institutions used as sites for education programs other than student teaching	8	42	12	48
Institutions used as practicum sites	14	70	19	76
Institutions used as field trip sites	17	85	23	92

4. TEACHER TRAINING

feel that because no formal arrangement exists, such services are not available.

Development of Cooperative Education Programs

Few educators from either group reported experiencing failure in initiating cooperative education programs or in maintaining them when once initiated, but those who did report having experienced failure tended to cite distance and lack of funds as causes of that failure. The citing of distance as a factor in preventing the development of successful cooperative programs is in contradiction to other findings of this study which indicate that cooperative programs tend to be established between facilities which are, on the average, about 100 miles apart, and that some programs have been successfully established between facilities as far distant from one another as 300 miles. It is possible that distance is frequently cited as a prohibiting factor, but that it is, in fact, not an insurmountable obstacle.

Attitude Scale

Replies to the attitude scale were received from 23 of the 34 institutions contacted, and from 25 of the 37 colleges and universities. Respondents could check any one of five response categories for each item, ranging from Strongly Disagree to Strongly Agree.

Summary of Findings

According to the results of the attitude scale, institutional respondents differ significantly in opinion from college/university respondents in four areas:

a) *Institutional practicum experience.* Institutional respondents tended to feel that special education students should have, as a regular part of their training, some practicum experience at a residential facility for the retarded. College/university respondents tended to disagree with this.

b) *Field trips to encourage special education students to become institutional teachers.* Institutional respondents tended to agree that a field trip to an institution might encourage a student to want to teach at that facility. College and university respondents tended to disagree.

c) *Special education instructors encouraging students to become institutional teachers.* Institutional respondents tended to feel that special education instructors do not encourage students to participate in institutional education programs or to consider institutional teaching as a possible career choice. College and university respondents seemed to feel that instructors do encourage their students to become actively involved in the work of institutional facilities.

d) *Expense of college/university consulting services.* Institutional educators tended to view college/university consulting services as too expensive for institutions to afford, while college/university educators tended to feel that such services are available and affordable.

The data and comments from the education program questionnaire suggested that institutional educators may not be aware of the availability of professional consultants from colleges and universities, while responses to questions on the attitude scale seem to indicate that, since many institutional educators regard consultants as too expensive, they may not even inquire into the availability of consulting services.

Both groups of educators surveyed tended to agree on several issues, including the desirability of establishing more cooperative education programs and the probability that such programs could be both successful and beneficial to both participants.

Summary and Conclusions

It appears that if the recommendations of the Accreditation Council for Facilities for the Mentally Retarded (1971) are to be implemented, institutional educators will need more intensive and specialized training in such areas as behavior management, language development, developing self help skills in the retarded, and other areas. It seems evident that to develop these competencies in institutional teachers, specialized training programs will have to be developed; these might logically be developed in cooperation with the special education professionals associated with various colleges and universities.

The opinions of the two groups of educators differed significantly in four of twelve areas. Three of the four areas concerned the institution as a training site for special education students or as a place of possible employment for college/university special education graduates. Institutional educators indicated that they believe college and university educators view the institution as a training facility in a negative way. College/university educators indicated that they do not so view institutions. It appears that there may be a serious lack of understanding between these two groups and that this lack of understanding may be preventing the best and fullest use of institutions as resources and training sites for special education students and potential teachers.

Behavioral Treatment Strategies of Institution Ward Staff

Irwin J. Mansdorf
Denise A. Bucich
Lawrence C. Judd

ABSTRACT. As the use of behavior modification techniques is increasing, so is the emphasis on training institution ward staff in these techniques. Several reports in the literature, however, cite difficulties in training ward staff in such principles. The present study attempted to isolate which behavioral training skills are the strongest and which the weakest in a group of institution ward personnel. Results generally show a reliance on verbal and physical prompts in training and a lack of use of either breaking down behavior into small steps or reinforcing behavior.

The use of operant treatment techniques in institutions serving the mentally retarded has increased tremendously in recent years (Watson, 1970). Psychologists and other therapists using these techniques are increasingly making use of nonprofessional staff in institutions (e.g., ward therapy aides) as agents of behavior change. This has been suggested by Tharp and Wetzel (1969), who, in formulating their "triadic model," felt that those persons in the natural environment who have greatest contact with the target are best suited to be behavior change agents.

Despite the attempts to train ward staff in principles of behavior modification, there has been no uniform success. Thompson and Grabowski (1972) note that a major difficulty in instituting their ward-wide programs in behavioral instruction was ward staff training and motivation. Gardner (1975) notes a host of factors, including experience and personality, which influence trainer quality.

The present study was undertaken in order to evaluate which behavioral treatment strategies institution ward staff use, in the absence of formal training in behavior modification. This, in fact, constituted a behavioral analysis of ward staff training skills, as the first step in behavior change is baseline assessment. With more exact knowledge of the operant level of various training behaviors in ward staff, appropriate training programs could be instituted to increase and/or decrease the strength of these behaviors.

Method

Participants. Five mental hygiene therapy aides (MHTA's) were selected by the ward supervisor to participate in a project of resident training. the MHTA is equivalent to most institution positions of "attendant," and is charged with the direct-care service of the institution residents.

Apparatus. A "Training Proficiency Checklist" (Table 1) was constructed and used to rate the behavior modification skills of the MHTA's. The checklist consisted of 10 behavioral skills which were considered necessary in any viable behavioral treatment plan. Each item was rated 0–3, depending on the frequency of the item. Scores were as follows: 0= did not occur, 1= occured two times or less, 2=occured more than two times but not consistently, 3=occured consistently. Thus, a maximum score of 30 for the entire checklist and 3.00 for any one item was possible.

TABLE 1
TRAINING PROFICIENCY CHECKLIST ITEMS

1. Modeled appropriate behavior.
2. Used verbal prompts.
3. Used physical guidance.
4. Contingent social reinforcement—descriptive.
5. Ignored inappropriate behavior.
6. Sought to break down behavior into small steps.
7. Specified "building block" behavior.
8. Sought to fade out prompts/guidance.
9. Used positive practice of attained step.
10. Gave reinforcement at end of training session.

"Behavioral Treatment Strategies of Institution Ward Staff," Irwin Mansdorf, Denise A. Bucich, and Lawrence C. Judd, *Mental Retardation*, Vol. 15, No. 5, October 1977. © 1977 American Association of Mental Deficiency, Washington, D.C. **169**

4. TEACHER TRAINING

Procedure. Selection of staff participants was followed by individual meetings between each MHTA and the building psychologist. At these meetings, MHTA's were told to select a resident with a particular behavioral deficit (e.g., cannot brush teeth), and train this resident. They were assigned specific blocks of time daily during which they were to work on these programs. None of the staff selected had ever received any formal behavior modification training. Twice weekly, videotapes were made of the training sessions of each MHTA. These tapes were later observed by two independent observers skilled in behavior analysis and rated according to the Training Proficiency Checklist. Inter-observer reliability (computed by total percentage agreement) was computed to be 95.5%. Each MHTA was rated five times, for a grand total of 25 observation points.

Results

Results are reported in terms of the average score per checklist item for all five participants. Table 2 shows the average score per item and the percentage of the total score this represents. Figure 1 illustrates the percentage of the total possible score per item.

Scores ranged from a low of .11 (3%) for item 7 to a high of 2.94 (98%) for item 2. The total average score for the entire checklist was 9.11 (30%). Only two items (#'s 2, 3) were above 50% in efficiency and most items (six) were below 20%.

TABLE 2

MEAN SCORE AND PERCENTAGE
TOTAL POSSIBLE SCORE
FOR ALL ITEMS

Item Number	Mean Score	Percentage
1.	.83	28%
2.	2.94	98%
3.	2.08	69%
4.	.94	31%
5.	.30	10%
6.	.47	15%
7.	.11	3%
8.	.55	18%
9.	.58	19%
10.	.36	12%

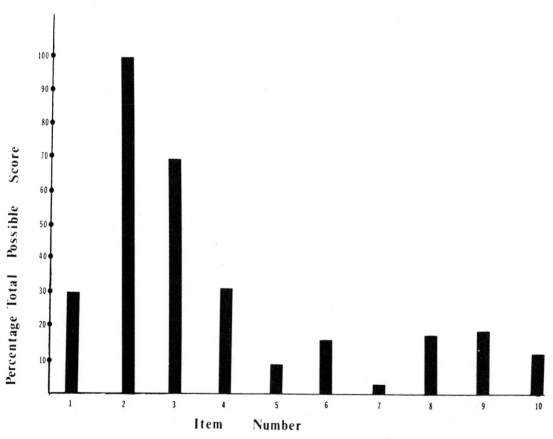

FIGURE 1
HISTOGRAM OF PERCENTAGE TOTAL POSSIBLE SCORE FOR EACH CHECKLIST ITEM.

Discussion

These results give an important insight into the behavioral training strategies of ward staff. There is a strong reliance on the use of verbal prompts and physical guidance, which is in fact simply telling a resident to perform a behavior and then leading him or her through it. It is clear that there is practically no attempt to conceptualize a behavior as a series of smaller steps, and to start at one point in training and move up from there. Similarly, there is little ignoring of inappropriate behavior, pointing out again the inability to focus in on the problem behavior itself. A significant finding is the lack of use of reinforcement for appropriate behavior. Ward staff viewed training as a mere exercise, and simply "ran" the residents through routine sequences.

The staff participants in the present study would benefit from a training package that emphasized looking at small parts of behavior and contingently reinforcing success. There would be little need to teach the use of prompts or manual guidance, but it would be important to indicate the proper fading out of these devices.

In planning training programs for ward staff, it would be important, as in the present case, to assess which skills are strongest and which are weakest.

Such an assessment would allow for a more efficient use of instruction time, and result in a more productive total training program.

References

Gardner, J. M. Training nonprofessionals in behavior modification. In T. Thompson and W. S. Dockens, (Eds.), *Applications of behavior modification*. New York: Academic Press, 1975.

Tharp, R. G. & Wetzel R. J. *Behavior modification in the natural environment*. New York: Academic Press, 1969.

Thompson, T. & Grabowski, J. *Behavior modification of the mentally retarded*. New York: Oxford University Press, 1972.

Watson, L. Behavior modification of residents and personnel in institutions for the mentally retarded. In A. Baumeister and E. Butterfield (Eds.), *Residential facilities for the mentally retarded*. Chicago: Aldine, 1970.

Authors: **IRWIN J. MANSDORF,** Ph.D., Psychologist and Program Coordinator, Adult Transitional Unit, Suffolk Developmental Center, Melville, New York; **DENISE A. BUCICH,** M.A. and **LAWRENCE G. JUDD,** M. A., Psychology Interns at Suffolk Developmental Center, Ph.D. students in Psychology at Hofstra University, Hempstead, New York.

Preparing "Paraprofessional" Personel for Education of the Severely Handicapped: The Teaching Associate

DENNIS TUCKER, JOHN HOLLIS, WAYNE SAILOR,
DON HORNER, PHYLLIS KELLY, DOUG GUESS

DENNIS TUCKER *is Co-coordinator of the
Teaching Associate Training Component of the
Personnel Preparation Program for Education
of the Severely Handicapped, Kansas Neurological
Institute;* JOHN HOLLIS *is Co-coordinator of
the Teaching Associate Training Component of the
Personnel Preparation Program for Education of
the Severely Handicapped, Kansas Neurological
Institute, Topeka, Kansas. He is also a Research
Associate, Bureau of Child Research, University
of Kansas;* WAYNE SAILOR *is Director of the
Personnel Preparation Program for Education
of the Severely Handicapped, Kansas Neurological
Institute, and a Research Associate, Bureau of
Child Research, University of Kansas.* DON
HORNER *is Coordinator of the Teacher Training Component of the Personnel Preparation Program for Education of the Severely Handicapped,
on subcontract to the Department of Special Education, University of Kansas, Lawrence, Kansas.*

Teacher and Teaching Associate Relationship

The educational teaching associate, in order
to effectively supplement the educational
opportunities for severely handicapped students, must have acquired the informational
and performance competencies directly related to changing the behavior of such
students. The teaching associates will be
directly supervised by the teacher and carry
out educational programs developed and
implemented by the teacher. In order to enhance implementation of educational programs, both the teacher and teaching associate should receive similar training in those
competencies directly related to the education of severely handicapped students.

Teaching Associate Preparation Model

The Kansas program (Sailor, *et al.*, 1975)
is designed to provide comprehensive, performance-based curricula for the preparation of both teachers and teaching associates
who will develop educational programs for
severely handicapped individuals, in accord
with the national mandate for equality of
access to education for all handicapped
children and youth.

The competencies identified through this
program provide both teachers and teaching
associates with requisite performance skills
to provide functional educational programs
for individuals who are severely and profoundly handicapped, including those with
severe or profound orthopedic impairments,
behavior disorders, perceptual, psycho-
motor, and/or medical disorders.

The competency-based curriculum model
was developed around two training components: informational competencies and
performance competencies. Informational
competencies are considered prerequisite to
the performance competencies. Each training module has a format which includes
the specification of the criterion required to
successfully demonstrate the acquisition of
the informational and performance competencies. The training modules are sub-
sumed under a sequence of courses leading
to college credit hours.

Competency Blocks. Three basic blocks of
"teaching" competencies have been identified: (a) those competencies that are directly
related to changing student behavior (e.g.,
measuring behavior, strengthening behavior, weakening behavior); (b) those
competencies that are indirectly related to
changing student behavior (e.g., writing instructional objectives, curriculum planning,
task analysis); and (c) those competencies
that have an unknown relationship to changing student behavior (e.g., issues in "right to

"Preparing Paraprofessionals Personnel for Education of the Severely Handicapped: The Teaching Associate," Dennis
Tucker, John Hollis, Wayne Sailor, Don Horner, Phyllis Kelley, and Doug Guess, *Education and Training of the Mentally
Retarded*, Vol. 11, No. 3, October 1976. © 1976 Council for Exceptional Children Division of Mental Retardation.

education," "normalization," counseling with parents).

Training Modules. Twenty-five training modules covering the three basic blocks of instructional competencies for teacher training were targeted for initial development. The topic covered by each training module was subjected to a content analysis and the informational and performance competencies identified (Horner, Holvoet & Rinne, 1976). The informational and performance competencies for teaching associates were specified by determining on *a priori* basis which competencies would provide functional classroom teaching assistance to teachers. Table 1 illustrates the relationship of the teacher and teaching associate training modules.

It was determined that the teaching associate should receive: (a) rigorous training in those competency areas that are *directly* related to changing student behaviors (i.e., concentration on competencies related to actual teaching skills); (b) training in some component parts of the areas *indirectly* related to changing student behaviors; and (c) minimal exposure to those areas that have an unknown relationship to changing student behaviors.

Informational Competencies. An example of the relationship between teachers and teaching associates with respect to informational competencies for a module is presented in Table 2.

Module A: Right to Education represents a competency area that falls into Block 3, having an unknown relationship to teaching students. Out of 20 informational competencies for teachers, only 6 apply to teaching associates. In addition (not illustrated), Module A contains 4 performance competencies for teachers as opposed to none for teaching associates. On the other hand, Module B: Introduction to Operant Behavior, exemplifies a competency area categorized as a Block 1 area. Module B contains 20 informational competencies for teachers all of which are applicable for teaching associates. The informational competencies are accompanied by 10 performance competencies for teachers of which 8 apply to teaching associates (see Table 3).

With respect to Block 2, areas *indirectly* related to teaching students, an example is Module P: Assessment Scales. A teacher is expected not only to administer assessment scales, but also to interpret the results for formulating instructional objectives and planning the curriculum. The teaching associate, on the other hand, is trained only in the mechanics of administering the assessment scale.

In addition to the informational and performance competencies, each module contains a reading list (academic modules only) which corresponds to the informational competencies and a system for evaluation. Both of the personnel training programs utilize written examinations for evaluating informational competencies.

Performance Competencies. The specific procedures being developed to train teaching personnel within the practicum component (Carpenter, 1975) are similar to those suggested by O'Brien and Azrin (1972) and Horner and Keilitz (1975) for training handicapped persons. Depending upon the trainee's ability to perform a specific task, the personnel trainer provides assistance in skill development at any one of four levels. In the development of applied skills, the four levels of assistance are: 1. No trainer assistance; 2. Corrective verbal feedback; 3. Model or demonstration of skill to be learned; 4. Verbal guidance or "verbal put-through" of trainee through the skill task.

The systematic application of operant techniques within the practicum component is evaluated by the use of a Teacher Proficiency Checklist (Horner, 1975). This system, which is currently undergoing revision and field testing, will when completed reflect trainee progress on instructional objectives measured against baseline performance in actual teaching situations with severely handicapped students.

Student Curriculum and Assessment. The ultimate goal of a teacher or teaching associate is, of course, to increase the number of functional skills of the child. Obviously, a teacher or teaching associate can perform perfectly according to academically structured objectives, but if the child fails to learn, any number of programmatic variables may be responsible. One common variable is the instructional program used to teach a specific skill. To increase the number of program resources available to teachers, the Project has compiled a continuously up-dated bibliography of existing curricula for the severely handicapped and is in the process of compiling a computerized prescriptive-retrieval system to be employed with an especially designed assessment technique for the severely handicapped. The TARC Assessment System (Sailor & Mix, 1975) provides a profiled assessment of a severely handicapped student, which, in turn, generates detailed information on the child's current level of functioning within the domains of Self-Help Skills, Motor Skills, Communication Skills, and Social Skills.

Career Advancement

The total program provides comprehensive,

4. TEACHER TRAINING

TABLE 1

**General Competency Area Curriculum Requirements: Teacher and Teaching
Associate Multiply/Severely Handicapped Program**

Module	Title	Teacher	Teaching Associate
Module A:	Right to Education	X	X
Module B:	Introduction to Operant Behavior	X	X
Module C:	Behavioral Approach to Special Education	X	
Module D:*	Basic Classroom Participation: Practicum I	X	X
Module E:	Measuring Operant Behavior	X	X
Module F:	Evaluation of Operant Procedures	X	X
Module G:	Strengthening Operant Behavior	X	X
Module H:	Weakening Operant Behavior	X	X
Module I:	Schedules of Reinforcement	X	X
Module J:	Generalization and Discrimination	X	X
Module K:	Programming for Normalization	X	
Module L:	Programming Prosthetic Environments	X	X
Module M:	Programming Engaging Environments	X	X
Module N:	Training Teacher Aides and Parents	X	
Module O:*	Intermediate Classroom Participation: Practicum II	X	X
Module P:	Assessment Scales	X	X
Module Q:	Writing Instructional Objectives	X	X
Module R:	Curriculum Planning	X	X
Module S:	Task Analysis	X	X
Module T:	Motor Programs	X	X
Module U:	Self-Help Programs	X	X
Module V:	Language Programs	X	X
Module W:	Socialization Programs	X	X
Module X:	Preacademic Programs	X	X
Module Y:*	Advanced Classroom Participation: Practicum III	X	X

* Practicum Modules consist of exercises designed to evaluate performance competencies.

performance-based training across a common set of competencies for both teachers and teaching associates, and an educational career ladder whereby teaching associates may advance across ranks to become teachers.

A program designed to train teaching associates for the severely handicapped will probably fail to attract many applicants unless some viable and objective method for advancement is built into the program.

Current salaries for teaching associates are inadequate in relation to the educational opportunities they provide upon completing a functional performance-based training program. Thus, potential career advancement is currently the only viable source of motivation for acquiring the competencies taught through a rigorous training program.

The staff of the personnel preparation program at the Kansas Neurological Institute in Topeka, Kansas, examined the issue of career advancement in terms of two potential career ladders. One potential ladder exists *within* a career as a teaching associate. Advancement within ranks would occur as a result of additional years of on-the-job experience and continuing education through workshops, in-service training, extension courses, etc. Although some benefits such as immediate and continuous employment, acquiring skills on the job and establishing seniority in preferential selection of classes may accrue, a within ranks advancement offers a very limited career ladder.

A second, and more promising career ladder for a teaching associate consists of advancing *across* ranks from teaching associate to teacher. The method of career advancement would consist of first completing a training program leading to an associate arts degree at a community college in or near the community in which the teaching assistant is employed.

Continuing competency-based education would then be arranged through either a combination of on-campus, continuing education, or extension programs of a four year college or university, culminating in a bachelor's degree and certification as a regular education teacher, followed by a graduate program in special education in order to receive certification as a special education teacher. This latter case represents a considerable investment in educa-

TABLE 2

Teacher and Teaching Associate Informational Competencies
Module A: Right to Education

Informational Competencies (Abbreviated)	Teachers	Teaching Associates
Prepare a written definition, description, statement of:		
1. Concept of "zero rejection"	X	X
2. Origins of "rights to treatment and education"	X	X
3. Constitutional provisions establishing "rights to treatment and education"	X	
4. Legal exclusion of handicapped from public education	X	
5. Difference between "class action" and "private action" suit	X	
6. Rationale for legal issue of equality of *access to* education	X	
7. Stages in Wyatt V. Stickney litigation	X	
8. The salient provisions of the Pennsylvania consent agreement	X	
9. Application of "least restrictive means" principle	X	X
10. "Cascade system" of educational placement	X	
11. Status of institutional residents in relation to "right to education"	X	X
12. Legally prescribed minimum standards for educational programs	X	
13. Economic aspects of court ordered minimum educational standards	X	
14. Court decision challenging use of testing instruments for special class placement	X	X
15. Negative aspects of purchasing special education services	X	
16. Concept of "institutional peonage"	X	X
17. Distinction between therapeutic and nontherapeutic work assignments	X	
18. Legal approaches to remediating "institutional peonage"	X	
19. Statutory definition of exceptional children	X	
20. Legal exceptions to providing special education services	X	

TABLE 3

Teacher and Teaching Associate Performance Competencies
Module B: Introduction to Operant Behavior

Performance Competencies (Abbreviated)	Teachers	Teaching Associates
Apply academic information by:		
1. Translating target behaviors from assessment scales into behavioral definitions	X	
2. Engaging in a procedure for identifying potential reinforcers	X	X
3. Using a measurement instrument to record performance of target behavior	X	X
4. Determining interobserver reliability of measurements	X	
5. Computing and plotting data points on a graph	X	X
6. Presenting programmed discriminative stimuli	X	X
7. Immediately presenting contingent reinforcers during training	X	X
8. Withholding the presentation of reinforcers during training contingent upon nontargeted responses	X	X
9. Interrupting responses which are incompatible with targeted responses	X	X
10. Following a specific programmed teaching sequence	X	X

tion and is based on the assumption that a regular education background is a valuable prerequisite to special education. The validity of this assumption is especially suspect in the preparation of teachers for the severely handicapped.

Summary

The personnel preparation model presented here provides the training requirements for a unified teaching team to provide functional educational opportunities for the severely handicapped. The training program specifies the competencies required of teachers and teaching associates and a suggested delivery model. The Kansas program is designed to fulfill the national mandate and to meet federal guidelines for the education of severely handicapped individuals through the public schools.

ENROLL IN WORK STUDY (Take extra turn.)

SPECIALIZED TRAINING APPROVED

GOOD PERFORMANCE RATING (Pick up salary bonus.)

COMPLETE APPRENTICESHIP (Pick up salary bonus.)

ADVANCE 5 SPACES

HANDICAPPED PARKING

EARN 4 COLLEGE CREDITS

GO BACK 2 SPACES

ADVANCE TO BONUS

CHANGE CAREER

OPPORTUNITY KNOCKS

PARKING

HANDICAPPED PARKING

Future Trends

It appears that the Federal government has again taken the lead in protecting the rights of another minority population. In this case the minority population is all handicapped children, and the right is for an appropriate, free, public education. With the enactment of Public Law 94-142, and other related legislation, the government has not only recognized these rights, but has attempted to secure and enforce them. Due process provisions, the right to be placed in the least restrictive environment, and the responsibilities for special educators to individualize educational plans are specific aspects of this law that should insure progress for the severely and profoundly handicapped. However, there is still a gigantic challenge ahead of us. The financial commitment required to implement the various educational, occupational, and social programs needed by the severely handicapped will be extensive. The issue of public accountability by those responsible for the education and treatment of the severely and profoundly handicapped must and will be examined. The development of appropriate educational goals and objectives that specify desired behavioral changes will require the coordination and cooperation of many professionals. Crucial questions must be resolved if education for the severely and profoundly handicapped is to be made meaningful. Some of those questions are:

— Who will define what is an appropriate education?
— Will there be adequate funds for expanded programs?
— What provisions will be made for the training of teachers and other specialists?
— Will the demands for interpretable and functionally useful research be met?
— Will this research lead to improved curricula and more sophisticated evaluative procedures?
— Will innovative efforts be disseminated in the literature?
— Will adovcacy groups grow in strength?
— Will interdisciplinary cooperation be found?

If these questions are appropriately addressed there will be no justification for inadequate education for severely/ profoundly handicapped youngsters. While these individuals will require some supportive services, every effort must be made to bring these human beings to their optimal potential.

The articles in this anthology highlight issues that may determine successful programming for severely and profoundly handicapped children in the future. Positive and accelerated change must continue to characterize this emerging field for the betterment of all.

Looking Toward the Future

The continuing expansion of educational opportunities for the handicapped at the State and local levels, a succession of court decisions affirming the rights of handicapped students, and climactic new Federal legislation have combined to create a firm foundation for further progress. What may and should lie ahead, both immediately and for the long range, is of particular concern to the National Advisory Committee, as part of its responsibility to review the condition of education of the handicapped and suggest optimum courses for the future.

In carrying out that responsibility the Committee sought to supplement the backgrounds and perceptions represented on the Committee itself by soliciting the views of a wide range of persons whose work and background promised valuable insights. Individual Committee members conducted interviews with State and local directors of special education, classroom teachers, school principals, university professors, private school directors, State hospital directors, handicapped individuals, and parents of handicapped children. In addition, meetings were held with concerned groups, including extensive sessions with the National Association of State Directors of Special Education, and NACH representatives attended professional conferences to solicit suggestions. The Committee also consulted with a number of distinguished authorities. There were "hearings" with members of the staff of the Bureau of Education for the Handicapped and its able leader, Dr. Edwin W. Martin, Jr., and with appropriate other Office of Education program officials. The Committee is grateful to all of these individuals and groups for their cooperation and their contributions.

Concerns of the Field

The interviews conducted by NACH members (about 100 in all) clearly do not represent a scientific sampling. Judging from the experience of members of the Committee, however, and from testimony offered at Committee meetings, the results do appear to be an accurate reflection of some of the basic viewpoints and concerns of special educators in the field and of parent and other advocacy groups.

There was considerable opinion that the importance of continued leadership and support from the Federal level should not be allowed to obscure the significance of activities at the State and local levels. Thus in discussions concerning the need for a deliniation of responsibilities (so that services will be more coordinated and comprehensive), the following observations emerged: Whereas Federal activity and leadership are especially important in the initiation and support of research, model program development,

"Looking Toward the Future," *The Unfinished Revolution,* Education for the Handicapped, National Advisory Committee on the Handicapped, 1976 Annual Report.

dissemination, and technical assistance, the delivery of services occurs primarily through local and State agencies. At both State and local levels, these services vary in quality and kind, and there are inconsistencies in full implementation of legislated mandates and guidelines. Protection of the rights of handicapped individuals cannot be viewed as the responsibility of any single agency or government unit, but rather must be accepted as the active responsibility of all.

In regard to training, it was widely felt that existing programs of professional preparation require reexamination and improvement if they are to meet the demands of the future. Particular stress was laid on the training of regular educational personnel to work with handicapped pupils, especially in view of the increasing participation of these children within conventional education.

In this latter connection it was emphasized that the philosophy of "the least restrictive environment" cited in the new Education for All Handicapped Children Act clearly requires that fundamental changes occur in regular school personnel and programs as well as in the specialized ones. This obviously implies such activities as preservice training and inservice retraining of regular school personnel, programs for "regular" school children who will interact with handicapped children, and programs for parents of both regular and special education pupils. Less obviously but probably of greater significance, it implies far-reaching attitudinal changes on the part of society as a whole. Given the magnitude of the changes called for, the complexities and needs of "mainstreaming" emerge as being so significant as to require considerably more study and debate than the concept has received to date.

In other areas, there was strong support for continued and expanded programs and services in early childhood education, vocational education, physical education, and leisure activities. A special need for these and other kinds of activities was seen as existing among five particular groups of handicapped persons—secondary school pupils, adults, the inner-city handicapped, handicapped persons from non-majority cultures, and handicapped people living in rural or sparsely populated areas.

Regarding priorities in serving these groups, many of those interviewed by NACH members spoke of the importance of research aimed at developing remedial and treatment techniques and programs directed at specific handicapping conditions. Several respondents observed that even where funds and personnel are available, uncertainty often arises as to which particular programs are most effective for what particular situations.

As regards possible new legislation, there was consensus that the essential issue is implementation and enforcement of existing legislation, rather than the development of new mandates. Where legislative changes were suggested, the emphasis was on protection of due process, guarantees of constitutional rights, and (as NACH has strongly recommended in previous reports) increased opportunity for decision making by handicapped individuals themselves. Said a handicapped respondent, "We need to move from 'tugging at the heartstrings' to letting handicapped people demonstrate what they can do." Another proposed that all local, State, and Federal institutions serving the handicapped be required to hire handicapped consumers as consultants or advisors.

Advocacy groups were held to be of critical importance in achieving success in these and other areas, and the National Advisory Committee was specifically singled out for its role as "the public conscience" in matters relating to the right of handicapped children to a good education.

There was much interest in the development of more effective techniques of data collection and distribution, in part to facilitate the monitoring of general progress in achieving goals spelled out in legislation, and with equal importance to provide better mechanisms for identifying effective practices and approaches and for disseminating information about them. Most of those interviewed felt that the Bureau of Education for the Handicapped was the logical (and perhaps only practical) entity to spearhead and coordinate this kind of activity.

Throughout these discussions it was repeatedly suggested that the single most important requirement for significant advances in education of the handicapped is an affirmative public attitude toward handicapped people and their rights and capacities. Most of the barriers to accomplishment by handicapped individuals, the respondents agreed, lie not so much within those individuals themselves as within the society in which they live and learn and work.

Farther Down the Road

The Committee also concerned itself with likely future trends, seeking informed speculation on what might lie down the road. We are

5. FUTURE TRENDS

under no illusion that the following represents a definitive list. Rather it might be thought of as a cross-section of impressions that might be found in a futurist's notebook.

One of the significant developments to be expected in the future is a greater *diversity* in the handicapped student population. The present trend toward serving younger and younger children will spread to all States, so that early and continuous intervention with handicapped youngsters will become standard. At the same time there will be greater insistence on the principle that handicapped people should not be considered ineligible for intervention simply because they have reached the age of 21. Thus it can be expected that Adult and Continuing Education will undergo an extensive reformation to the end that handicapped adults can enjoy the benefits of adult learning now effectively reserved to the nonhandicapped. As another aspect of special education's broadening spectrum, programs for the gifted and taltented can be expected to attract major new emphasis.

Many *labels* of handicapping conditions have been shown to stigmatize children without serving any useful educational purpose, and opposition to this practice can be expected to intensify, particularly as handicapped people become more militant in their objections. Because a child must in some fashion be designated as being in need of services in order to qualify for them, however, consideration will likely be given to developing less stigmatizing and more functional classifications. Ultimately there may evolve a well-refined classification system which conveys in brief phrases the major characteristics of handicapped children's learning and social behavior and implies appropriate treatment, as is often the case with medical terms for diseases. Until the development of such a system, however, there will be increasing insistence that efforts be made to avoid the stigmatization and deceptive oversimplification that labelling breeds.

The concept of *accountability* will more and more pervade special education, especially in connection with the development of precise and uniform measures permitting reliable assessment of the impact of various programs and approaches. Such a system of measurement would bear the same relationship to communicating progress in special education that having a common tongue bears on creating greater understanding among people in disparate parts of the Nation. With it improved practices not only could be clearly documented and displayed but could more readily be disseminated. Without it

each such gain must be translated into a variety of different measurement "languages." An important aspect of this work will be studies that specifically relate gains to the interventions that produced them, toward spelling out which interventions, under what conditions, are most productive, most cost-effective, and most likely to be applied, given the availability of the kinds of skills they require.

There will be continuing efforts in the general area of providing *service delivery*, with special emphasis on the search for a solution to the persistent problem of locating handicapped children who are not being served. This drive will be stimulated in part by a general recognition that early screening and identification methods now in use are unacceptably prone to error. Spurring it also will be the new "child find" provisions in the Federal Government's State assistance programs. Assuming the ultimate development of satisfactory identification methods, there is the further question of whether the services will be brought to the child or the child to the services. The latter method, being more economical and feasible in populous urban and suburban areas, is the more customary. To some extent even in these places, however, and more obviously in remote regions with scattered populations, services taken to children will be significantly broadened by such methods as telecommunications, travelling vans of Head Start teachers, video diagnosis of handicapping conditions, and others.

Personnel preparation also can be expected to acquire some new characteristics, chief among them an emphasis on interdisciplinary skills. The process of helping any handicapped children develop fundamental skills requires the efforts not just of special educators but of specialists from many fields—speech pathology, audiology, nursing, nutrition, medicine, psychology, physical education, recreation, and occupational and physical therapy among them. Increasingly the special educator will be required to have a firm grasp of what each of these disciplines involves and to be able to coordinate their implementation in educational settings involving both handicapped and nonhandicapped children.

In *research*, probably the most dramatic breakthroughs can be expected to come from medical, genetic, and pharmacological studies bearing on the prevention of handicaps with a biophysical cause. In particular, the next 25 to 50 years should see major breakthroughs in the prevention of handicapping conditions for which we now have some indication of cause. For example, since Down's syndrome is now known to be caused by a chromosomal anomaly, it is not unreasonable to expect that the cause of the anomaly itself will become known in the near future, and that this discovery will lead to prevention of the condition or its effects. Referring more specifically to special education, as research findings give greater precision to the early diagnosis of high risk infants and young children, it can be expected that prevention of the effects of handicapping conditions will come more and more to be one of special education's dominant functions.

No less significant departures from customary practice can be expected in other areas. The application of instructional *technology* will become far more general, and opposition to it far more muted, as electromechanical and other allegedly "dehumanizing" devices demonstrate their capacity to serve humanistic ends by opening up horizons in education for the handicapped that would otherwise remain closed. In *legislation*, the primary emphasis at the Federal level will be on securing appropriations closer to the amounts authorized for programs already enacted; and within the States the stress will be on removing age restrictions that limit the opportunities of handicapped persons. As for *litigation*, future suits may well

aim not just at securing new educational rights for the handicapped but at making sure agreed-upon rights are actually afforded. Much of what is accomplished both through legislation and litigation will result from the growing strength of the *advocacy* movement. To date the impetus for this movement has come essentially from parents of handicapped children. Parents will continue to be in the vanguard, but increasingly involved in advocacy activities will be persons with a direct or indirect professional interest in education of the handicapped. Particularly if handicapped children fail to receive the benefits now promised in legislation and ordered in court decisions, educators in particular can be expected to become among the most active champions of rights for the handicapped, to the point of initiating litigation and promoting new legislation to enforce those rights.

Summing up, the momentum that has been gathering during the past decade will gather further force, and major inroads will be made in the unfinished elements of the revolution in education of the handicapped. Neglect and pity will give way to respect for individual rights, and one day the handicapped will be regarded not in terms of their limitations but on the basis of their qualities as human beings.

Progress for the Severely Handicapped

PATRIA G. FORSYTHE

The ancient Greeks defined an idiot as a person who lived apart from his fellow man.

People are learning that persons who are severely handicapped, as well as those with other developmental disabilities, are entitled to be treated as individual human beings with basic rights. They are not for "warehousing." When walls are erected around them, their problems are not solved, but become more severe.

They are people. Although "severely handicapped" might be defined in technical terms in several ways (none of them precise), it is a relative term. Given the chance, retarded persons develop physically, socially, and intellectually like everyone else; not given the chance, they deteriorate.

Much has happened in developmental disabilities during the past 15 years. Organizationally, one might say, the country is ready to do some accelerated work on behalf of severely handicapped persons, and certainly, the knowledge for this work is not lacking.

It was 36 years ago—in 1939—when a man named Harold M. Skeels walked into the annual meeting of the American Association on Mental Deficiency in Chicago carrying a paper that reported the effects of environmental stimulation—or lack of it—on the mental development of children. He believed that cultural deprivation was a cause of mental retardation; it was, for that time, a radical idea. Three years later, he issued a follow-up report, and in 1966 Skeels reported on the same group over a span of 30 years.

He studied the mental development of 25 children. All were infants or of preschool age; all were wards of a state institution for dependent children; 20 were illegitimate. Most of their parents had been school dropouts and were generally on the lower end of the eco-nomic scale.

From this homogeneous background, two contrasting patterns emerged. Thirteen children who had shown *marked retardation* in infancy were judged to be of normal intelligence by middle childhood. "As adults," said Skeels, "these 13 individuals have continued to show at least average or better than average achievement as indicated by education, occupation, income, family adjustment, intelligence of their children, and contributions to the community." The developmental trend had been reversed by planned intervention, which included placing them in homes which provided love and normal life experiences.

What of the others? Twelve children who had been within the *normal range* in infancy showed such decline in rate of mental growth that by middle childhood, they were judged to be mentally retarded. This group had remained in the nonstimulating, emotionally barren environment of the original institution through childhood.

These 12 children had been selected because at the ages of 12 to 20 months, they had initially been of normal intelligence. By the age of six years there was an average loss of 26 points in IQ as compared with initial tests. A followup study showed that in spite of a small rise in IQ (associated with entrance to school), the children were still mentally handicapped. Nine of the 12 were remanded to institutions for the mentally retarded. One died in adolescence; one has become self sufficient at a middle class level; the rest are either in institutions or minimally employed.

Skeels felt that most of the children in both groups, had they been placed in suitable adoptive homes or the equivalent in early infancy, could have achieved within the normal range of development. This becomes even more signifi-

"Progress for the Severely Handicapped," Patria G. Forsythe, *Public Policy and the Education of Exceptional Children*, edited by Weintraub, Abeson, Ballard, and Lavor, Council for Exceptional Children, 1976. © 1976 Council for Exceptional Children.

cant when it is realized that the large majority of persons called retarded are only mildly retarded.

DYNAMICS OF INSTITUTIONALIZATION

The Willowbrook (NY) case is still in the foreground of many people's consciousness, although the indignities suffered by retarded youngsters there have occurred elsewhere. But this sad story should be remembered the way "we remember Pearl Harbor," because there are just as many lives involved. One of the strong impacts of Willowbrook has been the additional recognition from the courts that lack of meaningful help can be as damaging as overt cruelty in turning children into vegetables.

When Judge Judd of the District Court approved a consent decree in April 1975 securing the constitutional rights of the Willowbrook residents to protection from harm, he added a memo of his own. He said, "The consent judgment reflects the fact that protection from harm requires relief more extensive than this court originally contemplated, because harm can result not only from neglect but from conditions which cause regression or which prevent development of an individual's capabilities."

He accepted the argument of plaintiffs that in an institution for the mentally retarded, it is impossible for the condition of a resident to remain static. If his functioning is not improving, it will deteriorate. Thus, to keep the residents from being harmed, it may well be necessary to provide the full range of affirmative relief, which has been ordered in some court cases under a theory of right to treatment.

To insure safe custody, the theory of right to protection from harm has developed as set forth in 1973, based on the 8th Amendment to the Constitution: prohibition against cruel and unusual punishment. To insure habilitation, the theory of right to treatment has developed, based on the 14th Amendment of the Constitution and related to the clauses on equal protection and due process. So much for legal precedent; it helps turn good intentions into deeds.

There has been strong new interest in the total quality of life rather than in merely the length of life, strong new interest in the positive elements of good health rather than in merely the absence of disease and infirmity. Such interests are reflected in the work now going on throughout the country to make it possible for severely handicapped individuals to lead fuller lives.

More emphasis is placed on proper diet, especially during the younger years, as well as on the need for vaccination against rubella and other diseases. The school system is making education available to everyone, including severely handicapped children. This includes academic, vocational, and social skills which enable them to live up to their greatest potential. Recreation (a word whose origin is *re-creation*) is no longer busy work filling empty hours but an end in itself which provides not only therapy but many kinds of satisfaction. The physical environment finally has been recognized as important, and a handicapped person's relationship to his environment now is a major concern of architects, urban planners, behavioral scientists, and social workers.

PROBLEMS OF DEINSTITUTIONALIZATION

On the one hand, there are efforts to enrich the lives of persons who must remain in institutions, and on the other hand to make it possible for many persons in institutions to someday return to relatives and friends in a home environment. Deinstitutionalization has become a major objective of government. By 1980, a reduction of one third of the mentally retarded persons now living in institutions is to be effected. This takes planning, of course, and the normalization corollary is to have adequate supportive services in the community.

The new Developmental Disabilities Office (DDO), which recently became a separate agency in HEW's Office of Human Development, is coordinating this planning effort with the state DD councils. The state councils are the target groups, because they are both the planners and advocates for this group of disabilities.

DDO grants money to states provided there are state plans to make use of existing resources in helping people with developmental disabilities—education, rehabilitation, medical, welfare, and the like; in these instances where resources are not available, federal funds can be used to fill gaps.

The Developmental Disabilities Act specifies, "The state plan will describe how federal funds allotted to the state will be used to complement and augment rather than duplicate or replace services and facilities for the developmentally disabled which are eligible for federal assistance under other state programs." Emphasis on using what is already on hand has its organizational problems, such as "co-mingling of funds," but it does reduce cost greatly, and serves more people.

At the state level, there are three problems in planning for the use of existing resources: lack of information and a system for storing it; lack of staff and the analytic ability to assess the data; interorganizational problems. At the local level, problems of manpower can be turned to good advantage. Involving people can widen the base of support in the community and make it easier to solve the complicated problems of the severely handicapped.

The right of everyone to be well nurtured, well brought up, and well educated has been af-

5. FUTURE TRENDS

firmed since the first White House Conference on Children and Youth. Though society increasingly tries to ensure this right, for many years there will remain people to whom this has been denied and for whom society must provide both intervention and restitution.

REFERENCE

New York State Association for Retarded Children versus Rockefeller and *Parisi v. Rockefeller*, Case Nos. 72C–356 (E.D.N.Y. filed March 17, 1973) and 72C–357 (S.D.N.Y. 1972).

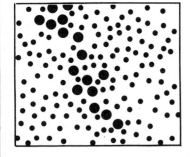

Perceived Responsibilities of Home and School for the Education of Severely Retarded Children

(A Summary of the Dissertion)

Thomas B. Bradley

Consumerism is a social force that has significant potential for influencing the direction of developments in the field of education generally and in special education specifically. This has been demonstrated beyond any reasonable doubt by recent court decisions involving cases where children have been denied access to educational services or where the preceived quality of educational services has been qustioned by parents representing the children consumers of educational services.

A useful model of the delivery system of health, education, and social services has been developed by Hurder (1973).

The Hurder Model of service delivery conceptualizes service delivery as a hierarchial series of producer/consumer interfaces. At higher echelons these interfaces are largely administrative and are responsible for accomplishment of administrative - programmatic (A-P) objectives. These objectives deal with those aspects of delivery of a general class of services to a general class of consumers which Hurder calls the "target population" (e.g., delivery of educational services to severely and profoundly mentally retarded children). These objectives are to a great extent administrative and supervisory in nature.

At the lower end of this chain of interfaces, services are delivered to individual consumers. Services are delivered to persons whom Hurder calls "target individuals" in an attempt to meet clinical-perscriptive (C-P) objectives. These C-P objectives relate to the delivery of specific services to specific individuals (e.g., severely or profoundly mentally retarded children). In this case, C-P objectives are the objectives selected by the teacher for the individual children assigned to his class.

The relationship between these two classes of objectives is interesting. A-P objectives must be achieved prior to developing the capacity to meet C-P objectives, but achievement of the C-P objectives is necessary to the achievement of the ultimate A-P objectives, effective delivery of services (Hurder, 1973). One does not know if services have been effectively delivered until the C-P objectives have been met and delivery of services evaluated.

At each echelon, the interface can be conceptualized as consisting of a producer and a consumer. In complex service delivery systems such as the educational services delivery system, a division of labor is essential. Those personnel who teach children cannot also be respon-

5. FUTURE TRENDS

sible for working with the state legislature, monitoring and evaluating service delivery, coordinating services, planning transportation, preparing budgets, and so forth. Rather, a service or standards for service, originate (or is mandated) at the highest levels of the system and flow toward consumers through the series of administrative - programmatic echelons. The service begins in gross terms and is refined at each echelon until it is ready for delivery to a target population at the clinical-prescriptive level.

Hurder described two criteria of service delivery in his paradigm. For service delivery to be achieved **both** criteria must be adequately met. One of those criteria is **access** which Hurder defines as **availability** of a service. Availability of a service can be evaluated in terms of easily quantifiable variables such as distance (geographic proximity) and staff/client ratios. Hurder has written that "Most thinking about service delivery, as well as research, forcuses on access. This focus leads to such questions as, is the service . . available to all? If it is available, how long does it take to get it? How far must one travel to get to the source?" (1973, p.10)

The other criterion of service delivery is **disposition.** The disposition criterion is met when the service to which a consumer has access is also acceptable. The variables which determine whether this criterion will be met are difficult to study since they are predominatly qualitative in nature. Despite the difficulty, it remains imperative that the educational establishment develop and maintain configurations of specialized knowledges and specialized personnel that are congruent with the configuration of consumer needs.

To facilitate the development of this congruence, Hurder (1974) has recommended that service delivery be conceptualized as consisting of three phases, the definition-negotiation phase, the operating phase, and the evaluation - replanning phase. The first phase, the definition - negotiation phase, is the one during which the provider of service and the consumer attempt to define the consumers' needs and specify the mutually acceptable characteristics of the desired services. When these services are implemented, the operating phase has begin. Ongoing formative evaluation leads to a reformulation of the desired service which again must be mutually acceptable to both provider and consumer of service during phase three.

Since meeting the disposition criterion is essential to effective service delivery, the need for formal evaluation of qualitative variables can be significantly reduced if the providers of services and the consumers of services can negotiate this consensus of the definition of the consumer's needs and a consensus of the specification of the desired service. Such a negotiated consensus is the essence of the disposition criterion.

The probability of service delivery is affected by how well the disposition criterion is met by the educational establishment. Consumer (parent) satisfaction with the services would facilitate effective service delivery. Dissatisfaction on the part of consumers would indicate a high probability that they would attempt to alter those services in the direction of greater conformity with their perception of what the services should be. Hurder (1973) has written " . . . *when the . . . (producers' and consumers') attitudes are incompatible (sic) service delivery is made much more difficult and problematic"* (p.11).

The implications of the foregoing discussion of the Hurder Model are clear. For service delivery to be consummated with greatest efficiency (i.e., in the least difficult and least problematic fashion), the services made accessible to a target population must coincide with the consumers' perception of what that service should be. It should also be evident that the Hurder Model can be used to interpret consumer (parent) activism in education.

In the Pennsylvania Right to Education Consent Agreement (**PARC v. Commonwealth of Pennsylvania, 1972),** the parties agreed to delivery appropriate service to retarded children regardless of the severity of retardation. Access to these services was provided through the intermediate unit administrative structure of the Commonwealth's educational service delivery system. Efforts to include the parents of severely and profoundly retarded children in program planning were made by the Pennsylvania Department of Education. Indeed, such parental input was mandated by the Consent Agreement.

Though this effort to meet the disposition criterion was mandated and did occur at the highest echelon of the service delivery system, it is not known if similar efforts were made at lower echelons of the service delivery system. Of particular importance is the issue of meeting the disposition criterion at the level of service delivery where teachers interface with parents.

Failure to meet the disposition criterion at this level would make the delivery of services more difficult and   problematic . Indeed, from the perspecetive of the Hurder Model, failure to meet   the disposition criterion is, by definition, equivalent to a failure to deliver   services. Therefore, a study   of the disposition   criterion of service delivery in the context of Pennsylvania's Right to Education Consent Agreement was undertaken.

Sampling Procedures

Fifteen of Pennsylvania's 29 intermediate units were randomly selected to participate in the study. Parents of severely and profoundly retarded children, teachers of classes which included severely and profoundly retarded children, and supervisors of such classes were randomly selected from these intermediate units. Packets containing cover letters, a copy of the two part questionnaire, and a stamped self-addressed envelope were sent to each participant in the study. The number and percentage of instruments sent and returned are reported and summarized by groups in **Table 1.**

TABLE I
Summary of Percentage of Questionnaires
Returned by Group . . . .

Group	No. of Questionnaires Sent	No. of Questionnaires Returned Prior to the Termination	%
Parents	98	71	72.4%
Teachers	70	55	78.6%
Supervisors	33	29	87.9%
All Groups	201	155	77.1%

5. FUTURE TRENDS

Data Collection Instrument

Part I of the questionnaire requested the "thoughtful opinion" of the respondents in assigning responsibility for the accomplishment of 20 educational objectives. The respondent indicated his response by checking the appropriate blank on a seven-step scale which included the bipolar choices of "total home responsibility" and "total school responsibility" and five central blanks if he wished to indicate any of five levels of shared responsibility.

The 20 objectives were selected from COMPET (Pennsylvania Department of Education, 1972a). Ten objectives were selected as having traditional academic connotations and ten were selected as being more closely associated with self-help skills.

Scoring was accomplished by assigning values of one to seven to the blanks beginning with the left blank.

Each item of the data collection instrument was treated as a dependent variable. A one way multivariate analysis of variance (MANOVA) was used to test the hypothesis of equal mean vectors for the three groups.

Results and Discussion

The MANOVA resulted in a F-ratio of 2.215 (df = 40, 266). The probability of obtaining such a value by chance is less than .01. Therefore, the null hypothesis of equal population mean vectors was rejected. This decision indicated a lack of congruence among the perceptions of parents, teachers, and supervisors regarding the degree of reponsibility the home or school should be assigned for accomplishing educational objectives. Thus, within the Hurder Model, the disposition criterion has not been met and services have not been delivered.

To further explore the nature of group differences in the assignment of responsibility, discriminant analysis was performed. Group mean vectors, univariate F-ratios, scaled discriminant weights, and discriminant score centroids for the three groups were studied. Group means, standard deviations, and univariate F-ratios for the 20 dependent variables are reported in **Table 2.**

Discriminant analysis is a procedure that has been described by Tatsuoka (1973), Kerlinger and Pedhazur (1973), and Tatsouka and Teidman (1963) as a means of examining the dimensions along which several groups differ. The procedures determine the linear combination of dependent variables that reveal large differences in group means. These linear combinations are called discriminant functions.

Multiple discriminant analysis resulted in only one of the two possible discriminant functions being statistically significant. The significance tests on the two discriminant functions are reported in **Table 3.** The non-significant orthogonal discriminant function was regarded as immaterial since group differences could have resulted from sampling error.

The plot of discriminant function centroids, revealed that the first discriminant function separated the three groups in approximately equal steps. Teacher and parent centroids were separated by the greatest distance on this discriminant function.

Based on the scaled discriminant weights for the first discriminant function reported in Table 4, the variables which contributed most to the differentiation of the groups were number 2, *(brushing teeth)*, 7, *(Discrimination of shapes)*, 8, *(Learns names of common objects)*, 10, *(Zipping and unzipping a coat)*, and 14, *(Spoon feeding)*. Since

TABLE II

Means, Standard Deviations, and Between Group
F-Ratios for Parents (n=71), Teachers (n=55),
and Supervisors (n=29) for 20 Dependent Variables

	Parents		Teachers		Supervisors		
Variable	Mean	S.D.	Mean	S.D.	Mean	S.D.	F.Ratio[a]
1	4.24	1.29	4.98	1.05	4.62	1.19	5.91***
2	2.34	1.49	3.29	1.06	2.97	1.03	8.87***
3	4.13	1.07	4.44	0.91	4.03	1.00	2.04
4	4.39	1.35	4.75	0.96	4.31	1.23	1.75
5	3.21	1.52	3.62	0.82	3.28	1.03	1.79
6	3.42	1.47	3.87	0.97	3.34	0.99	2.62*
7	4.72	1.38	5.49	0.91	5.03	0.89	6.93***
8	4.54	1.39	4.56	0.80	4.38	1.10	0.25
9	2.70	1.46	3.44	0.80	3.14	1.04	5.91***
10	3.37	1.40	3.85	0.86	3.31	0.91	3.40**
11	3.85	1.03	4.18	0.66	3.86	0.63	2.68*
12	4.61	1.18	5.05	0.92	4.48	0.77	4.03**
13	3.00	1.36	3.70	0.75	3.31	0.91	6.32***
14	2.72	1.41	3.82	0.69	3.24	0.97	14.72***
15	4.92	1.68	5.25	1.05	5.10	1.37	0.86
16	4.77	1.59	5.11	1.06	4.90	1.12	0.95
17	5.17	1.59	5.49	0.91	5.34	0.92	0.98
18	3.10	1.47	3.67	0.79	3.34	0.80	3.75***
19	4.00	1.15	4.42	0.68	3.90	0.96	3.82**
20	4.63	1.39	4.76	0.87	4.90	0.88	0.58

a df = 2,152
***p .01
**p .05
*p .10

TABLE III

Significance Tests of the Two Discriminant Functions

Functions	Non-Zero Eigenvalues	χ^2	df	P
I	.59416	66.92	21	.001
II	.12095	16.38	19	.50

three of these are self-care in nature *(2, 10, and 14)* and two have academic connotations *(7 and 8)*, the self-care or academic nature of the objectives did not appear to be a factor distinguishing the groups. The group differences, rather, appear to be associated with individual items of the data collection instrument.

5. FUTURE TRENDS

TABLE IV

Scaled Discriminant Weights of the 20 Dependent
Variables for the Two Discriminant Functions .

Variable	Function 1	Function 2
1. Discrimination of sounds	-.20	0.65
2. Brushing Teeth	4.05	3.19
3. Playing cooperatively with other children	-2.18	-2.09
4. Focusing attention on a speaker	-1.39	-1.18
5. Putting on a pullover sweater	-0.66	2.96
6. Buttoning and unbuttoning a shirt	2.50	-3.40
7. Discrimination of shapes	6.89	-0.34
8. Learns names of common objects	-7.01	0.73
9. Washing hands & face	0.43	2.76
10. Zipping & unzipping a coat	-3.66	-5.25
11. Moving about in the environment	2.18	-1.65
12. Discrimination of colors	-0.37	-5.75
13. Toilet training	-1.22	1.64
14. Spoon feeding	6.79	1.16
15. Visual tracking of objects	0.91	1.30
16. Learning about the concept of numbers	-1.17	1.38
17. Learning basic number concepts	0.98	2.45
18. Putting on & taking off shoes	-0.75	-0.67
19. Responding to verbal commands	1.69	-5.67
20. Expressive language development	-1.14	5.60

An examination of unvariate F-ratios indicated that 6 were significant at the .01 level, 4 were significant at the .05 level, and 2 were significant at the .10 level. (The liberal alpha level was decided upon after examination of the comparative risks of not identifying pertinent differences between groups vs. possible identification of non-real differences). Eight of these 12 significant F-ratios were of a self-care nature, while only four had academic connotations, indicating that self-care objectives may be the area of greatest misunderstanding between teachers and parents.

Teachers as a group had the highest meanscore on all but one of the questionnaire items. On all but four of the twelve significant objectives the parent group scored at the other extreme. The teachers seem to be willing to accept significant levels of teaching responsibility, but parents seem reluctant to "impose upon" teachers.

Differences exist among groups of teachers, supervisors, and the parents in assigning responsibility for the accomplishment of selected educational objectives. These differences are typically greatest between parents and teachers, indicating possible failure to meet the disposition criterion at the clinical - prescriptive level.

Implications

The result of this study clearly indicated a need for better lines of communications between teachers and parents at the clinical-prescriptive echelon of the service delivery system. Twelve of the twenty educational objectives revealed significant discrepancies, and in the case of eight of those objectives, teachers and parents had the most discrepant mean scores. It is also interesting that 8 of the 12 significant discrepancies were associated with educational objectives with self-care connotations. Parents seem to be ignorant of the willingness of the educational system to provide training assistance in self-care skills.

In light of the research available that has indicated increased effectiveness when coordination of the training efforts of home and school exists (Staats, 1971; Margo, 1973; Staats & Staats, 1963; Freeman & Thompson, 1973; Gallagher, 1974; Ryback& Staats, 1970), these results are doubly crucial. Efforts cannot be coordinated when effective lines of communication either are not available or are not frequently utilized.

There is also the issue of consumer knowledge regarding the product he buys or the services he receives. In recent years this knowledge has become increasingly essential since it is basic to wise decisions in the "marketplace" (Aaker & Day, 1971). Once it is understood that, despite the compulsory nature of educational services, the consumer of these services still has recourse to sources of change through the agencies of the delivery system and ultimately even through the legal system, then the importance of such knowledge can be clearly perceived.

This study has explained the group discrepancies in terms of a failure to include a definition-negotiation phase at the clinical-prescriptive level in the planning of the delivery of the right to education services. While this explanation suffices to account for a failure of the service delivery system to achieve congruence of the configuration of service characteristics and needs of the consumers that is essential to the disposition criterion, it does not explain **why** the differences exist.

Several possible explanations of those differences exist. First, parents may distrust a provider of services who for years deprived them of services to which they were constitutionally entitled. If a consumer must bring suit to secure needed educational services to which they are entitled under law, then it is likely that suspicion will exist regarding the quality of services provided by this reluctant educational establishment.

A second possible source of differing group perceptions is that the teachers and supervisors are affected by professional training programs in colleges, universities and inservice workshops while parents are not. This source is further confounded by the fact that training programs for teachers of children who are severely and profoundly retarded are relatively new to the curricula of most training institutions where they exist at all. Therefore, not only do teachers and supervisors differ from parents in the fact of professional training, but in some cases the appropriateness of that training for this level of child can be questioned.

Parents, teachers, and supervisors also differ in the extent of their experience with severely and profoundly retarded children. Parents obviously have the most contact with their children, and similarly teachers spend a significant portion of the day with these children. Supervisors, who are preoccupied with administrative and supervisory responsibilities on the other hand, rarely have time to be in direct

5. FUTURE TRENDS

contact with these mentally retarded children. These varying degrees of proximity would be expected to result in differing perspectives of the needs of the children and, therefore, in differing perspectives of the characteristics of service that the educational establishment should provide as well.

Other variables which may contribute to the failure to meet the disposition criterion are differences of cultural values, social class, family traditions, and personal beliefs (Hurder, 1973).

These causes may indeed overlap and interact with each other; they need not always function in a simple and discrete fashion. The interesting fact is that there is a common solution to these problems, communication. Communication which seeks to define the needs of consumers and to negotiate specific services which are mutually acceptable to the provider of services and the consumer as well is the essence of the crucial disposition criterion.

Policies established by school districts and intermediate units may serve to either impede or facilitate the development of lines of communications between teachers and parents. The establishment of policies that encourage parent-teacher interaction is often made more difficult by teachers' contracts which specify the time commitment required of teachers in terms of instructional time and inservice time. Inclusion in future contracts of time allotted for meetings of parents and teachers seem desirable. Communication with parents through meetings of the Parent-Teachers Association (PTA), Association for Retarded Citizens, open-house arrangements, and home visits should be encouraged by responsible administrative and supervisory staff. Such additional commitments of teacher time would assist in maximizing coordination of educational efforts of the home and the school as well as opening essential lines of communication through which parents of severely and profoundly retarded children could be provided with the knowledge essential to their roles as consumers of special education services.

Increased efforts of the service delivery system at the clinical-prescriptive level would appear to be essential for maximizing the effectiveness of training efforts with severely and profoundly retarded children. In the absence of increased efforts to meet the disposition criterion, serious doubt can exist regarding the consummation of service delivery as conceptualized by the Hurder Model.

References

Hurder, W.P. Personal Communication, September 21, 1974.

Hurder, W.P. The Primary Physician and the delivery of mental health services. Essay presented to students of University of Illinois School of Medicine, March 15, 1973.

PENNSYLVANIA ASSOCIATION FOR RETARDED CHILDREN, NANCY BETH BOWMAN ET AL., v. COMMONWEALTH OF PENNSYLVANIA, DAVID H.KURTZMAN ET AL., E.D. Pennsylvania Civil Action No. 71-42 (1972).

Pennsylvania Department of Education. COMMONWEALTH PLAN FOR EDUCATION AND TRAINING OF MENTALLY RETARDED CHILDREN. Harrisburg, Pa. Pennsylvania Department of Education, 1968.

Tatsuoka, M.M. Multivariate analysis in educational research. In F.N. Kerlinger (Ed.), REVIEW OF RESEARCH IN EDUCATION. Itasca, Ill. F.E. Peacock Publishers, 1973.

Tatsuoka, M.M. MULTIVARIATE ANALYSIS: TECHNIQUES FOR EDUCATIONAL AND PSYCHOLOGICAL RESEARCH. New York: John Wiley & Sons, 1971.

Research Implications

EDWARD L. MEYEN
REUBEN ALTMAN

Public School Programming for the Severely/Profoundly Handicapped:
Some Researchable Problems

Programming for the severely and profoundly handicapped in public school settings is fast becoming more than an innovation. This is not to suggest that school administrators, boards of education, and/or special educators have responded to the needs of this population on their own initiative. It does, however, represent a response to the federal and state legislation which has resulted from the advocacy efforts of parents and social groups. While the success of this movement is not assured nor is there uniform agreement on the school's role among professionals and lay groups, there is evidence that public schools are moving forward in meeting legislative commitments to the severely and profoundly handicapped.

The establishment of programs for the severely and profoundly handicapped in the public schools does reflect a change in public policy and, hopefully, public attitudes toward the handicapped. Because this change did not occur as a result of an evolutionary process, we are without a meaningful history to draw upon in developing specifications for public school programs. Certainly the experiences of institutions and day care programs offer a base for planning, but that base is totally insufficient when compared to the decision making required by public school personnel in program planning. One could argue that the experiences of institutional settings is in general not relevant to public school settings because of the differences in the mission of residential centers versus public schools. Residential centers, by design, have assumed a total care posture in programming

for this population, whereas public schools are oriented toward meeting the educational and social needs of a population of independent learners. In public schools, students are assumed to be capable of making decisions regarding their futures and destined toward further training beyond the aegis of the public schools. The achievement orientation of the schools is real and operationalizes into a particular definition of education. The contrast between residential centers and public schools complicates the process of generalizing between the two settings. It also inhibits the communication required to transmit that which is generalizable.

Having no history of serving the severely and profoundly handicapped and little history in working with agencies serving this population, schools are placed in a position of implementing programs without sufficient direction. For the researcher interested in the severely and/or profoundly handicapped or in the public school setting, generally, the establishment of programs for this population represents a research laboratory without precedent. Almost every decision made by public school administrators and instructional personnel regarding this group poses a research question or has implications for research. Certainly these decisions call for research evidence. Most of the research available to program developers concerned with the severely and profoundly handicapped stems from basic research in the areas of discrimination, generalization, linguistic development patterns, reasoning, retention, stimulus control,

"Public School Programming for the Severely/Profoundly Handicapped: Some Researchable Problems," Edward L. Meyen and Reuben A Altman, *Education and Training of the Mentally Retarded*, Vol. 11, No. 1, February 1976. © 1976 Council for Exceptional Children Division of Mental Retardation.

inhibition, operant strategies, etc. As significant as this research is, it is not directly applicable to the current readiness level of the public schools in programming for the severely/profoundly handicapped. For the most part, such research is primarily applicable to curriculum developers and teacher trainers who must assume responsibility for the transition of research findings into application. The paucity of activity in this area by curriculum developers and teacher trainers minimizes the impact of the research which is available. At least two problems emerge, i.e., the processing of available research into a usable form and the focusing of attention of researchers on priority problems of a practical nature which are occurring in the public schools and impeding progress. Unless the everyday problems of programming in a public school setting are subjected to research, or at least to systematic review procedures, what will become routine practices in 1985 may be the result of arbitrary responses to immediate problems today. This becomes particularly disturbing when one recognizes that most programs today are being established using minimally trained instructional personnel. The involvement of researchers in programs as they evolve can have a formative effect on such programs and at the same time accummulate needed research data to resolve the problems being encountered and/or anticipated as programs are implemented.

At the risk of over simplifying the task of delineating areas of needed research pertaining to programming to the severely/profoundly handicapped in public school settings, two general domains are proposed. Both are couched in the context of curriculum. The first pertains to the general area of curriculum development and curriculum research. The second encompasses an array of programming concerns which represent instructional problems related to curriculum implementation. This approach argues for the placement of curriculum related research as the major priority at this point in time in serving the severely/profoundly handicapped. It also argues against an emphasis on research which does not incorporate the cycle of moving from an identified learner need — to remediation — to generalization.

Curriculum Development/Research

In contrast to the pattern of prioritizing concerns which occurred relative to the mildly handicapped, funding agencies have responded quickly to the obvious need for curriculum development and research for the severely/profoundly handicapped. Curriculum development as a priority was largely ignored during the early years of programming for the mildly retarded. Instead, the investment of professional energy and financial resources was directed toward procedures for determining eligibility, administrative arrangements, and the retraining of teachers. The task of curriculum development was left to the special class teacher. It was not until the late 1960's or twenty years after the trend toward special classes began that curriculum development emerged as a priority. Before that, what was accomplished in curriculum development was carried out in SEA's and LEA's with insufficient funds and too frequently without the necessary expertise.

Curriculum development is costly, time consuming and complex, but it is the basis of instruction. From an instructional perspective Special Education should be synonymous with special curriculum. Unfortunately too often the focus is on classification, organization and teaching methods. These are obvious concerns in programming for exceptional children. But one can be effective in the process of teaching only to find that the skills or concepts taught were inappropriate and experiences of a high priority were overlooked. In the case of the severely/profoundly handicapped, the Bureau of Education for the Handicapped is supporting curriculum development projects directly applicable to the target population as well as projects having curricular implications. Figure 1 describes selected projects having direct or indirect application to the severely/profoundly handicapped.

These projects are examples of the kinds of efforts required to answer questions related to content, sequencing of skills and integration of instructional strategies. For the most part, the magnitude and interrelatedness of curriculum development tasks preclude undertaking by individual researchers. They require substantial resources. However, problems related to curriculum and program implementation constitute an array of problems which in general can be sufficiently circumscribed for researchers with limited resources. The following discussion is intended to set forth an array of needed research directly related to the immediate concern of public school programmers. It should also be mentioned that the residual effects of large scale curriculum development projects yield research problems of reasonable dimensions. Too often such residual research problems or peripheral data are obscured by the narrow sightedness of the project personnel whose primary concern is for the broader project they have designed. It is a rare curriculum project which effectively uses more than 25% of the data collected in the researching of curriculum problems. The consequence is that many questions for which answers may exist are not effectively pursued. Researchers would be well advised to affiliate with curriculum development projects with the motive of gaining access to the residuals of curriculum development.

FIGURE 1

Curriculum Related Projects Directly or Indirectly Applicable to Severely/Profoundly Handicapped*

PROJECT	Project MORE	Project MAZE	Debbie School Program	Programmed Environment Project	Portage Project**	I CAN**
Title	Mediated Operational Research for Education	Madison Alternative for Zero Reject Education	Debbie School Program	Programmed Environments Projects	Portage Project	Individualized instruction to create social leisure competence, associate all school learning, and narrow the gap between theory and practice.
Developer(s)	Dr. James R. Lent, Carol Foster, Barbara M. McLean	Dr. Lou Brown	Dr. William Bricker, Dr. Diane Bricker, Laura Dennison, Richard Iacino, Jacques Davis, Linda Wahlin, Gisela Chatelanat, Betty Vincent	Dr. James W. Tawney	David Shearer, James Billingsley, Alma Frohman, Jean Hilliard, Frances Johnson, Marsha Shearer	Dr. Janet A. Wessel, Dr. Paul Vogel, Dr. Claudia Knowles, Mary Jane Green, Jane Watkinson
Model	Behavioral Task Analysis	Behavioral Task Analysis	Integration of Cognitive and Behavioral Models into a Constructive-Interaction-Adaptation approach to training	Behavioral	Developmental	Developmental
Curriculum Product(s)	How to Do More Eating Program, Nose Blowing Program, Handwashing Program, Toothbrusing Program (others in press)	(Skill sequences are prepared by project staff, but the organization or development of an instructional program is left to the teacher.)	(Curriculum lattices are prepared by project staff, but the organization or development of a program is provided through skillful arrangement of environmental interactions by the teacher.)	Systematic Language Instruction Automated and Non-automated Programs	Portage Guide to Early Education	Primary Skills Modules, Leisure Modules, Teacher's Manual

FIGURE 1 (Cont.)

	Edmark Associates Bellevue, Washington	Madison Public Schools Madison, Wisconsin Department of Behavioral Disabilities University of Wisconsin	Mailman Center for Child Development University of Miami Miami, Florida	Department of Special Education University of Kentucky Lexington, Kentucky	Cooperative Educational Service Agency 12 Portage, Wisconsin	A publisher for the final version is currently being selected.
Source						
Designed to be used by:	Professionals and paraprofessionals, as well as parents, aides and volunteers	Teachers, Researchers and Teacher Trainers	Early Intervention Personnel	Special Education Teachers and Teacher Trainees	Professionals, Paraprofessionals and Parents	Special Education Classroom Teachers Physical Education Specialists Therapeutic Recreation Specialists Curriculum Consultants
Designed to be taught to:	Persons who are moderately to severely retarded	Severely handicapped students from birth to at least twenty-two years of age	Infants or Profound-Retarded Individuals	Individuals assumed to be severely retarded	Preschool Normal or Handicapped Children	Preschool through primary age group, three to fourteen years of age
Designed to be used in:	One-to-one teaching situation and small groups in the home, classroom, or institution	Heterogeneous settings (not self-contained schools) in which severely handicapped students are integrated with normal students	Early Intervention Program	Programmed Environment Preschools	One-to-one teaching situation and small groups in the home, classroom, or institution	Self-contained classrooms, resource centers, or integrated programs for mainstreaming handicapped children
Content	Activities of daily living	Preacademics and Basic academics	Conceptual frameworks of such areas as sensorimotor and and language development	Programs to evaluate the effectiveness of potential reinforcers, train such specific behaviors as grasp and pull motions, establish simple responses to visual and auditory stimuli, promote general-	A sequential checklist of behaviors which usually appear in normal children between birth and five years of age divided into cognitive, self-help, motor, language, and socialization areas	Primary Skills Modules are Aquatics, Body Management, Fundamental Skills and Health/Fitness. The Leisure Modules will include Dance, Neighborhood Games, Outdoor Education

FIGURE 1 (Cont.)

			ization of responses, and determine response retention	and suggested activities and materials for teaching each item on the checklist	and Camping, and Special Games/Events.
Teaching Format	A four-stage teaching strategy progressing through NO HELP, VERBAL DEMONSTRATION and PHYSICAL HELP	A variety of strategies are presented for tailoring skill sequences to individual students through adapting instructional procedures, adapting tasks, and adapting response modes.	The use of operant procedures to decelerate socially maladaptive or inappropriate behavior and the substitution of adaptive or appropriate behavior and the arrangement of antecedent events to assist students in the development of new adaptive skills.	A seventeen-step format including objectives, rationale, materials, directions, antecedent stimuli, demonstrations, arranging stimuli, response requirements, criterion performance, conditions, reinforcers, correcting, recording, evaluating, storage ststyem, modification of program, and systematic stimulus changes	Suggested activities	An eight-step format including goals, performance objectives, criterion referenced tests, short-term objectives, instructional program of teaching/learning activities and and monitoring of progress
Evaluation procedure	Use of the programs by nonstaff trainers with a multiple baseline design across students. In addition, trainers complete a Trainer Reaction Scale and a Student Reaction Questionnaire.	Use of the programs by teachers and teacher trainees using evaluation procedures suggested in the skill sequence.	Use of the programs by early intervention personnel within applied behavioral analysis. Experimental designs incorporated into a Problem Oriented Educational Record.	Use of the programs by teachers and teacher trainees using evaluation procedures presented in the program	Experimental comparisons and use throughout the country in home-based and classroom programs for normal and handicapped preschool children	Use of the programs by teachers in the field and analysis of completed teacher feedback forms, program feedback forms consultant monitor forms, student data sheets, student performance score sheets, and a developmental inventory
Project Organizational Base	University Bureau of Child Research	Public Schools and University Department of of Studies in Behavioral Disabilities	Research and Service Project based in University Affiliated Facility	University Department of Special Education	Public School Cooperative Educational Service Agency of State Department of Public Instruction	Curriculum Development: Project in University Department of Physical Education

*Modified from chapter by Meyen, E.L. and Horner, R.D., to appear in J. Wortis, *Mental Retardation and Developmental Disabilities*, VIII, Brunner/Mazel, New York, N.Y.

**Not specifically oriented toward the severely/profoundly handicapped but applicable with modification

5. FUTURE TRENDS

Implementation Related Problems

There is an initial simplicity surrounding problems encountered in working with the severely/profoundly handicapped which when subjected to careful scrutiny emerge as complex and many faceted. It would be naive to suggest that the following questions will yield to short-term efforts. But they are real questions and deserving of attention. Each question relates in some way to the interaction among the instructor, student, environment, and curriculum. Even questions related to equipment have curriculum implications.

Researchable Questions:

—What kinds of data collection procedures can a teacher effectively employ to help in instructional planning for the severely and profoundly handicapped?

—What activities are effective in engaging the severely handicapped in elements of their environment?

—How can teachers structure activities which hold the involvement of the severely handicapped for short periods of time, so that his/her efforts can be directed to others?

—What baseline data should be retained as a baseline for later comparison in measuring progress of the program?

—What are the most generalizable skills needed by a teacher?

—What anecdotal evidence is meaningful in working with parents?

—What basic guidelines should be followed in establishing classes for the severely/profoundly handicapped in a regular attendance center?

—Given a finite budget, what are the essential expenditures or priority items basic to a new program for the severely/profoundly handicapped?

—How can the instructional needs of this group be illustrated effectively to administrators and teachers who possess an academic orientation to education?

—What strategies can a teacher use in sampling student progress as it evolves, so as to check on retention and cumulative progress?

—What constitutes an optimal physical setting for instruction?

—What kinds of social interactions on a group basis are effective with the severely/profoundly handicapped?

—Is there a preferred process for integrating new students into class membership?

—What kinds of responses are prerequisite to participating in group situations?

—What kinds of materials, apparatus, activities, etc. stimulate independent or semi-independent behavior of a short-term nature?

—How does a teacher effectively work with paraprofessionals?

—What kinds of cumulative performance data are most meaningful for instructional planning and for communicating with parents?

Researchers need to be attracted to the problems surfacing in public school programming for the severely/profoundly handicapped. The pressures to establish programs will cause instructional and programmatic decisions to be made. Such decisions could greatly benefit from the rigor of the research community. The conditions may not be as clean as the traditional laboratory, but at least the results will be subjected to application. An additional benefit will be a dialogue with practitioners who ultimately apply research results — if they are to be applied. They are in fact the generators of research questions.

The Intent of Congress

The importance attached by the Congress to the individualized education program called for in Public Law 94–142 is suggested by the emphasis placed on it in the Act itself, in the Senate and House colloquy prior to the law's enactment, and in special congressional reports.

What the law says

Quoting first from the law itself, section 4(a)(3) provides the following definition:

The term "individualized education program" means a written statement for each handicapped child developed in any meeting by a representative of the local educational agency or an intermediate educational unit who shall be qualified to provide, or supervise the provision of, specially designed instruction to meet the unique needs of handicapped children, the teacher, the parents or guardian of such child, and, whenever appropriate, such child, which statement shall include (A) a statement of the present levels of educational performance of such child, (B) a statement of annual goals, including short-term instructional objectives, (C) a statement of the specific educational services to be provided to such child, and the extent to which such child will be able to participate in regular educational programs, (D) the projected date for initiation and anticipated duration of such services, and (E) appropriate objective criteria and evaluation procedures and schedules for determining, on at least an annual basis, whether instructional objectives are being achieved.

Under the heading "Eligibility," section 612 provides that "In order to qualify for assistance under this part in any year, a State shall demonstrate to the Commissioner that the following conditions are met," and in citing those conditions goes on to say—under section 612(4)—that "Each local educational agency in the State will maintain records of the individualized education program for each handicapped child, and such programs shall be established, reviewed, and revised as provided in section 614(a)(5)."

Under section 613, dealing with "State Plans," section 613(a)(11) declares that these plans shall, among other things, "provide for procedures for evaluation at least annually of the effectiveness of programs in meeting the educational needs of handicapped children (including evaluation of individualized education programs), in accordance with such criteria that the Commissioner shall prescribe. . ."

Regarding the review alluded to above in connection with section 612, section 614(a)(5) states that any local education agency or intermediate educational unit that wants to receive funds under the law shall "provide assurances that the local educational agency or intermediate educational unit will establish, or revise, whichever is appropriate, an individualized education program for each handicapped child at the beginning of each school year and will then review and, if appropriate revise, its provisions periodically, but not less than annually."

Comments in the Senate

As reflected in the *Congressional Record*, the debate in the Senate regarding the proposed Education for All Handicapped Children Act was launched with the issuance on June 2, 1975, of Senate Report No. 94–168, prepared by the Senate Committee on Labor and Public Welfare. On page 4 the report noted that:

"The bill provides for an individualized planning conference, to be held at least three times a year, involving the parents or guardian, an individual representing the local educational agency qualified to provide special education, the child's teacher and the child when appropriate who will meet jointly to develop and review a written statement describing the educational services to be provided and, when ap-

"The Intent of Congress," *The Individualized Educational Program: Key to an Appropriate Education for the Handicapped Child,* 1977 Annual Report. National Advisory Committee on the Handicapped, U.S. Government Printing Office, Washington, D.C., 1977.

propriate, to revise such statement with the agreement of the parents."

Then on pages 10 and 11 the report goes into the subject of the IEP more deeply, as follows:

"The Committee bill defines individualized planning conference as a meeting or meetings to be held at least three times a year for the purpose of developing, reviewing, and when appropriate and with the agreement of the parents or guardian, revising a written statement of appropriate educational services to be provided for each handicapped child. The planning conference shall be conducted with the joint participation of the parents or guardian, the child (when appropriate), the child's teacher and a representative of the local educational agency who is qualified to provide or supervise the provision of special education.

"In reviewing the testimony on this bill and after consultation with professionals in the field, the Committee recognizes that in order to derive any benefit to the child, parent, and teacher an individualized planning conference must be held a minimum of three times per year. The frequent monitoring of a handicapped child's progress throughout the year is the most useful tool in designing an educational program for not only the child but those who are responsible for his management in school and at home.

"There is evidence that an individualized planning conference on an annual basis is insufficient. It is the Committee's intent in requiring that individualized planning conferences be provided for each handicapped child that these conferences be utilized as an extension of the procedural protections guaranteed under existing law to parents of handicapped children, and that they be the logical extension and the final step of the evaluation and placement process.

"They are not intended to be the evaluation process itself. Thus, it is the intent of this provision that local educational agencies involve the parent at the beginning of and at other times during the year regarding the provision of specific services and short-term instructional objectives for the special education of the handicapped child, which services are specifically designed to meet the child's individual needs and problems. The Committee views this process as a method of involving the parent and the handicapped child in the provision of appropriate services, providing parent counseling as to ways to bolster the educational process at home, and providing parents with a written statement of what the school intends to do for the handicapped child.

"It is not the Committee's intention that the written statement developed at the individual planning conferences be construed as creating a contractual relationship. Rather, the Committee intends to ensure adequate involvement of the parents or guardian of the handicapped child, and the child (when appropriate) in both the statement and its subsequent review and revision. The Committee has included a requirement that any revision of the statement be done only with the agreement of the parents or guardian in order to ensure that services to the child are not arbitrarily curtailed or modified.

"During the hearings on this bill, the Committee received testimony that the individualized written educational plan (as contained in the bill introduced in January) would require school systems to develop an expertise and ability to provide services guaranteed to assure educational progress. The Committee recognizes that in many instances the process of providing special education and related services to handicapped children is not guaranteed to produce any particular outcome. By changing the language of this provision to emphasize the process of parent and child involvement and to provide a written record of reasonable expectations, the Committee intends to clarify that such individualized planning conferences are a way to provide parent involvement and protection to assure that appropriate services are provided to a handicapped child. The Committee has deleted the language of the bill as introduced which required objective criteria and evaluation procedures by which to assure that the short term instructional goals were met. Instead it has required the Commissioner of Education to conduct a comprehensive study of objective criteria and evaluation procedures which may be utilized at a later date in conjunction with individualized data available through the individualized planning conference to determine the effectiveness of special education and related services being provided.

"The Committee further points out that it intends that a copy of the statement thus developed be retained on file within the school district with copies provided to parents and others involved subject to strict procedures for protection of confidentiality. While it believes that such statements may be useful to a State educational agency for purposes of audit and evaluation, it does not intend that such records be forwarded to the State agency, but be available for inspection."

Several pages later the report added that the law

". . .requires that the State assure that local educational agencies provide and maintain records of the individualized planning conference for each handicapped child including the written statement developed from the conferences, and that such conferences will be conducted at least three times a year to develop, review and, with the agreement of the parents or guardian, revise the statement. Fifth, the bill requires that the State educational agency be responsible for insuring the implementation of and compliance with provisions of the Act, and for the general supervision of educational programs for handicapped children within the State, including all such education programs administered by any other State or local agency. Finally, to assure orderly due process with regard to carrying out the provisions of the Act and to assure compliance with provisions of the Act, the Committee bill provides that the State shall establish policies and procedures to provide consultation with persons involved in or concerned with the education of handicapped children including handicapped individuals and parents of handicapped children. Further, in this regard, the State shall establish an entity to assure compliance with the provisions of the Act which shall conduct periodic evaluation and be empowered to receive, and take such necessary steps as are required, to resolve complaints of violations of the requirements of the Act."

In its final reference to the IEP the report notes that

"The Committee has designed the individualized planning conferences as one method to prevent labelling or misclassification. Furthermore, the Committee points out that due process requirements in existing law were designed specifically to protect against this abuse, and should be examined by the Commissioner and the State educational agency to assure that they are effective in this regard."

Subsequent to the issuance of this report, on June 8, the debate got underway with remarks by Senator Jennings Randolph of West Virginia, Chairman of the Senate Subcommittee on the Handicapped. In analyzing the various provisions of the proposed Act—at that time referred to as S. 6—Senator Randolph noted that

"A feature of the measure that will promote the educational development of handicapped children is the individualized planning conference. It has long been recognized by educators that individualized attention to a child brings rich rewards to the child, his teachers, and family. Handicapped children have been a neglected minority in our school system; individualized planning conferences are a way of targeting the resources of our school systems on handicapped children. These conferences are to be held at least three times a year and will represent a cooperative effort on the part of the school, the parents, and the child himself, when appropriate, to meet the unique educational needs of the child. Frequent monitoring of a handicapped child's progress throughout the school year is a vital component of the individualized planning conference. Preliminary evidence on annual planning conferences indicates that the usefulness of the individualized planning conference would be nullified if held only on an annual basis."

Senator Robert T. Stafford of Vermont then spoke about the makeup of the planning conferences, noting that

"The participants will include the parents, the teacher, and a qualified supervisor or provider of special education services. This provision is extremely important if the child's progress is to be adequately monitored and if appropriate steps are to be taken to assure that the problems with the educational process that the child is having are met in a timely and consistent way. An additional benefit that will result from these conferences is one that is too often overlooked. Not only will the child be better served, and the parents better informed of the limitations their child has due to a particular handicap, but the teacher will learn from this experience as well.

"As we look more and more toward children with handicaps being educated with their normal peers, we must realize, and try to alleviate, the burden put upon the teacher who must cope with that child and all the others in the class as well. The teacher needs reinforcement and a better understanding of the child's abilities and disabilities.

"It is hoped that participation in these conferences will have a positive effect on the attitude of the teacher toward the child, and an understanding of the child's problems in relating to his or her peers because of a handicapping condition."

Commented Senator Randolph:

"Mr. President, the Senator from Vermont explained one feature of this bill, and I will try to emphasize his point. We will promote the educational development of handicapped children through the process of individualized planning conferences.

"What the Senator has stated is very important. Educators generally have begun to realize that some personal attention must be given to a child. I am sure that the child is the better for it. Individual attention is one of the benefits of a good education in institutions of learning for all the people of the United States, not only the handicapped.

"Throughout this country, our schools, colleges, and universities long have stressed the need for individual attention to students. It is the heart of our educational process and it has stood the test of time.

"Perhaps this is not the occasion to mention it, but I do so. I look back upon my school days, and I say to the Senator from Vermont that I recall those teachers who not only were informed, but also were inspiring. They were those men and women who gave of their time a

little after the class actually had closed. They gave one the opportunity to come and talk with them. They were there to counsel the students. In a sense, that can be carried over into the specific that the Senator mentioned here—the individual attention to children.

"The individual planning conference is a cooperative effort. It is an effort that must include the teacher, the representative of the local educational agency, the parents, and, when appropriate, the boy or girl who is handicapped. When we do this, we have the opportunity to keep in touch with that child. We monitor the child's progress, as one might say, and that frequent monitoring is a vital component of this training planning conference process. It helps the child, it helps the parents or guardian, and it helps the teachers.

"For these reasons, I comment on what the Senator has said."

Subsequently, following a discussion regarding other provisions of the bill, Senator Williams had this further comment about the IEP:

"In order to involve the parent and the child—when appropriate—in the educational process so that they may fully participate in making decisions regarding their child's education, S. 6 provides for an individualized planning conference, to be held at least three times a year, involving the parents or guardian, a person representing the local educational agency qualified to provide special education, the child's teacher and the child, when appropriate. These persons will meet jointly to develop and review a written statement describing the educational services to be provided for the particular child and, when appropriate, the statement will be revised with the agreement of the parents.

"This conference is intended also to serve as a method of providing additional parent counseling and training so that the parent may bolster the educational process at home. This involvement is particularly important in order to assure that the educational services are meeting the child's needs and so that both parents and child may be part of the process from which they are so often far removed. The conference is not a contractual relationship, but rather a cooperative effort. It serves to fully extend the procedural protections and parent involvement which was initiated last year in the Education Amendments of 1974."

In a query addressed to Senator Randolph, Senator Richard B. Stone of Florida said:

"There is a question which has been raised by some of my constituents concerning the individualized planning conferences.

"Was it the committee's intent that these planning conferences be held three times a year and attended by a small group of persons for the purpose of developing a plan for each child, or was the intent to hold a large meeting three times a year to draw plans for many children?"

Responded Senator Randolph:

"In answer to my colleague, it was the intent, and I believe I can speak for the subcommittee and the committee in this matter, that these meetings to which the Senator makes reference be small meetings; that is, confined to those persons who have, naturally, an intense interest in a particular child, i.e., the parent or parents of the child, and in some cases, the guardian of the child. Certainly, the teacher involved or even more than one teacher would be included. In addition, there should be a representative of the local educational agency who is qualified to provide, or supervise the provision of, specially designed instruction to meet the unique needs of handicapped children.

"These are the persons that we thought might well be included. That is why we have called them individualized planning conferences. We believe that they are worthwhile, and we discussed this very much as we drafted the legislation.

"We thought they should be held three times a year because we have the belief that a lesser number of such conferences would not be productive.

"If the child is not progressing as he or she should, it would be best to identify the problem as quickly as possible. Then we would have the opportunity of correcting the difficulty before a long period of time goes by. Sometimes we bring into focus the needs of a child simply by discussion of his problems.

"We believe, as I said in my opening statement, that frequent monitoring of the child's educational development is certainly valid."

Regarding the burden that might arise from the IEP requirement, Senator Jacob Javits of New York expressed reservation about

". . .the dynamics by which the local educational agencies handle a three-times-a-year planning conference for each handicapped child, and a written record. I do not think there can be any objection against maintaining a written record. We do that for every student anyhow.

"As to the three-times-a-year conference, I believe we ought to think about that. That is a lot. It is 21 million conferences. . . . If there is any amendment addressing this issue, we will deal with it, and if there is not, we will probably deal with it anyhow in the House-Senate conference.

"As to the general requirements of the State entity, the amendment which Senator Dole will introduce, in which I very much wish to join, will deal with that situation, so I hope it should obviate reasonable objection to that proposition."

The observations by Senator Javits led to the following colloquy involving him and Senators Randolph, Stafford, Williams, and Robert J. Dole of Kansas:

Mr. DOLE. It was the intent of the Senator from Kansas to offer an amendment which would either delete the planning conference or at least to make it discretionary, because it just seems to me, as I have indicated earlier, if we are going to hold at least 3 times a year an individualized planning conference for everyone who is handicapped, according to the definitions of this act, that is going to be about 24 million conferences and 24 million pieces of paper. That could be an administrative nightmare.

Now the Senator from Kansas understands the problem of the handicapped to some degree. There may be some who need 10 conferences or more per year, there may be some who need one. It would seem to the Senator from Kansas that one thing that we could do between now and October 1976 would be to conduct a pilot program, that has been suggested, in the States of Texas, Florida, and Wisconsin, where they have ongoing programs or at least could have a pilot program to see if a nationwide program were appropriate.

5. FUTURE TRENDS

Mr. RANDOLPH. Mr. President, will the Senator yield?

Mr. DOLE. Yes.

Mr. RANDOLPH. What is being done in the State of Kansas on this matter?

Mr. DOLE. We allow the State agency to have as many conferences as they want. I do not believe we require any certain number of conferences. As this Senator understands, the purpose is to sit down with parent or guardian and if appropriate, the handicapped individual and establish a clear and meaningful plan.

Mr. RANDOLPH. The only reason I come back to Kansas is because that is the State represented by the Senator and sometimes if we look at our own situation we assess it in view of the national needs. As I understand, these conferences for handicapped persons are held about once a month at the medical center.

Mr. DOLE. But I do not think the number of meetings—whether it be an individual conference once a month or once a year—is set by law or otherwise made inflexible.

Mr. RANDOLPH. There is a file on every handicapped child, starting with an evaluation following right through diagnosis and service. I think this is correct.

Mr. DOLE. This may be technically correct but as far as the conferences, I do not think we have been discussing this but have been discussing whether the number of conferences should be set in law by the Federal Government.

Mr. RANDOLPH. What is being done in some Kansas programs is what we want to do in other States.

Mr. DOLE. Right.

Mr. RANDOLPH. The Senator can understand that. I would hope in this instance that the Senator would not press for this amendment, but let it be a part of the discussion here today. We shall give very careful study to this in the future.

Mr. DOLE. The Senator from Kansas does not quarrel with the conference. This Senator does not quarrel with whether it is 3 or 6 or 9 or 12, but again it is a Federal dictation to a State agency that they must comply; they must have at least three individual conferences. And later on in the bill there are other sections where the

States must have statistically valid data based on these individual conferences.

Mr. RANDOLPH. I add further to the Senator, this is only if they desire to participate.

Mr. DOLE. If they do not want to participate in the program, they would not be so constrained.

Mr. RANDOLPH. That is correct.

Mr. DOLE. But the Senator from Kansas is trying to figure out some way that, before we launch into this massive effort, we have some history. And since the Senator from Washington has delayed the effective date until October 1976, it would seem to me that we should make some legislative history that HEW should conduct a pilot program in at least three States, and maybe Kansas would be a good State.

Mr. RANDOLPH. That is presently being done by DHEW. There are projects in Florida and in Texas. Let us remember that we have adequate time until October 1, 1976 to see the results of these studies, which I feel will prove that this provision will be beneficial.

Mr. JAVITS. Exactly. Mr. President, if the Senator will yield, I commend that, too. I was going to modify an amendment to make it annual so that we do not start out quite so tough.

Also Senator Randolph has now defined in the Stone amendment the matter of the conference and that, therefore, somewhat relieves the strains. Somewhere between one and three we ought to be able to let the matter move from here and strike a fair balance. My suggestion, because I know how strongly Senator Randolph feels about it, to Senator Dole would be to make it twice. In other words, instead of three times, make it twice with the understanding that the pilot work is being done and that seasonably, before the operative date, we will review the figure of two. Then at least you have a mandate which is one-third less, and we have committed ourselves to reducing even further depending upon the actual work of the HEW. I think that is probably the best way.

Mr. RANDOLPH. Will the Senator from Kansas permit me to comment on the words of the Senator from New York.

Mr. DOLE. Yes.

I yield.

Mr. RANDOLPH. I would rather not have it

twice, for the reason that the Senate works with. . .

Mr. DOLE. The House has one conference in their bill.

Mr. JAVITS. I will agree. I will be a conferee, Senator Randolph will be a conferee, and Senator Stafford will be a conferee. I think the Senator should leave it to us, with the legislative record, and he has our feet to the fire. He has agreed to listen to the House and give attention to the findings where the words are being experimented with.

Mr. DOLE. I have no quarrel with that. If all these studies should prove that there is really no benefit from the individualized conferences, whether they are 2 or 10 or whatever number.

Mr. RANDOLPH. I would be ready to amend it.

Mr. DOLE. That is what I am seeking.

Mr. JAVITS. I make the same commitment.

Mr. DOLE. The Senator does not wish to impose any burden on educators, or parents, or handicapped children that does not benefit the handicapped.

Mr. RANDOLPH. No Member of the Senate is more concerned about the handicapped than is the Senator from Kansas. He has been a leader in this field. All of us working on these matters want to do one job, and that is to benefit the handicapped—in this particular instance, the education of the handicapped.

Mr. DOLE. That satisfies me. My concern is that we make every resource, or as much as possible, available to the direct activities and the direct programs that are going to benefit the handicapped.

Mr. WILLIAMS. Mr. President, if the Senator will yield, I think that one of the greatest benefits that can come to the handicapped child is to have the parents brought into this conference, because the education of the child continues after the school doors close and that child is at home. This is part of the educational process. That is one of the reasons why we have developed the idea of the mandatory conference, to make sure that the parent is part of the education of the child. We have to have more than one, it seems to me. That is almost a "get acquainted" meeting, and a followup meeting is essential. I support the three meetings that Senator Randolph put into this bill, and I hope we can keep it at that, at this point.

Mr. JAVITS. Mr. President, if the Senator will yield, as the ranking member, I pledge to Senator Dole to pay the most serious attention to the findings of the work which will be done in the interim until the new operative date. As will Senator Randolph, I will be perfectly willing to advocate even its entire omission, if we are convinced that it is a drag instead of an aid to everything that is being done.

Mr. WILLIAMS. It is an absolute promise to do that, because the ends are what we are interested in here. We want to see the best possible approach to education. We will be watching very closely during this period to see how it develops, particularly in the area that the Senator from Kansas has brought forth.

Mr. DOLE. I appreciate the assurances from the Senators from New York, West Virginia, and New Jersey. Their concern for the handicapped is genuine, as is that of the Senator from Kansas. But hopefully we do not want to burden some State agency with a requirement that may prove to be counterproductive. Based on the assurances, the Senator from Kansas will withdraw the amendment.

Mr. STAFFORD. Mr. President, while assurances are being given, I would like to join my three colleagues in offering the same assurance on that.

Mr. DOLE. I appreciate that. It means a great deal to the Senator from Kansas.

Mr. President, I withdraw the amendment.

The PRESIDING OFFICER. The amendment is withdrawn.

The final comments on the IEP during this phase of the debate were offered by Senators Alan Cranston of California and Walter F. Mondale of Minnesota.

Said Senator Cranston:

"S. 6 as reported also would add a new provision that establishes procedures to insure that handicapped children and their parents or guardians are given an opportunity to participate in the planning and development of the educational program, including the assessment of the handicapped child's present educational performance, the specification of instructional objectives, and identification of the specific educational services to be provided.

5. FUTURE TRENDS

"Mr. President, there are many other significant provisions in S. 6. I am particularly pleased with the specific guarantees of due process of law provided for handicapped children and their parents in all matters relevant to identification, evaluation, and placement, and the prohibition against the classification of children in a manner which promotes racial or cultural discrimination."

Added Senator Mondale:

"This bill represents a major step toward the identification and education of all handicapped youngsters in the near future. In the past, many children have been simply placed in institutions or segregated in schools and classes with little emphasis on adequate education and training. Under S. 6, an individual planning conference, will provide a tailored program for each handicapped youngster to meet his special educational needs.

"In the past, many children have been left to sit at home, providing little opportunity for adequate training and development. Under S. 6, priority is given to provision of a free appropriate public education to children not currently receiving any, as well as those currently receiving inadequate assistance.

"In the long run our whole society will benefit by timely, effective identification and treatment of the needs of those individuals and their families."

Comments from the House of Representatives

Meanwhile the House Education and Labor Committee was busy preparing a report on its companion bill, H.R. 7217. Issued on June 26 and labeled No. 94–332, the report says the following (on page 13) about the individualized education program:

Why does the bill provide for prescription of an individualized education program?

The movement toward the individualization of instruction, involving the participation of the child and the parent, as well as all relevant educational professionals, is a trend gaining ever wider support in educational, parental, and political groups throughout the Nation.

Therefore, this legislation would require each local educational agency to develop with a child's teacher in consultation with the parents of the child (and in appropriate instances the child) an individualized education program. Such a prescription responds to 3 fundamental tenets:

(a) each child requires an educational plan that is tailored to achieve his or her maximum potential;

(b) all principals in the child's educational environment, including the child, should have the opportunity for input in the development of an individualized program of instruction;

(c) individualization means specifics and timetables for those specifics, and the need for periodic review of those specifics—all of which produce greatly enhanced fiscal and educational accountability.

Parenthetically, it may be noted that the 93rd Congress, and, more specifically, this Committee, have already expressed their concern about the need for increased individualization in at least 2 public laws: Public Law 93–112, the Rehabilitation Act Amendments of 1973, and Public Law 93–380, the Education Amendments of 1974 (Title I).

Then five pages later the report adds this:

H.R. 7217 defines "individualized education program" as an educational plan for each handicapped child developed jointly by the local educational agency and an appropriate teacher, in consultation with the parents. This plan would contain a statement of the present levels of educational performance of the child, desired instructional objectives, a statement of the specific educational services provided the child, and the extent to which the child will be able to participate in regular educational programs, a projected date for initiation and anticipated duration of such services, and an annual evaluation of the procedures and objectives.

Agreeing on the bill's IEP provisions

In the subsequent debate on the House floor, as recorded in the *Congressional Record*, Representative John Brademas of Indiana commented as follows regarding the IEP:

"Mr. Chairman, we also provide that an individualized plan of instruction must be provided for each handicapped child and evaluated at least annually. Individualized plans are of great importance in the education of handicapped children in order to help them develop their full potential."

Representative Albert H. Quie of Minnesota also discussed the IEP, noting that the bill

". . .includes a requirement for the development of individualized education programs for each handicapped child. This would be an educational plan which is developed jointly by the local education agencies, a teacher involved with the specific education of the handicapped child, and his parents or guardian. The plan would include a statement of the child's present level of educational performance, a statement of the goals to be achieved, a statement of the specific services which will have to be provided, a projected date for initiation and duration of the services, and criteria and evaluation procedures for determining whether the objectives are being met. Because handicapped children are unique, setting up plans for each one makes good sense and by involving the parents in the development of such plans, the benefits begun in school hopefully would be continued at home. It is important to point out that it is an educational plan developed jointly, but it is not intended as a binding contract by the schools, children, and parents."

Conference Report

Although the two measures subsequently passed by the Senate and the House were alike in their broad outlines, they differed in detail. Thus it was necessary to appoint a conference committee, composed of representatives of each branch of the Congress, to work out the differences. Out of those deliberations came House of Representatives Conference Report No. 94–664, which says on pages 30 and 31:

The Senate bill and the House amendments add to the definitions in the Education of the Handicapped Act a definition of individualized instructional planning for each handicapped child which includes a statement of the child's present level of educational performance, statement of the instructional objectives to be achieved, statement of the specific educational services to be provided to the child, the extent to which the child will participate in the regular educational program, and the projected date

for initiation and anticipated duration of such services.

The Senate bill designates this individualized instructional planning as an "individualized planning conference"; the House amendments designate the planning as an "individualized education program." The Senate recedes.

The Senate bill provides that the individualized planning conference is a meeting or meetings for the purpose of developing a written statement; the House amendments provide that the individualized education program is an educational plan. The House recedes.

The Senate bill provides that the written statement shall be developed by a representative of the local educational agency, the teacher, the parents or guardian of the handicapped child and the child when appropriate; the House amendments provide that the educational plan shall be developed jointly by the local educational agency and an appropriate teacher *in consultation with* the parents or guardian of the child, and the child, whenever appropriate. The House recedes.

The Senate bill, but not the House amendments, provides that the representatives of the local educational agency shall be qualified to provide, or supervise the provision of, specially designed instruction to meet the unique needs of the child. The House recedes.

The Senate bill provides for a statement of *short-term* instructional objectives; the House amendments provide for a statement of *desired* objectives.

The conference substitute provides that the individualized educational program shall include a statement of the annual goals and short-term objectives to be achieved by the child. It is intended that each individual handicapped child will have an educational program which states the annual goals as well as including short-term instructional objectives to be achieved within shorter time perods.

The House amendments, but not the Senate bill, provide that the individualized instructional planning shall include objective criteria and evaluation procedures and schedules for

5. FUTURE TRENDS

determining, on at least an annual basis, whether instructional objectives are being met.

The Senate recedes with an amendment specifying that such objective criteria and evaluation procedures shall be "appropriate." The conferees intend that this amendment clarify that any criteria and evaluation procedures used are to be consistent with the requirements regarding testing and evaluation procedures in existing law.

The conferees further clarify that it is not intended that the individualized educational programs be forwarded to the U.S. Office of Education or the State educational agency. The individualized educational programs are intended to be retained in the local educational agency. Where inspection or review of such programs may be useful to the Office of Education or State educational agency for purposes of audit or evaluation, it is intended that such activities take place within the local agency, subject to strict procedures for the protection of confidentiality.

The House amendments, but not the Senate bill, add to the Education of the Handicapped Act, a definition of *public educational agency* defining such agency as any State educational agency or any other public agency approved by a State educational agency to provide special education and related services to handicapped children within the State involved. The conference substitute includes a definition of intermediate educational unit, defining such term as any public authority established by State law for the purpose of providing free public education on a regional level within the State which provides special education and related services to handicapped children within that State and which is not a local educational authority but which is under the general supervision of the State educational agency. The conferees include this definition in order to cover certain unique situations in States where public bodies established by State law provide special education and related services for handicapped children, but where the definition of local educational agency does not necessarily apply, e.g., intermediate units in the Commonwealth of Pennsylvania. Generally, the term "intermediate educational unit" is used throughout

the conference report wherever the term "local educational agency" is also used.

Requirements for individualized planning conference. The Senate bill requires that the State give assurances to the Commissioner that each local educational agency in the State will maintain records of the individualized planning conference, including the written statement developed pursuant to such conference, and that such conference shall be held at least three times each year to develop, review, and, when appropriate, and with the agreement of the parents, revise such statements. The House amendments require the local educational agency in its application to provide satisfactory assurance that it will maintain the individualized program for each child, and will review the program at least annually, and revise its provisions in consultation with the parents or guardians.

The conference substitute requires that the State give assurances as a condition of eligibility that each local educational agency will maintain records of the individualized education program for each handicapped child, and to provide assurances that each local educational agency within the State shall establish, review and revise such program consistent with requirements on local educational agencies under the local application provisions of the Act.

The conference substitute also requires each local educational agency to provide assurances that it will establish, or revise, whichever is appropriate, an individualized education program for each handicapped child at the beginning of each school year and will then review and, if appropriate revise, the provisions of such program periodically, but not less than annually. In the initial year of a handicapped child's participation in a program of free appropriate public education the individualized education program shall be established at the beginning of the school year and reviewed at least once during that year. Thereafter, the conferees intend that this provision requires at least one annual review of the child's individualized education program.

The conferees have defined the individualized education program as a written statement (including the educational status of the child, the annual goals and short-term instructional objectives, and specific educational services to be provided) for each handicapped child which is jointly developed by the local educational agency, the teacher, the parents, and the child, whenever appropriate. It is intended that *all* parties (the local educational agency, the teacher, the parents, and the child, whenever appropriate) will be involved throughout the process of establishment, review and revision of this program.

Concluding debate—House
In the House following the issue of the conference report, the remarks of Representative Brademas included the following:

"Mr. Speaker, the conference bill, as did the House version, requires the development of an individualized written education program for every handicapped child served, to be designed initially in consultation with parents or guardian, and to be reviewed and revised as necessary at least annually."

To which Representative Quie added the following:

"Not only have we guaranteed (handicapped children) a right to an education, but I think we have written adequate provisions which will protect those rights and guarantee that a child will not be improperly labeled or improperly placed in an educational setting which will not suit his or her unique educational needs. The bill further guarantees that each handicapped child will have an individualized program which is designed to meet his or her special needs. As you know, not every handicapped child is the same; and by designing educational programs which specifically address specific needs and problems, I believe that handicapped children will benefit more from our educational programs. One of the reasons why I feel so strongly that the individualized education program will be so beneficial is that we require that it be developed with the involvement of a child's parent or guardian. By having a child, the parent, and his or her teacher involved in planning, it is my belief that the end result has to be positive."

Concluding debate—Senate
In the Senate following the issuance of the conference report, Senator Harrison A. Williams, Jr., of New Jersey, said the proposed law "assures the individualization of the educational process by requiring an individualized education program tailored to the unique needs of each handicapped child," and subsequently added:

"The provisions requiring an individualized education program for each handicapped child are extremely important protections to the parents and child, and highly necessary to proper planning and programming for the school district. Under the conference agreement, a local educational agency or intermediate unit receiving assistance must assure that this provision is carried out for the handicapped children within their jurisdictions, and the State is required to provide assurances that the program is carried out for all other handicapped children within the State. The Senate bill required a conference to be held at least three times a year for developing, reviewing and revising the plan, in order to assure that changes were made in the plan as appropriate to the child throughout the school year, while the House bill required that this occur on an annual basis. Once again, the conference substitute represents the essence of compromise. For under the conference agreement, this program must be established or revised, whichever is appropriate, for each handicapped child at the beginning of the school year, and must then be reviewed, and if appropriate, revised periodically during the school year, but not less than annually.

"The conferees have further defined the individualized education program as a written statement—including the educational status of the child, the annual goals and short-term instructional objectives, and specific educational services to be provided—for each handicapped child which is jointly developed by the local educational agency, the teacher, the parents, and the child. It is intended that all parties will be involved throughout the process of establishment, review and revision of this program."

Said Senator Stafford:

"The Senate passed bill contained a provision for three individualized planning conferences for each child each year. These conferences were to include, but not necessarily be limited to the teacher, the parent or guardian, a representative of the educational agency responsible

5. FUTURE TRENDS

for the child's education, and the child when appropriate.

"The conference agreement changes the name of such conferences to an individualized educational program, but retains in the definitional sense much of the Senate language. The difference is the way in which it will operate. The agreement clearly specifies that there will be two conferences in the first year of the handicapped child's schooling and provides that it will be reviewed at least annually. I wish to point out, however, that the conference clearly did not wish to preclude more than one conference per year.

"The conferees recognize that each child is affected in a different way by a handicap. Some may be more severe for some children than they would be for others. We want to encourage as many conferences a year as any one child may need. It is felt that in some cases numerous conferences would be desired. We did not preclude that possibility."

Concluding the debate, on November 19 Senator Randolph again emphasized that the agreed-upon version of the law

". . .calls for the development of an individualized educational program for each handicapped child, in which there is participation by the parents or guardian of the child, the teacher, a representative of the local educational agency qualified to provide or supervise the provision of special education and related services, and the child when appropriate. Individualized attention to educational needs has and will continue to be one of the most important elements to a child's success in school. By monitoring a child's progress, a teacher can aid the child in achieving educational goals as well as determining where a potential educational problem may arise."

INDEX

STAFF

Publisher	John Quirk
Editor	Irving Newman
Editor	Robert Piazza
Director of Production	Richard Pawlikowski
Staff Consultant	Dona Chiappe
Permissions Editor	Audrey Weber
Customer Service	Cindy Finocchio
Administration	Linda Radomski

Cover Design	Donald Burns

SPECIAL EDUCATION SERIES

- ● Autism
- * ● Behavior Modification
- Biological Bases of Learning Disabilities
- Brain Impairments
- Career and Vocational Education
- Child Abuse
- Child Psychology
- Child Development
- Cognitive and Communication Skills
- Creative Arts
- Curriculum and Materials
- * ● Deaf Education
- Developmental Disabilities
- * ● Diagnosis and Placement
- Down's Syndrome
- ● Dyslexia
- Early Learning
- Educational Technology
- * ● Emotional and Behavioral Disorders
- Exceptional Parents
- * ● Gifted Education
- Hyperactivity
- ● Individualized Education Programs
- * ● Learning Disabilities
- Learning Theory
- ● Mainstreaming
- * ● Mental Retardation
- Multiple Handicapped Education
- Occupational Therapy
- * ● Physically Handicapped Education
- Pre-School and Day Care Education
- * ● Psychology of Exceptional Children
- Reading Skill Development
- Research and Development
- * ● Severely and Profoundly Handicapped Education
- Severe Mental Retardation
- Sex Education for the Retarded
- Slow Learner Education
- Social Learning
- * ● Special Education
- * ● Speech and Hearing
- * ● Visually Handicapped Education

● Published Titles   • Major Course Areas

Exceptional Children: A Reference Book

An updated and welcome resource for educators and librarians.

COMMENTS PLEASE:

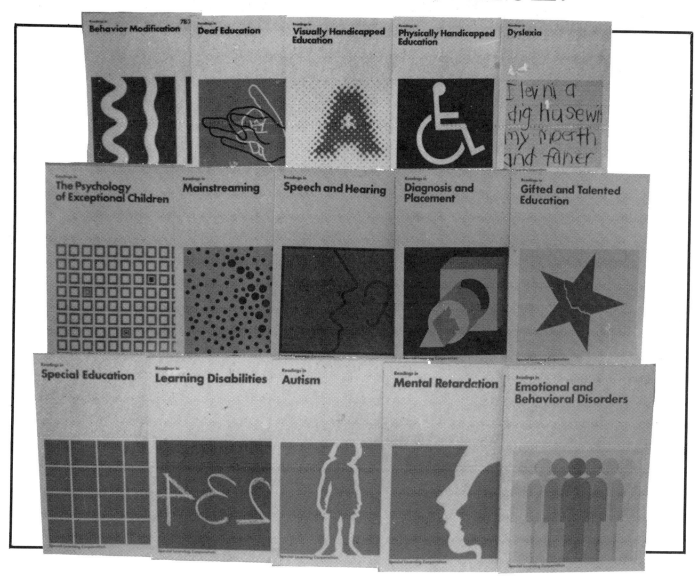

SPECIAL LEARNING CORPORATION
42 Boston Post Rd.
Guilford, Conn. 06437

SPECIAL LEARNING CORPORATION
COMMENTS PLEASE:

Does this book fit your course of study?

Why? (Why not?)

Is this book useable for other courses of study? Please list.

What other areas would you like us to publish in using this format?

What type of exceptional child are you interested in learning more about?

Would you use this as a basic text?

How many students are enrolled in these course areas?

_____ Special Education _____ Mental Retardation _____ Psychology _____ Emotional Disorders

_____ Exceptional Children _____ Learning Disabilities   Other _____

Do you want to be sent a copy of our elementary student materials catalog?

Do you want a copy of our college catalog?

Would you like a copy of our next edition?   ▱ yes ▱ no

Are you a ▱ student or an ▱ instructor?

Your name _____ school _____

Term used _____ Date _____

address _____

city _____ state _____ zip _____

telephone number _____

S/P